PRAISE FOR *SHUT OUT*

Selected as a finalist by the *Society for American
Baseball Research* for SABR's Seymour Award for
Best Baseball Book of the Year

"A fine, lively dissection of not only race and the Red Sox, but race relations
in Boston in general, and the city's legendary sportswriters as well. A must-
read for not only Red Sox fans, but those who love and follow the game."
—JULES TYGIEL, author of *Baseball's Great Experiment:
Jackie Robinson and His Legacy*

"*Shut Out* is an important book that reaches beyond the borders of the City of
Boston and the Red Sox. With courage, eloquence, and hard-nosed reporting,
Howard Bryant asks the tough questions others have not and explores base-
ball's ongoing struggle with race as played out in the history of one team. *Shut
Out* is as fearless as the truth."
—GLENN STOUT, co-editor of *Red Sox Century*
and *Yankees Century*

"Brace yourself for *Shut Out,* the story of the Red Sox and race relations,
written by Howard Bryant . . . Bryant grew up around here and did his
homework on this one."
—DAN SHAUGHNESSY, Boston *Globe*

"What was the best sports book of 2002? Howard Bryant's *Shut Out: A Story
of Race and Baseball in Boston* is a brilliant dissection of the racial problems of
the Red Sox, the last team in baseball to integrate. Bryant does a great job of
showing how the legacy of the past infects the present and how the media in
Boston played a crucial role, for good and ill."
—JEFF BAKER, *Portland Oregonian*

"A long overdue look at the history of racism not only in Boston, but in baseball."
—REGGIE JACKSON

"A courageous, well-written and important book . . . scrupulously researched . . . . *Shut Out* does an exemplary job in locating the problems of the Red Sox within the context of Boston's racial history."
—BRUCE DANCIS, *Sacramento Bee*

"One of the most anticipated baseball books of the summer."
—Boston *Herald*

"There's no mistaking the view afforded us by Howard Bryant—up close, in our faces, so raw and unfiltered, it forces us to entirely rethink Boston's baseball history. Bryant compels us to ask: do we have the guts to do it?"
—BOB KLAPISCH, baseball columnist and author of
The Worst Team Money Could Buy

"The romantic view of the Red Sox revels in the notion that the team is a victim of history, its last 84 empty-handed years the byproduct of calamities from fate to curses to mismanagement. But in *Shut Out: A Story of Race and Baseball in Boston*, author Howard Bryant turns that perspective on its head, issuing a crucial lesson about the team's role as an agent, and not a victim, of injustice."
—ALEX SPEIER, Boston *Metro*

"In *Shut Out: A Story of Race and Baseball in Boston*, journalist Howard Bryant . . . is historian enough to chronicle honestly what went on throughout the bad old days at Fenway Park . . . [and] also explore the circumstances behind the failure of the local press to tell the story of the last baseball club to hire a black player, an organization capable of fielding a team with only one black man on it 30 years and more after Robinson retired, and brazen enough to claim the idea was just to put the best possible nine on the field."
—BILL LITTLEFIELD, Boston *Sunday Globe*

"An unflinching exposé . . . While some may disagree with Bryant's assessment, the book will likely create an important dialogue on why so many African American athletes have felt unwelcome in Boston. Rather than sweeping the franchise's flaws under the rug, *Shut Out* calls for some serious soul-searching before the Red Sox can move on."
—*Providence Journal*

SHUT OUT

(Photo by Bill Chapman)

SHUT OUT

A STORY OF RACE
AND BASEBALL
IN BOSTON

HOWARD BRYANT

BEACON
150

BEACON PRESS   BOSTON

Beacon Press
25 Beacon Street
Boston, Massachusetts 02108-2892
www.beacon.org

Beacon Press books
are published under the auspices of
the Unitarian Universalist Association of Congregations.

08 07 06 05 04 03   10 9 8 7 6 5 4 3 2 1

This book is printed on acid-free paper that meets the uncoated paper
ANSI/NISO specifications for permanence as revised in 1992.

Library of Congress Cataloging-in-Publication Data

Bryant, Howard, 1968–
   Shut out : a story of race and baseball in Boston / Howard Bryant.
      p. cm.
   Includes bibliographical references and index.
   ISBN 0–8070-0979-2
      1. Boston Red Sox (Baseball team) 2. Baseball—Massachusetts—Boston—History—20th
century. 3. Discrimination in sports—Massachusetts—Boston. 4. Boston (Mass.)—Race
relations. I. Title.

GV875.B62 B79 2002
796.357'64'0974461—dc21   2002069950

In memory of Robert N. Downes, for making a difference

FOREWORD

This book is Howard Bryant's first turn at bat in what Ring Lardner, Sr., called "the lit-ry league," fast company, and it is a pleasure to observe that Mr. Bryant himself is in no way shut out. He takes on a formidable trinity—race, the press, and baseball—without fear or favor, and if I were going to use further baseball metaphors to describe his book, I'd say dinger, over the wall, a home run.

Scores of baseball books reach my cluttered desk each year, but few are memorable. Many are simply imitative. Jim Brosnan, a bespectacled journeyman pitcher, kept a diary of his 1959 adventures in the National League that Harper & Row published as *The Long Season*. It is touching and bittersweet. Since then ballplayer diary books have sprouted like mushrooms in a rainy August, but as far as I know Brosnan is the only athlete who composed his diary without bringing a ghost into the privacy of his boudoir. The only diary book, then, that really was a diary.

The first baseball oral history was *The Glory of Their Times*, by Lawrence Ritter, published by Macmillan in 1966. Ballplayers from the early twentieth century "spoke" this beautiful work. Since then we've seen perhaps fifty baseball oral histories. Some, notably those collected by Donald Honig, are splendid. None matches Larry Ritter's original. My own *The Boys of Summer* has been imitated more times than I care to count, and not even the sanctity of my title, which comes from a Dylan Thomas poem, is respected. A few seasons back someone even wrote a quick book about women soccer players and called it *The Girls of Summer.*

A salient fact of *Shut Out* is that it is wholly original. Nothing quite like it exists in the literature. Bryant sees baseball, the press, and the city of Boston as parts of the whole on which he focuses. And that whole, of course, is racism; alive, but hopefully weakening in America.

He describes the Red Sox's rejection of Jackie Robinson, who worked out before the owner, Tom Yawkey, and some others in 1945. At one point someone, probably Yawkey, probably drunk, bellowed, "Get the nigger off the field." Breaking baseball's color barrier—even *attempting* to break a barrier of bigotry that had been in place for six decades—was a major story. Where were the armies of the press, monitoring to see that the tryout was fair? That is just one of the good questions Howard Bryant asks. Later, Red Sox scouts turned down a young centerfielder with the Birmingham Black Barons named Willie H. Mays. Let me here quote from Hank DeBerry, a Southerner, assigned to report on Mays a few seasons later, after the New York Giants had signed Willie and sent him to Minneapolis of the American Association: "Sensational. Hits all pitches and hits to all fields, with power. He has made the most amazing catches. Slides hard, plays hard. The Louisville pitchers knocked him down plenty but it seemed to have no effect at all. This player is the best prospect in America. It was a banner day for the Giants when this boy was signed." What were the Red Sox looking at when they saw Mays? Color. Nothing else, and that is a disgrace to Boston, to baseball, to America. (Sadly, a season afterward, when Willie was turning heads all across New York, Hank DeBerry, one honest scout, died at the age of fifty-five in the town of Savannah, Tennessee, where "integration" still was a dirty word.)

As an enthusiastic but hardly conventional Boston baseball man, Howard Bryant speculates about a Red Sox team that could have included Robinson and Mays. I will go a step further. Suppose the Red Sox had scouted the Negro Leagues as intelligently as did their neighbors, the Boston Braves. They would have found the kid from Mobile, Alabama, Henry Aaron, who, by the end of his career, had hit 755 home runs for the portable Milwaukee-Atlanta Braves. Had the Red Sox fielded a team with Robinson, Mays, and Aaron, one phrase would long since have dropped out of the English language: Yankees Dynasty.

As *Shut Out* makes clear, Boston newspapers included many gifted sportswriters. But none was an effective champion of equal rights or even of the simpler matter, fair employment. Instead there developed prattle among the crowds walking in the Boston Common about "the Curse of the Bambino," which is every bit as catchy as it is irrelevant. At this writing, the Red Sox have not won a World Series since they shipped Babe Ruth to New York for what was then a fortune: $125,000 and a $300,000 loan. But the curse was not that deal, even though, as Ed Linn has written, if Harry Frazee, the Red Sox owner, could have been squeezed into a tea bag, locals would have dumped him into Boston Harbor. The curse was bigotry.

Bryant cites David Halberstam, who has attributed the Yankees' dreary stretch in the late 1960s mostly to Bronx racism. Halberstam is a global writer, given to sweeping statements; the Yankees situation was a bit more subtle than he seems to recognize. True, the Yankees did not integrate until 1955 and unlike, say, the Dodgers, the Giants, and the Braves, had no black superstar until Reggie Jackson arrived, to a flourish of trumpets from Olympus, in 1977. But the ancient régime, the scouts who signed Rizzuto, Mantle, and Berra, simply grew old. They didn't sign great blacks, but they didn't sign great whites either. Surely the Yankees stumbled because they had failed to seek out black ballplayers. (They too passed on Willie Mays.) But their afflictions also included incompetence and senility. Integration, while morally right, is no guarantee of baseball success. Consider the Cleveland Indians; under Bill Veeck the team began integrating in 1947. They won the World Series in 1948 then finished behind the all-white Yankees for five consecutive seasons. The St. Louis Browns integrated in 1947 and finished last. As Ron Shelton wrote in a lovely piece of irony in *Bull Durham*: "It's a simple game. You throw the ball. You catch the ball. You hit the ball. Sometimes you win. Sometimes you lose. Sometimes it rains."

Contrasting the Yawkey Red Sox and the Branch Rickey Dodgers is worthwhile. Rickey signed Jackie Robinson in 1946, and in spring training 1947, when it was clear Robinson would be promoted from the International League to Brooklyn, a significant number of Dodgers signed a petition. The signers swore that they would never play on the same team as Robinson. Pee Wee Reese, the splendid Dodgers shortstop and a man of great nobility of character, refused to sign. The movement wavered. Then the manager, Leo Durocher, called a sudden late-night meeting. "I hear some of you don't want to play with Robinson," Durocher began in a voice that set vertebrae vibrating.

"Well, boys, you know what you can use that petition for. . . . I'm paid to win and I'd play an elephant if he could win for me and this fellow Robinson is no elephant. You can't throw him out on the bases and you can't get him out at the plate, this fellow is a great player and he's gonna win pennants.

"And here's something else. He's only the first, boys, only the first! There's many more colored ball players coming right behind him and they're hungry boys. They're scratching and diving. Unless you wake up, these colored ball players are gonna run you right out of the park.

"I don't want to see your petition. Fuck your petition.

"This meeting is over. Go back to bed."

Racism is as old as the country, and Robinson's problems did not end there. Some St. Louis Cardinals organized a strike movement in May. They would strike rather than appear on a ball field with a black A great sports editor, Stanley Woodward, a New England man who was thriving on the *New York Herald Tribune*, found out and confronted Ford Frick, the president of the National League. Under pressure Frick conceded the reports were true. He had called in eleven individual Cardinals and said, "If you strike you will be suspended. I don't care if it wrecks the National League for five years. This is the United States of America and one citizen has as much right to play as another. You will find, if you go through with your intention, that you will have been guilty of complete madness." After Woodward wrote his story, the baseball strike movement, like the anti-Robinson petition, shriveled. Woodward failed to win a Pulitzer Prize, which suggests another area where racism was flourishing in 1947.

Opposition persisted in nasty chatter. Once, when Robinson was batting against the Cardinals in 1953, Ed Stanky, the St. Louis manager, held up a pair of spikes and shouted. "Hey! Boy! Shine these!" When Jack told me what he'd heard, I wrote a strong story for the *New York Herald Tribune*, but Stanley Woodward had been fired and replaced by a Yalie who could not spell "social consciousness." My story slipped into one edition, then it was killed, and the assistant sports editor wired me: "We will not be Robinson's sounding board. Write baseball not race relations." Although I did not know it at the time, my career as a newspaper sportswriter was fast winding down.

Opposition to integration began to form around what John Lardner called "the fifty-percent color line." That is, it was fine and American to play four blacks and five whites in your starting lineup. But play *five* blacks and you upset white supremacy, which of course threatens motherhood, the food chain, and the Republic. To avoid starting five blacks the Dodgers shipped Roberto Clemente to Pittsburgh, where he tore up the league for eighteen years, until his tragic death in 1972.

In 1953, the Dodgers did bring up Jim Gilliam, and one spring training game fielded a lineup of five blacks. That night I heard rumblings. "It's all right to have them in the game," a pitcher said, "but now they're taking over." An infielder was more direct. He said, "How would you like a nigger to take your job?"

I wrote the story for the *Trib*, and when it was published, columnists swarmed to Vero Beach. One, writing for the *New York Post*, immediately began a multipart series "The Roots of Bigotry." If nothing else, at least it made the appropriate noise.

My point here is that the Jackie Robinson experience was watched over by committed journalists, and wherever Woodward or I found a bigot, we smoked him out. In 1961 Robinson presented me with the book called *Wait Till Next Year*, which he had written with the black journalist Carl T. Rowan. The inscription reads: "To Roger with respect and admiration. It has been good working with you and knowing you over the years." I showed the book to Yogi Berra a few years ago. Yogi thought briefly, then he said, "You know, you really ought to keep that."

Traveling with the Dodgers long ago, I heard reports about the racist Red Sox, but nothing as detailed, as painful, or as convincing as the stories that Howard Bryant tells. Pumpsie Green, the first black Red Sox player, who could not stay at the team hotel during spring training but had to live in a ramshackle rooming house seventeen miles away. Big, handsome Earl Wilson, a right-hander who never found his rhythm amid Boston racism but later won twenty-two for

Detroit. Jim Rice, one of the great modern hitters, who found that even when he became the most valuable player in the American League, much of Boston remained closed to him.

Howard Bryant ends with a bright note of hope. Pedro Martinez, the great right-hander, is coming to be recognized as the leader of the current Boston team and has gained wider acceptance than any previous black Red Sox player. My own bright note of hope is Howard Bryant. Someone finally has found the discipline and energy and courage to write this marvelous book.

Roger Kahn
Stone Ridge, NY
May 2003

INTRODUCTION

The future of the Boston Red Sox stood next to me behind the Fenway Park batting cage one April afternoon, staring out at a canvas both lush and decrepit, one that for nearly three-quarters of a century owned the name of only one architect, Thomas A. Yawkey.

Suddenly and completely, the Red Sox, Fenway Park, and its legacy now sat in new hands, in the hands of this man, tall and gaunt, whose eyes looked over his investment behind sunglasses, but were fixed on the game he calls his passion.

The conversation was both quick and intense, and it was clear that the meter was running for John Henry, the new principal owner of the Boston Red Sox, the oldest professional sports team in Boston and easily its most valuable and evocative. That Henry surveyed the storied and venerable Fenway Park landscape on April 12, 2002—hours before a Patriots' Day weekend clash between the Red Sox and New York Yankees—was ironic but not surprising, for the Red Sox more than other franchises have always found themselves linked with the larger Boston story of abolition, opportunity, politics, and clannish insularity. He says without assumption that he is undergoing a crash course in such far-reaching but wholly New England principles.

Having met Henry only minutes earlier, I would find it impossible to glean his thoughts through his mannerisms or expressions, but it was clear that he was not surprised by the details of our impromptu discussion. He stood coolly, appearing concerned about a subject that he knew of only by piecemeal anecdote. He wanted to know if the relationship of the Red Sox with black players and the African-American community was as damaged and intractable as he'd heard it was.

Bluntly, John Henry cut to the issue. He asked what the perception of the black community was toward the franchise he'd paid $700 million to steward. We shared stories. I told him of a revealing moment in my early teens, growing up in the city's Dorchester section, during the 1982 World Series playoffs. A group of family members, led by my gruff and unmovable grandfather, admonished me for rooting for the Red Sox instead of the National League Cardinals and Dodgers, teams that had embraced integration while the Red Sox had not.

"We don't care for the Red Sox around here, because the Red Sox have never had any niggers," my grandfather said, speaking harshly but truthfully for an entire black community, embittered and distrustful of the Red Sox. "Never have, never will. You think about that."

The sunglasses came off, and the story made Henry wince a little, as did hearing the belief known throughout the black network of baseball that Boston is so much more difficult, so much less welcoming a place to play for African Americans. Many superstar black ballplayers over the years, starting with Jackie Robinson and funneling down, from David Justice, Albert Belle, and Tim Raines, to Gary Sheffield and Dave Winfield, have all either expressed hesitancy about playing in Boston or inserted language into their contracts that expressly prevented them from ever being traded to the Red Sox.

Though he owns no responsibility, John Henry seemed to know that as much as he controls the Red Sox future, he can also be susceptible to the touch of its past, a past that—in the framework of race—was never truly confronted by his predecessors.

The result would be a history that is always maddeningly and importantly present. The memory of Pumpsie Green's early days as the first black player on the Red Sox—a dozen years after Jackie Robinson made it permissible to open the doors of the game—would decades later maintain a sort of relevance in Boston that it would not in other cities. Earl Wilson's difficult navigation of a segregated South and the club's uneasiness about racial questions would seem alive a quarter century later when Ellis Burks found himself isolated by race in the Red Sox clubhouse, as Jim Rice had been before him. Reggie Smith's anger toward Boston would be felt a generation later, a mystery but a topic of discussion, even as Mo Vaughn and Dan Duquette were seminal figures in creating a better, healthier environment for players of color in Boston. Unspoken, the bitter feelings would persist.

Henry and I talked about the muddled and contentious history between the club and the black community, in which Boston's blacks have always felt a certain hostility and distance toward the Red Sox while the club has always been frustrated that its best efforts for outreach have been received with lukewarm enthusiasm.

The past would never seem to fade, and the Red Sox and the city continued to struggle with racial unease. Playing for the Red Sox wasn't always required to feel the racial distance that existed; visiting black players could feel the tension.

"I used to love to play the Red Sox, just to beat them," said longtime New York Yankees second baseman Willie Randolph. "It wasn't just because of the rivalry, although that was part of it. As a black player, the Red Sox brought out that little something in all of us. Black players knew that it was always a little harder for other blacks in Boston, the environment a little rougher.

"We knew Boston's reputation and as a player you always look for that something extra. I have family there and I know the city from spending time with them. It was the reputation of the city that made me want to beat them that much more. You want to win every game, of course, but believe me, every black player in that Yankee clubhouse wanted to beat Boston even more."

John Henry nodded without revealing much emotion, acknowledging that the Red Sox still pay a price not only in the Boston black community he seeks to cultivate and also in the won-loss column—imagine not the Curse of the Bambino but Willie Mays, Ted Williams, and Jackie Robinson on the same team—but in its overall baseball legacy for being the last team to integrate and for its humiliation of Robinson during the final days of World War II.

What John Henry wanted to know wasn't if the Red Sox live in racism's shadow, for he knows his new franchise most certainly does. With that recognition, he stood already quantum leaps ahead of his predecessors, who often seemed to believe that forceful, impassioned denial could somehow alter the facts.

Instead, he reacted with dynamism, free of the cynicism that has handcuffed both the Red Sox and those who have sought relief from a cold war of sorts. He wanted to know what could be done about it. More to the point, he wanted to know what he could do about it.

"It doesn't *have* to be this way," Henry said of the lingering animosities between the community and team, the trepidation between players—potential championship-winning players—and the Red Sox, his Red Sox. "You have to just decide you want to make the effort. If you make the effort, I believe people will respond."

In the voice of John Henry was the confidence of hope, perhaps naïveté to the more hardened of Red Sox watchers who don't believe that the Red Sox or the city of Boston will escape a decades-old notoriety. A notoriety fueled by the Tom Yawkey legacy that respected sports and news commentator Clark Booth calls with conviction a "perverse farce." Yet it seemed to me that Henry understood that in his hands lie an opportunity if not to rewrite history then to chart a new course for a franchise long weighted by entrenched racial attitudes.

For Henry's future to be realized—and for the Red Sox to begin a day where the club is not forever reminded it failed to integrate quickly and thus is forever suffering from a competitive disadvantage—there must be a recognition of the past, for too many voices have felt stifled or gone completely unheard. This is the story of the African-American experience in Boston, through the eyes of one of its greatest institutions, the Boston Red Sox.

After a handshake, John Henry left, with more education about the culture he has bought into and the challenges ahead. For both him and his ownership group, the complexity of Boston and the Red Sox's past should not be a source of pessimism, as it had been in the city for decades, but a blueprint for hope. With that hope stifled but important voices begin to reemerge.

Luis Tiant, the great Red Sox pitcher, believes himself to be lucky in the sense that he was fortunate enough to enjoy all that Boston had to offer, even though applause for him was tempered by the experiences of a Jim Rice or Reggie Smith.

"I heard so many people say that Boston is racist," he said. "Some people had problems there, and I really do feel sorry for all the Afro-Americans there and what they went through. But what happened to me, I can't say a bad word about Boston.

"People loved me there, and when the team wins, there is no place like Fenway Park in the world. Everyone should be able to feel what I have felt there."

Tiant, weary but resilient, said he grew tired of Boston's constant racial struggles and hopes that within the rubble of hard years exists the key to a newer, brighter chapter for the future.

Howard Bryant
Provincetown, MA
New York City, NY
May 22, 2002

SHUT OUT

ONE

There was no reason to be optimistic. The Boston Red Sox of 1959 were expected to be mediocre, as they had been for nearly a decade. The writers, in fierce competition for headlines in what was then an edgy, eight newspaper town, were desperate for a story. In March, they got one.

Pumpsie Green to be first Negro to play for Red Sox. Beats out Jackie Robinson and Willie Mays.

The headline is made up, but it is not fiction. Pumpsie Green did beat out Robinson and Mays, and beat them by a long shot, because the other two were courted by the Red Sox years earlier and were never even issued a uniform. Green was just a ten-year-old shrimp in 1945, when the Red Sox sent Robinson packing, humiliated after inviting him to Boston to try out with the club. Green was in high school when a Red Sox scout was tipped off to the kid prodigy Mays, playing on the no-name fields and dirt lots in Westfield, Alabama. But scouts are busy people, too busy, busting up and down the dusty back roads and getting paid only when a kid pans out. This scout, a Texan named Larry Woodall, had other things to do, and said so, proudly. "I'm not going to waste my time," he said, "waiting on a bunch of niggers."

And he didn't. Woodall went home, and Mays went to the Hall of Fame.

The price the Red Sox would pay, of course, was winning, and history. Surely a club with Mays, Robinson, Doerr, and the Splinter would have beaten those Yankees at least once, and Williams would have been more than just a hitter, but a champion as well. DiMaggio and Williams would always be rivals, linked to history like Magic and Bird, but DiMag and Teddy weren't playing on the same stage. In private, DiMaggio said it in a way you couldn't confuse. "Sure, he can hit," the Clipper said. "But he never won a thing." This inability—for many years unwillingness, really—would to a major degree prevent the Red Sox from what they wanted to do: win.

While the rest of baseball would to a large extent evolve and distance itself from the nascent days of integration, the end of roster segregation in the major leagues would only be the beginning of a greater challenge for the Red Sox. In Boston, the consequences would be severe and lasting.

What hastened the fall of the Red Sox and separated the team from its rivals was the culture of racism that coursed through the organization. It was not a secret around the game. In fact, the Red Sox were merely carrying out baseball's strictest order of maintaining segregation as all teams had, but Boston seemed to have missed the memo that the sixty-year agreement had been permanently dissolved with Robinson's arrival in 1947. Nevertheless, it was a topic that went largely unreported in Boston, for the organization merely reflected the most rigid sentiments held by much of the society at large.

The unspoken policy of the Red Sox organization to ignore the wealth of black talent that was now being admitted into the game was a simple enough order, one that was carried out so efficiently that integration forces could never pin down any member of the team's hierarchy to explain how so many gifted players—starting with Robinson and Mays—were slipping through the net of what was the richest team in baseball. For the Yankees, baseball's most successful team, an explanation came easily. The team's management would often say for the record it had no intention of integrating. The Red Sox were different. The public face of the organization, usually a general manager, was insistent that the club did not discriminate, but within the organization scouts who discovered gifted black players were discouraged from cultivating and signing these youngsters to contracts. Organizations that tried to trade black players to the Red Sox found Boston reluctant to deal for them. The few newspaper reporters attempting to gain clarity as to why the Red Sox seemed to show such little interest in blacks were met icily and sometimes with outward hostility. When tensions grew, the veneer could sometimes fade. As a young reporter for the Boston *Herald,* Bud Collins was one of the few reporters who openly questioned the Red Sox regarding hiring black players. Once, Red Sox manager Mike "Pinky" Higgins rewarded Collins for his intrepidness by dumping a plate of beef Stroganov in his lap. Forty years later, Collins would begin an essay with the lingering culinary question from that evening, "Who was Stroganov?"

The Red Sox of 1959 were expected to be mediocre because they had been for so long. They couldn't pitch and, oddly for any Red Sox team, weren't expected to do much at the plate, either. Ted Williams was at the close of a legendary career. During the decade he had fought in Korea, retired for the first month of the 1955 season, had only participated in one pennant race, and was fending off an increasing vocal press corps that encouraged his retirement. The 1950s were a decade dominated by New York baseball, and the powerhouse Boston teams of the late 1940s led by Williams, Junior Stephens, and Doerr were long gone, replaced by a club that was consistently below average.

But in the spring, and almost by accident, the Red Sox invited an unknown black infielder named Pumpsie Green to spring training. If it was not a historic moment in the game—by 1959 every other team in baseball had integrated except the Red Sox, and the novelty of seeing a black player on the field had largely dissipated—the news in Boston was nonetheless welcomed as painfully overdue. When he arrived in Scottsdale, Arizona, in March, Green would be the latest prospect poised to do something that couldn't be done. Pumpsie Green would be the latest hope to integrate the Red Sox since Jackie Robinson left Fenway Park bitter and humiliated fourteen years earlier.

For an infielder of limited skills, playing in the major leagues was a difficult enough challenge; baseball is only fun for those good enough not to worry about making the club, and Pumpsie Green always worried. He was expected to compete for the starting shortstop job not because of any special skills of his own, but because the incumbent, Don Buddin, wasn't much of a player. Buddin was known as much in the press box by the nickname "E-6"—the official scoring designation for "error-shortstop"—as by his own first name.

Breaking into the majors was difficult enough. Green wasn't a touted prospect, a "can't miss," in scout parlance. He was just a guy trying to win a job. Being black made it all different. Add color into the mix and Pumpsie Green was no longer a limited shortstop trying to win a spot on a mediocre ball club. He was a pioneer, storming the castle sword in hand. Anyone who took an interest in the story transformed an unassuming kid with a suspect swing into a piece of history. Pumpsie Green would say often that he didn't want that kind of scrutiny, that responsibility. That didn't matter, though, because it wasn't his choice to decide. That was a fact. So was this: Jackie Robinson, of all people, was watching, too.

Everyone in the game knew what the Red Sox were, and that's why no one was particularly envious of Pumpsie Green as he packed up and made his way down to Arizona for that first spring training. The Red Sox were tired. The owner, Tom Yawkey, was for years the richest man in baseball, but he was tired of losing ballgames, and even more tired of throwing money into a ball club that produced in the 1950s sorry finishes year in and year out while the Yankees owned the planet. What really drove him crazy were those politicians, and that funky ballpark. They loved it. He wanted another one, and if they weren't careful, he might just pack up shop sell the club, or worse, move it to another city. The National League Braves had packed up and moved to Milwaukee, so Yawkey had Boston all to himself. Nobody told Tom Yawkey what for.

In the meantime, though, what Yawkey did best was drink, and no one likes to drink alone, so he brought in his boys and while the club was losing, Yawkey tuned out. He let them—one particular man named Pinky Higgins— run the show. While the rest of the baseball world moved forward, the Red Sox stood still. That's what Pumpsie Green had to look forward to.

It was with this knowledge that he prepared for the spring, and if by chance Green did not know what to expect of the Red Sox, Pinky Higgins spelled it out with brutal directness to the local reporters that covered the team. "There will never," Higgins said to reporter Al Hirshberg, "be any niggers on this team as long as I have anything to say about it."

They were crushing words, and they hovered over the Red Sox, a reminder of perpetual torrent. Immediately upon his arrival in Scottsdale, there was but one certainty: Pumpsie Green would not only have to win a job, but would have to make history in doing it.

To understand the world of Pumpsie Green is to accept a baseball establishment that had spent the first decade and a half following World War II integrating its ranks and undergoing the greatest change in its history. But by no means was it seamless or always welcome, for the men who ran baseball—despite Robinson's success—were unconvinced that the country was prepared for, or even wanted, integrated baseball. George Weiss, the architect of the New York Yankees dynasty in the 1940s and 1950s and one of the most strident racists in the game, believed that his white players did not want to play with blacks and pointed to the decrease in attendance of both the rival Brooklyn Dodgers and New York Giants—two teams that integrated quickly and heavily but were also subject to the severe and rapid shifts of New York's demographics—as sure evidence that integration would hurt baseball financially. The Dodgers, incidentally, were the game's best road draw in 1947.

The nation—largely two separate societies when Robinson arrived in 1947—lagged behind baseball as a social engineer. The country was on the verge of entering a major stage of the civil rights movement, but it was not there yet, and any organization taking real steps toward integration was if not radical, then clearly progressive. The legendary Supreme Court *Brown vs. Topeka Board of Education* decision had passed, but its implementation was hardly peaceable or universal. Segregation, still rigid, continued to be the order in the South, but in a relatively short time it was apparent that sweeping and major change was inevitable. A full four years before Pumpsie Green faced the Red Sox's strict color line, Martin Luther King, Jr., had already arrived on the national scene, having scored his greatest victory. The Montgomery bus boycott, now famous, was just the start. Wrote David Halberstam—in his book, *The Fifties*:

> An AP reporter handed him [King, Jr.] a note that included an AP bulletin reporting that the Supreme Court had judged the Montgomery bus-segregation law to be unconstitutional. The blacks had won. . . . So the battle was won. But the war was hardly over. It was a beginning rather than an end; the boycott became the Movement, with a capital *M*. The blacks might have alienated the local white leadership, but they had gained the sympathy of the white majority outside the South. In the past, the whites in Montgomery had been both judge and jury: Now, as the nation responded to the events there, they became the judged.

The Boston Red Sox were not physically located in the South, but they too were the judged. Even in the late stages of the 1950s, they were not alone in their recalcitrance, yet in a very short time they would stand in total isolation.

In 1957, neither the Philadelphia Phillies nor the Detroit Tigers had fielded a black player, prompting Jackie Robinson to thunder in his retirement speech, "If the thirteen major league clubs can come up with colored players, why can't the other three?"

Robinson made his first visit to Philadelphia in 1947, and Phillies General Manager Herb Pennock—a former pitcher with the Red Sox and member of its front office—made his sentiments clear. He pleaded with Dodger GM Branch Rickey to keep Robinson from Philadelphia. "Branch, you can't bring the nigger here. Philadelphia's not ready for that yet." Fifty years later, when Pennock's hometown of Kennett Square, a middle-class, integrated community near Philadelphia, sought to erect a statue celebrating the old pitcher, his comments were unearthed and caused a minor scandal.

In the early fifties, American affluence produced a flood of movement to the suburbs, initiated by the housing phenomenon of Levittown, the planned housing community about forty minutes outside of Philadelphia. Yet the postwar boom didn't apply to blacks. The Red Sox organization would be castigated for charges of racism, but Philadelphia in those days was equally if not more foreboding. Consider the position of Bill Levitt in the early 1950s, a man who did not allow black families to move into his sprawling new—and immensely popular—suburban communities until nearly two decades later—in *The Fifties*, Halberstam constructed the argument:

> The Negroes in America are trying to do in 400 years what the Jews in the world have not wholly accomplished in 600 years. As a Jew, I have no room in my mind or heart for racial prejudice. But . . . I have come to know that if we sell one house to a Negro family, then 90 or 95 percent of our white customers will not buy into the community. That is their attitude, not ours. . . . As a company our position is simply this: we can solve a housing problem or we can try to solve a racial problem, but we cannot combine the two.

Yet by 1959, the Red Sox grew to be an embarrassment, even to the right of the most conservative baseball organizations. They represented the most rigid example of the old guard unwilling to recognize the inevitable changes taking place. Even Philadelphia and Detroit, two northern cities that weren't by any means progressive, had integrated their rosters, leaving the Red Sox as the only all-white team in the majors. If the hearts and attitudes of the men who ran baseball teams had not changed, even the most virulent of race-conscious owners had fielded black players, if only for the novel reason of trying to improve their teams. Clubs hiring blacks were no longer special, wrote the black periodical *Chicago American*, the teams without them were.

Jackie Robinson was three years retired by 1959, but he was by no means out of the game. Real pioneers don't fade softly into the horizon. He zeroed in on Yawkey—he would never forget that first slight fourteen years earlier—

pointing straight to the top for an explanation. Robinson's ferocity stayed with him long after he hung up the spikes. Through the press, Robinson needled Yawkey, just like he used to pester all those pitchers by feinting, darting, and dancing off third base. If no one else would, he would hit Yawkey between the eyes with the truth. If Yawkey had a hired a black player or two, "Maybe he would have won a few more pennants," Robinson said. Not winning the World Series, that was a sore subject all along New England. Since the end of World War I, it always has been.

Yet what really galled Robinson was not just Yawkey's club, but the converging myths of the Red Sox and the city. For two centuries, Boston was supposed to be a social leader, a beacon of tolerance.

Robinson knew firsthand that a strain of liberalism had existed in the city, for he was befriended by Isadore Muchnick, a Jewish city councilor who had clashed with the Red Sox through Yawkey's top baseball man Eddie Collins. Two years before Robinson joined the Brooklyn Dodgers, Muchnick welcomed Robinson to Boston with the promise of integrating the Red Sox. The Red Sox in 1945 could have been the first team to integrate, with Robinson, but instead would be the last. The missed opportunity would sharply mirror a reversal of the city's own racial fortunes.

Yawkey's racial belief system would be a question throughout his lifetime, and after, but to Robinson and the black press, there was no real quandary. Yawkey did not want blacks on his team.

In 1959, the pressure was on. The Red Sox still did not have a black player on the roster, nor did they seem particularly interested in finding one. Yawkey frustrated the integration forces in Boston by feigning ignorance about his team's racial makeup. Save for a few reporters, the Boston media showed little interest in pressing Yawkey on racial issues. Boston as a newspaper town left much to be desired in those days. It was, thought Marty Nolan, who started at the *Globe* in 1961 and would become one of the most respected political journalists in the country, like Chicago journalism in the 1920s, "lots of papers, all of them bad." Bud Collins, who would go on to prominence as a columnist for the *Globe* and as a television color commentator on NBC's tennis broadcasts, remembers a silent edict at the *Herald* generally prohibiting reportage on the club's racial transgressions because it also owned the radio station WHDH, which happened to be the Red Sox flagship station. Most of the best reporting about the Red Sox and its failure to hire black players appeared outside of the city.

Over the years, a few Boston reporters, such as Dave Egan, a Harvard-educated columnist for the Boston *Record,* challenged the team, but focused not on Yawkey, the person most responsible for the direction of the franchise, but on lower personnel who lacked the same authority and presence. A defining characteristic of the Boston press in those days would be never to challenge Yawkey directly to explain the team's racial direction, even when powerful city and state agencies would take an active role in challenging Yawkey to explain his hiring policies.

Unlike other baseball cities, an old abolitionist activism still existed in Boston. Boston was the home of a host of firsts for the nation, and for years it liked to be considered by its citizens—both black and white—as especially racially progressive. For the better part of the nineteenth century the city had built a powerful reputation on its noble accomplishments, but like most of the nation in the early part of the twentieth century Boston had exhibited a massive retreat from the concept of racial equality and owned little new history on racial issues about which to be proud. In truth, Boston was always a city confused about its moral direction. Its abolitionist pedigree was more the result of a relatively small but influential group of anti-slavery leaders than any form of citywide enlightenment. Still, the idea of Boston as a racial beacon not only captured the imagination but would also be a heady legacy to live up to. Dealing with its significant past and its quite different present, Boston was perhaps as morally conflicted as any city in the country about race, a characteristic that would curiously grow worse as the rest of the country seemed to improve. Because of its prominent past many of the city's blacks believed in a special bond with Boston that dated back to slavery; they possessed a pride in self and in the city that was markedly different than, say, how a black person would view his condition in the South. Boston's pedigree was well documented and enhanced by the black press. Runaway slaves found refuge in Boston. Long before it was commonplace, Boston opened up its prestigious universities to blacks, and as a city it lacked the overt racial hostility that marked much of America during those times. Although much of these accomplishments occurred in the nineteenth century, the sentiment existed that Boston was insulated from the racism that would tear at the rest of the nation. It was a last vestige of this old spirit that on the verge of the 1960s attempted to prod the Red Sox.

The Boston Ministerial Alliance, the NAACP, the American Veterans Committee of Massachusetts, and the Massachusetts Commission Against Discrimination (MCAD) challenged the Red Sox to explain why it was the only major league team without a black player. As of 1958, Yawkey did not employ a single black person—not with the grounds crew, custodians, concessionaires, or office staff—at any level of the organization. Local NAACP president Herbert Tucker attacked the team. "The Red Sox are suspect," Tucker said. "Their past record makes them vulnerable to the charges hurled against them."

Yawkey, the wealthiest owner in the game, would neither explain nor defend his hiring practices. That responsibility usually went to a person of lesser authority, usually a general manager, while Yawkey remained in the background. Bucky Harris, the Red Sox general manager in 1959, represented the organization in front of the MCAD with testimony that infuriated Robinson especially. "The primary concern of the Red Sox is to give the fans of New England a winning ball club. When capable players are available, they will be used regardless of race, color, or creed." The stalemate was a telling reflection of Yawkey's indifference to integration and provided a clear window into the minds of the men who ran the club under him. Yawkey's old shortstop, manager, and general manager, Joe Cronin, was both curt and pugnacious about the issue over the years. Cronin, nearly as much as Yawkey himself, would wield an immense amount of power in the shaping of the personality and culture of the club. He was a great player in the 1930s and 1940s and was groomed by Yawkey over the years to be a defining voice in the franchise. Cronin was like the rest of his generation, who came of age between the two great wars and knew nothing other than a segregated society. He believed in his heart that if blacks were not inherently inferior to whites, then both societies benefited from segregation. These feelings were revealed both by Cronin himself and more importantly by the complexion of the players he chose to play for the Red Sox. Still, he would claim otherwise. "The Red Sox care nothing about a man's color," Cronin said in 1958. "They only want good ballplayers."

The Red Sox further benefited from Yawkey's silence because it was such an extreme departure from other baseball owners, such as the Yankees' Weiss, Walter Briggs in Detroit, and Larry MacPhail of the Yankees, who voiced racist opinions with impunity. Briggs was a segregationist to an almost proud degree, who like Higgins vowed never to hire a black player. It was not mere bluster. The Tigers did not employ a black player until five years after Briggs' death in 1952. Wendell Smith, the respected sportswriter for the black weekly Pittsburgh *Courier*, characterized Briggs as, "Oh, so very prejudiced. He's the major league combination of Simon Legree and Adolf Hitler."

But if Yawkey and his lieutenants claimed victory by not being forced into integrating by protestors or state agencies, they failed to recognize the mounting, lasting, and unflattering portrait the organization was constructing for itself. Here, the Red Sox would not escape so cleanly. Yawkey may have held out on integration, but the word was out. Blacks who played in the majors for other teams claimed—and members of the black press wrote fiercely—that the Red Sox were no longer just another team, but the living symbol of racism in baseball. It was in this environment that Pumpsie Green reported to Red Sox camp in 1959.

He still doesn't know how he received the nickname, but everyone would call Elijah Green "Pumpsie." He was born in 1935 and grew up in the working-class neighborhood of Richmond, California. During the World War II shortage of men in the country, his mother Gladys was a welder on the docks in Oakland. His father Elijah worked in nearby Richmond for the city's public works department and also for the Oakland Army Base. Elijah Green, Sr., was a direct, hard-working man.

For blacks, California was not a promised land, for if its racism was not as virulent as in other places around the country, the rules were still rigid. What blacks did find on the West Coast was work. The rules in the Green household were simple: Stay in line and do as you're told. In those days, especially for a black family in Depression-era America, there simply wasn't time for frivolity.

Elijah Green, Sr., was himself an athlete but denied himself the strong impulse to meddle in the athletic growth of his children. He let his children play, and two of his boys would grow into exceptional athletes. "He never pressured us," Pumpsie says of his father. Pumpsie would play major league baseball. His older brother Cornell would later become a star defensive back for the Dallas Cowboys.

Almost immediately, there was a charge to the spring air. The Red Sox for the first time in their history were faced with a legitimate opportunity to integrate, and the confrontation of its rigid culture with this new prospect was fascinating.

Under the most tense of circumstances, Green and Higgins never wanted to meet. Pumpsie Green's ultimate dream was not to play for the Boston Red Sox, but in the Pacific Coast League, home of the most competitive baseball on the West Coast. It was where the great Joe DiMaggio began his career with the San Francisco Seals; Ted Williams and Bobby Doerr also started out there. Perhaps more than anything else, Pumpsie Green owned an ability—very important for black people in the 1940s and 1950s—to accommodate his aspirations to conform to the social limitations of the day. He was content to play ball with the West Coast teams familiar to his youth, such the Seals, the Mission, and the Oakland Oaks, in a league that was once segregated but had opened its doors to blacks in 1948 without the hostility that peppered the major leagues. That was fine, for Pumpsie Green was not by nature a trailblazer. When he finally arrived in Boston, he liked to say he needed a map just to find it. He grew up in California and felt comfortable with the more relaxed racial climate there.

Nor were the Red Sox particularly enthused about Green. He was an infielder for the Minneapolis Millers, a minor league outfit that Yawkey purchased in 1957. The Red Sox were a bad team in those days, hardly aggressive in the pursuit of top ballplayers. Racially, the Red Sox showed little interest in black players in general, which, thought Earl Wilson, a pitcher who would be the second black to play for the club, created a dubious side effect. If the members of the Red Sox hierarchy felt pressured into signing a black player, the conditions would be even worse for the unfortunate black prospect who arrived.

Spring training was a disaster from the very start. When he arrived at the posh Safari Hotel in Scottsdale, Green was turned away. He said he was with the Boston Red Sox. That didn't matter. He found out the hard way that the Safari didn't accept black guests. Pumpsie Green underwent his indoctrination. If you were black, you went through it, too. Robinson did, as did Bob Gibson, the great pitcher for the St. Louis Cardinals. Curt Flood remembered a similar dignity-stripping moment when he arrived at the Floridian Hotel, reporting to his first spring camp for the Cincinnati Reds in 1957. The front deskman must have thought that Flood didn't understand English, and for an instant, Flood had wished he hadn't.

The deskman repeated himself sharply. Yes, Flood may have been with the Cincinnati Reds baseball club, and yes, the ball club was staying there, but the Floridian Hotel admitted only white guests. With that, Flood was instructed to follow the black bellhop who suddenly emerged, leave the hotel through a side door, and then head to the boarding house where the black ballplayers lived. Flood stood for a minute, gathered himself, and did as he was told. The words resounded as if they were a thunderclap, ripping through every part of his body.

"Until it happens you literally cannot believe it. After it happens, you need time to absorb it," Flood wrote. "The black cab took me five miles out of town and deposited me at Mrs. Felder's boardinghouse. When I saw who was there—Frank Robinson and four or five other black ball players—my knees began to knock. Rules had been enforced. . . . Officially and for the duration, I was a nigger."

The Red Sox didn't know what to do, so the club glossed the truth. A lot. Jack Malaney, a team official, said the Safari was booked because of "the normal seasonal traffic jam." Malaney had really put his foot in it, because it wasn't just the Safari that barred blacks, but *the entire city of Scottsdale!* In those days, Scottsdale was completely segregated. Blacks were permitted to work in the city as day laborers and domestics, even as baseball players, but none were permitted within city limits after dark. Green was taken to the Frontier Motel, in Phoenix, seventeen miles from his own team.

The daily routine was mortifying. Each day, a member of the Red Sox staff would pick up Green at the Frontier and drive him to the Red Sox spring training facility. When the day ended, a Red Sox representative would drive him back and deposit him at the front door.

On the field, things weren't much better. Higgins was omnipresent, his dislike for blacks palpable. While addressing reporters, Higgins would commonly refer to blacks as "niggers" and rarely made eye contact with Green or Earl Wilson. Higgins was also known to be a heavy drinker, which unnerved Green. Higgins was coarse by nature, and he was close to Yawkey. That meant, in Yawkey's especially crony-oriented world, that Higgins had a job for life. In the first five years Yawkey owned the Red Sox, Higgins played third base, driving in 106 runs in both 1937 and 1938. In so many ways, adjusting under Higgins was a difficult process for Green, who liked his minor league manager, Gene

Mauch, immensely, for obvious reasons. Nor did he feel particularly comfortable in Arizona. How could he? Arizona in 1959 was an empty dustbowl, where the tumbleweed outnumbered the people. Scottsdale was not the tony boutique haven it would become—you needed air-conditioning for that—but a desert that was only hot, dry, and conservative. It was Goldwater country.

There was little communication with his teammates outside of the ballfield, few of the beers and laughs that come with the easy climate of spring and are crucial for a player to adjust to major league life. Green spent the weeks of spring training, in usual circumstances crucial to creating the camaraderie so essential to a team, completely detached from his teammates. By comparison, the San Francisco Giants, having been an integrated team for more than a decade, stayed at a hotel in Phoenix, the Adams, that admitted the entire team.

For Green, it was another unfortunate illustration of how insensitive many organizations of the day could be about race, that the Red Sox were not even aware of the segregation laws of the city where it played. Nor did Yawkey use the club's influence—as Branch Rickey of the Dodgers and Gussie Busch of the Cardinals would—to promote any type of change. Pumpsie Green was an outcast.

"From night to morning," wrote Milton Gross, "the first Negro player to be brought to spring training by the Boston Red Sox ceases to be a member of the team he hopes to make as a shortstop."

Yawkey was merely a millionaire, thought David Halberstam, not a moral or social crusader. Nor—as in the case of a Rickey or Bill Veeck—did Yawkey seem to be particularly hounded by his conscience. He owned no personal desire for racial justice. He was merely and totally a product of his times, insulated by his affluence and the high privilege of being white. Occasionally, Green would see Yawkey on the spring training grounds. The exchanges between the two were always pleasant, Green recalled, often ending with an open invitation from Yawkey for Green to visit him on any matter. Recognizing his place in the team's social and professional order and the reality that Higgins was watching him every day, Green never complained to Yawkey about being situated seventeen miles from his teammates.

The Boston press did just as little.

"Agitators may try to make something of the Pumpsie Green case," wrote the *Herald's* Bill Cunningham, who in some clearly conservative quarters was regarded as something of a liberal champion. "In fact, they've been at it already. . . . There seems, however, to be nothing to the present arrangement but social accommodation."

Green took the silent approach, offering little insight into his isolated world. Gross, however, would be moved by how Green lived.

"But segregation," Gross wrote,

> doesn't just come in buildings, such as the Safari Motel in Scottsdale, where the white Red Sox stay, or the Frontier Motel, where Red Sox secretary Tom Dowd deposited

Boston's first Negro when he arrived at camp. It comes in a man's heart, residing there like a burrowing worm. It comes when a man wakes alone, eats alone, goes to the movies every night alone because there's nothing more for him to do and then, in Pumpsie Green's own words, "I get a sandwich and a glass of milk and a book and I read myself to sleep."

Emotional turbulence carried over to the field. Green's physical isolation was worsened by the constant questions of his place in history. Attempts to protest his position only enhanced his status. "So far as I'm concerned, I'm no martyr," he said. "No flag carrier. I'm just trying to make the ball club, that's all. I'm not trying to prove anything else but that. I'm not even interested in being known as the first Negro to make the Red Sox. I just want to make the Red Sox and all the rest of it can wait."

When he played well, Green uplifted the city's integration forces. The Associated Press reported the story of a picketer in front of Fenway hoisting a sign that read, "We want a Pennant, not a white team." According to the story, the picketer was attacked by three youths and the sign was destroyed.

When he struggled, Green believed he let down not only his teammates, but also the people in Boston—the NAACP, for example—who had so tirelessly petitioned the Red Sox on his behalf. The spring turbulence continued. He spoke to his wife Marie, but kept the anxieties mostly inside. He had started the spring hitting a robust .449, but in his final nineteen at-bats, Green produced just two hits. He lost games with his defense, once overthrowing the first baseman on a throw from shortstop by an estimated thirty feet. There was no encouragement from management; Higgins' feelings about black players were a matter of record. Green knew he would have to be perfect to make the club.

There would be one final indignity that first spring. Bucky Harris, the Boston general manager, intimated to reporters that Green had made the club, and even allowed him to travel north for a few final exhibition games through Texas. Green believed he would return to Boston to start the regular season not just as a major leaguer, but also as the first black player in Red Sox history. Then, at the last minute, Higgins sent Green to the minor leagues, ordering him to report to triple-A Minneapolis.

T W O

The notion of Boston as the moral voice of a nation, as social beacon and the home of abolition in the eighteenth and nineteenth centuries, was a myth, really. Schoolchildren, both white and black were fed this version not only as history, but as fact, as something to be proud of. This was the special heritage of Boston, what would separate her and her ideals from the rest. The story would be not just history, but a living blueprint of how to conduct oneself in a society. It would be plenty to live up to.

Yet this myth was so strong, so appealing and sexy to the city's citizens—both white and black—who both clung to it and would pay dearly for its responsibilities and expectations. For the small but vocal anti-slave leadership in New England, the idea of a special relationship between blacks and whites was necessary to build fame and a powerful legacy for both themselves and the region. It was a legacy that would endure long after their days on earth.

For the blacks in Boston, so desperate to be separate from the bitter and squalid lifestyle that came with being a step above slavery, the mere hope that a place of possibility existed in America was attractive enough.

The history books would propagate the notion that Boston was the epicenter of tolerance, and it sounded good. Everybody rode along, too. The city would bask in the comfort of being set apart from the rest of a racially torn, morally confused nation, as Boston would boast a society more integrated than any other major city.

The reality was that it was a big set up, and the bill wouldn't come due for years. How trapped they would all be, Bostonians black and white, when cotton candy fiction met his uncompromising older brother, concrete fact a century later in the streets, on the first day of school.

There were big names in Boston. Wendell Phillips and William Lloyd Garrison were the dominant figures of the anti-slavery movement. They were moralists in their oratories, decrying the inequities of rights. Garrison, in particular, incensed southern leadership not only by words, but actions, for everyone knew Boston was a destination for runaway slaves; or at least a rest stop until they could get to Canada.

Phillips and Garrison were the true beneficiaries of their renown, but blacks benefited, too, secure that no matter how miserable black life was in America, in Boston it was just a little better.

If the idea of a special relationship was profitable for a time, Boston would also be held hostage by it in the twentieth century, for when the city erupted in violence in the 1970s, it fought not only the crisis but also the attitude that these problems couldn't be happening in Boston. When the grandmothers of New England traveled to the Deep South in the 1960s to be arrested in a public show of support for civil rights, they were embarrassed by their conspicuous silence when those same racial battles exploded in Boston. When the Boston Red Sox followed the same gentlemen's agreement as the other fifteen major league clubs in keeping blacks out of the game, it was not only the act of a mismanaged baseball team but also proof that the city couldn't live up to its pedigree. Like the average child of prestigious parents, Boston would forever be a prisoner of its past, of expectations it could never fulfill.

The truth about Boston was something very different—while the abolitionists stole the headlines, the roots of the distance between the city's blacks and Irish were being planted during the nineteenth century, at the same time Garrison spoke of slavery in simple but inflexible terms:

> Reader! Are you with the man-stealers in sympathy and purpose, or on the side of their downtrodden victims? If with the former, then are you the foe of God and Man. If with the latter, what are you prepared to do and dare in their behalf? Be faithful, be vigilant, be untiring in your efforts to break every yoke, and let the oppressed go free. Come what may—cost what it may—inscribe on the banner which you unfurl to the breeze, as your religious and political motto—"NO COMPROMISE WITH SLAVERY! NO UNION WITH SLAVEHOLDERS!"
> WM. LLOYD GARRISON
> BOSTON, November 1, 1845

Whoever spoke the loudest received the attention, and the voice of Boston was that of Garrison and the abolitionist movement. For Garrison, abolitionism was a calling. Slavery was the evil, there could be no debate. Garrison's life was devoted to its elimination.

The more difficult concept was Garrison's and the abolitionists' perception of the slave himself. Here, Boston found itself to be as conflicted as the rest of the nation, for until the arrival of Frederick Douglass, the movement contained no blacks in its leadership. It was, at some level, an irreconcilable conflict, one that over time would not only begin to taint the nobility of the anti-slavery movement but would also mischaracterize Boston as a city far more cultivated racially than it really was. Adelaide Cromwell, one of the earliest black Boston writers, suggested in the 1800s that the abolitionist deplored slavery while simultaneously deploring the slave. Discussing a thesis written by Arthur

Makechnie on the Boston abolitionist Theodore Parker, J. Anthony Lukas concurred, writing, "Nor did Arthur disguise the central contradiction in Parker's world view: his zeal for the black man's abstract rights, his intense distaste for the Negro as a particular person."

Such an inseparable conflict created a predictable hypocrisy, and the result would be decrying slavery in far-away places but practicing segregation at home.

The result was the formation over the years of a much-debated special relationship between the two races. Boston's black population, so small and unthreatening to the white populace, enjoyed a standard of living superior to that of other blacks across the nation. The city's Brahmin ruling class, the white, Protestant gentry that descended from England, lavished freedoms upon blacks that even allowed the formation of a small black middle class.

The list of early abolitionist achievements was impressive. In the First African Church, Boston's oldest black church, Garrison's first anti-slavery society was formed. By the mid-1850s, Massachusetts had eliminated segregation in public schools. Negro citizens were allowed to appear on jury rolls, and for a period of nearly twenty years, a black candidate won election to the city council in each election. Seating in railroad cars was no longer segregated. Moreover, public facilities—museums, the opera, playhouses—had long accepted black patronage. During the Civil War, the most notable event was the valor of the 54th regiment—the first black fighting unit in the North. Its story offered another important mark that Boston stood well ahead of its nation in race relations. The weary Regiment, badly outnumbered in its assault on Fort Wagner in South Carolina, died along with its white commander, Robert Gould Shaw. "Their common martyrdom," wrote J. Anthony Lukas, "helped cast a glow of brotherhood over the city's race relations." A century later, Hollywood would even make a movie, *Glory*, about Boston's nobility.

The result of these early freedoms was an uncommonly strong belief on the part of the city's blacks in the whites who controlled power in the city. In Boston, dissent would be less confrontational than in other cities. Over the years, it would be the blacks in Boston who trusted the vision of Massachusetts as much as any white; this trust would lead to animosity not just between the races when Boston inevitably retreated from these ideals but also between blacks, who would forever be perplexed by why Boston's blacks appeared so submissive to the white power structure.

For a runaway slave named Frederick Baily, Boston was still the ultimate destination. He eluded slave catchers in Rochester, New York, before fleeing to Boston:

> I was afraid to speak to any one for fear of speaking to the wrong one, and thereby falling into the hands of money-loving kidnappers, whose business it was to lie in wait for the panting fugitive, as the ferocious beasts of the forest lie in wait for their prey.

The motto which I adopted when I started from slavery was this—"Trust no man!" I
saw in every white man an enemy, and in almost every colored man cause for distrust.
It was a most painful situation; and, to understand it, one must needs experience it, or
imagine himself in similar circumstances. Then, and not till then, will he fully appreciate the hardships of the toil-worn and whip-scarred fugitive slave.

In New Bedford, the whaling town forty miles southeast of Boston, Baily
boarded at the house of a relatively wealthy black man named Nathan Johnson,
who was reading Sir Walter Scott's *Lady of the Lake*. Johnson had an idea.
Perhaps, to make it more difficult to be tracked and caught by bounty hunters,
he should change his name to a character in the book. It was a good suggestion.
From that day forward, Frederick Baily would be known as Frederick Douglass.

With the addition of Douglass, the Boston anti-slavery movement grew in
power, and Boston's reputation as the destination for blacks crested. He was not
only the ranking Negro voice for the better part of the century, but he also
championed women's suffrage. In part because of his efforts, Boston even
hosted a conference of Negro women voters.

Boston's legend as receptive to blacks was greatly influenced by the black
writers of the day, who were given to hyperbole. One described Boston as a "city
of refuge, place of light, life, and liberty."

"I have been in many states and cities, and in each I have looked for liberty and justice, equal for the black as for the white," wrote ex-slave Susie King
Taylor in 1902. "But it was not until I was within the borders of New England,
and reached old Massachusetts, that I found it."

Wrote early Boston black advocate William Monroe Trotter—himself
Harvard educated—in the Boston *Guardian,* "Welcome to the Home of
Abolition, where it is no crime to be black."

In later years, this position of pride and ownership that Boston blacks held
toward their city would anger emigrating blacks from the South, who viewed
Boston's blacks as bourgeois, unable to recognize the racism that had always
existed and had deluded them into thinking they stood on equal footing with
whites. These early victories in Boston would be exposed later, in the 1970s,
when both blacks and whites in the city would be taken by surprise at the level
of animosity that existed between the races.

Yet the relationship of blacks with whites was by no means ever one of
absolute or even near equality. Boston judge Lemuel Shaw introduced in 1850
the infamous "separate but equal" doctrine that provided a legal foundation for
the 1896 *Plessy v. Ferguson* case and the legal segregation that lasted until the
mid-1950s. When Frederick Douglass fled Rochester, he sought a job as a
caulker. When he arrived in New Bedford he found whites unwilling to accept
him as a skilled worker. He settled for a job as a day laborer. This was in 1845,
at the very same time so many Negro writers spoke of Boston as a paradise.

With such a strong desire to believe in some form of special bond, it was relatively easy on the part of the city's blacks to ignore the powerful elements of the city that truly defined it. Boston's blacks and Irish were already on poor terms, the result of the insistence by the Catholic Church that its members oppose abolition. The Irish were already bitter toward blacks for attempting to emulate the Yankee ruling class. Indeed, as early as the mid-1850s, blacks and the Irish were fighting for a foothold in society's pecking order. A century and a quarter later, the same two groups, still poor, would fight each other over school integration.

As the Irish political position grew more powerful and the Brahmin sphere of influence declined—the Yankee ruling class would cede the mayoralty but would control the city's banks and financial and philanthropic institutions—blacks would not escape the ferocity of the Irish mandate.

Two of the leading Irish orators of the nineteenth century, Daniel O'Connell and John Boyle O'Reilly, dreamed wistfully of an Irish-black alliance as revenge for the Brahmins and their exploitative treatment of both, but it was a romantic notion that died within the ranks of a hostile Irish community. When the Irish began to seize the power they were long denied, it was not done with coalition-building in mind. Thomas O'Connor's continuing history of Boston, described the roots of Irish political hunger:

> For two centuries Catholics were persecuted in Boston, a city which tolerated an annual event called "Pope's Day," when unruly parades from the South End and North End would meet, battle, then join in burning their effigies of the pope. Finally, Gen. George Washington ordered the Continental Army in Cambridge to cease "that ridiculous and childish custom." By the 1830s Boston's Catholic population numbered 8,000, a threatening mass to Yankee residents. Lyman Beecher preached that Catholicism was incompatible with democracy because the Pope controlled the thoughts of his flock. A campaign against Catholics by "Native Americans" set the background for the burning of the Ursuline Convent, Charlestown, in 1834. Francis J. Grund, one of the few native Bostonians who took a sympathetic interest in the fate of the Irish newcomers, warned them to remain orderly and to seek their place in Boston through the political system. Boston's growing Irish-Catholic community took this advice with a vengeance in the next century.

Simultaneously, black life in Boston eroded. The generations who bene-fited from more tolerant times aged and were replaced by a people who may have heard stories of Boston's abolitionist past, but knew nothing but segrega-tion and poverty. Phillips was gone. So were Garrison and Douglass, replaced by only a worn legend of activism. Boston's public schools, integrated in the mid-1800s, were now segregated, as were hospitals and mass transit. Higher-paying union jobs became prevalent, but blacks were largely excluded from the country's labor unions until after World War II.

The black writers once so optimistic about Boston's future scolded the abolitionists once committed to their freedom, who now abandoned the struggle. The Yankee gentry did disappear, fighting a losing battle for political control with the Irish. They still controlled the banks and other financial institutions, and were immensely powerful backroom brokers, but Yankee political power in Boston slipped greatly. Irish politicians first secured Boston's mayoralty in 1905; for the remainder of the century, the city would elect only two non-Irish mayors. In 1895, the city approved redistricting of its voting wards, splitting the already small black population. The result for Boston's black communities would be shattering. Boston would not elect a black politician to its city council until Tom Atkins in 1967. In turn, not only were the Irish political blocs able to control the city's local wards, but their growing numbers also allowed them to elect officials citywide.

And through it all, the tensions simmered. Blacks watched the Irish leapfrog over them politically and economically and their numbers were too small to do anything about it. Black prosperity depended on the goodwill of the politically weakened Brahmins.

That was black life in Boston, and it stirred its own kind of resentment. Dependency was a dangerous thing, but that was the reality. When white political or social leadership took an interest, black fortunes could flower. When other items on the political agenda took priority—or when an issue would be politically beneficial for whites but not blacks arose—black status would effectively crumble, and crumble it did.

Black disenfranchisement in Boston was merely following a national trend after the Civil War. Liberal Republicans, led by Massachusetts senator Henry Cabot Lodge, lost a bid to implement an important voting rights act that would have guaranteed the black vote in 1890. It was, thought historian Mark Schneider, the final, and, with the exception of emancipation itself, perhaps most significant moment in black political history in the nineteenth century.

> The failure of the bill marked the end of an era in American race relations, and the beginning of the nadir of African-American history. Mississippi disenfranchised its black voters during the course of that very year, followed by South Carolina in 1895 and Louisiana in 1898. Lynching reached an all-time high in 1892. . . . It is a significant testimony to the primacy of Massachusetts in the civil rights crusade that the fight for the election bill was led by Bay State Brahmins Lodge and Hoar. These politicians were both descendants of Boston's political antislavery movement and the tradition of Charles Sumner and John Quincy Adams. This, however, was the last fight of powerful Bostonians for civil rights in Congress. Their retreat greatly facilitated the national advance of racism.

The Boston Evening *Transcript* wrote in a September 1885 editorial: "The Southern issue is the question whether the colored men of the South shall enjoy their political rights. Those rights are given them by the Constitution. They are deprived him by fraud." Periodically, as in the *Transcript* editorial, the old

Boston spirit would shimmer, but more often was engulfed by the more vivid realities of the time.

For a brief moment, Irish leaders such as Daniel O'Connell and John Boyle O'Reilly sought fruitlessly to coax Boston's Irish if not into abolitionism, at least into dialogue with the Negro struggle. O'Connell was the legendary Irish patriot known as "The Liberator." His example spawned a generation of freedom seekers such as O'Reilly, who arrived in Boston in 1870.

O'Reilly might be best characterized as a rebel romantic. If Jackie Robinson presented Boston with an opportunity to change the course of its history, so too did O'Reilly. He was a passionate patriot who first gained renown for his poetry and speeches in Ireland, but it was not long before he was sentenced to hard labor in Australia and, presumably, left to die. A daring escape on a New Bedford whaler bordered, in the words of his countrymen, on the wondrous, and O'Reilly, in exile from Ireland, made his way to Philadelphia, then Boston. He arrived in Boston, settled in Charlestown, and began to follow in the ideological footsteps of the legendary O'Connell. It was O'Connell who was the inspiration for O'Reilly and his egalitarianism. If his nationalism to Ireland was unquenchable, O'Connell grew as a world figure for incorporating the imperiled into the same struggle.

Such communication, indeed friendship, disappeared between the blacks and Irish by the end of the century. In 1885, the hundredth anniversary of O'Connell's birth elicited celebration throughout the United States. Observations were held in no fewer than a dozen states. But reality persisted. A small item on the front page of the Boston *Transcript* highlighted life for Negro America:

> The Gazette's Knoxville special says Mrs. John Howard of Athens, McMinn County, Tenn., was stopped in the road by a Negro who attempted to rob her. It is also asserted he tried to violate her person. The Negro was captured and lodged in jail. Last night, a party of 30 masked men took him out and shot him seven or eight times. He was found dead this morning. The citizens were arming themselves, fearing the Negroes will attack the town, but later reports state that quiet has been restored.

In Boston, Yankee abolitionist Wendell Phillips offered to the overflow crowd at Boston's Music Hall examples of O'Connell's reach and spoke of O'Connell's reverence from black leaders. He told a story from Sir Thomas Fowell Buxton, the British abolitionist who fought for anti-slavery treaties between Britain and African countries. O'Connell stood alone in 1830 in his anti-slavery voice when addressing Parliament. At one point, a bloc of West India planters offered O'Connell a political bribe. O'Connell was to resign from his anti-slavery campaign. In return, the West India bloc would guarantee him "twenty-seven votes for you on every Irish question," but "if you work with those abolitionists, count us always against you."

Phillips retold the story and it all sounded so good. O'Connell responded with purpose when he said, "Gentleman, God knows I speak for the saddest people the sun sees, but may my right hand forget its cunning and my tongue cling to the roof of my mouth if to save Ireland—even Ireland!—I forget the Negro one single hour."

The National Conference of Colored Men in Cincinnati sent a dispatch, which Phillips read. It concluded: "to recall with gratitude his eloquent and effective pleas for the freedom of our race . . . we earnestly commend his example to our countrymen."

The staid Yankee Boston *Evening Transcript* noted bitterly Phillips' lionizing tribute to O'Connell. "When Music Hall resounded with applause at Mr. Phillips' eulogy of O'Connell because of his antislavery labors, it was hard for some of us to forget that the great mass of his countrymen in America were deaf to his appeals, and were, for years, willing tools of the slave power."

That was the rub. The Irish leaders made an attempt at coalition; the rank and file weren't listening. Why should they? For as romantic and interesting as a black-Irish bond fighting the well-heeled Brahmins sounded in theory, the truth was this: these two groups were pitted against each other every day for jobs, for housing, and for status. Everybody knew the talk and the consequences, both economically and socially. *Don't let a nigger take your job.* There was no way to bond across racial lines when putting food on the table was at stake.

Competition along class lines wouldn't stop there, and the same Irish argument that thwarted O'Connell and O'Reilly in the nineteenth century would be voiced in the 1970s, when school desegregation pitted the poor and black against the poor and white.

In the face of those realities, O'Connell and O'Reilly could only offer blacks their sympathy and individual support. O'Reilly needed a vehicle for his political oratory, and soon took over as editor of the Irish *Pilot*, long the voice of the city's Irish and Catholic Church. Though it would never translate into any time of coalition, O'Reilly did feel a connection to the city's blacks. Being a political prisoner could do that. Garrison and Phillips may have fought on the side of abolition, but O'Reilly *suffered* as had the blacks, and as such he brought to the discourse a voice that Yankee sympathizers—sincere as they might have been—could not match.

On an icy December night in Fanueil Hall in 1885, O'Reilly told the audience at the legendary Boston meeting house of his time in a Tennessee train station. He was struck and embittered by Jim Crow:

> I went into that room and saw it as close, confined and crowded with people of both sexes, with mothers surrounded by little children, young girls and young men who sat on bare, comfortless seats attached to the wall.
>
> I went into the waiting room for white people and found it large, airy and com-

fortable, one for men and another for women and children. . . . If ever the Negro question comes to the front as long as I live I shall be counted with the black man.

O'Reilly also brought forth a kind of radicalism foreign to Boston blacks, whose strategy to gain a foothold in America had always been assimilation with whites. In Boston that meant parroting the Yankee culture, which even included vacationing on Martha's Vineyard. Indeed, to this day, the section of Oak Bluffs—long the black enclave of the island—owes its roots to the black middle class of nineteenth-century Boston who vacationed there.

The great abolitionist struggle contained a deep paternalism, but here was O'Reilly, an Irishman at that, demanding self-sufficiency. It was a strain that would often be voiced by black leaders such as W. E. B. DuBois, but the idea of individualism coming from a white man was radical indeed. "The Negro is a new man, a free man, a spirited man," he said that night. "And he can be a great man if he will avoid modeling himself after the whites."

An Irish patriot to the end, O'Reilly never lost his relevance. But like O'Connell before him, the black cause was not one that Irish Bostonians would ever embrace. There would be no alliance. By the turn of the century, death had claimed the most powerful of the abolitionists' voices. Garrison died in 1879. Frederick Douglass, who had long since left Boston, died in Washington, DC in 1895. Politically, Boston's Brahmins were exhausted, defeated in Congress by a national hardening of spirit and outnumbered at home. The Irish had claimed a majority in Boston's population and soon seized political and religious power as well. Phillips died in 1886. O'Reilly's voice succumbed first to the recalcitrant Boston masses and then to an accidental death in 1890, extinguishing whatever hopes existed for an Irish-black conduit. His oratory, although eloquent, necessary, and for Boston a missed call to racial harmony, fell upon a populace uninterested in race. The *Pilot,* partly owned by the conservative Catholic Church, became the Church's official vehicle following O'Reilly's death.

Few of O'Reilly's overtures to Boston's blacks are now mentioned. Even if overlooked, an important portion of the O'Reilly legacy is that of an Irishman committed in the O'Connell tradition to bringing the races together. With O'Reilly gone, O'Connell's still-legendary spirit did not translate into any form of meaningful black-Irish caucus, nor did a new voice emerge.

This was black life in America, and black Boston was not going to escape. While the Irish grew to power, as did other ethnicities around the country—the Italians and behind the scenes the Chinese in San Francisco—black life sank deeper into the morass. There was a final, crushing episode that severed once and for all the notion that Boston was a welcome destination for blacks. It happened in 1915, when Boston's outraged black community failed to prevent the showing of D. W. Griffith's *The Birth of a Nation.* The film was famous for its technical breakthroughs for the motion picture industry as well as for its overt racism. Boston's blacks knew that to ban the film, which depicted the antebellum black as a savage and the Ku Klux Klan as heroes, they had to rely on their relationship with Boston Mayor James Michael Curley. William Monroe Trotter, a Harvard-educated black activist and publisher, was publicly defeated by Curley's refusal to ban the film. It was a telling moment for Trotter, who felt Curley's rebuke to be the clearest example of Boston's crumbling abolitionist spirit; Curley's inaction was proof of a questionable interest in his black constituents. "Unless this play is stopped," Trotter said, "Boston will never be as Boston of old to the colored people who live here."

The defeat was also a signal that black Boston did not have a reliable ally in Curley, who was, thought longtime Boston *Globe* political columnist Marty Nolan, "the mayor of the dispossessed." It was also a mortal wound to the O'Reilly/O'Connell romantic vision of a black-Irish coalition of the downtrodden. "Where is valiant Jim Curley of old?" Trotter asked. "If this was an attack on the Irish race he would find a way pretty quick to stop it."

The *Globe* largely ignored the political ramifications of the film. "As a work of art it is so wonderful and so beautiful that it robs one of the power of criticism." Curley biographer Jack Beatty said the episode "jarred Boston's blacks out of the their complacency about living in the capital of abolition, the city of Garrison and Sumner, and into an awareness of the racial chasm separating them from Boston's whites."

Thus by 1916, virtually every gain enjoyed by Boston's black community had been eliminated, leaving only the vapor of harmony with whites. The city that had once fancied itself as standing so far ahead of the rest of America in terms of being racially progressive was, at the very least, in step with the rest of the nation. Some black writers in Boston, Trotter especially, believed the Irish enmity toward blacks made Boston a city that would ultimately provide even fewer opportunities for blacks than other cities, with the hostilities potentially greater. The defeat was made worse by the fact that Curley had enjoyed a black majority in his previous election. This realization was a bitter moment for blacks and whites alike who knew of Boston's special racial achievements and expected the city to stand at the moral center of a tattered nation faced with reconstruction. There was, however, a new history awaiting Boston. Instead of being a voice of tolerance, Boston followed the nation and would fully retrench into the most racially discordant period in American history. It would take two world wars, an economic depression, and nearly thirty years before Boston would have another opportunity to fulfill its past nobility. It would come from baseball. The Boston Red Sox would be given that chance.

THREE

Virtually everything about Boston baseball is conditional. *What would have happened if . . .* The fight is with history, and for some seemingly inexplicable reason, the punches were always thrown at the wrong guy. Boston would be frustrated by history but rarely by the people who ran the Red Sox themselves, the ones who made the history. Led by Tom Yawkey—though it would become popular for Yawkey to be considered victimized by his unsavory cocktail mates—the Red Sox would always seem to come to the fork in the road, and wind up driving in the wrong direction.

So who knew that on April 16, 1945, the Red Sox would once more approach history's intersection? With FDR on his deathbed and World War II winding down, fate and the last vestige of a city's social conscience conspired and put the Red Sox in a historic position.

As an issue, civil rights had been largely dormant for years, but with the defeat of Nazism, it drew new strength. Black soldiers had fought valiantly in segregated units to defeat fascism. At the end of World War II, the question of black rights in America was again relevant. Asking black soldiers to fight and die for the liberty denied them at home created renewed dialogue. It was a question that was asked in Boston nearly two hundred years earlier, when the city's leadership began studying the essential contradiction of slavery in Massachusetts at a time when the colonies sought freedom from England.

Now, baseball found itself at the center of the argument. Black soldiers could not die on the battlefield and still be prohibited from playing center field in the major leagues. Baseball had retreated from race as steadily and completely as the rest of the nation during the first forty years of the twentieth century.

Segregation was an unbreakable rule. That blacks played in separate leagues was a practice that went largely unquestioned. When debate was stirred, either from a relentless black press or from the few mainstream white reporters who made integration a cause, there was always a reason why the time was not prudent for the majors to open their doors to blacks. The only groups that were truly vociferous in their appeals, such as the Communist Workers Party, stood on the fringes of the mainstream.

But during the latter half of 1944 and in the early months of 1945, Eddie

Collins was uncomfortable. He was the vice president and general manager of the Red Sox and was now being pressured by Isadore Muchnick, a liberal Jewish city councilor, who demanded the Red Sox begin offering some form of talent evaluation of black players.

It was a threatening concept. Baseball prohibited black players from the major leagues in 1884, and no serious challenges to that authority had arisen. The desire to keep blacks out of the major leagues existed in great degree from the players all the way to the commissioner's office; Judge Kenesaw Mountain Landis was, with a few peers, one of the great racists in baseball history.

Shunned, blacks created their own leagues, the Negro National League and the Negro American League, and the races played the same game on patently uneven tracks. To some, the very existence of the Negro leagues was proof that blacks didn't care to play in the big leagues.

Yet here was an emboldened Muchnick, potentially unsettling the balance. For emphasis, he approached Collins with a hammer. In those days in Boston, a permit was required to play baseball on Sundays. The city council required a unanimous vote for the permit to be granted. Muchnick told Collins he would withhold his vote unless the Red Sox agreed to sponsor a tryout for black players, a potentially crippling financial blow.

Collins had felt pressure before, on the baseball field at Columbia and in winning world championships as a second baseman with the Philadelphia Athletics. He had also deftly escaped tarnish by distancing himself from his scandal-ridden teammates on the 1919 Chicago White Sox who threw the World Series. After his playing days ended, his paternal relationship with a young Tom Yawkey developed into a business partnership; Yawkey idolized the great Collins to such a degree that when he bought the Red Sox in 1933, he would only complete the purchase if Collins ran the franchise for him.

This was a new pressure. Led by Muchnick's threat and with consistent commentary in the black press (and to a lesser degree the mainstream), integration advocates pushed baseball as they hadn't before the war. In Boston, the approach was typically parochial. Integration should begin in Boston, where abolition was born. It made for a nice symmetry.

Pedigree didn't matter to Yawkey, for cold dollars were at stake. Yawkey was a member of the infamous 1946 baseball steering committee that suggested too many blacks attending baseball games would scare away white customers and ruin the national pastime. Say what you want about Tom Yawkey, but he wasn't going to let any moral issue stand in the way of making his cash. Was he rich? More than that, Yawkey was so rich the Boston papers used to call the Red Sox "the millionaires" in print. This was during the Depression. In the *Red Sox Century*, Glenn Stout and Richard A. Johnson called Yawkey "the richest boy in the world." Did he get a free pass from all of Boston because he "saved" the Red Sox? Absolutely, and everybody loves a rich man who throws money at the city's passion.

Tom Yawkey might be many things, but the one thing he was not was a leader. He would follow the market instead of move it, and this would make him beloved among the rank-and-file attitudes in baseball because he could be trusted not to be a maverick. He could be trusted not to be the one to open up his doors to blacks. He would see to it that they remained where they belonged, in the Negro leagues.

Morals? Forget it. Yawkey took the "no blacks allowed" edict to the extreme. If the game prohibited them from playing center field, they could at least sweep up the place after the game, right? Wrong. During hearings before Massachusetts' civil rights agencies in the late 1950s, it came out that not a single black was employed at Fenway Park in any capacity, not even to scrub the bathroom.

Not that Yawkey was a bad guy. You'd never read about him railing on about blacks in print, or on the radio like Briggs in Detroit or guys he would later hire, like Pinky Higgins. Yawkey knew better than that. He did it the right way, by appearing interested, even sympathetic, then letting progress take its slow winding course. Tom Yawkey knew how to buy time. Now, about this Jewish City Councilor . . .

As Muchnick circled, Collins hedged. Dave Egan from the Boston *Record* pushed in his column for the Red Sox or the Braves to be consistent with the Boston pedigree and lead the major leagues into a new, integrated era. Egan, best known for his contentious, often spiteful treatment of Ted Williams, was known as a heavy drinker whose binges periodically left him so drunk that his column would have to be ghostwritten.

Dave Egan could often be a brilliant writer. He was Harvard educated, and remained one of the few media members who steadily challenged baseball's exclusion of blacks. "We are fighting, as I understand it, for the rights of the under-privileged everywhere," he wrote in 1945. "We weep for the teeming masses of India. Down the years we have contributed millions of dollars to the suffering Armenians. We have room in our souls to pity the Chinese and the Arabs and the brave Greeks. Could we, by chance, spare a thought for the Negro here in the United States? Do we, by any chance, feel disgust at the thought that Negro players, solely because of their color, are barred from playing baseball?"

He often wrote without fear of the club and did so before it was fashionable. For his crusading efforts, the NAACP Boston office often cited Egan.* It

---

* At an NAACP testimonial dinner in October 1948, Williard Smith presented Dave Egan with a scroll from the Boston branch. Isadore Muchnick introduced Egan with the following words:

[Egan] has played an inspiring and effective role in shattering the stupid baseball taboo by which white players have maintained a sports monopoly for years. The knot has been cut and if the diehards and the still unconvinced need further awakening, they got it Saturday when Larry Doby cracked his home run at Cleveland. People who only give lip service and fail to follow the example was a position, thought Glenn Stout, that likely made Egan an unfair target. He was out front on an issue about which the rest were, at the very least, ambivalent. Egan attacked Williams, but it wasn't, Stout thought, so much crueler than the rest of the writers that Egan would become the symbol of anti-Williams journalism. There was something else that set Egan apart, and that something else was Egan's position on racial questions. Egan's college education likely spurred resentment. Wendell Smith seemed to believe the same. Smith remembered that the writers used to call Egan, "Dave Ego."

The black press in Boston was less provocative because of its size. The old Trotter spirit dissipated as Boston blacks saw the steady erosion of their place in the city. Mabray "Doc" Kountze, a black journalist from nearby Medford, was perhaps the preeminent black reporter in the city.

Kountze was born in 1904 in the Boston suburb Medford and was a member of the school of Boston blacks who believed in the special heritage of blacks and whites in the city. He wrote for the black Boston *Chronicle* as well as Trotter's *Guardian*. If Kountze was aware of the emerging new attitude of Boston, where hostility would replace accommodation, he did not allow it to sap his enthusiasm for the city's old abolitionist spirit. Doc Kountze was an integrationist before the civil rights movement, when the label would in many circles be a pejorative term, a sign of weakness. Where others surrendered hope of integration with exasperation, it was Kountze who believed that the relationship between blacks and whites in the city was not a myth, but a powerful example of what was possible.

In 1935, ten full years before the Robinson tryout and a dozen before Robinson made his debut, Kountze met with Phil Troy and Ed Cunningham at Fenway Park. Troy was the secretary of the Red Sox, Cunningham of the Braves. Both Troy and Cunningham told Kountze that they personally believed the segregation in the game should be lifted. Troy, while sympathetic, was pessimistic about the real prospects of the conversation. Tom Yawkey had owned the club for only two years, but already it appeared that Troy knew that Yawkey would not be the one to move forward on such a prickly issue. At the meeting, Kountze recalled Troy "shrugging his shoulders" and pointing his finger upward, indicating the decision to scout and sign black players belonged solely to the Red Sox front office.

Kountze found a more receptive response from the Braves' Cunningham. The National League club had a greater interest in the idea of integration, if for no reason other than economic survival. The Braves were for years a horrible

---

of Dave Egan in actually fighting through for the end of injustices are cluttering up the scene. They are fooling a well-meaning but ineffectual people into a bad case of goodwill-itis. And the only cure for that is do-it-ism. Get it done. Crack a taboo. Smash a tradition. Open job opportunities. Break down restrictive covenants. Storm the walls of medical colleges until they come clean with training for young men and women of all groups. In short, be a Dave Egan.

baseball team. After finishing third in 1916, the Braves would finish no higher than fourth until winning the pennant in 1948. As a franchise, they treaded water. The "Miracle Braves" won the World Series in 1914 only to see attendance *decline* the following years. When the Red Sox won the 1918 World Series, the Braves' attendance was a miserable 84,938. After the Warren Spahn team lost the World Series to Cleveland in 1948—that year the Red Sox and Braves were on the cusp of a Boston-style Subway Series—the team's attendance dropped again in 1949. Unable to compete, they would move to Milwaukee following the 1952 season.

The Braves were suffering not only on the field, but also with the daunting handicap of never being fully accepted by the city. Boston was an American League town. Perhaps, Kountze thought, integration might be the answer to reverse sagging fortunes. By making history, the Braves might be to stay afloat in Boston.

Kountze was persistent, and he bided his time to present such a strategy to the Braves. In 1938, he traveled to Braves Field for a meeting with Bob Quinn, Sr., the venerable Braves president. The two enjoyed a spirited conversation. Even in 1938, nearly fifty years after the death of O'Reilly and Garrison, the Boston mythology gripped Kountze. Quinn was, like Kountze and unlike Tom Yawkey, a New Englander, and he suggested to Kountze that the integration of baseball should start in Boston, the home of abolition. For Kountze, it was a hopeful moment. "I sat with the, even then, elderly grey haired Bob Quinn, Sr. and talked about bringing Colored teams to Braves Field in order to help break the color line and make Boston take the lead, as the Cradle of Liberty should."

Kountze was surprised that the two men were in agreement that segregation should be ended, and Boston was the city to do it. Quinn, however, told Kountze that it was not going to happen, not in 1938:

> Bob Quinn, Sr. left no doubt in my mind he would have voted to remove the Major League Color line in 1938. But he told me, at that time, the other club owners would have voted him down. Quinn agreed the League, and especially the Boston Braves needed extra attraction to rival the American League Clubs in some cities, including Boston. . . . But in our interview, President Quinn prophesied the National League would have Colored players before the rival league, and the Braves would have Colored before the Red Sox. Bob was a true prophet.

Wendell Smith, columnist from the black weekly Pittsburgh *Courier*, joined Egan in challenging Collins as well as other general managers across the league to offer tryouts to black players. Sam Lacy of the Baltimore *Afro-American* had vainly tried to push for integration in 1939 with well-known integration foe Clark Griffith, owner of the Washington Senators. In 1945, Lacy and Collins began corresponding about integration.

It was, however, Muchnick's voice and clout that turned a cadre of disparate voices into something of a movement. Doc Kountze referred to Muchnick as a "white modern abolitionist." Over the course of history Muchnick would be a figure mischaracterized in the story of baseball's integration. Muchnick was an important Boston figure who may have been as pessimistic as Bob Quinn about the realistic chances of the major leagues integrating. Unlike Quinn, he pressed forward. That was a big difference.

Muchnick was the first person in the modern era to pressure baseball's power structure and come away with a tangible result. The Boston Red Sox would be the first team in the twentieth century to hold a tryout for black players.

It was not a reflection of the Red Sox's heightened willingness over other clubs to integrate or a remembrance of a city's proud past that brought Jackie Robinson, Sam Jethroe, and Marvin Williams to Boston during the second week of April in 1945. Eddie Collins was a known insider and a bigot. He played his entire career in a segregated game and saw no reason to change. If change was inevitable, he wasn't going to help it along. For Collins, it wasn't just blacks, either. During his time with the Red Sox, the club suffered from the ironic reputation of being horribly anti-Catholic and anti-Semitic as well. Back in the old, old days, the great center fielder Tris Speaker was a proud member of the Ku Klux Klan back in Texas.

As a city, the optimism of Doc Kountze notwithstanding, Boston was in 1945 a perilous place for blacks, having long ago abandoned any pretense of welcoming them. In fact, the opposite was occurring. The war was nearing an end, and southern blacks had already begun the great migration north, a source of great contention. Even fellow blacks in Boston were not glad to see more blacks enter the city.

The reason the Red Sox were faced with trying out black players was the by-product of two factors: the persistence of Isadore Muchnick and the arrogance of Eddie Collins.

"I cannot understand," Muchnick wrote to Collins in late 1944, "how baseball, which claims to be the national sport and which . . . receives special favors and dispensation from the Federal Government because of alleged moral value can continue a pre-Civil War attitude toward American citizens because of the color of their skins." What Collins did next was a clear reflection of both the unassailable mindset of baseball as well as the arrogance of the Red Sox. Collins had been able to pacify integrationists in the past with his charm. He would simply return phone calls and engage in the philosophical debate of integration, which was more than most baseball men were willing to offer. He gave the integrationists, Dave Egans, Wendell Smiths, and Sam Lacys the illusion of being open to change. With Muchnick, Collins failed to realize he was dealing with someone who could not be so easily charmed.

"As I wrote to one of your fellow councilors last April," Collins replied to Muchnick in a letter, "I have been connected with the Red Sox for twelve years

and during that time we have never had a single request for a tryout by a colored applicant. It is beyond my understanding how anyone could insinuate or
believe that all ball players, regardless of race, color or creed have not been
treated in the American way so far as having an equal opportunity to play for
the Red Sox."

Collins was polished, an easy and well-read Ivy Leaguer. He was clearly
one of the brightest people in the game, a position enhanced because of the
times; few baseball people in those days attended college at all, never mind a
university as prestigious as Columbia. Muchnick was not pleased when Lou
Perini, the owner of the Boston Braves, flatly refused Muchnick's request for a
tryout, which was the ultimate repudiation of any hope Quinn may have given
Kountze during their correspondence.

Collins, however, promised dialogue, which was a signal of hope.

Collins' cordial inaction insulted Muchnick, who pressed further. Like
Perini and the rest of the owners in baseball, Collins had no intention of even
granting the tryout, but he had badly underestimated Muchnick's tenacity.
Collins was used to being in a position of strength when he dealt with baseball
issues, but it was clear that he couldn't say a few positive, encouraging words to
rid himself of Isadore Muchnick, a man who was determined to see tangible
progress. When he received no satisfaction from their written correspondence
in 1944, Muchnick alerted Collins to his intention to block the Red Sox from
playing baseball on Sundays. It was a potentially crippling blow, for these were
the days before billion-dollar television contracts, multimillion-dollar local
cable TV deals, and regularly scheduled night baseball. In the 1940s, baseball
clubs were almost completely dependent upon gate receipts as a revenue source.
To infringe on that would surely get the attention of any baseball owner, even
one as wealthy as Tom Yawkey. With that Collins agreed.

On March 3, Sam Lacy of the *Baltimore Afro-American*, wrote Collins a letter containing suggestions on how to facilitate the integration process. He sent
copies to Larry MacPhail, president of the New York Yankees, and Bob Quinn
of the Braves. The letter was intended to keep the question of integration at the
forefront of baseball's priority list, but it also contained a proposal. He advocated
that the sixteen major league clubs hire a chief scouting director of sorts, a person who would troubleshoot potential problems that would arrive in this nascent
venture as well as create a talent database of Negro league players who possessed
the skills—and temperament—worthy of being the first black major leaguers.
The letter's tone suggested that Lacy himself was angling for the post. He also
added language that sought to assuage the owners into accepting integration as
a community partnership of sorts, a progressive and voluntary venture instead of
the result of a civil rights action or political demand.

"I know," he wrote, "that there will be no hiring of colored players as a
direct result of the . . . Boston ban on Sunday baseball, but such an appointment

as I recommend here will indicate that the owners involved are interested in working out a feasible plan of action."

Lacy never received a response from the Braves or the Yankees, but Collins curiously replied with a cordial note dated April 11, 1945, a mere five days before Robinson arrived at Fenway Park for the tryout. If it was his intention to ignore Lacy in the manner of the Braves and Yankees, Collins could no longer do so with the tryout looming. Instead, Collins reversed himself and attempted to show enthusiasm for Lacy's idea. He explained allowing five weeks to pass before responding to Lacy's letter by suggesting that Lacy dated his March 3 letter erroneously, as if Lacy did not know what day it was.

The truth is probably closer to this: While Lacy's letter sat on Collins' desk, he succumbed to Muchnick and hastily agreed to the tryout. Cornered, he then replied to Lacy, stating, "I think your suggestion contains a lot of merit. I hope you will feel that as far as the Boston Red Sox are concerned, we want to make every effort to avoid anything that savors in any way of discrimination of race, color or creed in the selection of our ball club." Collins, perhaps aware that Robinson's imminent arrival would create a severe backlash from other teams for breaking the gentlemen's agreement barring blacks, needed a plan of action. Collins fired off a quick and revealing letter to American League president Will Harridge, which characterized himself not only as a progressive but also, in knowing Robinson was nearing town, as a collaborator with baseball on the issue. "I would appreciate it if you have any suggestions to offer in this regard," Collins wrote Harridge. "I personally feel that is an issue that we are going to be faced with in the future, possibly the immediate future."

When Collins rescheduled the original date of the tryout, Muchnick contacted columnist Dave Egan, who knew that Wendell Smith had arranged for three black players to arrive in Boston. "Eddie Collins is forgetful. He forgets that this is not 1865; he forgets that this is not Mobile, Alabama; and he forgets, most of all, that exactly one month ago today he wrote a letter to City Councilor Muchnick. It was full of injured innocence."

Jackie Robinson was already fatalistic about the tryout. He didn't believe the Red Sox were serious about integration and wasn't especially thrilled about his own situation. He had only played for the Negro League's Kansas City Monarchs for a few weeks and was already disappointed by the league's air of gambling and disorganization, the very type of lowbrow behavior that made white baseball people hesitant about allowing blacks into the big leagues. Robinson was fastidious in his adherence to his own personal code, and seeing the chaos of the Negro leagues only frustrated him further. It was the stereotypes of corruption and anarchy that not only plagued black baseball, thought historian Edmund G. White, but also gave whites a secure excuse to keep blacks out of the major leagues:

When the Negro Leagues had come within the consciousness of those within organized baseball, they had been seen as a reverse mirror image. If Organized baseball was
free from gambling and corruption, the Negro Leagues were run by racketeers. If
Organized baseball was premised on the roster stability of the reserve clause, the Negro
Leagues were the province of contract jumpers. If Organized baseball was structured
around the permanent franchise cities and regular schedules, the Negro Leagues were a
kaleidoscope of changing franchises and whimsical scheduling. If Organized baseball
was a clean, wholesome, upwardly mobile sport, Negro League games were the scenes
of rowdy, disorderly, vulgar behavior. By being the opposite of Organized baseball's ide-
alized image, the Negro Leagues served as their own justification for the exclusion of
blacks from the major leagues. They appeared to demonstrate just how "contaminated"
major league baseball would become if blacks were allowed to play it.

When Robinson arrived in Boston, the tryout was delayed for two more
days in the wake of Franklin Roosevelt's death. He told Smith of his disappointment during the days of delay. "Listen, Smith, it really burns me up to
come fifteen hundred miles for them to give me the runaround."

Nearly fifty-five years after Cap Anson engineered the removal of the last
black major leaguers in the late nineteenth century, the tryout finally took place
at Fenway Park at eleven on the morning of April 16, 1945. Two above-average
Negro leaguers, Sam Jethroe and Marvin Williams, joined Jackie Robinson.
The Red Sox players were white and were mostly minor league pitchers.
Starting the season the following day in New York, the big league roster was
given the day off by Joe Cronin. The routine was mundane. The players fielded,
threw, and took batting practice. Hugh Duffy, the former great Red Sox outfielder, ran the tryout and took notes on index cards. Cronin sat, according to
one account, "stone-faced." Another depicted Cronin barely watching at all.
Muchnick marveled at the hitting ability of Robinson, whose mood apparently
darkened. When it ended, he, Williams, and Jethroe received platitudes from
Duffy. Joe Cashman of the Boston *Record* sat with Cronin that day and reported
that the manager was impressed with Robinson. He wrote cryptically, with virtually little comprehension, that he could have been witnessing a historic
moment. "Before departing, Joe and his coaches spent some 90 minutes in the
stands at Fenway surveying three Negro candidates. . . . Why they came from
such distant spots to work out for the Red Sox was not learned." The Boston
Globe did not cover the tryout.

Robinson himself was satisfied with his performance, although by the time
he left Fenway he was smoldering about what he felt to be a humiliating cha-
rade. As the three players departed, Eddie Collins told them they would hear
from the Red Sox in the near future. None of them ever heard from the Red
Sox again.

Eighteen months later, the Dodgers signed Robinson, who would begin a
legendary career a year and half later. Jethroe, at age thirty-three, integrated

Boston pro baseball with the Braves in 1950 and would become the National League Rookie of the Year. Williams would stay in the Negro leagues, never again coming so close to the majors.

The remaining details of that morning are completely speculative. Robinson never spoke in real detail about the tryout. Joe Cronin, who next to Collins and was the most powerful member of the Red Sox next to Yawkey, also never offered a complete account about the tryout except to say that he remembered that it occurred, although he and Robinson would never speak.

Thirty-four years later, Cronin would discuss the tryout; he explained the Red Sox position as well as the game's:

> I remember the tryout very well. But after it, we told them our only farm club available was in Louisville, Kentucky, and we didn't think they'd be interested in going there because of the racial feelings at the time. Besides, this was after the season had started and we didn't sign players off tryouts in those days to play in the big leagues. I was in no position to offer them a job. The general manager did the hiring and there was an unwritten rule at that time against hiring black players. I was just the manager.
>
> It was a great mistake by us. He [Robinson] turned out to be a great player. But no feeling existed about it. We just accepted things the way they were. I recall talking to some players and they felt that they didn't want us to break up their league. We all thought because of the times, it was good to have separate leagues.

Clif Keane would give the day its historical significance. A reporter for the *Globe*, Keane said he heard a person yell from the stands during the tryout. The words—"Get those niggers off the field"—were never attributed to one person, but they have haunted the Red Sox as much as Pinky Higgins' proclamation a decade and a half later. Numerous Red Sox officials, from Joe Cronin to Eddie Collins to Tom Yawkey himself, have been credited with the taunt, if it was ever said at all. Keane has always believed it was Yawkey.

What cannot be disputed about the events of that April day are the final results and the consequences that followed. It was an episode from which the reputation and perception of the franchise have never recovered.

"I still remember how I hit the ball that day, good to all fields," Robinson later said. "What happened? Nothing!"

Back with the Negro League's Cleveland Buckeyes, Sam Jethroe told his teammates about the Boston way of doing business. "Sam told us what a joke that so-called tryout was," his teammate Willie Grace said. "He said you just knew it was a farce because when the guys were out there Joe Cronin—who was managing the club—didn't even bother to look. He was just up in the stands with his back turned most of the time. He just sent some of his men out there and told them to throw some balls, hit some balls to us, and then come back and say we had ability."

In January 1951, six years removed from the morning tryout, Jethroe met

Eddie Collins again at a Boston Baseball Writers dinner, the same annual dinner where a decade later Pinky Higgins would drop beef Stroganov into Bud Collins' lap. Jethroe had just won the Rookie of the Year award in the National League, and the Red Sox still had not integrated. A smiling Collins sat next to Jethroe and told him he was happy to see Jethroe succeed. Jethroe thanked him and without bitterness replied, "You had your chance, Mr. Collins. You had your chance."

If Robinson was properly pessimistic about the tryout, Doc Kountze was devastated. He was a believer in the Boston ideal and was convinced that morning of the tryout was to be a day long remembered in Boston. It would be, of course, but for completely opposite reasons than Kountze had envisioned.

> In Boston, we all expected a fair trial at the Hub's Fenway Park. [I] . . . was already keenly anticipating the end of the Color Ban beginning at Fenway Park and Braves Field. Whether Robbie and his mates made it or not, I could see the Sox extending invitations to many others who definitely could. . . . Tom Yawkey . . . failed his big chance. . . . That same year, Brooklyn signed Robinson to the Dodger farm club in Montreal. I think this is one of the biggest letdowns the author ever experienced in his entire career of sportswriting. I could see it happening in Mississippi, but not in Massachusetts.

Thus the tryout ended bitterly for Jackie Robinson. But that evening, he accepted a dinner invitation at 9 Powelton Road in Dorchester. It was the home of Ann and Isadore Muchnick, the city councilor who pressured Eddie Collins and arranged the Boston tryout. Why young Robinson, who was twenty-six at the time, would be invited to dinner made perfect sense to Ann Muchnick. Fifty years later, she would recall the reason with a warm smile. "Because no one else asked him."

Isadore Harry Yaver Muchnick was born on January 11, 1908, in Boston's West End, on a residential neighborhood that no longer exists. There existed among the four children of Joseph and Fannie Muchnick strong beliefs in justice, fairness, competition, accomplishment, and the power of education. All four children of these Russian Jewish immigrants would attend college. Muchnick's older sister Eva would become the first Jew to head New York's Rochester Public Library. His older brother Louis boxed at Boston University. Izzy received the first double promotion at the renowned Boston Latin School since Benjamin Franklin. He played goal in college hockey and lacrosse, lettering in lacrosse for Harvard in 1928.

Activism was a trademark for Izzy Muchnick from almost the very beginning. When he married, he and his wife Ann were active in HIAS, the Hebrew Immigrants in America Society, and Hadassah, the women's Zionist organization, as well as numerous other Jewish organizations in Boston. Muchnick involved his children in public service at an early age. David Muchnick recalls giving out his father's palm cards to voters from his baby carriage at a polling place on Columbia Road on election day 1947. He also remembers being left at his grandfather's tailor shop while his mother and father went to Boston Harbor to greet and assist Jewish survivors from Europe and World War II. Muchnick's daughter Fran accompanied her parents to the docks on the Boston Harbor. She was but a child, but the vision of seeing Jews arrive from Europe with worn, cardboard tags affixed to their coats never left her memory.

Izzy Muchnick commanded a principled, homespun rhetoric and possessed a natural political sense that would serve him well throughout his life. He taught his children lessons laced with humor, always containing morals of family and simple decency. David Muchnick remembers that his father told him before his first date, "Treat the girl the way you'd like your sister to be treated." Baseball advice was, "If at first you don't succeed, try the outfield." In the supermarket, it was a favorite act for Muchnick to approach a child in line and whisper, "Did you know that your mommy told me that you're the best little boy in the whole world?"

Being Jewish in 1940s America carried a considerable weight of prejudice, but Muchnick possessed a skill and integrity that allowed him to navigate Boston's difficult, tribal quarters. It allowed him to be respected by both the Irish, who controlled city government, and the entrenched Yankees, who dominated Boston's cultural, legal, and financial world. He did this without becoming an outcast from his own community, and such a balance required real political skill. He was aided by a strong faith. Fran Goldstein remembers her father as very serious about his Judaism, attending synagogue every Friday. Muchnick countered the anti-Semitism of the day by becoming a power broker in a city where survival meant balancing between the two worlds of the powerful Irish and the city's Yankee elite. During Jack Kennedy's senate run in 1952, it was Muchnick who was instrumental in delivering the Jewish vote. On the train from Boston to New York for the 1953 Harvard-Princeton football game, Muchnick's family and the Massachusetts junior senator enjoyed a special camaraderie, reminiscing about the election results the year before. Coming through for Kennedy was not easy, for his father Joe had angered the city's Jews with what was seen as his anti-Semitism.

Muchnick graduated from Harvard College in 1928 and from Harvard Law in 1932. A Harvard Law graduate is a desired commodity, and Izzy Muchnick was no different. The Yankee law firms that wanted him also wanted something else in return for their lucrative offers: A name change. "Muchnick" was too ethnic, too Jewish. How about something more assimilated, something less ethnic? It wasn't a request that Muchnick was asked to think over. That was a condition of employment. Muchnick responded by opening up his own law firm, in the heart of the Yankee financial center at 148 State Street.

If there existed in Isadore Muchnick the indignant streak of a person straddling two entrenched worlds, it was in the political realm where he felt he could best remedy injustices. Politics often demanded suppression of one's principles. This would be especially true in Boston, and after being elected to the city council in 1941, Muchnick found himself in constant opposition to the majority. He fought for equal pay for women in the city's patronage jobs and supported a redistricting of the city's schools that would have created some integration of public schools long before the eruptions of the 1970s. He was a classic East Coast liberal.

There was something about Muchnick, something both admirable and self-destructive about his unfailing adherence to his principles, for his adherence to a high personal code often conflicted with Boston's insularity. He did not play the game. Both of his children would marvel at the number of times their father would align with the underdog, especially in a city such as Boston, with its go-along to get-along political credo. In her personal papers, his wife Ann would note how much her husband gave of himself, often at the expense of more lucrative prospects. He consistently found himself on the minority side of issues, dedicated to public service in a town that survived on an almost clannish credo of ethnic solidarity and the greased wheels of political patronage.

Nor did he shrink from a fight. In 1947, Robinson's year, the Boston city council drew sharp fire for allegations of corruption. The city's mayor, the legendary James Michael Curley, was in jail, and when the process for a water-taxi license proceeded sluggishly, it was Muchnick who confronted his colleagues, charging that the license was being stalled because members of the council awaited a kickback. In a moment of individual bravado, East Boston councilor James Coffey considered Muchnick a hypocrite. "Who the hell does Muchnick think he's kidding? Especially me. I will take a buck and have guts enough to say I will take a buck. I would like to see the guy who does not . . . let me know the guy who does not." But it was Muchnick who won the respect of his peers.

Perhaps even had he wanted to opt for safer ground, his personal convictions wouldn't allow it. In this regard he found kinship with the uncompromising Robinson.

The duplicity of baseball angered Izzy Muchnick. He was a Red Sox fan, but the game's contradictions conflicted with his worldview. If it was the game that was supposed to represent the goodness of America, the ultimate arena of fairness, how could it be staunchly segregated? How, he wondered, could this impregnable line of segregation—which baseball maintained did not exist—go unchallenged for so long? Blacks were relegated to the inferior Negro leagues, went the baseball rhetoric, because they liked it there.

Perhaps even more than the game's obvious contradictions, it offended Muchnick that its government-endowed protection against competition and uncontested national standing produced in team owners a certain kind of arrogance. Their dance around integration, exemplified by his dealings with Eddie

Collins, was especially off-putting to a man of his credentials. No law prohibiting black players existed in the league's charter, although no team had fielded a black player since 1884.

For a man for whom standing on the right side of an issue was an absolute must, history would not be kind to Isadore Muchnick. Jackie Robinson became a star, and the wall preventing blacks from playing baseball began to crumble. Branch Rickey as much as Robinson received the justified credit as the co-architect in baseball's desegregation. Writers Wendell Smith and Sam Lacy both would wind up in the baseball Hall of Fame.

Baseball is full of homespun myth, ones that elevate their participants into the culture, the very fabric of the game. Without the mythology, of course, there is no game, and baseball is then just another pointless exercise where people run around for fun.

Izzy Muchnick would not be inflated by one particular myth of the game; his reputation, in fact, would be destroyed by one that would be repeated so often that it became fact. Instead of being known as the first politician to use his clout courageously and confront a resistant power structure, Muchnick emerged as something worse than forgotten, but as the opportunistic, oily politician who sought to exploit both Robinson and the black struggle for civil rights.

Al Hirshberg, one of the first Jewish sportswriters in Boston, wrote in his 1973 book *What's the Matter with the Red Sox?* that Wendell Smith was the architect behind the tryout and that Muchnick saw a solution to a precarious political future:

> Wendell Smith, a television news announcer in Chicago before his death, had been fighting the color line for years as sports editor of a Negro newspaper in Pittsburgh. Because of a quirk in Boston's Sunday baseball law, he saw a chance to force one of the Boston clubs to give black players a tryout in the spring of 1945.
>
> At the time, although Boston had had Sunday baseball for some years, the law Smith found was that it had to be voted on unanimously for renewal every year by the Boston City Council. One of the council members, Isadore H.Y. Muchnick, represented Roxbury, originally a Jewish stronghold but becoming predominately black. Smith suggested to Muchnick that he could insure a big black vote in his district by withholding his vote for Sunday baseball until one of the two ball clubs tried out a few black players.

In *Baseball's Great Experiment: Jackie Robinson and His Legacy*, Jules Tygiel wrote that in Boston, "The Red Sox and Braves found themselves in a curious position as they prepared to start the new season. The city council, under the leadership of Isadore Muchnick, a white politician representing a predominately black district, was pressuring the two teams to employ blacks."

Arnold Rampersad's thorough *Jackie Robinson: A Biography* stated, "behind the tryout was the action of a Boston city councilman and Harvard College graduate Isadore H. Y. Muchnick. In 1944, seeing his constituency change steadily from mainly Jewish to mainly black, Muchnick joined the ragtag band of critics fighting Jim Crow in baseball."

These historical accounts were not only inaccurate but were also a reflection of the crudity of the conventional thinking. The only reason Muchnick would become involved, so went the thinking, was to win a political prize. In the eyes of his children, it was not an innocent journalistic mistake that snowballed. Rather, the result, thought Fran Goldstein, was the permanent besmirching of her father's name. Muchnick was accused of acting to ingratiate himself to a new black constituency, but in 1940, Izzy Muchnick's Mattapan district was 99.69 percent white. In 1950, it was 99 percent white. During that year, 439 nonwhites lived among the district's 51,170 residents. In two of his elections, Muchnick ran unopposed. In short, there was no black vote for Muchnick to exploit, nor was there during the 1940s any difficult election year for him. It wasn't until the middle to late 1960s, after Muchnick was dead, that his old district turned from Jewish to black, which occurred long after Muchnick traded bitter letters with Eddie Collins. Hirshberg once apologized to Muchnick's son David for the error.

Outside of his personal commitment to fairness, Izzy Muchnick had no political motive to act on behalf of blacks. There weren't yet many blacks to work for in the first place.

How Muchnick's name was not only omitted from the Robinson tryout but was also subsequently brutalized in the retellings of the event is open to troubling interpretations. The simple answer—that an early account was taken as gospel, repeated, and never checked—does nothing to mollify Muchnick's children. These errors bore into Fran Goldstein's skin like a cigarette burn. "I never understood," she said, "why people had to attach a motive to what he did. My father did not act out of any kind of personal motive. It was how he was. If something wasn't right, he wanted to fix it. And most times, he paid an unreasonable price for it."

Fran Goldstein believed her father was an unfortunate victim of something of a power grab for credit of baseball's integration. In the Hirshberg account Smith appears to take credit for recognizing the Sunday ban on baseball and alerting Muchnick.

In his telling of the details of the tryout, it was Smith who first suggested that Muchnick was a political opportunist and assumed credit for the entire birth of the tryout:

> In February 1945, maybe it was early March, I contacted a Boston councilman by the name of Isadore Muchnick. He was white, in his forties. I saw this little piece in the paper where he was running for reelection in a predominately Negro area and was having quite a hard time getting reelected. I called him and told him he should include in his platform a program, or a threat that he would protest Sunday baseball in Boston if the Braves and the Red Sox didn't express interest in our campaign. The

churches in Boston frowned on Sunday baseball. . . . I telephoned him from Pittsburgh and told him, "If you want some Negro votes why don't you stand up in the City Council and threaten to vote against Sunday baseball?" It hit home with him. He said he would, and he did.

This, thought David Muchnick, was preposterous. Smith couldn't possibly have known of or understood the workings of Boston's city council, while these arcane procedures were Izzy Muchnick's everyday business. Once the subject of integration became popular to research in the 1970s and 1980s, Muchnick wasn't around to explain himself, but Wendell Smith and others were. Fran believes, as does David Muchnick, that the survivors inflated their early roles in the drama at the expense of their father. Otherwise, it would have been impossible for such glaring errors to exist. Only a person who didn't know Boston could have suggested that in the 1940s any Boston neighborhood could turn black overnight or that the black population was substantial enough to produce a swing vote. Even in 1960, Boston's black population was less than 10 percent of the total. Fran Goldstein believed these character-distorting mistakes—and not the notion of credit itself—to be the most unforgivable of offenses.

The truth, however, is that the first American politician to disrupt the idea of segregated baseball and emerge with a result was Isadore Muchnick, the former Hebrew School teacher who could have made a fortune in a Yankee law firm had he only changed his name.

Muchnick pressured the Red Sox to integrate because he was the rare person who—like Robinson—often placed principle in front of political or personal pragmatism. He was rarely rewarded for this. His son David, who followed in his father's footsteps and worked in the city's political arena, said of his father that "this role of progressive reformer was not ultimately rewarded nor universally admired by the general public, obviously, because he never won another election after the school committee."

Boston City Councilman William Foley, Jr., respected Muchnick, although he acknowledged that his zeal for the underdog probably cost him a longer political career. It made, David Muchnick thought, for a bittersweet commentary on his father. "Bill also said that dad was always way ahead of his time and the reason he basically couldn't win big in Boston was that he had 'smarts disease.' Foley was brilliant himself and I've done enough campaigning so I can understand that explanation as expressing great respect and admiration as well as an underlying sadness about what might have been."

Glenn Stout, who along with Dick Johnson would write the most complete book ever on the history of the Red Sox franchise, never believed, either, that Muchnick approached the Red Sox with the intention of receiving anything.

"It's much more the opposite. Looking at what he did I'm sure was not very popular. Otherwise, he wouldn't have been the only one hanging out there. You could say that what he did was political suicide."

What did emerge after the failed tryout of 1945 was a legitimate friendship between Jackie Robinson and the Muchnick family. When Robinson was
signed by the Dodgers, Muchnick wrote him a letter that read in part, "My con-
gratulations and best wishes to you on your well-deserved promotion to the
Brooklyn Dodgers! Since the day when you first came here with Wendell Smith
of *The Pittsburgh Courier* and I arranged for you and two other boys to get a tryout with the Boston Red Sox, I have naturally followed your career with great
interest. I have every confidence you will make the grade."

The Muchnick house became a regular stop for Robinson when the
Dodgers came to town to play the Boston Braves. After Robinson retired, he
sent Muchnick a copy of his autobiography with journalist Carl Rowan with
the inscription, "To my friend Isadore Muchnick with sincere appreciation for
all you meant to my baseball career. I hope you enjoy 'Wait Til Next Year.'
Much of it was inspired by your attitudes and beliefs."

Izzy and Jackie remained in frequent contact over the years. Robinson and
one of his sons came to Boston in 1950 or 1951 at Muchnick's invitation to speak
at a father-and-son breakfast at Muchnick's synagogue. The two men engaged in
heated debate about the 1960 presidential election. Muchnick was a lifelong
Democrat, and Robinson, in a move he would later regret, backed Nixon. At the
time, his reasoning was that Kennedy simply knew little, and cared to know even
less, about the black condition. To Robinson, such a quantifiable lack of desire to
understand the black dilemma disqualified Kennedy as a viable political option.

Neither man would lose the pioneering instinct. Jackie, Izzy, and David
went to the Kenmore Hotel for dinner once in the early 1950's. David still cher-
ishes the autographed team ball Robinson gave him that night. He remembers
that they were met with a mix of curiosity and suspicion. Rudeness at a distance
followed. "I don't know whether our presence unwittingly broke down another
barrier and integrated a whites' only dining room, but it could have. We didn't
seem to be part of the usual clientele."

During the summer of 1963, Fran never knew her father had taken ill.
Thinking only of her and her happiness, he wouldn't let anyone tell her, as she
was spending her honeymoon on a work-study program in Israel at the hospital in Beer Sheba. Only ten days after her return, on September 15, 1963,
Isadore Muchnick died of a heart attack. "I'm convinced," David Muchnick
said, "he willed himself to stay alive until she had returned."

There was a clear spiritual connection between Robinson and Muchnick.
Robinson, battered and weary from the fight, died too young of a heart attack
in 1972. He was only fifty-three years old; his hair was snow white, his eyes
blinded from the effects of diabetes. Isadore Muchnick died nine years earlier,
in 1963, but he was just as young, fifty-five at the time. His will to live, David
Muchnick believed, was enormous. Over his final five years, Muchnick suffered
seven heart attacks. On a rainy night in 1957, Muchnick received a frantic call

at 5 A.M. from a former city councilor's wife. Her husband had gone out drinking and had not come home that night. Muchnick crawled out of bed and went out into the drizzly Boston night to look for his old colleague. At 9 A.M., Ann Muchnick received a phone call of her own. Izzy had suffered a major heart attack and had been rushed to Massachusetts General Hospital, which sits in Boston's old West End near Izzy Muchnick's boyhood home.

It was Muchnick who used his influence to push the door open, to force the Red Sox and baseball to publicly face itself. Even if Joe Cronin and Eddie Collins weren't paying attention, Branch Rickey most certainly was. Slowly, the landscape began to change.

In 1998, Ann Muchnick died. She was eighty-nine. In prior years, the daughter asked for family information and the mother obliged with poignant recollections. She wrote that her husband "was a wonderful man . . . helped so many, so many abused his help, took advantage of him. I could name dozens, but better forgotten." They also spoke of Jackie Robinson not as the man spurned by the Red Sox, but as their friend.

"It was the Red Sox's loss," Ann Muchnick said of the whole tryout affair. "It wasn't his loss. Look at the career he had. He lost nothing. It was the Red Sox who lost everything."

In Robinson's autobiography with Carl Rowan lay another tribute to Muchnick. "Without the pushers and the crusaders, the waiters wait in vain; without people like Damon Runyon, and Branch Rickey, Wendell Smith and Isadore Muchnick, Jackie and the Negro might still be waiting for their hour in organized baseball."

In the end, the Robinson tryout failed because the Boston Red Sox were reticent from the outset. Led by Eddie Collins, the club had no real intention of acting beyond that April morning or as history would show for more than a decade thereafter. Within the organization, there was no guiding force, no catalyst with the vision to make integration a reality, and in years to come this would become the critical characteristic of the Boston Red Sox regarding race. Had there been a central figure in Boston, a Branch Rickey or even a Gussie Busch, who provided some form of vision, the Red Sox script would indeed have been different. It is more than a little damning that the months before the tryout and even after, it was Collins who represented the club and not Tom Yawkey, who stood invisible. At a time when the Red Sox stood at the precipice of baseball history, the team's owner lay deep in the background. Tom Yawkey was the only figure in the organization with the power to act boldly, and whether or not he harbored a personal dislike for blacks is secondary to his silence. That silence, in effect, would become a closing indictment. No different than the curved maze of streets in its city, the Red Sox lacked a clear-cut moral direction on race; against this, the combined pioneering spirit of Isadore Muchnick and Jackie Robinson never stood a chance.

FOUR

Had the Robinson tryout been an isolated incident, the Boston Red Sox would have been no different from the rest of the baseball world, for in April 1945 no one in the game—not future crusaders such as Branch Rickey or Bill Veeck, the irreverent Cleveland Indians owner—was ready to end its segregation. The Red Sox would not be faulted in those days, but privately applauded for remaining in step with the status quo.

In fact, instead of becoming a flashpoint for change, the Robinson tryout would for years be one of the least known pieces of both Red Sox history and the Robinson legend. A great collegiate athlete, Robinson was a baseball unknown. He had only been playing baseball for the Negro League's Kansas City Monarchs for three weeks. Few major newspaper outlets covered the event, and when Robinson, Jethroe, and Williams left Fenway Park that afternoon, nobody, except maybe Izzy Muchnick and Dave Egan, complained that nothing ever came of it. As sparse as the coverage of the tryout was, the follow-up reporting was largely nonexistent. Even Clif Keane—the *Globe* reporter who gave the tryout an inflammatory edge by charging that Tom Yawkey yelled, "Get those niggers off the field"—never reported the event for his paper.*

For a time, tryouts were commonplace. Before Robinson joined Brooklyn in 1947 and changed American life forever, both the Chicago White Sox and the Dodgers held tryouts for black players; like the Boston workout, nothing ever came of them. What doomed the Red Sox would be what the organization did after 1947, and how they did it.

For the next decade, black players revolutionized the game, and to no small degree; the sight of the two races competing on the ballfield—instead of playing the same game in separate worlds—began the slow disintegration of strict, previously unmovable racial barricades. Before baseball integration, it was as if

---

* This may not be completely true. As Marty Nolan pointed out, Keane may have very well covered the Robinson tryout and written an account of it, but for varied reasons—ranging from the various quirks of a newsroom to the Globe's potential unwillingness to publish the piece—Keane's story never made the paper. What is true, however, is that no account of the tryout ever appeared in surviving editions of the Globe during the week of April 16, 1945.

black people were invisible, thought longtime baseball writer Leonard Koppett. As a race of people, blacks resembled extras in a movie, Koppett thought, filling the background, but seldom heard. "With Jackie, black people became *present*. You couldn't ignore Jackie Robinson, and thus with black people, you now saw them as three-dimensional characters. They were now people, where before you rarely, if ever, had any real contact with any of them."

Brooklyn was the first, but the rest of the game soon followed. The silent, sixty-year gentlemen's agreement now broken, black players were now part of the talent pool, and the teams that exploited this sudden fire sale—as businessmen instead of social engineers—were handsomely rewarded. The Dodgers, Cleveland Indians, and New York Giants all signed talented black players at prices well below market, always a winning formula. The result was a model for an economics class. The Dodgers appeared in the World Series in Robinson's first year, in 1947; then again in '49, '52, '53, and '55, where they won it; and once more in his final year of 1956. The Indians won the World Series in 1948 and appeared again in 1954. The Giants went to the World Series in 1951 and won it in 1954. With the exception of the St. Louis Browns, who hardly ever won before moving to Baltimore and becoming the Orioles in 1954, teams that embraced integration won championships.

The Boston Red Sox did neither. They refused to sign young, talented players that were available for much less than they were worth and in the process saw their on-field fortunes decline steadily. In 1946, the year before Robinson, the Red Sox were the best team in baseball. They won 104 games and were in first place every day of the season. Even when they were stunned in the World Series by the St. Louis Cardinals, there was a feeling that it was a disappointment that would be long forgotten in the shadow of the numerous and glorious world championships that were to come.

The Red Sox, however, got old quickly, and because of the heavy strain of racism that ran throughout the organization, they would not sign the cheaply priced, highly talented, and readily available black players that surely would have kept them competitive. In this instance, thought Koppett, the Red Sox committed the worst of many sins. They allowed their racism to affect their economics. Instead of 1946 being the initial step of a dynasty, the Red Sox lost two bitter pennant races in 1948 and '49, fell out of contention late in 1950, and, after falling out of the race with three weeks to go in 1955, would not challenge the American League again until 1967.

Koppett was not surprised by the shortsightedness of the Red Sox and would offer a biting appraisal of Yawkey as a businessman.

> The Red Sox have always been one of the worst-run teams in the history of the game. Let me tell you something about the Boston Red Sox. Even when the game was all white, they made horrible business decisions. They had an owner who allowed his friends to hold positions of high, important baseball authority, and the result was dis-

aster. They never had solid baseball men making personnel decisions when the game was all-white, so why is it a surprise that they dropped the ball so badly on race?

If the tryout fiasco exposed Eddie Collins as a man reluctant to confront race as an emerging and ultimately unavoidable factor in the game, it was under Joe Cronin that the Red Sox were exposed as a racist franchise, for the team's characteristics mirrored the attitudes of these two men. Understanding the Red Sox of the 1940s and '50s under Tom Yawkey is to accept one overriding principle: Collins and Cronin were his most powerful deputies.

It went back to when Yawkey first purchased the Red Sox in 1933. He had admired Collins since childhood, when Collins was a star second baseman in the American League. Yawkey may have had more wealth than most men in America, but Eddie Collins could do something Tom Yawkey never could. He could play ball. Yawkey idolized Ty Cobb, the great and terribly racist Detroit Tigers outfielder. Indeed, when Yawkey was young it was Cobb who first suggested that Yawkey one day buy a baseball club. When Cobb and Yawkey had a falling out during a hunting trip over whose turn it was to shoot, Yawkey began to keep his eye on Collins to one day help him create a baseball powerhouse. In 1933, Collins accepted the position of vice president and general manager of the Red Sox.

Yawkey was rich, but when it came to baseball players, he was something of a sycophant. He had the money, but they had the talent. He liked nothing more than to be around the rugged, often coarse element of the game. When he owned the Red Sox, he would take batting practice at Fenway Park when the team played on the road. He wanted nothing more than to be a baseball player himself. He would have to settle for being an owner.

In 1935, in the throes of a spending spree previously unseen in baseball history, Yawkey asked Collins who he believed to be the best player in the game. When Collins responded that it was the Washington Senators shortstop Joe Cronin, Yawkey immediately acquired Cronin for $250,000, an exorbitant sum, especially during the Great Depression. Yawkey and Cronin would soon develop a closeness that rivaled that of him and Collins.

It was during these years that Tom Yawkey made the most critical decision as owner of the Red Sox: He would trust completely the baseball judgments of Eddie Collins and Joe Cronin. From 1933 until 1958, these two men would control virtually all player movements of the Red Sox organization. In 1941, Yawkey got drunk and he got mad. Bill Evans, his farm director paid the price when Yawkey fired him. Generally, however, the decisions belonged to Collins and later Cronin.

The foundation of the Red Sox attitudes as a franchise would be formed when Jackie Robinson was in grade school. Even in a whites-only environment, the Red Sox would hire some of the game's worst racists. Collins hired Herb Pennock, a Hall of Fame pitcher, to be his scouting director in 1935. Pennock would serve Collins for eight years before taking over as general manager of the Phillies, where he would protest Jackie Robinson's promotion to the major leagues. Pennock is but one example of the type of personality that existed within the Red Sox organization. In 1938, he convinced Collins to sign Ben Chapman, a rugged outfielder who had won championships with the New York Yankees. Chapman was a southerner, born in Tennessee and raised in Alabama. He made no secret about his distaste for blacks. When Pennock took over in Philadelphia, he soon hired Chapman to be his manager. Chapman would be celebrated as one of the worst tormentors of Jackie Robinson. The abuse Robinson took at the hands of Pennock and Chapman was so bad that National League President Ford Frick once placed a call to Pennock to demand he reprimand Chapman. The Phillies, largely a team created by Pennock, would be considered the most racist franchise in the National League, rivaling the Red Sox in their aversion to integration. The Phillies, unsurprisingly, would be the last National League team to integrate, just one and a half years before the Red Sox.

The lingering effect of the Pennock-Chapman Phillies was so severe that in 1969 Curt Flood refused a trade to the Phillies (which set up his landmark challenge of baseball's economic system), and in 1997, on the fiftieth anniversary of Robinson's debut, the Phillies apologized to Robinson's family and to Major League Baseball for Pennock and Chapman's treatment of him.

As scouting director, Pennock also suggested to Collins that the Red Sox reacquire a third baseman named Mike "Pinky" Higgins. Higgins played two years with the Red Sox and would become one of Tom Yawkey's fondest hunting partners.

Under Collins, with Yawkey's blessing, the Red Sox would adopt the characteristics of a southern team, and naturally the environment would be considerably unfriendly to blacks. When the Red Sox began to develop its farm system, Yawkey purchased clubs in Louisville and Birmingham, which were two of the worst regions to nurture black players, and over the years Cronin would use the location of these two farm teams as convenient reasons to avoid integration. Nothing, however, could be farther from the truth. Had the Red Sox wanted to sign a black player, the organization surely could have, for in those days it was commonplace for teams to loan players to different organizations. Cronin could have purchased a black player and assigned him to a more tolerant region. It wasn't as if the Red Sox didn't know about players, for the organization's tentacles stretched across the North and South. The Red Sox's own farm system team, in the nearby city of Lynn, often rented out its facility to black barnstorming teams. Two great players, Roy Campanella and Don Newcombe, played in Nashua, New Hampshire.

In addition, Yawkey owned a sprawling plantation in South Carolina to which he would invite his hunting and fishing friends. Yawkey also financed a notorious brothel, the Sunset Lodge, which was located in nearby Georgetown and used as a stopover and gentlemen's perk. It was yet another example of the club's old-boy atmosphere.

Initially, these traits had no immediate effect on the Red Sox, for the game was still largely segregated, and whatever disputes players had with their teams, they were unable to move between franchises. The results would only be seen later, when black players began to trickle into the major leagues and the Red Sox at first refused to scout and sign black players and then in later years were unable to communicate with either blacks or Latinos who were new to the game. When the time finally came for blacks to play in the majors, the negative effect of the team's ingrained culture—created steadily over the years by the hiring of southerners adamant against the notion of an integrated game—was embarrassingly apparent.

"The Red Sox have always been an agenda-driven franchise," said San Francisco *Chronicle* columnist Ray Ratto, who saw the Red Sox for years in their perennial battles with the Oakland A's. "It wasn't so much that racism was their M.O., but it was yet another agenda that prevented them from thinking about winning ball games. If ever there is any agenda outside of winning baseball games, you're going to lose."

Cronin was the player-manager of the Red Sox during the Robinson tryout, and while Collins may have been the public face of the franchise, Cronin clearly possessed no great desire to hire blacks. Cronin, who was from San Francisco, would have many powerful allies in the press and over the years would be portrayed as sensitive to integration, despite little proof. Joe Cronin was no friend of integration. He felt no moral fire to alter the social fabric, but over the years would be politically savvy enough to sound conflicted in the press over the integration issue. In 1949, his second year as general manager, Cronin was the lucky benefactor of serendipity. With the rest of major league baseball scurrying to find the next great player, a youngster named Willie Mays was available exclusively to the Red Sox. It was the by-product of a lease arrangement between the Birmingham Barons, an important Red Sox affiliate, and the Negro League Black Barons. As one of many conditions of the lease, the Black Barons' manager, Piper Davis, would tip off the white Barons to any special prospects. The Barons, in turn, would alert the Red Sox, Birmingham's parent club.

As the eighteen-year-old Mays dominated the competition, a Barons official made a quick call to Cronin in Boston, alerting him to a player who quite possibly was the best prospect in America. Cronin dispatched Larry Woodall to Birmingham to see Mays. Woodall, a Texan and not particularly thrilled about the assignment of watching black players, reluctantly arrived in Birmingham. Upon arrival, Woodall was greeted with three days of rain. Insulted that remaining in Birmingham was beneath him, Woodall said, "I'm not going to wasty my time waiting for a bunch of niggers." He wrote an unenthusiastic scouting report back to Cronin. It was widely suggested he never even saw Mays play. Wrote Al Hirshberg:

> That year the Red Sox had a working agreement with the Barons as Boston's Class Double-A farm club. The Barons tipped the Red Sox on Mays and they sent Larry Woodall, like Higgins a Texan, to Birmingham to look at him. It rained all the time

Woodall was there. Without ever watching Mays play, Woodall gave the front office a more accurate report on the weather than on Mays and, as I heard the story, when he came home he still hadn't seen Mays in action. Everyone I asked around Fenway Park denied that this ever happened. But I would have denied it, too, if I had had let a Willie Mays slip away right from under my nose. Imagine what the Red Sox would have done to the American League with Jackie Robinson and Willie Mays joining Ted Williams at Fenway Park!

Another version of the story has the Red Sox dispatching a scout named George Digby to scour the South looking for ballplayers; he came across an eighteen-year-old phenom who was in his words "the single greatest talent I have ever seen." Digby burned up the phone lines to Boston with his enthusiasm for the prospect only to be met by the cool response of Joe Cronin, something to the effect of, "We have no use for the boy at this time." The "boy," of course, was Mays. Still another story has the Red Sox, Yankees, and Dodgers passing on Mays because a scouting report circulated that Mays possessed a "mediocre" throwing arm and could not hit breaking pitches.

For Mays, it was a crushing moment. In his youthful zeal, he told all of his friends back in his small town of Westfield that a major league scout was coming to see him play and that he was going to play center field for the Boston Red Sox. It never happened, and Mays would go on to become arguably the greatest player who ever lived. When they would meet over the years, Mays would always tell Ted Williams that they should have played together.

One night in San Francisco nearly fifty years later, Willie Mays sourly remembered being an eighteen-year-old who thought he was on his way to play for the Boston Red Sox. "There's no telling what I would have been able to do in Boston. To be honest, I really thought I was going to Boston. They had a guy come down to look at me. They had a good team, with [pitcher Mel] Parnell, and [Vern] Stephens and of course, Ted. But for that Yawkey. Everyone knew he was racist. He didn't want me."

Like Robinson, Mays did what few observers of the Red Sox would do: He went straight to the top of the organization and blamed Tom Yawkey for passing on a legend. Yawkey may not have been enthusiastic about integration, but in 1949, Joe Cronin was clearly against it.

Having failed with Robinson and Mays, two players who could have altered the history of the Red Sox, Cronin in 1950 signed his first black player. It was Lorenzo "Piper" Davis, Mays' old manager with the Birmingham Black Barons. Davis was signed for $7,500 and promised another $7,500 had he remained on the Scranton, Pennsylvania, roster until May 15. A tall infielder at six-foot-two, Piper Davis was a natural athlete who, like Bob Gibson, played for a time for the Harlem Globetrotters. He grew up in Piper, Alabama, and thus the name of the town became his nickname. In 1950, Davis was thirty-three years old, fourteen years older than the lithe and wondrous Mays. A New

York Yankees scouting report believed Davis to be at least thirty-four in 1950. When he signed with the Red Sox, either he or the Red Sox lied to reporters about his age, as Cronin announced Davis as a "26-year-old sleeper."

Davis played well at Scranton, the one Red Sox affiliate that was not in Jim Crow country. On May 13, with Davis leading the club in home runs, batting average, RBIs, and stolen bases, manager Jack Burns told Davis the club was releasing him from his contract. The reason, Burns said, was economics.

It was a bitter blow. Davis knew that his only probable chance to make the majors had quickly disappeared. At thirty-three, there would not be too many teams interested in developing him. If this opportunity failed, he ran the very real risk of joining the ranks of Buck O'Neil and Josh Gibson, players who were too old to play major league ball when segregation finally ended. Davis had been hurt before. Before Robinson joined the Dodgers, Davis had been rumored to be the one who would end the color line.

He felt deceived. Whatever the real reason, Davis wasn't released because of economics. Ever since Tom Yawkey bought the club in 1933, money would never be an issue for the Red Sox. Scranton Manager Burns, too, was hurt by the club's decision to release Davis. Two days away from a $7,500 payday, Davis was sent back to Birmingham without train fare. His major league chance had disappeared.

Fate had yet another humiliation waiting for Piper Davis. He met Joe Cronin while his train stopped in Washington to segregate the seating for trains heading south. As Davis walked to the black section of the train, he saw Cronin. Cronin told him the same story. The Red Sox were financially challenged and thus could not afford Davis. The two parted ways and later Cronin reimbursed Davis for his travel expenses.

"They told me, 'we got to let you go because of economic conditions,'" Davis said bitterly of the experience with the Red Sox. "Tom Yawkey had as much money as anyone on the East Coast. I don't talk about it that much. It wouldn't help. Sometimes I just sit there and a tear drops from my eye. I wonder why it all had to happen, why we had to have so much hate."

The black press took an activist role toward the cause of integration. The two leading writers of the period, Sam Lacy and Wendell Smith, had clearly seen enough. Both had dealt for years with Eddie Collins and now his successor Joe Cronin. The result—active denial of discrimination while the Red Sox remained a segregated club—was the same. Neither Smith nor Lacy needed any more proof that the Red Sox were a racist franchise. The stories of how Robinson and Mays were both rejected by the Red Sox circulated from the black papers—the Chicago *Defender*, Smith's Pittsburgh *Courier,* and Lacy's Baltimore *Afro-American* were nationally distributed—and began the trail of evidence that the Red Sox were perhaps the worst organization in baseball toward blacks. The *Defender* was circulated through the South using a sophisticated network of black railroad car porters. At one point, its circulation reached 230,000, the majority of which came outside of Chicago. The stories of the Red Sox's treatment of black players trickled through major league club-houses—none of which contained more than one or two black players at a time. When they then filtered down into the barbershops—the true epicenter of sports opinion shaping the black community—the Red Sox would forever be suspect.

The mainstream press in Boston avoided confrontation with Cronin on racial issues. He offered a hollow denial—"The Red Sox care nothing about a man's color. They only want good ballplayers"—that, as the team continued to be completely white, sounded like a punch line. In 1953, the Red Sox signed a black catcher named Earl Wilson. It was a hopeful sign until the organization decided to convert him to a pitcher, setting Wilson's expected timetable to the majors back and giving the appearance that the Red Sox would always find a reason to deny a black player a spot on the roster. "The Red Sox," wrote Sam Lacy, "will never have a colored player as long as Tom Yawkey is owner." While Lacy's prediction was exaggerated, the Red Sox would never employ a black player while Eddie Collins, Joe Cronin, or Pinky Higgins controlled player movement.

Bud Collins arrived in Boston to work at the *Herald* in 1954 from Cleveland and was immediately struck by two traits about Boston journalism. The first was its provincialism. If an event occurred outside of New England, it was treated as a foreign affair. Collins remembered the 1959 NCAA title game when North Carolina was in the process of stunning Wilt Chamberlain and his Kansas Jayhawks. Collins not only thought the story worthy of the front page, but was surprised the newspaper hadn't sent a reporter to the game. "The response in the office was, 'Who cares?'" Collins recalled.

The second staple of newspaper work in Boston was the strict code of denial that existed about confronting the racial problems that were beginning to percolate in Boston as well as around the nation. He remembered complaining that the Red Sox's refusal to hire a black player was one of the biggest stories concerning the team. Collins was never the beat man who traveled with the club, but he covered nearly every home game and wrote features and sidebars. The response from the *Herald* sports editors was one of condescension. "'Take it easy, Junior,'" Collins remembered. "That's what they would tell me. They told me I had a lot to learn about their town."

Bud Collins never thought Yawkey to be a racist, but a victim of the trinity of Collins, Cronin, and Higgins. He was a person, thought Glenn Stout, who not only hired his drinking buddies, but also placed them in positions of such powerful authority that they ultimately controlled the direction of the franchise more than he. Unlike many of the journalists and historians who studied Yawkey, Stout, like Willie Mays, ultimately holds Yawkey—and not his wingmen—accountable for the club's racial attitudes. He did, after all, sign the checks. Richard A. Johnson, who coauthored a thorough history of the Red Sox with Stout, refers to the Red Sox, particularly the Yawkey style of management, as "Crony Island."

In 1954, while Willie Mays was winning the World Series for the New York Giants, Cronin hired Pinky Higgins, Yawkey's old hunting partner when Higgins played third base for Boston in the late 1930s, to manage the Red Sox. Higgins, as Pumpsie Green would soon find out, hated blacks as much as did Ben Chapman and Herb Pennock. The Sox finished sixty-four games out of first place under Higgins. Ted Williams would fight in Korea and return to a Red Sox team that still hadn't joined the ranks of the integrated.

For the next few years, the Red Sox faded from view in the American League, while in baseball the emergence of the black player represented the single greatest change in baseball history since the dead ball was eliminated. For a time, the men who controlled the Red Sox were no different than the rest of baseball in how severely they misread the type of player that had entered the game. While much of the white baseball hierarchy viewed the desegregation of baseball in strictly racial terms, what had emerged was an especially motivated ballplayer, the kind of player who knew what success could bring. Conversely, this new player—because he knew what awaited him back in the Negro leagues or, worse, as a black man struggling to find work out of the game—understood that failure was not an option. Baseball executives liked to say that most players "needed a steak" in front of them to motivate them to play hard every day. This new wave of black player—hungry to prove to the white baseball world they belonged long before this chance and dreading the return to that harsh world—would need no such encouragement. That the Red Sox would so completely and totally underestimate the hunger of the post-Robinson black player was one of the strongest illustrations of the depths of the racism that existed in the organization.

Buck O'Neil would never have the chance. He was the American tragedy, the black player who was once talented enough to crack the major leagues but was too old now that the chance had finally arrived. When he talks about that first wave of black player, his eyes light. He would lose his youth to racism but not his heart. Baseball would always bring a glint, a kind of electricity to his mannerisms. He would always become quick and defiant when considering just how completely baseball's leadership had misjudged the ravenous hunger. His face would contort, as if he fouled off a letter-high fastball instead of driving it out of the park. "Those players wanted to show them that not only were they wrong for keeping us out, but that they made a terrible, terrible mistake." O'Neil is now animated. He leans close and flashes a wrinkled index finger. "And they would have to pay for that mistake." Monte Poole, who would write columns for the Oakland *Tribune*, would notice something unique in the demeanor of those first players, scarred but determined. Even in the 1990s, nearly a half-century removed from the fight, black players of that era possessed an edge that even in the most serene setting would not allow them to show weakness. They were, Poole thought, still playing out parts of the game in their everyday lives. Even when their eyes closed, they never could quite erase the sting of segregation and the humiliations with which it came, of being told you weren't good enough. It was as though the true victory—for a black person to be judged equally and treated fairly—had still not yet been attained. To those men, even after a career of applause, there was not yet cause for celebration.

It would never be more pronounced than with the great Henry Aaron, who would never forget the slights of his youth and the pain that would come as he assaulted the all-time home run record. "There wasn't much white people would allow us to do in those days. You could be a schoolteacher or an athlete to get away from the manual labor and servant-type jobs, but there wasn't much else they were going to allow you do." Aaron's emotions snowballed. His soft, steady anger was apparent, and there wasn't much—perhaps nothing—that could assuage him. "I came from a family of eight. We only had outdoor plumbing. We would see white people live in a way we couldn't dream of, because if we did think we could live like that, we were simply being foolish and we would get depressed at our own lot in life. You have to understand what that could do to a person. A lot of players who came up through Mobile went through the same thing. . . . Watching that type of disparity had a direct effect on all of us, and it was just a matter of time before it had to stop. I wanted to make my mark, I wanted people, white people in power especially, to know that I was alive and when it came time for me to confront them, I was going to do that by hitting the baseball. *Hard.*"

The Red Sox misread a generation of black players as completely as any team in baseball. The Phillies did, too, for the bloodlines of the Philadelphia front office could be traced to the Red Sox of the 1930s. The mighty New York Yankees were perhaps worse than the Red Sox in their resistance to this new element in the game. The Yankees were the most successful team in all of baseball and as such carried a great deal of clout. Lesser teams immediately attempted to emulate their habits and mindset, thus making people like George Weiss, the team's openly racist general manager, that much more influential. Emulating the Yankees explained in some degree why the American League integrated much more slowly than the National League, which followed the pioneering Dodgers. For the decade of the 1950s, the Yankees did not feel the effects of their institutionalized racism. They fielded their first black player in 1955, catcher Elston Howard.

If the Red Sox were immediately affected by ignoring a plentiful talent source, the Yankees—thanks to a great farm system and numerous players in their prime—would not begin to feel the erosion of talent in their system until a decade later, in the 1960s. After the 1964 World Series appearance, the Yankees wouldn't see a pennant race consistently for more than a decade. It wasn't readily apparent, but Weiss, thought David Halberstam, had set the Yankees back a generation:

> The Yankees were paying much more heavily for George Weiss's racism than anyone had realized at the time. That racism was an unfortunate reflection of both snobbery and ignorance: Weiss did not think that his white customers, the upper-middle-class gentry from the suburbs wanted to sit with black fans, and he did not think his white players wanted to play with blacks, and worst of all, he did not think in his heart that black players were as good as white ones. He did not think that they had as much courage or played as hard.

The Gentlemen's agreement was airtight for sixty years. Yawkey didn't break it, so he was just like the rest. When black players did come to the game, the attitudes about black inferiority remained the same in the early days, and every now and then someone would get careless, like that New York Yankees scouting report that was proof of just how the Yankees felt about integration:

> There isn't an outstanding Negro player that anybody could recommend to step into the big leagues and hold down a regular job. The better players in Negro baseball are past the age for the big leagues. Several years ago I could have named several players that could more than hold their own in the big leagues. In fact, several would have been stars but now I know of not one that would stick. If they come up with certain named players please advise me and I will give you the low down on them. As I previously stated, there are no outstanding Negro players at this time.
>
> I am aware of how these committees apply the pressure on the big leagues to hire one or perhaps two players. If you hire one or two, then they will want you to hire another one. There will be no compromise with them.

In 1958, Joe Cronin left the Red Sox to become president of the American League. He was the ultimate insider, a loyal soldier to Tom Yawkey, popular with the press, and well known throughout baseball for thirty years. He had served Yawkey for nearly twenty-five years, and on Yawkey's strong recommendation Cronin became the first former player in baseball history to become a league president.

In many ways, the promotion of Cronin was a tacit condoning of the Red Sox way and a clear example of the deep levels of entrenchment that existed in Major League Baseball with regard to racial questions. The Red Sox had been one of the most resistant to the admission of blacks into the game, but far from being held accountable for their opposition, Cronin was rewarded with even greater prestige. Yawkey benefited, too; having one of his own as a league president was a reflection of his power and reach as an owner.

Bucky Harris, an old baseball man who guided the Washington Senators to a World Series title in 1924, and the Yankees in 1947, took over as the general manager of the Red Sox. For the rest of the league, integration was an important first step the Red Sox had yet to take. Boston, isolated as one of the only teams to have failed to integrate, would lag behind for years on the next phase—hiring blacks and Latinos within the organization as scouts and talent evaluators. Doing so would mean that organizations would be forced to learn how to deal with the differences in culture, language, and style and no one was quite ready for that. The team's players, coaches, and management would have to learn how to coexist with black players, a new, foreign concept that would prove far more difficult than the mere hiring of a black player. It would mean that these men who spent so long in a segregated game would now enter into the difficult challenge of trying to win while confronting deeply held racial beliefs.

That left Pinky Higgins. Collins was dead and Cronin was now gone to the AL, but like his mentors, Higgins swore never to field a black player. As a final act in the spring of 1959, he had sent Pumpsie Green back to the minors in a spiteful, last-second gesture. The Red Sox struggled early in the season with poor infield play, and Larry Claflin, a columnist for the Boston *Record American,* asked Higgins if he would bolster the infield by recalling Green, who, in the minors, was hitting over .300 and playing solid defense. Higgins responded by calling Claflin a "nigger lover" and spit tobacco juice on him.

FIVE

The historic moment came on July 21, 1959, in the eighth inning of a completely meaningless game. He stepped on the field in what would be a 2–1 loss in Chicago as a pinch runner for Vic Wertz, the man robbed by Willie Mays five years earlier in the 1954 World Series. Pumpsie Green had completed the final step of the first phase of baseball's integration. In a private moment back in the clubhouse after the game, he cried.

It was over. Pumpsie Green had joined the major leagues and in the process the Red Sox had joined the present. Baseball, some fourteen years after Jackie Robinson's infamous tryout at Fenway Park and twelve years after his Brooklyn debut, was now integrated. If the Boston press had characterized Green—more than a little unfairly—as a man oblivious to his role as a central figure in a larger social drama, he quickly understood when hundreds of supporters met a foundering team at the airport in Boston and the popping of flashbulbs alerted him to his position as a pioneer.

He was the celebrity of the moment. When he arrived in the Red Sox clubhouse at Fenway Park days later, he received a dozen phone calls, mostly from the organizations—the NAACP, for one—that had bitterly protested the Red Sox for his return. One call stood out above the rest. It was from Robinson himself, who was in his third year of retirement. More than to congratulate, Robinson called to remind Green of his historical place, that the two were, in a way, bookends to the long story of baseball's integration. Robinson told him more than a little prophetically that Green's achievement was by no means anticlimactic, but equally historic, for the last team to integrate likely suffered from an ingrained, deeply entrenched form of racism that was possibly worse than anything Robinson himself ever endured.

For Jackie Robinson to call—he was nothing short of a living legend for black players everywhere—was a defining moment for Pumpsie Green. It reminded him that in his own way, the son of a California public works laborer had made a significant difference in the world. Even if he never hit a game-winning home run or won the World Series, for this he would always be remembered. It also quieted to some degree the many voices that pierced him, unkind voices that suggested cynically that he had been chosen to fail, for the

Red Sox had for years passed on more gifted players, men like Willie Mays and Robinson himself. Surely, the thoughts went, if the Red Sox were serious about integration, they would have chosen someone with the opportunity to be a real impact player instead of Green, a player who would have to fight every day to remain on a major league roster. But he did not fail, Pumpsie Green thought to himself. He was a major leaguer.

It was, of course, inevitable that one day the Boston Red Sox would field a black player. That it took until nearly 1960, nearly two decades after the Robinson tryout, reflected the collective will of Eddie Collins, Joe Cronin, and Pinky Higgins.

The Red Sox didn't integrate because Collins, Cronin, and Higgins had suddenly become enlightened. The Red Sox brought a black player to Boston finally because none of the three were around to stop it. Collins was dead, Cronin was president of the American League, and new general manager, Bucky Harris, fired Higgins seventy-three games into the season, replacing him with Billy Jurges. A mere month later, Pumpsie Green suited up for the Red Sox.

If Pumpsie Green was unsure of what to expect from his teammates, Ted Williams provided the answer. The great, aging star chose Green to warm up with him before every game. It was the symbolic gesture of a true leader, for even if anyone did harbor a problem with Green's arrival, no one would cross the mighty Williams. Then it became a habit. Green, as was his way, immediately tried to downplay his arrival in Boston and the potential for discomfort with his teammates. He knew many, he said, from the minor leagues and in spring training and thus there was no real need for an adjustment period. This was Green's attempt at normalizing his potentially incendiary situation, for there was nothing normal about the Red Sox having a black player in their ranks. It had never happened before.

Arriving in Boston was not the end of the story, but merely a beginning. If Pumpsie Green never wanted to come to Boston—something he had said often—he soon found out that among certain neighborhoods, the feeling was reciprocated. He lived in Roxbury and Dorchester happily, he recalls. In fact, his temperament—easygoing and friendly—would serve him well in a place such as Boston, with its hidden presuppositions of how black people should act, especially around whites. Indeed, Pumpsie Green found out about Boston's harsh underside not from personal trauma but from a towering and unlikely sponsor, Boston Celtics star Bill Russell.

They were both from the San Francisco Bay Area, and when Green arrived in Boston that summer, it wasn't long before he and Bill Russell gathered for the first of many social occasions. By the end of Green's rookie year, he had eaten so many meals at the homes of Russell and K. C. Jones, he liked to say, that he feared the two would begin charging him. Russell could be dark and moody, but Green remembered him to be welcoming. Russell's presence, and the interest he took in the young infielder, gave Green's arrival that much more cachet, for by 1959, Bill Russell had already transcended the world of basketball. He had only been in the league three years and his skill as not just a great player but a revolutionary one was apparent. He led the Celtics, a team that before his arrival was good but hardly dominant, to titles in two of his first three years, and Russell had not even come close to reaching his prime. He would be, in terms of his effect on the game itself, the single greatest champion the NBA would ever know.

Bill Russell was miserable in Boston, suffering from bouts of terrible loneliness and frustration at the racial climate in the city. Having another Californian in town, Pumpsie Green felt, must have provided Russell with some form of comfort. Although the height of his power—Russell would go on to win eleven championships in his thirteen years with the Celtics—should have been the best years of his life, it would be take nearly forty years before he and Boston ever reconciled from those bitter, early days. It was not that northern California lacked racism or segregation. Russell's hometown of Oakland suffered its own damning polarity, for affluent whites there carved out the Piedmont section of the city as an exclusive region, geographical protection against the huge numbers of blacks that had moved west after World War II. Russell recalled his early years growing up in the black ghetto of West Oakland being fraught with racism, the kind of soul-torturing structure that destroyed the weak and sowed a foundation for the violent racial confrontations of the 1960s. "The police represent society. White society," he wrote. "The Negro learns to hate authority and he also begins to hate himself. They are taught through repetition that they are the scum of the earth and that they are bad. They have nothing in common with anyone, not even with each other. They are at the bottom of the heap, the bottom of the dung heap." During Russell's first years in Boston, San Francisco Giants star Willie Mays would have embarrassing difficulty finding a realtor to sell a house to him in the affluent neighborhoods along the peninsula towns south of San Francisco.

Boston, with its jagged notions of race and deeply segregated neighborhoods, was by its own complex design a racial powder keg. The city was woven into ethnic enclaves that were tight and inflexible. It wasn't only the societal racism that unnerved Russell; that existed in Oakland and in Monroe, Louisiana, where he was born. It was that Boston possessed an insularity that was by definition exclusionary. In Boston, Russell thought, you had to be an insider. If you were white, you had to be Irish. If you were Irish, you had to subscribe to the proper strain of Catholicism. Then you had to belong to the right clubs, attend the right schools, and know the right people. If you were none of these things—or worse, if you were black and thus could never become part of that club—Boston, even for Bill Russell, was a very hard city to navigate. "I had never," he wrote, "been in a city more involved with finding new ways to dismiss, ignore or look down on other people."

Russell found whites in Boston to be duplicitous and blacks curiously passive in the face of their clearly inferior status. Russell was a well-read man, coming of age politically in a time when colonial and imperial notions around the world were being confronted, often violently. This was no good in a place like Boston, where blacks were not to be seen or heard. His political awakening forced a hard look at Boston. He believed he was living in a city known for Paul Revere and its legacy of abolition and liberty. He found a place suffering from a deep moral confusion, rife with denial on the part of both blacks and whites as to the city's racial realities and a cauldron of simmering anxieties just beneath the city's surface. Well-meaning whites owned a latent, condescending view of black people that offended Russell almost as much as the virulent, angry racists who made no secret of their dislike of blacks. Blacks, meanwhile, because they had so thoroughly believed that Boston was a different city, one more racially tolerant than the rest of America, were incapable of grasping just how deprived they truly were. It would be a sentiment that a former Boston resident, Malcolm X, would articulate in later years.

With the exception of the multiracial South End and Roxbury neighborhoods, the city's racial boundaries were strict and foreboding, and any shift, however marginal, in the city's delicate racial balance could unsettle a tenuous peace. Blacks lived in Roxbury, one slice of Dorchester, and slowly more so in Mattapan, a neighborhood long Jewish and Eastern European that over the course of the 1960s would turn almost completely black. Mattapan was Izzy Muchnick's old neighborhood. Italians lived in Boston's North End and East Boston, while the city's Irish dominated Charlestown, South Boston, and the other half of Dorchester. The other major sections of the city, Allston and Brighton, were Irish, but would in later years become a destination for students, for the neighborhoods rested along Commonwealth Avenue between Boston University and Boston College. The Protestant gentry still controlled the prestigious brick-hued slopes of Beacon Hill, which in the nineteenth century was so dominated by blacks that it was nicknamed "nigger hill."

Within the city, there was little overlap of these strict boundaries, and generally speaking, an unspoken pact among the races meant that this arrangement suited all groups, especially the immigrant populations that preferred rapid assimilation. Even where blacks weren't concerned, Boston had long been ravaged by a century-long transfer of power from the Protestant Brahmins to the Irish Catholics, a bitter political and social conflict that would forever shape Boston and have real and dire consequences for the city's blacks.

Russell was perceptive to the city around him. He called Boston a "flea market of racism." If the lack of deadly and constant race rioting gave the city a collectively false sense of its racial climate, Russell knew just how unstable the city truly was. Other cities in the 1960s would suffer the effects of explosive racial conflicts, and Boston remained fairly peaceful. That, however, did not move Russell, who seemed to be more inflamed by the city's seemingly collective insistence that it lacked the same structural and emotional problems that plagued race relations in the entire country. It was an arrogance that marked the city's personality and would later leave it completely unprepared when racial resentments finally did roil to the surface.

He knew this from the experiences and the prejudices that he—a legendary athlete—had faced. What then, he wondered, could the average black in Boston be subject to? There was segregation in Oakland, but one still saw prominent black faces in the city. In Boston, black professionals were almost nonexistent. In the downtown financial districts, a black face that did not belong to a janitor was a rarity. Also, the black community, considerably smaller than those in Chicago, New York, or Philadelphia, was surprisingly passive, unable through its miniscule numbers to assert itself politically. He saw the black community in Boston as a permanent underclass, if not economically, then socially. Boston, he felt, was a tinderbox in denial. Already, subtle signs began to arise around the city that Boston's ethnic clans were not living in the harmony that was so often espoused by both blacks and whites. The city had not elected a black public official since before 1900, and the public school system, integrated in 1855, had quietly over the previous century begun a sharp and permanent reversal. Legally, Boston's schools were integrated. In practice, because of the rigid patterns of segregation that defined the city—especially in the hardcore white sections of South Boston and Charlestown and the overwhelmingly black areas of Roxbury and Dorchester—the two races rarely attended the same schools. The conventional belief was that residential segregation of the city was the reason for this, but the truth is that the Boston School Committee, an elected body known for its partisanship, wanted no part of integrating the city's schools. Marty Nolan, who covered the school committee in the early 1960s for the Boston *Globe* and would go on to become a prominent political reporter, knew firsthand the disturbing racial belief systems of many members of the committee. "They would try to blame it on how the neighborhoods were set up, that there was no racist thought that went into those policies, but that wasn't true," he said. "The truth is that there were some truly bad people on that committee in those days."

A very important but largely ignored phenomenon had also taken shape over the previous twenty years, the sudden migration of blacks to the North, which would mushroom the black population in Boston as well as create a severe cultural conflict within the city's black communities. In 1960, just as Bill Russell came into his own and Pumpsie Green began his first full season with the Red Sox, a new generation of black activists would begin to challenge the city's longstanding customs.

It was the city's treatment of Russell—and how he perceived Boston—that would begin to separate the city from the rest of the sports world. The Red Sox were considered a racist franchise, but Russell would provide the lightning rod for scrutiny upon the city. That the average black person had a rough go of it in

Boston was one thing; that Bill Russell, the greatest basketball player on the planet, felt so ostracized and so bitter about a place that should have idolized him was quite another. It was, felt Jack O'Connell, the veteran baseball writer for the Hartford *Courant* who in a career covering baseball would be confronted with the distance black players would feel toward the city, the first major point of demarcation. Black athletes, just coming into their own both athletically and socially in the 1960s, slowly viewed Boston with great trepidation. The general wisdom for athletes had been simple: If you play hard and win, the paying white customer will embrace you. But here was Russell, winning championships every year—the Boston Celtics won eight straight titles from 1959 though 1966— and responding to life in Boston with real vitriol. "I would rather be in a Sacramento jail," he once said, "than be mayor of Boston." His teammate Tommy Heinsohn said of Russell, "This was a great man. The people of the city didn't understand him. They belittled him, and he deserved better than that."

During impromptu car rides with Russell, Pumpsie Green would learn the depths of Russell's anger and discomfort in Boston. The routine, Green recalled, would often be bizarre and, at times, chilling. There was Russell, the greatest basketball player in the world, cramped behind the steering wheel of his Cadillac, immersed in deep, tortured thoughts with Pumpsie Green, the utility infielder for the Boston Red Sox. Most times, he would just listen to Russell, who was talking as much to himself as he was to Green. There were the times his house was burglarized in the affluent suburb of Reading. One time, thieves broke into Russell's house and didn't steal a thing. In fact they left him a gift, by defecating in his bed. That's right. Someone took a shit right in his bed, in his house. They would wonder, those Boston fans, where the rage came from. *Hey, big fella. These are the best years of your life. Why are you so mad?*

Green and Russell would drive around the city and Russell served as something of a tour guide, alerting the young Green to the perilous areas of Boston. South Boston was the Irish-Catholic stronghold, violently clannish and unwelcoming to blacks. They were the "brick-throwing racists, " as Russell called them. There were the writers, the ones that could be trusted and the ones that certainly couldn't.

What Bill Russell revealed to Pumpsie Green was the many faces of his soul. Russell's tortured soul spoke of the humiliations, of the whites who would always view blacks as dirt. He described a racist personality he believed was special to Boston—one in which a white person would approach him, impressed that he didn't possess the usual stereotypes that whites held of most black people, telling him that because of this, he was *one of the good ones, not like the rest.* Russell's energized soul would point out Washington Street, Boston's bustling black thoroughfare. The elevated subway rumbled above, there was nightlife nearby. There were jazz clubs, such as Connolly's and the Hi-Hat, as well as Slade's, the restaurant that doubled as a legendary jazz spot and in which

Russell himself owned an interest. Russell's angry soul would mention nothing but the slights. Boston, he told Green, was the most segregated city he knew.

Green would sit in the passenger seat perplexed, wondering why he was the recipient of Russell's force. Part of it was the great gap in their personalities. If Pumpsie Green did not accept racism, he also knew it was an intractable and unavoidable part of his life. He would not allow it to bore at his soul. Russell, meanwhile, was proud and defiant, demanding to be recognized on his own terms. Where Green tried not to complicate his life with the burgeoning questions and choices now being asked of the black man, Russell sought the debate and the resolution. The distances in their personalities would provide a blueprint for virtually all black players that would come to Boston over the ensuing decades. The players closer to Pumpsie Green's temperament—mild and less threatening to whites—usually managed Boston without much trouble. An introspective, Russell-like mind—both unafraid to voice controversial questions and unaccepting of the smallest racial slights—usually found Boston a resistant, prickly city, one often aggressive in its distaste for black assertiveness.

Russell may have heard the stories about Boston's proud pedigree as a racial champion, but it was a history remote and distant from his current reality, a history that had created a city that suffered from a true moral dilemma. It was a Boston, Bill Russell knew, that no longer existed except in the imaginations of Bostonians black and white who lived in denial, unable to face a new and harsh reality. Each time Russell drove him around the city, Pumpsie Green would find this out firsthand.

During those days, Pumpsie Green could only listen to Russell's searing troubles. Only years later, after watching a documentary about Russell's life, did Pumpsie Green truly grasp just how much emotional turmoil Bill Russell endured in Boston and how in many ways he served as a catharsis for Russell's beleaguered psyche.

There would be times when Green himself would be forced into the social fray, an unwilling ballplayer sucked into a city's racial dilemma. For him, it did not manifest in ugly confrontations with the city's whites or even in being subject to racial slurs at the ballpark—a tradition that would torment many blacks at Fenway Park. Green resented being the sudden spokesman on racial issues, and it created a clash with the Boston media, which wanted him, Green felt, to do their jobs for them. He was offended that reporters—who lived in the same conditions as him and often by virtue of being white enjoyed better privilege—needed him to explain realities about American society they already knew.

It was a feud whose roots went back to that first spring training in 1959. The writers knew Green was segregated from his teammates, that Scottsdale was restricted, and that Boston had never fielded a black player. Their colleagues wrote the stories of the lawsuits and protests against the Red Sox for the team's hiring practices. These, Green thought, were facts. Worse was that Green

believed these white reporters were living off of, in fact benefiting from, the segregated conditions of the day at his expense while he lived a dozen and a half
miles from his own team. They knew as well as he did the impossible chasm that
existed between their two worlds and hardly needed him to spell it out. As such
it confounded and at times angered him that writers would ask him if he was living a segregated life or if Boston or Major League Baseball had a racial problem.

"I mean, people—reporters, that is—would ask me the dumbest questions,"
he says, decades removed from those days, for the first time beginning to reveal
a personal passion for his story. "They would ask me about the things they
already knew the answers to. They would ask me about Boston, about the racial
situation in Boston, and I would think to myself, 'That's a stupid question. You
don't know already?' He responded with little candor and generic quotes, and
the press responded by depicting Green as something of a buffoon, oblivious to
his own social and historical importance. That first day in Chicago, the
Associated Press considered Green aloof, the "unwitting center of a storm of
protest charging racial discrimination." Earlier, when he was sent to the minor
leagues at the end of spring training, Bob Holbrook, the *Globe*'s baseball writer,
asked Green if he felt the move racially motivated. Green replied glibly, "I
haven't made any comment, and you can quote me."

Partly, he decided, the Boston press was trying to set him up, to goad him
into saying something inflammatory, and he would not accommodate them.
Robinson enjoyed the backing of management and was a legitimate superstar, and
thus could voice opinions with less fear of reprisal. Green was a black utility player
in an unsure environment that possessed a terrible history. He refused to offer any
insights that could be considered incendiary. Such action could quickly end his
career in Boston, he thought. It had happened with other black athletes, and
would happen in the future, especially in Boston. "They just wanted me to say
what they already knew, so I just didn't say anything," Green said years later. "In
a way, I didn't give them a lot. I was very protective of what I said."

Green loved playing for the Boston Red Sox. More accurately, he loved being a
major leaguer. There was wonder in being part of such a special fraternity, and
there was for him something special about witnessing the game played at the
highest level firsthand. There was the marvelous day in Boston when Frank
Malzone, playing third base for the Red Sox, found himself caught in an in-
game drama with the great Baltimore third baseman Brooks Robinson. Early in
the game, Malzone robbed Robinson of a hit, and in the bottom of the inning,
Robinson returned the favor. By the seventh inning, both fielders had taken hits
away from each other. After Malzone had stolen yet another hit from Robinson,
the Hall of Fame third baseman stood on the top step of the visitors' dugout,
ironically waving a white towel, in mock surrender. For a marginal player like
Green, it was an awe-inspiring moment to see baseball played this well.

"Brooks was in the dugout waving a towel and said to Malzie, 'truce.' It was like you were watching a movie. Things like that just don't happen in baseball, for those two guys to even have the opportunity to rob each other like that so many times in one game."

Later in his Boston career, there would be a well-publicized incident that would rank in the annals of Red Sox lore and cement Green's rep as a clown. After a series in New York, the team bus headed for Washington, where the Red Sox were to open with the Senators. The bus, mired in New York traffic, stopped in the gridlock, and frustrated by both the heat and the crush of cars, Green and pitcher Gene Conley got off the bus and went drinking around New York, resolved to meet the team in D.C. before the next game. At one point during the binge, Conley came up with a bizarre, spontaneous idea. The two should hop on a plane and go to Israel. Conley was serious, Green thought him crazy. Green, fearing for his baseball life, headed to Washington and rejoined the team. Both were threatened with hefty fines, but while it solidified their place among the great characters in Red Sox history, no one took Green seriously after that.

Without the daily influence of Cronin and Higgins, the flagrant air of racism that was so much a part of the Red Sox atmosphere dissipated slowly. Jurges was no genius, and the Red Sox were not considered serious contenders, but Green felt a great difference in the team climate without Higgins. There was, however, the question of living conditions. With Green the only black member of the team, he would have to room with a white player, a racial taboo that still existed. So Green needed company. A week after his arrival, the Red Sox recalled Earl Wilson, the hard-throwing black pitcher from Louisiana. He was 10–1 in the minors, and unlike Green, Wilson's arrival could not be debated in terms of social experiment. Had it not been for a two-year military commitment, Wilson likely would have been the first black player in Boston. He was drafted by the Red Sox in 1953 as a catcher but didn't hit well enough to be developed as a position player. Converted into a pitcher, Wilson flourished. He was wild, needing to harness his great power, but to Pumpsie Green there was no question that Earl Wilson possessed the physical tools and the desire to succeed required to be an above average major leaguer.

The two roomed together and in short time, Earl Wilson and Pumpsie Green forged a real friendship. Their position in the organization contrasted greatly. Green could never play consistently enough to nail down a permanent infield position, while Wilson was a budding star. Both, despite their position as Major League Baseball players, suffered the humiliations that came with being black.

Once, driving through Louisiana, the two men drove slowly through a school zone, only to be accosted by a white policeman. Wilson, the native, told Green to be quiet, to let him do all the talking. After the officer let the two men drive away, Green was at once stunned and frightened by condescending tones of the officer and, more, by the power of the police. He and Wilson, he thought, could have been shot to death for driving too quickly in a school zone.

On another occasion, Green drove home from Boston after one season and was stopped by two white officers in Texas. Green knew it was because of two things. First, his car bore out-of-state license plates, always a reason to be harassed by police. Second, he was black. As the officer spoke, Green answered his questions dutifully. He told the officer that he played for the Boston Red Sox and that in the trunk was baseball equipment so he could work out during the off-season. The officer told him to open the trunk.

While the first officer inspected the trunk, Green noticed the second with a steady hand on his gun. One unexpected flinch, Green thought, and I'm a dead man. The officer began the questioning anew.

"Who are you with again?" he asked.

"I'm with the baseball club. The Boston Red Sox."

The cop didn't care. He looked over the equipment once more and asked Green for the second time why he had it. Green told him the equipment was for his off-season training.

"How do I know," the cop said menacingly, "that you didn't steal this stuff?"

The second cop squeezed the butt of his gun a little tighter, but kept it in his holster. Green watched the second cop even more closely than the first.

"Officer," Green said. "If you think I stole these things, you can have them. All of it."

There was one problem. At the end of the 1959 season, Tom Yawkey fired Billy Jurges and rehired Pinky Higgins. Pumpsie Green remembered Higgins' famous proclamation, the one about there never being any niggers on the Red Sox under his watch. Higgins was a nightmare for Earl Wilson, who was on his way to becoming a special pitcher. "It's not very hard to tell if a guy likes or dislikes you," Wilson once said of Higgins. "It's like if a dog comes into a room, he can tell if a person likes him or dislikes him, just by the vibes."

Higgins hadn't changed a bit. And why would he? The Red Sox may have integrated, but the club's racial attitudes of the 1950s were perfectly intact. Higgins was known throughout the league as an alcoholic and a racist, the classic old-boy drinking buddy of Tom Yawkey's who always found himself with a job in the Red Sox organization.

On the Red Sox, Green had to learn to ignore the chatter in the dugout. Wilson, who owned a more fiery personality, tried too to subdue his feelings. There was another black on the team, Willie Tasby, who started 105 games for the Red Sox in 1960. Tasby was the first black player acquired by trade by the organization. They couldn't help the feeling of being outcasts. The concept of jockeying—the attempt to unnerve an opponent with taunts and insults—was commonplace. In the old days, white players ripped each other's ethnicity mercilessly. The Irishman ragged the Jew who ragged the Kraut who ragged the Wop. Not everybody liked it—indeed, the great Detroit slugger Hank Greenberg suffered similar taunts to Robinson in the 1930s and '40s—but nobody stopped it, either. It was part of the game.

Vestiges of this gamesmanship still existed in the 1960s, but with the addition of black and Latino players in the game, it contained a different, less tolerable meaning. During a regular season game against the Chicago White Sox at Fenway Park, the great Cuban outfielder Minnie Minoso ripped a line drive in to the right field corner, a chance for an easy triple. Yet Minoso, who was known for his great speed and acceleration, curiously slowed and stopped at second, which caught the eye of Red Sox coach Del Baker.

"Did you see that?" Baker yelled in the dugout. "The way he can run, he should be on third. That nigger's got to be hurt or something. Niggers usually run better than that, especially him."

It was an embarrassing moment for Pumpsie Green, who was the only black in the dugout at the time. As Green sat on the bench, mortified, a white teammate angled up to Baker and said, "Hey, you can't talk like that anymore. We got Pumpsie with us now." Baker stopped talking, didn't apologize to Green, and the rest of the Red Sox sat in an uncomfortable silence.

Green believed that Higgins thought of him as a troublemaker because of the fanfare surrounding his not making the big league club in 1959. Higgins said he would never have any blacks on the team, Green thought, and while he couldn't change the times, he certainly could make a few strategic eliminations.

Pumpsie Green's problem was his hitting, and his fielding was average. He hit only .233 in fifty games that first season. The major leagues may have integrated, Hank Aaron claimed, but the white baseball establishment would only make room for exceptional black players. It was, he thought, one of the least-discussed examples of the game's ingrained racism. While marginal utility players such as Pumpsie Green always had to keep their suitcases packed, it was precisely this class of player who generally became a field manager. Green played fifty-six games for the Red Sox in 1962 and was traded during the off-season to the Mets for Felix Mantilla.

While his roommate Earl Wilson grew to prominence, throwing a no-hitter in 1962 against the Los Angeles Angels, baseball ended quickly for Green. He was not a star, but a player whose survival was tenuous each season. For such men, baseball is not fun. Joe Morgan, another baseball product from Oakland, remarked that baseball is only fun when you are a superstar. For the player trying to survive in a game where a hungry teenager awaits on every sandlot, eager to take your job, there is little time to enjoy the game. Green played seventeen games for Casey Stengel's New York Mets in 1963 before being sent to the minor leagues. After fighting a hip injury that never improved, Green was released by the Mets in 1964. He played 344 games over five seasons. Green packed up, went home to California, and never looked back. He would work at

Berkeley High School for years, for some as the baseball coach. There would be
no major league comebacks. He understood.

It should have been Jackie or Willie who integrated the Boston Red Sox,
but it wasn't. It was Pumpsie Green, the final link to Robinson's gallant quest.

"I had an arthritic hip that just never got better. I got tired of cortisone
shots and in September of '65 I came home. I never thought about coming back
or trying to be a coach or anything. My thought was 'been there, done that.'
That was enough for me."

Earl Wilson felt that without Pinky Higgins and men like him in the Red
Sox organization, Green may have been developed into a better player. Boston,
he thought, was an unhealthy organization for black players, the pressures to
succeed much greater than the level of encouragement received.

When Tom Yawkey fired Higgins as manager in 1962, Earl Wilson felt for
a moment that the Red Sox finally understood what a divisive influence Higgins
was on the club. But Yawkey did the unthinkable. He didn't fire Higgins, he gave
him a promotion, moving him up to general manager. Now, Pinky Higgins
enjoyed total control over the player personnel decisions of the club. It was a
bizarre decision, emblematic of the insider nature of the Red Sox. Higgins was a
drinking partner of Yawkey's and instead of just finding a place for an old friend
on the team's payroll, Yawkey gave Higgins the title of general manager, the most
critical role in the construction of a ball club. Higgins was no exceptional baseball
mind. He was not a brilliant manager, or even a good one. His teams never finished higher than third place. He was a proud and devout racist, which was the
worst credential to own in a game that was changing as dramatically as the society around it. For the next three years, the Red Sox would founder, and if Higgins
could no longer keep black players off the Red Sox with impunity, he could certainly refuse to acquire or develop new ones.

On September 16, 1965, Red Sox pitcher Dave Morehead threw a no-hitter against the Cleveland Indians. It was a great day, but the more significant
act occurred directly following the game. Unable to control his drinking,
Higgins was fired by Yawkey, who replaced him with Dick O'Connell, a New
Englander from the Boston suburb of Winthrop. It received little attention
then, but it would soon become a decision of major impact, the best move the
Red Sox made in a generation.

God has a sense of irony, so fate had something else in store for Pinky
Higgins after Tom Yawkey—the only man who would hire him—fired him that
day of Morehead's no-hitter. One day in Louisiana, Higgins got drunk, then
got in his car, and plowed right into a group of black highway workers. He did
time, and two days after his release in 1969, Pinky Higgins dropped dead of a
heart attack. Earl Wilson was in Detroit at the time, and took a minute to think
about his old skipper. "Good things," he said, "happen to some people."

SIX

In 1966, Ted Williams was inducted into the Hall of Fame. Ever the iconoclast, Williams used his induction speech to send a unique message that needed to be heard. As surely as himself, he said, the great black players such as Josh Gibson and Satchel Paige of the Negro leagues should be inducted into the Hall of Fame. They would already be there, Williams argued, had they only been given the chance to play. Their only crime was being born black in the wrong era.

It was a telling speech. Because the National League moved much more aggressively in embracing integration, Williams played in All-Star games against black major leaguers for more than a decade. In those All-Star games, he teamed with few black stars from other American League teams. Minus nearly five years of military time, Williams played twenty-one seasons under Tom Yawkey; only in his last, in 1960, did he play on an integrated team for a full season.

Yawkey said nothing publicly, but some players at the time believed he groused at his greatest star using a great moment to further a cause about which he felt considerably ambivalent. Yawkey had always wanted to be close to Williams, the greatest hitter in history and the greatest star ever to wear a Red Sox uniform. Williams lauded Yawkey as a great owner, and Will McDonough, the influential columnist for the Boston *Globe*, believed that Yawkey wasn't as accessible to the Boston press in protest of the harsh manner in which the city's media treated Williams. Yawkey and Williams, however, would never become confidants, never as close as Yawkey would be toward Carl Yastrzemski, his next great star. And how could he? Williams and Yawkey looked at life in completely different terms. Yawkey was an old boy who never lifted a finger to earn the tremendous wealth bestowed upon him. Williams' mother worked for the Salvation Army—much to Williams' embarrassment—and dedicated her life to poor people, people who never had a chance. Williams would train himself to be great. Yawkey woke up one morning—thanks to a fat inheritance—and wound up on top of the world.

Then there was the drinking. Yawkey, when disinterested in his ball club, was famous for it, as famous as that night in New York when he agreed to trade Williams for DiMaggio straight up. Done deal, until Yawkey woke up hung over, freaked that he'd get crucified by an entire city and pulled the deal off the table.

Jackie Robinson would go to his grave bitter at the Red Sox—Joe Cronin, in particular—for the farcical tryout in 1945, but he cheered Williams' ability to see beyond himself, even during such a personal moment, when he would be justified in speaking only in self-congratulatory terms. Pumpsie Green was out of baseball and living back in California. He would work at Berkeley High School near where he grew up for years as a baseball coach and athletic director. After hearing of Williams' speech, Green remembers smiling to himself. Williams would always be his favorite. It went back to Green's rookie year when no other Red Sox player would even warm up before games with their new black teammate. As much as it became a superstition for Williams to warm up with Green, Green remembered Williams as one of the few players that first year that made him feel like both a ballplayer and a man. Using the day he was enshrined as a baseball immortal to propose a way of making amends for the game's most shameful period made Ted Williams all the more a hero to Pumpsie Green.

Williams' speech came as a complete surprise, for there was little in his public background as a player that offered clues into his feelings on baseball's segregation. For many years, Doc Kountze believed Williams to be the secret engine behind the Red Sox mandate of segregation, for Kountze thought Williams never wanted to play with blacks. While Kountze never wrote about this suspicion in the black press, he always harbored it against Williams. During the early 1990s, and very late in his life, Kountze was told by Glenn Stout about Williams' Hall of Fame speech and immediately recoiled with embarrassment. For all those years he was wrong about Williams. Kountze sent Williams a letter apologizing to the great star for even *thinking* Williams was a racist when he was in fact an ally. His conscience was cleared months later when he received a warm response from Williams himself.

Ted Williams was not a pioneer in the sense of crusading for racial justice, nor was he an outspoken protector of the old guard. Perhaps the most important aspect of Ted Williams was that he was a perfectionist who viewed life in linear, apolitical terms. Either you could hit a baseball or you could not. It was, in his world, just that simple. Once, according to baseball legend, Williams slept in a lawn chair near the batting cage during an exhibition game. He laid with his eyes closed and listened to the perfect sound of the bat making contact with the ball. There was, thought Williams, no more sweet or gratifying sound in the universe. Such a swing, coupled with the same, consistent pitch each time the bat struck the baseball, convinced Williams he was in the presence of not just a natural hitter, but a potentially great one like himself. Williams asked around. The hitter was a young Henry Aaron, who in time would become the greatest home run hitter ever. It was a story Aaron himself believed to be true. For Ted Williams, the politics of race had no place in between the lines of the baseball diamond. It was, in Williams' mind, one of the few places in the world where merit was the only judge, and not allowing a player, never mind an entire race of players, the chance to prove himself was in direct opposition to the belief system of Ted Williams. For a member of the Red Sox to issue such a public indictment of the game, and by clear extension the team's longstanding policies, was a sign of real change.

Along these lines, the hiring of Dick O'Connell as the team's general manager in 1965 would be the single most important front office move in Red Sox history; it was first concrete step the franchise took outside the usual Yawkey cronyism, and it would pave the way for what would be the most progressive era the franchise would enjoy until the mid-1990s. O'Connell, thought Glenn Stout, was the first member of the Yawkey regime—a regime that by O'Connell's hiring was more than three decades old—who received his title based on merit. He was not a Yawkey crony. He did not receive his job by being a drinking buddy of the owner or a former player whose skills Yawkey admired.

Equally as critical, O'Connell was also the first executive under Yawkey to be free to maneuver within the organization without the influential trio of Eddie Collins, Joe Cronin, and Pinky Higgins. With all three gone and Yawkey disinterested in the direction of the franchise—the Red Sox in 1965 drew 652,201 fans, an average of 8,052 per game—O'Connell could then construct the team of his own vision.

O'Connell had started from the bottom rungs of the organization. He was a Boston College–educated World War II veteran who worked in Navy intelligence at Pearl Harbor. During the war, he met Jim Britt, a Navy officer who happened to broadcast for the Red Sox before the war. To O'Connell, who grew up twenty-five minutes from Boston, it was fortuitous contact. If he was not athletic, he was certainly physical, having worked his way through college as a longshoreman at a time when Boston was one of the busiest ports on the eastern seaboard. It was a tough assignment and a reflection that Dick O'Connell certainly did not fear hard work. Baseball intrigued him, and he and Britt made a pact to reconnect in Boston after the war.

In 1946, O'Connell decided to take Britt up on the offer. They met for lunch one day at Fenway Park, and during the afternoon, O'Connell met George Torporcer, a man was aptly nicknamed "Specs" for being one of the first major leaguers in history to wear glasses. Torporcer, who lived on Long Island and wanted to spend more time with his family in New York, hired O'Connell to handle the day-to-day operation as business manager for Boston's minor league affiliate in nearby Lynn. It was a small operation, one that required an aggressive self-starter. O'Connell handled virtually every facet of the operation, from bookkeeping to ticket taking, and during that time realized he had a knack for administration. He also had a growing idea of how to construct a ball club.

As O'Connell worked his way through the organization, he also noticed something telling about the Red Sox: He was an outsider, ironically in part because he was a New Englander. If the Red Sox of today represent New England in heart and soul, it was not true in those days before the watershed year of 1967, before the perception of the entire franchise—and its place in New England—forever changed. Nineteen sixty-seven was the year when the Red Sox became New England's team. Glenn Stout believes that without Dick O'Connell, the glory of 1967 would have never happened.

Before that, however, the Red Sox were a decidedly southern team devoid of much magic or fanaticism. Yawkey may have grown up in Michigan and gone to the same Tarrytown, New York, boarding school as Eddie Collins, but the institutional flavor of the Red Sox was a very southern one. It could be seen in the construction of the organization, where for years its top farm teams resided in Louisville and Birmingham. This, and not any racial agenda, thought Boston *Globe* columnist Will McDonough, was the true reason the Red Sox lagged behind in their pursuit of black players. In fact, McDonough believed that men such as Yawkey and Cronin wanted to integrate quickly, but were hamstrung by societal limitations.

While McDonough would be a steadfast supporter of this notion, there is no evidence supporting him. In fact, there is only proof of the contrary. The final three teams to integrate—the Detroit Tigers, the Philadelphia Phillies, and Boston Red Sox—all have one man in common: Tom Yawkey. Yawkey learned the game from his uncle and adoptive father Bill Yawkey, who owned the Tigers. Tom Yawkey's introduction to the game began with baseball men whose views on integration are well documented. He idolized Ty Cobb, who along with Cap Anson was perhaps the most famously racist ballplayer in history. It would be on Bill Yawkey's 25,000–acre retreat on the South Carolina coast, immersed in the viewpoints of men like Cobb, where Tom Yawkey's baseball world would be shaped. Cobb's influence could not be underestimated, for not only was he considered the greatest player who ever lived but his relationship to the Yawkeys was so close that Cobb was present at Bill Yawkey's deathbed. Taking his adult role models into account, it is not difficult to envision how the Red Sox would mirror the Tigers.

As a player in the Philadelphia Athletics, Eddie Collins grew to know a young third baseman named Mike "Pinky" Higgins. They played together in 1930, and Higgins played on the Athletics for three more seasons while Collins served as bench coach to legendary manager Connie Mack. Higgins also played third base for the Red Sox under Collins in 1937 and 1938, driving in 106 runs both years. As general manager of the Red Sox in 1946, he would acquire Higgins to play third base for him. When Higgins retired, Collins found him a job managing in the Red Sox farm system, a system overseen by Herb Pennock, who would become the general manager of the Phillies and instill in that club a racism that was similar to that of the Red Sox. Pennock's son would marry Collins' daughter.

This is how it would go in Boston, a neverending game of pass the buck. Yawkey could be charming that way, of course he also had the power of that bottomless wallet he carried. It was a great weapon against attack, and make no mistake, Tom Yawkey was a Boston giant in name, if not in his passion for the city. That would be the rub of the man. He gave money—tons of it—to the cancer foundation, the Jimmy Fund, but behind the scenes, watching his nine lose a hundred games a year deepened his conviction that the Olde Towne Team was better off somewhere else. He wanted a new stadium—those damned Boston pols left him in musty old Fenway—and nobody would budge.

So Yawkey sat in the background or way out of sight in South Carolina, letting men like Higgins and Larry Woodall run the show. Al Hirshberg, the old beat writer for the *Herald* and Dominic DiMaggio collaborator, thought that was precisely the problem. If Yawkey had taken a more active hand in matters, who knows? Maybe he would have reeled in Collins, Cronin, and Higgins—not likely, since he gave them the deed to the house in the first place—and maybe history would have been completely different.

In any case, Yawkey took a backseat, and the housecleaning began. Dick O'Connell had been in Yawkey's employ since 1946, but he wasn't one of them. Dick O'Connell was out of that loop, and when the Red Sox crashed to the bottom of the league in both attendance as well as with a 62–100 record, O'Connell was given the job. Part of the reason for his hire, Stout thought, was out of expediency. Yawkey was barely interested in the team, and O'Connell was already a part of the organization, allowing him to quickly move into the position. O'Connell also did so well with his assignment in Lynn that he turned the club into a profitable enterprise. There was no reason to look outside of the organization.

Before O'Connell, the Red Sox were the backroom team, an unimaginative franchise that overpaid for underwhelming prospects. They had not contended—except for one season, 1955, when they wound up finishing twelve games out of first place—since 1950. The Red Sox were the team, in Leonard Koppett's estimation, that had all the money in the world but not a single person in the organization who knew how to build a ball club. They were a country club. Dick Johnson recognized O'Connell's significance in changing the culture of the Red Sox. His reference to the Red Sox as "Crony Island" would never be more appropriate than during the first half of the 1960s.

Under O'Connell, the Red Sox would be different. He was the first real talent evaluator in the Red Sox organization, and unlike the Collins-Cronin-Higgins trio, carried no baggage concerning the changes in the game. Black and Latino players had now been a part of baseball for twenty years, but for the first time Latinos constituted a real part of the talent pool for the Red Sox. Part of the difference with the old Red Sox regime was purely racist, but another part was generational. Collins, Higgins, and Cronin had all played their entire careers in a segregated game and, although it was happening in front of them, none of the three could envision playing with or against black players.

O'Connell had never played the game, and the majority of his time in base-ball had been post-Robinson. It was, thought Dan Shaughnessy of the Boston *Globe*, one of O'Connell's great hidden strengths, for he did not harbor any of the residual racism that existed with Cronin, Collins, or Higgins. He knew the Red Sox had needs, and instead of satisfying an agenda, he attended to them. To Leonard Koppett, O'Connell was not a particularly remarkable baseball man, except in the framework of the Red Sox, a team that for decades would never produce the results equal to what Tom Yawkey was spending. In Boston, any executive who received a job on merit was unique. As such, O'Connell's arrival represented a sea change in the way the franchise did business.

Thus the Red Sox front office began to evaluate all players on merit, at least more than before. It wouldn't, however, be as simple as acting colorblind, which, based on the explosive times and the deep gaps in social experiences, would be a near impossibility.

The Red Sox would soon find out what the St. Louis Cardinals already knew, that integration was one matter, and true acceptance and teamwork across intractable racial lines was quite another. The reward for success, thought Tim McCarver, could be plentiful even if the process would be decidedly painful. Where the Red Sox avoided even the discussion of race as an impor-tant topic, the Cardinals underwent the difficult, often agonizing process of real integration.

At first glance, St. Louis would be one of the more unlikely places for social engineering, especially in a baseball clubhouse. Jackie Robinson entered the majors in 1947, and many members of the Cardinals had signed a secret peti-tion to boycott the season. The National League president ultimately quashed the insurrection, but a residual effect remained. When the Dodgers played the Cardinals, the racial bench jockeying against Robinson was, with the possible exception of Philadelphia, at its most fierce. In the eyes of needling white play-ers, dark skin was simply another target used as an attempt to unnerve. The Cardinals consistently would yell out at Robinson, "Hey porter, get my bags." Robinson complained. Newspaper stories were written. White players, already stung that baseball was integrated in the first place, complained that if Robinson and the blacks couldn't handle the taunts, maybe they didn't belong in the game. Before he was a celebrated writer, Roger Kahn covered the Dodgers beat for the New York *Herald-Tribune*. Once, confronted by Dodgers relief pitcher Clem Labine, Kahn understood the white perspective.

"Look," he said, "maybe if someone called me a French-Catholic bastard, I'd tell him to go fuck himself. I wouldn't come crying to you."

"It's not the same thing," Kahn responded. Labine was unmoved. He wanted to know why not. "Because in Mississippi, they're not lynching French-

Catholic bastards, only niggers." Labine, in Kahn's words, "winced and then he nodded."

For black players in the 1950s, there were three cities in the National League where nobody wanted to play: Philadelphia, Cincinnati, and St. Louis. By the 1960s, a Cardinals team full of extraordinary young men began to emerge. More than playing baseball, the players on that team illustrated in so many ways the American dilemma of how to be different and succeed as a group simultaneously. The team had cultivated talented players from disparate racial and ethnic backgrounds, and the challenge—to find a way to work together and maximize each other's talent within the staid, old-school environment of Major League Baseball—mirrored many of the challenges taking place in each corner of the country.

The Cardinal team became perennial champions in the 1960s, and much of the team's success was rooted within many of the players' earlier struggles. Bob Gibson, the great pitcher, was from the black ghetto of Omaha, Nebraska. He was so athletically gifted he once played for the Harlem Globetrotters after attending Creighton, but quit because it simply couldn't satisfy his fierce competitive urges. "I couldn't stand the clowning," he once told Roger Angell. The center fielder, Curt Flood, was from the ghettoes of West Oakland, and attended McClymonds, Bill Russell's old high school. Flood, always underestimated because of his size, would become perhaps the single most important figure in baseball's economic history when he challenged the reserve clause that kept players bound to one team for life.

The tough Irish catcher Tim McCarver, the son of a Memphis policeman, before joining the Cardinals had little contact with blacks. Bill White, McCarver thought, was quite simply the most mentally tough person he'd ever met. Dick Groat, the shortstop, who attended prestigious Duke University, was part of the emerging number of college-educated players in the game. Lou Brock attended Southern University, the traditionally black college, and his will to succeed was only surpassed by his desire to be treated with decency and fairness, despite the racial climate of the country.

The Cardinals as an organization were a charter member of the National League, and in St. Louis then, as today, they stood as the single largest sports team in the area. Like the Red Sox, St. Louis is more a regional team than a local one. The Cardinals organization, initially resistant, made a conscious decision to confront integration and the difficulties that came with it. Owned by the powerhouse Anheuser-Busch brewery, the Cardinals ultimately used its influence to promote social changes, changes that were at first limited, but would become broader over time. Black players were assisted in finding housing, even in areas that may have been historically segregated. When the local customs would not bend, The Brewery bought a motel in Florida in order for the entire team to be housed together. It was a move similar to that of the Dodgers, which had used the converted Army barracks in Vero Beach for spring training and in a way circumvented the prejudices of the Deep South. It was a great contrast to how the Red Sox treated Pumpsie Green during his first spring training in Arizona. Bill White, the conscience of those Cardinal teams, applied to The Brewery to use its influence during spring training by pushing local communities to integrate spring training facilities. A man of Bill White's inner strength and sensibilities, thought Tim McCarver, created a powerful moral center for the Cardinals.

By no means, thought McCarver, were the Cardinals a crusading organization, yet by the strength of the considerable personalities on those teams, the Cardinals became committed to the idea of racial acceptance. It was first White, then Gibson and Flood, who prodded The Brewery into a significant role.

Tom Yawkey with all of his millions had ample influence in Boston, Arizona, and Florida during spring training, but it was The Brewery that used its leverage. Curt Flood may have had differing opinions about Cardinals management over the years, but he agreed that the franchise did more on balance for black players than most. Segregated facilities in Florida, fearing the loss of lucrative baseball business, began a slow bend, contributing to the demise of segregation in its own small way. The Brewery, using its power to force change, Tim McCarver thought, was one of most important but least mentioned aspects of the Cardinals' story. Without that pressure, he said, there would have been no incentive for Southern businesses to relax and ultimately eliminate the segregated order.

The promotion of black players was a by-product of the Cardinals seeking out the best possible talent. While it hardly took a brilliant baseball man to see that Bob Gibson was a great talent, the power of convention cannot be underestimated. Few teams actively pursued black players, and even fewer recruited black pitchers, since the stereotype dictated that blacks lacked the intelligence or discipline to play that position. Solly Hemus, Gibson's first manager on the Cardinals, would not pitch Gibson regularly and often insulted his intelligence by suggesting in meetings that the young pitcher could not grasp the finer aspects of pitching. "Just throw it over the plate, Gibson, if you can," was the extent of Hemus' teaching of Gibson. While the front office and General Manager Bing Devine in particular took the raw talent of a Bob Gibson, Bill White, or Curt Flood and incorporated it into the Cardinal system, it was not a smooth transition. The Cardinals, like the Red Sox and many other clubs, had powerful strains of racism that ran throughout each segment of the organization. Flood remembered his constant clashes with Hemus, a southerner who was convinced Flood would never be a major league hitter. Hemus, Flood wrote, never looked him in the eye and "acted as if I smelled bad." It was no different from how Earl Wilson was treated by Pinky Higgins. Black players believed Hemus managed them based on his own racial stereotypes. Flood explained Hemus brutally:

During a game against Pittsburgh in 1959 or 1960, Hemus inserted himself as a pinch hitter against Bennie Daniels, a black man. Daniels knocked him down with the first pitch. On the second, Solly swung, missed and let go of the bat. It flew to the pitcher's mound. Tit for tat. Nothing wrong with that. Daniels' third pitch hit Hemus in the back. As our manager trotted to first base, we saw him shouting at Daniels, but we could not hear what he was saying. Neither did we particularly care.

The next day, Hemus called a team meeting in the clubhouse. "I want you to be the first to know what I said to Daniels yesterday. I called him a black son of a bitch." End of statement. End of meeting. Not one word of regret. No hint that he had perhaps acted excessively in the heat of combat. Gibson, White, Crowe and I sat with our jaws open, eyeing each other. We had been wondering how the manager really felt about us, and now we knew. Black sons-of-bitches. . . . The meeting had been his way of revealing the principles for which he stood. The great beliefs that prompted him to bench a good center fielder, ignore a good pitcher and play a good first baseman out of position.

Bill White, the first baseman whom Hemus embarrassed by once playing him in center field, and Harry Walker, the former Cardinals great, collided along racial lines with great frequency. Yet between the two men existed a competitiveness and professionalism that forced them, however grudgingly, to work together. David Halberstam's remarkable *October 1964* offers a tense portrait of the difficult times between the two men.

The Brewery had economic motives as well, Tim McCarver felt. And as the Cardinals became a strong club, which also happened to be integrated, it wasn't long before the St. Louis black community warmed to the Cardinals and The Brewery's principal product: Budweiser. It was a strategy that rarely received proper credit, McCarver thought. Indeed, as much as moral certitude played a role in the gains of the civil rights movement, nothing would have been accomplished without the accompanying economic pressure.

"Too many times people think that moral fortitude is all it takes, but that's not true," McCarver said. "The Brewery and Mr. Busch had another motive. People, black and white alike, drank beer. There was a market out there that he needed to cultivate. This was an example where racism was bad for business." Hence, the Cardinals would never be saddled with the seemingly impenetrable belief among the black community in St. Louis that would haunt the Red Sox.

Personally, it was in the clubhouse where Tim McCarver felt his life change. His contact with black people was, by his own admission, extremely limited. But he found himself surrounded by men like Flood, Gibson, and White, whose viewpoints on similar subjects were often widely different from his own. It revealed to him not only the great divide that existed between blacks and whites in America but also the falsity of stereotypes he had believed about black people. The awakening in the Cardinals clubhouse was nothing short of remarkable.

Joe Torre, then a young catcher with the Milwaukee Braves, would remember being largely oblivious to the wide racial chasm that existed between black and white teammates on his team. He was an Italian kid from Brooklyn and while neighborhoods may have been strictly segregated, New York was as cosmopolitan as cities could be. Two events reminded him of the fragile balance. The first was that as late as 1963, blacks lived in separate facilities during spring training. The next year, the entire team moved into a hotel that would accept the whole team.

The second was during a road trip, when a fight broke out between the great Hank Aaron and Rico Carty, the Dominican outfielder. It was a complete surprise, for Torre remembered Aaron as one the great gentlemen of the game. He was provoked by Carty, who called him a racial slur, and soon punches were being thrown. Torre would never forget, even between teammates, what tensions roiled just beneath the surface.

For the most part, McCarver hadn't given race much thought, but being in a room with such a mix of teammates taught him how growing up in a segregated community where blacks were subjected to horrific second-class status had affected him. During those years McCarver came to unshakeable but true conclusions about himself.

Halberstam told a story that would be McCarver's favorite example of his growth in the Cardinals clubhouse. Once, he was drinking a soda with a straw and Gibson asked him for a sip. At once, McCarver was gripped with dual strains of fear. He believed the old line of southern folklore about blacks having animal germs, which justified the Jim Crow black and white drinking facilities. But here was Gibson, not just black but the emerging power pitcher and premier clubhouse leader, asking white McCarver, young and unwilling to anger such an important member of the club, to let him drink off the same straw. McCarver pulled the old playground line out of his back pocket.

"I'll save you some," he said to Gibson.

"I'll save you some!" Thirty-five years later, Tim McCarver would echo his own words with a curved, cherubic Tennessee accent. He would be at once incredulous about the virulent prejudice of those times and self-deprecating at his own culpability. He spoke in high, excited bursts of energy laced with wisps of hard reflection, almost evangelical about those important, formative years. "Learning about each other made us better in every way. Some of the difficulties we went through reflected that growth and change. When I think about the things we went through, if you allow them to happen, to learn from the whole experience, I really believe it will change your life for the better.

"We had incredible personalities on that team. Men like Bob Gibson and Curt Flood and Bill White," McCarver said. "It was Bill who asked the question in his way, not forceful, except in its truth. How can we stay in different parts of the city and still be a team? We had a bunch of tough people on that team, in their attitudes and convictions. None of us were wealthy growing up. Dick Groat went to Duke, so maybe he came from greater means. My father was a policeman. His top salary was $417 a month."

The years made McCarver not just a better ballplayer, but, because of the constant challenge and discussions of the racial order with men like Lou Brock, Gibson, and Flood, a better man. In turn, they learned from him and the result of those countless, tense hours was a lifelong friendship with Gibson. Another important by-product from those hard years was the concrete-solid belief each player had in one another. "We had gone through so much learning about each other as men," McCarver said, "that when it came down to a seventh game, we never had any doubt where each of us stood. We were a family."

When Flood misplayed a ball in the seventh game of the 1968 World Series that wound up being the critical play in the Cardinals' defeat, he received solace from a most unlikely source, his old manager Solly Hemus, the man who Flood felt treated him as less of a person. Still, it was an example of McCarver's belief that through struggle, men often gain a newfound respect for one another:

> Dear Curt:
>
> After reading all of the articles in the newspapers, I still feel that you are one of the greatest defensive center fielders that I have seen play. Don't let all the second-guessers upset you, because without you in the lineup, the Cardinals would not have been in the Series this year and would have missed the two previous times.
>
> If I ever missed on evaluating a ballplayer, it was you, and I admire you for all of your determination, guts and pride in your work. You are not only one of the finest outfielders I have seen play, but you are a gentleman, and I admire you for this. Stay healthy and best of luck in the future. Congratulations on a fine year.
>
> Sincerely,
>
> Solly

"I don't usually save letters," Flood wrote, frustrated by the wasted energy of bigotry. "But I could not part with that one. Every time I look at it, I get sore."

Dick O'Connell began rebuilding the Red Sox, and for the first time in the team's history, some nineteen years after Robinson's debut, the Red Sox signed black talent. Red Sox teams would not have such remarkable moments of self-discovery between black and white players, and what existed in its place would be a clubhouse that for decades would be known as the most self-centered in baseball.

O'Connell acquired Reggie Smith, a black switch-hitting center fielder who grew up in Los Angeles. There would be a twenty-two-year-old rookie named George Scott, and that season the Red Sox would acquire John Wyatt and Jose Tartabull.

It all went back to the day that O'Connell was hired and Dave Morehead threw a no-hitter against Cleveland. It was, thought Glenn Stout, not only one of the first positive signs on the ballfield in years for the Red Sox, but a sudden suggestion that the Red Sox may have some talent on a sagging club.

Earl Wilson, the first black player ever signed to a big league contract by the Red Sox and the second one brought up by the club in 1959, was already on the club, and he believed that 1966 would be an important year for him. After almost four full years in the majors, he believed he was finally coming into his own as a pitcher. Wilson was always big and strong, but wildness kept him from being a consistent winner. It was never Wilson's stuff that was questioned by baseball people. Indeed, his fastball was considered by scouts to be better than average; more importantly, his ball contained a natural movement that would make it difficult to hit.

No matter how hard a pitcher can throw, a good major league hitter will eventually hit a straight fastball consistently, and Wilson's exceptional movement gave him a greater edge. But he was wild and was prone to giving up home runs. It was a bad combination for a young pitcher; Wilson would give up a walk or two, then a home run. In 1964, Wilson gave up a team-leading thirty-seven home runs. The year before, he'd led the team in walks. Once he learned how to control his enormous talent, Wilson could become a standout pitcher in the major leagues.

Earl Wilson fared much better on the field than Pumpsie Green had. If the weight of discrimination lawsuits and an undercurrent of skepticism existed about the club's motives in promoting Green, there would be no question that Earl Wilson was a legitimate major league prospect. He was physically more gifted than Green, his raw talent quickly visible. Where Green was never given a real opportunity to win out a starting job at either second base or shortstop, Earl Wilson's talent forced him into the starting pitching rotation. He was a right-hander who owned a pitcher's disposition—fierce, strong, and fearless. The 1960s were dominated by Bob Gibson and Sandy Koufax, but Pumpsie Green believed that while Wilson may have lacked the overwhelming slider of Gibson or the devastating curve of Koufax, he could be every bit was intimidating. He was totally unafraid to pitch inside or occasionally deck a hitter who leaned out over the plate.

He was a natural athlete. Quick, strong, and powerful, Wilson would be the type of athlete today who would have his choice of avocations—baseball, but maybe basketball or football. Wilson was the rare black athlete in those days to be first a catcher, then later a pitcher. Such a conversion went against the conventional wisdom that blacks weren't considered intelligent enough to handle "thinking" positions of the battery. Prejudice played a large role as well; it was widely believed that white pitchers would not to take orders from a black catcher. Even the success of Roy Campanella, Elston Howard, and Johnny Roseboro did not easily change this mindset of most baseball men.

Off the field, Wilson was as frustrated with being a black player on the Red Sox as Green was, but unlike Green, Wilson possessed a lower tolerance for the racism that existed around him. He was humiliated from the start. A Boston scouting report on Wilson leaked out that was not only crushing to Wilson but also revealed the bigoted train of thought that ran through the organization. It referred to Wilson as a "well-mannered colored boy. Not too black. Handles himself as a gentleman."

Part of the reason Wilson arrived in the majors was that he was 10–1 in the minor leagues and was as dominant a pitcher as his record had suggested. The other reason for his promotion was both common and sinister. Pumpsie Green needed a roommate. Baseball management was skittish about the idea of blacks and whites rooming together, thus Pumpsie Green needed a black companion. The Red Sox were especially cautious about the mixing of whites and blacks. Dick Radatz, the monstrous relief pitcher, often noted that the Red Sox players were very much aware of the quota system. On the Red Sox, there would always have to be an even number of blacks on the team, in order for them to room with each other on the road.

Wilson's first years with the Red Sox were marked by high successes followed by inconsistency. In his debut, he walked nine hitters but won the game. He threw a no-hitter in 1962, and Tom Yawkey responded by handing Wilson a $1,000 cash bonus. For a time, Earl Wilson believed 1966 would be his big year in Boston. He began slowly to understand the rhythms of being a pitcher as well as the ticks of the organization. He had won forty-seven games over the previous four seasons, and in 1965 had won thirteen, his high for a single season. Unlike Bill Russell, Wilson was less affected by the fatiguing polarity of Boston's neighborhoods and enjoyed the city's nightlife, especially in the heavily black areas of Roxbury and Dorchester.

Then it all collapsed. A few weeks into spring training, Earl Wilson was faced with the ultimate test of his faith. On balance, the events of that evening may have been nothing more than another of a million humiliations that came with being black in the South, but Wilson had grown tired of being humiliated. He grew up in Louisiana and knew all too well being the recipient of yet another slight at the hands of whites.

To his employers, the Red Sox, however, Wilson's situation was infinitely more than routine; it was a source of potential embarrassment and unwanted publicity should the probing Boston press find out.

So what happened on that steamy night Wilson and two white pitchers, Dennis Bennett and Dave Morehead showed up at the Cloud Nine bar in Lakeland, anyway? The first thing to remember is that spring training in the 1960s did not exist for the sake of commodity. It wasn't yet a business, and those flat and nasty Florida towns did not easily welcome blacks, even if they were ballplayers. Spring training wasn't yet "family entertainment," and those old towns were strictly Klan. Bradenton, Sarasota, Port Charlotte were all run by the local KKK. Even the slightly more cosmopolitan St. Petersburg held a rigid social order. That meant no blacks and no Jews.

Lakeland was north of Tampa, but even forty years later owned its fair share of Confederate flags hanging in the yard or affixed to the front license plate of the family truck. So when Wilson entered the Cloud Nine, the needle screeched off of the record.

Bennett was infamous. Before joining the Red Sox, he was a member of the 1964 Philadelphia Phillies who lost the pennant despite leading by six games with ten to play by losing ten games in a row. He would—because of his penchant for carrying a suitcase filled with handguns—also become one of the game's more colorful and potentially dangerous players. Morehead had thrown the no-hitter that preceded the firing of Pinky Higgins and prompted the Red Sox to again become serious about winning.

As Wilson remembers it, the scene at the Cloud Nine was brief and hostile. Bennett ordered a beer. The bartender looked at Morehead, who like Bennett was white, took his order but followed by angling toward Wilson and telling Morehead, "We don't serve niggers here."

Wilson left the bar, teeth clenched. A million images flashed. It was he and Pumpsie Green being rousted by cops one night in the South. It was more than just another humiliation; it was also a reminder that in certain parts of his country he was just another nigger, so beneath human decency that he couldn't even order a cold beer without being harassed.

To Wilson, the Cloud Nine represented the exclusivity of the white world. It was just a seedy, worthless bar. But, Wilson thought, what was I if I couldn't even drink a beer there? He had served the country for two years, and for what? The anger continued to well. This may be life in the South, but it was time for it to stop.

Wilson went to Red Sox management, expecting to be backed by the organization. With thirty-five years of perspective, he still isn't exactly sure what he expected the Red Sox to tell him. Perhaps a team official would console him or even speak to the bar owner and threaten some type of economic sanction. The Red Sox, as a valuable spring training tenant, held significant economic clout in the region. With the weight of a powerful baseball franchise behind him, perhaps the rigid customs of the region would begin to change. All he knew is that he didn't expect to hear what he was told.

Billy Herman, his manager, coldly rebuffed him. Forget the incident. It never happened, he was told. Also, should any members of the press ask, Wilson was told in no unclear terms to tell them nothing. It was this point that the Red Sox were most strident. To Wilson, the club's chief concern was that the press did not write about the incident.

A piece of him had been stolen and it could not ever, it seemed, be returned. "Having that happen and then being told not to say anything about it," Wilson said, "was the most humiliating experience of my life."

Nothing about the South surprised Earl Wilson. He was born in the deepest of the South, in Ponchatoula, Louisiana. He was well schooled in its customs. What surprised him most about Boston was what little support he received from management. That the Red Sox did nothing was consistent with baseball custom in those days. Most organizations flinched at the prospect of disturbing local custom, especially in the explosive issue of race in the South. It was another unfortunate example of baseball's unwillingness to use both its power to challenge the racial customs of the day as well as to provide an accommodating atmosphere for the growing number of black players in the game.

For a time, the matter remained quiet. The *Herald*'s Larry Claflin, who prided himself as a liberal, heard about the incident and confronted Wilson. He confirmed it, but asked Claflin not to write the story. Within days, the entire Boston press corps approached Wilson one morning before stretching. The Red Sox told him to stay quiet, but here was Earl Wilson, a religious and thoughtful man, being asked to lie to reporters about an incident that was so clear, so vivid and infuriating to his sensibilities as a man.

He decided to take a walk to clear his head, but that didn't work. Wilson just got madder at the whole thing. Sure, it was just a beer, and he knew how things worked in this backwards part of the world, so maybe it would just be better to go back, forget about it. This was 1966 and all over the country, especially in the South, the mortar bricks of the movement had been built on slights just like this one.

Wilson was no fool, either, and as he found out from the Red Sox earlier, they weren't going to back him. They didn't need this kind of heat. He didn't have any rights, for free agency was still a decade away. If the Red Sox dumped him, how much life existed out there in a segregated world for a thirty-one-year-old black man that would be better than what he had? To have his name in the papers, branded as some black troublemaker would quickly derail all that he had worked for to this point. It was just a beer, after all. There would be many more after that.

Wilson had owned something of a reputation of a guy who liked a cold one; he was a favorite in Roxbury, during the hot summer months in Boston, when Slade's and the Hi-Hat were jumping. Professionally, he was close. He could feel it. Control of the fastball was improving all the time. Sixty-six was going to be a big year, his year.

So that was the question: Was it worth it?

His mind was made up. For a redneck at the Cloud Nine bar to call him a nigger and refuse him service was degrading. For the Red Sox to tell him to cover up the story was cowardly. For him to lie to protect both was not only immoral, Earl Wilson thought, but also made him something he never wanted to be, the willing agent of a segregated order.

The choice was clear. He would tell the press the story in its entirety. The Red Sox would now have to respond.

The end for Earl Wilson in Boston came quickly. All it took was a hot Florida night during spring training in 1966. Wilson learned that the Red Sox weren't about to defend a black ballplayer against the customs of the South. The culture of the organization, from the front office down to the clubhouse, was not merely conservative, but was also still uneasy about the racial transformation in the game. Instead of the issue being one of racial fairness, Red Sox manager Billy Herman labeled Wilson a drinker and a troublemaker. On June 13, the Red Sox acquired two black players, Jose Tartabull and John Wyatt, which was a telltale sign. The running joke among the blacks on the team was that with four blacks on the roster, a trade certainly had to be coming, for the Boston Red Sox would never have so many blacks on the same team.

Four days later, it was official. Wilson was traded to the Detroit Tigers for Don Demeter and a pitcher named Julio Navarro. On the outside, it was a bizarre trade. Wilson was emerging, and the two players O'Connell received weren't much more than a bag of balls. Wilson would believe that the incident at the Cloud Nine bar finished him as a member of the Red Sox, for clearly it was not a good trade. Wilson would hit more home runs as a pitcher for the Tigers than Demeter would as an outfielder for the Red Sox, and Navarro never pitched a game for Boston. It would be Dick O'Connell's first major mistake as general manager; he gave away a pitcher just entering his prime under very questionable circumstances and received nothing in return.

For Earl Wilson, being traded was at first a bitter blow. He had finally believed in his ability to excel as a pitcher, and he would never shake his belief that he was traded for speaking out against the racial customs in 1960s Florida. Over the next season and a half, he would win thirty-five games for the Tigers, including a league-high twenty-two in 1967. He would harbor bitterness toward the Red Sox but would win thirteen more games and a World Series title with the Tigers in 1968. He played three more years; after his playing career ended in 1970 with the San Diego Padres, Wilson returned to Detroit, where he would remain for the next thirty-three years, working as a businessman. He would remain active in baseball, but baseball would not define him.

He never looked back and thus would be an example of how Monte Poole described the attitudes of those black players of the 1950s and '60s. Nothing could pierce that tough, protective hide. Wilson didn't look back on the Red Sox, didn't reflect. There would be no revision, no new introspection, and certainly no forgiveness.

SEVEN

Bill Russell's mood darkened. Nineteen sixty-six marked his tenth year in Boston, and he became solid in his conviction that for a black person like himself, it was a place with which he could not reconcile. If anything, his fame made life worse. He had been the anchor of the greatest basketball dynasty the National Basketball Association had ever known; for in his ten years, the Boston Celtics had won nine championships. Through it all, for him Boston had become the site of his greatest athletic triumphs and at the same time an untenable place for him to exist.

Russell's distance with the city had not been the by-product of one sensational event, but the confluence of dramatic forces at large. He was growing into a political person, one who didn't want to merely be known as a basketball player. Articulating new positions was both exhilarating and daunting for him. It was unprecedented that black rage and anger became a necessary part of the country's overall discussion on race. Russell found himself questioning the entire society as a whole, not merely his part in it as a basketball player. In fact, he diminished his role as a superstar athlete as never before, for too much recognition of his basketball skills would in his eyes overshadow the burgeoning opinions and perspectives of a young black man in a rapidly changing society.

Bill Russell was undergoing a total political awakening. His reading list became more diverse. His personal appearance changed, as he sported a goatee and wore African dashikis, cosmetic alterations that intimidated some whites— and many blacks, who believed society may have been moving *too* quickly. Questioning the accepted mores of society, Russell believed, angered a predominantly white fan base that was less concerned with his mental and social developments than his ability to play basketball. Such a conflict made basketball even less enjoyable for him, for Russell did not see himself as the average fan did. To them, he was a basketball star who happened to be politically active. To him, such a characterization trivialized what he was, a critically thinking black person living through an extraordinary moment in time who also excelled in sports.

It was a conflict that could never be easily resolved; Russell could not enjoy the perks of celebrity, and it was inconceivable to the average fan—who would give everything he owned to enjoy just a single day of Russell's gifts—that

Russell could be anything but blissful. Russell's skin was thin, and he remembered *everything*. How could he not? How could he forget that day at the Cleveland airport at the baggage claim? All he was doing was waiting for his luggage. That's it, nothing more. Then this fan comes over to him and says, "How about an autograph, *Wilt?*" Russell sat there and took it, and waited for his bag. The price of fame, he thought. But the guy doesn't let up.

"You got some nerve, Wilt. The public made you what you are!" This disconnection would become more pronounced over the years, especially as player salaries increased. For Russell, however, there was too much at stake around the nation for him not to notice and be moved. He found himself interested not merely in the civil rights struggle in the United States, but also in the issues of racism and nationalism in South America, Haiti, Vietnam, and the tribal-colonial struggles in various African nations. His was a complete political stimulation.

He would not make it easy on the resentful fan that wanted nothing more than for him to deliver winning basketball to the Celtics, for most fans wanted their heroes to be uncomplicated. That, too, lessened him as a person, cheapened his growth. Bill Russell was everything but simple. He was, along with Jackie Robinson, one of the first professional athletes to combine the political with the personal. There would always be in Bill Russell during those years a desire to curb his excitement about the great accomplishments on the basketball court, for he feared the role of being another dumb, black jock. Worse for Russell was that the average fan didn't find himself caught up in the larger social drama in which he was awash. The implications may have been greater for a black man, but the end results would certainly contain powerful consequences for whites as well.

In Boston, as well as most other sports towns, the concept of black assertiveness was not particularly welcome, much of it for the basic reason that most sports fans take a certain position of ownership over the local athlete. For a man such as Bill Russell, who felt the same low self-esteem, limited opportunity, and need to question his place in society because of his race that other blacks felt, it was a terribly offensive phrase to use because of its latent, sinister accuracy. You did make me what I am, Russell thought to himself, and that is precisely the problem.

That Russell underwent such intellectual growth in Boston, a city that suffered from erratic mood swings in its level of racial acceptance, created an irrevocable conflict between him and the city. Part of his difficulty with the city was his own belief that black players were never amply compensated for providing the city with high sporting moments. He bristled at the prevailing wisdom that only whites received television and radio shows and greater opportunities for product endorsements. What bothered him further was the notion that he was to accept this duality happily, that he was a malcontent for disagreeing with the double standard.

The other part was the city itself. The hypocrisy of its pedigree, known for years, was now being realized. Boston was a city whose politics, unions, and public school systems were dominated by the Irish, and if there had been small but vocal strains of abolition and liberalism, Boston was never the place of refuge espoused by the history books or the black press of the previous century. It was always a tenuous, clannish place, and the idea of a special relationship between blacks and whites wilted in the face of the cold facts of the city. Blacks and whites in the city may have clung to the idea of Boston as a place that had found middle ground between the races, but no black had been elected to public office during the entire century. Boston blacks enjoyed the idea that as a race they lived in a manner superior to other blacks around the nation, but their children attended the oldest, most decrepit schools in the city and—except for certain magnet schools—were isolated from the rest of Boston's students. Earlier, in 1964, William O'Connor, who succeeded Louise Day Hicks as president of the Boston School Committee, illustrated his views on the city's black school students when he announced, "We have no inferior education in our schools. What we have been getting is an inferior type of student."

Thus, during the middle of the 1960s, Russell watched intently and with no small degree of fury when the Boston political leadership retrenched as the city's black parents began to assert themselves for rights that were long overdue. For Russell, it wasn't only white resistance that angered him, but the apparent black passivity. For generations, black Bostonians attempted to live in harmony with whites. It wasn't only out of convenience, but necessity. In other cities, pressing city government may have been an effective means of politics, but life was different in Boston because the black community was so small. A 1949 charter change made it virtually impossible for even predominately black neighborhoods to elect a black to citywide public office. The struggle that came with the migration north was no different than what occurred in many northern cities. Without a weighty political base, Boston's black community relied on good relations with whites, especially with the Yankees in the previous century. As the Irish dominated the city's politics, such goodwill missions proved fruitless.

Another element of Russell's political awakening required the choice of the fiery Malcolm X over the nation-building Martin Luther King. For him, it was a simple choice because so many whites feared Malcolm X while favoring King. If whites so preferred King, Russell surmised, there had to be some truths to what Malcolm X said. "Martin Luther King had more followers," Russell wrote, "but Malcolm X opened eyes."

Jackie Robinson disagreed, which was his right, thus exhibiting the pick-a-side mentality that would define the followers of Malcolm X and Martin Luther King. It had to be one or the other. Robinson was an integrationist aligned with Martin Luther King, Jr. He and Malcolm clashed in dueling newspaper columns concerning the proper tactics needed to set a course for black empowerment. Malcolm was too militant; Robinson—ironic considering his playing days—was in the 1960s considered not militant enough. Robinson and King looked for hope, whereas the followers of Malcolm X saw none in the current black experience. After Malcolm's assassination, Robinson said, "A lot of blue went out of sky and warmth out of the sun." Malcolm X and Martin Luther King were seemingly caught in the same trap, set in opposition only by strategy. Robinson's sadness over Malcolm's death echoed the lament in his testimony against Paul Robeson in front of the House Un-American Activities Committee in 1949. Robinson never outwardly expressed regret—he was too tough and had too much pride—but after twenty years he came to recognize that, like him, Robeson "sacrificed himself, his career and the wealth he once enjoyed because, I believe, he was seriously trying to help his people."

Malcolm X knew Boston well—too well. If Russell's disdain for Boston came as an outsider, Malcolm's analysis of the city came as a person with firsthand knowledge of the peculiarities of Boston's struggle. As a young man, he lived in Roxbury with his half-sister Ella in the Roxbury/South End neighborhood and spent six years in prison after committing a series of robberies in Harvard Square. Before his assassination in 1965, Malcolm often returned to Boston and predicted—as did some others—the violence that would mar school integration in the 1970s. Like Russell, he viewed Boston as a cauldron of latent frustrations, in no small part exacerbated by the attitudes of Boston's old-line black families, whose actions he viewed as embarrassing, almost minstrel-like:

> In those days on the hill, any who could claim "professional" status—teachers, preachers, practical nurses—also considered themselves superior. Foreign diplomats could have modeled their conduct on the way the Negro postman, Pullman porters and dining car waiters of Roxbury acted, striding around as if they were wearing top hats and cutaways.
>
> I'd guess that eight out of 10 of the Hill Negroes of Roxbury, despite the impressive-sounding job titles they affected actually worked as menials and servants. "He's in banking," or "He's in securities." It sounded as if they were discussing a Rockefeller or a Mellon—and not some gray-headed, dignity posturing bank janitor or bond-house messenger. "I'm with an old family" was the euphemism used to dignify the professional of white folks' cooks and maids who talked so affectedly among their own kind in Roxbury that you couldn't even understand them. I don't know how many 40 and 50–year old errand boys went down the hill dressed like ambassadors in black suits and white collars, to downtown jobs "in government" in "finance" or "in law." And it has never ceased to amaze me how so many Negroes, then and now, could stand the indignity of that kind of self-delusion.

The words held meaning for Russell, who, like Malcolm X saw this behavior most in Boston's black population. Like the rest of the north, Boston dealt with the hard transition of southern migration after World War II, but unlike cities such as Chicago, Cleveland, or Newark, New Jersey, the arrival of blacks to Boston did not create a powerful voting bloc; rather, it lead to difficult culture clashes between southern blacks, Caribbean blacks, and the old black gentry who were descendants of the freedmen that lived in Boston from before the Civil War.

For a young white kid growing up in the integrated Roxbury neighborhood of Boston, Marty Nolan did not understand completely the prickly class struggles that were taking place among those various groups of blacks, but he saw the effects. It was, he thought, no different that the similar struggles that were happening in South Boston and in Charlestown, neighborhoods that were being transformed as a new and somewhat more prosperous generation of Irish moved from Boston and into the suburbs. Nolan remembered the harshness with which blacks in those neighborhoods treated one another.

The migration of blacks to Boston was far less than that to Chicago, which during one stretch in the 1940s saw African Americans moving in to the city at a rate of two thousand per week. Instead of building a coalition, and thus a stronger political base with which to gain a stronger foothold, blacks from each camp held on to debilitating stereotypes of one another that only made harmony impossible. The old-line, so-called black Brahmins believed the newly arriving southerners lacked the social graces that would have endeared them to Boston's white gentry. Theirs was an angry community. They felt sold out by the weakened Brahmins and left out of the political order by the Irish. That left the southern blacks, the only group lower on the social totem pole, to absorb the brunt of black anger. They expected these southern blacks to model themselves in the old and traditional Boston way. Certain Boston neighborhoods contained three-decker apartments that contained porches in both the front and back of the unit. Laundry was to be hung on the back porch, not the front.

The Caribbean blacks brought with them a self-reliance and work ethic from the islands that, it was widely believed, the southerners lacked. If the incumbent Bostonians believed the southerners to be unrefined, Caribbean blacks believed the southerners—the "Homies," they called them—to be lazy, waiting to be taken care of by welfare. Perhaps more than any other group in black Boston, the southerners endured the most withering of taunts and stereotypes. It was the worst kind of infighting, for it did nothing except divide an already small political base. For their part, the southern black new to Boston was largely struck by how completely black Bostonians had adopted the customs of the very Yankee culture that kept blacks in second-class status. Not everyone stood in agreement that the southern black expedited any souring of a special black-white relationship in Boston. Malcolm X viewed this infighting as a pitiful yet brilliant example of a still-prevalent slave culture, as well as a clear illustration of the Boston blacks' desire above all else to be viewed favorably by whites:

Any black family that had been around Boston long enough to own the home they lived in, were considered among the Hill elite. It didn't make any difference that they had to rent out rooms to make ends meet. Then the native-born New Englanders among them looked down upon recently migrated Southern homeowners who lived next door. Usually it was the Southerners and not the New Englanders who not only managed to own the places where they lived, but also at least one other house which they rented as income property. The snooty New Englanders usually owned less than they.

The result was a black community in Boston that was as splintered as it was small. With the Irish in Boston firmly in power, black forces in Boston would need to marshal its strength. Instead, the opposite was occurring as factions split in class warfare. Russell, both cerebral and passionate, could not watch idly as Boston's political drama played itself out. The combination of the dominance of the Irish in city government as well as the inability of the city's minority communities to gain any type of civic foothold drove Russell to impenetrable views about Boston as a city. Its complexities were the result of an oppressive Irish majority bent on exacting the same suppression of minorities as the Yankee majority had done in the century previous. In a maddening dynamic, Russell was angered that these very same people to a large degree cheered him on the basketball court.

Bill Russell's experience underscored an emerging truth about black athletes in Boston. There was a certain black personality that could thrive in those days and one that would likely endure hardship. The difference, thought Boston *Globe* writer Dan Shaughnessy, could be seen easily in the contrast of K. C. and Sam Jones against Russell. The Joneses were more easygoing, more tolerant of Boston's quirks and personality. They were not to engage themselves in any of the emerging debate on race taking place in the city. Pumpsie Green was the same way. There was, thought Glenn Stout, a certain subjugation that had to take place for the black athlete in Boston to exist well. The players who could do this would have fewer problems in Boston and were not apt to view the city with such permanent disdain.

A deep-thinking person such as Bill Russell would be too quick, too unafraid to voice unpopular opinions. Most importantly, a man like Bill Russell would be too sensitive and too aware not to notice the virulent contradictions that were taking place in Boston and the rest of the nation. It is questionable that during a time of such radical upheaval a man as aware as Bill Russell could have been happy anywhere in the United States. In 1966, the Boston Red Sox would call to the major leagues a young, black outfielder from Compton, California, who was cut from a cloth similar to Russell's. His name was Reggie Smith.

By 1967, the Red Sox had a new manager, the fiery Dick Williams. Williams had been Jackie Robinson's teammate in Brooklyn in the 1950s, and if he took a no-nonsense approach with the players, he was also fair in his seeming disdain for all of his players instead of embracing the country club attitude of the previous regime, where the rules were different based on a player's batting average. The 1967 Red Sox began winning ball games in such heady, surprising fashion that it was impossible not to be caught up in them. New England, dormant during the slumbering years of Higgins and Cronin, was now awake in a flowering that revived a region and a franchise. It couldn't have come at a better time for the city, for during the first half of the 1960s, Yawkey had become so frustrated with both the sour fortunes of the franchise and his bitter battles with the state legislature that he threatened to sell the club. Without 1967, Yawkey likely would have disassociated himself from the Red Sox in some way, either by selling the club or even allowing it to be moved. As drastic and inconceivable as this notion would become, relocating the Red Sox in the mid-1960s was not then so unbelievable.

Without 1967, Yawkey may have seriously considered selling or even moving the team from Boston. The team continued losing—the Red Sox hadn't won a pennant in twenty-one years and weren't in a pennant race during the final weeks of the season since 1950—and Yawkey, during the few instances when he was visible, began to push the Boston political leadership for a new stadium to replace Fenway Park.

One summer changed everything. In addition to their own magic, the 1967 Red Sox thrived for two important reasons that were beyond their control. The first was that the club's rise came at a time when the Yankees were down. The Yankees, arrogant and resistant to integration in the 1950s, were now in the midst of freefall in the second half of the 1960s. The rules for signing players had changed during the decade, and New York was no longer able to simply outspend for the best young prospects. They were now susceptible to a draft. There were no readily available players in the Yankees farm system to replace the great Mickey Mantle and Roger Maris because of those days a decade earlier when the Yankees passed on the talented black and Latino players who were available. Where failing to sign cheap talent in the 1950s affected the Red Sox immediately, the more talented Yankees did not feel the effects until the latter part of the 1960s.

Hence, the northeast corridor now had a team to connect with. The Red Sox were a young, integrated team coming of age at a time when young people across the country were breaking with convention. That a staid game like baseball had a team like the Red Sox, one that was young, energetic, and reflected small parts of the social discussion, elevated the Red Sox of 1967 into a mythic symbol. That it was happening in Boston, the ultimate of college towns, was possibly the most important cog in the "Impossible Dream" phenomenon.

Perhaps the greatest change in the Red Sox during 1967 was that for the first time, the Red Sox were a truly integrated team that relied on players of all races to succeed. It was a by-product of O'Connell being able to acquire and develop talent without the specter of the old prejudices that governed the organization. Despite the protestations of the influential Will McDonough, it would not be a coincidence that when Joe Cronin and Pinky Higgins vacated positions that oversaw player personnel in 1958 and '59, the Red Sox quickly integrated. Nor is it a coincidence that when Higgins was finally cut free from the Red Sox in 1965, it was in 1966 and '67 under O'Connell that the Red Sox farm system began churning out its first wave of black and Latino players. Marty Nolan would only be half-joking when he referred to the Red Sox during the Higgins era as "the Klavern."

In addition to Smith, the '67 team started two other black players, first baseman George Scott and third baseman Joe Foy. Cuban outfielder Jose Tartabull was a backup, and in midseason, the Red Sox acquired former Most Valuable Player Elston Howard from the New York Yankees. In 1955, Howard became the first black player in the history of the Yankees. For Howard, the trade was a bitter one, for he believed what Yankees management had always told him, that he would always be taken care of by the organization. But Howard immediately provided the veteran leadership a young club needed in the heat of one of the greatest pennant races in American League history. That the Red Sox would make a late-season deal for an important black player was another sign that under Dick O'Connell, the pre-1967 Red Sox way of doing business was dead.

Even so, an old nemesis was not convinced. During the pennant race of 1967, Jackie Robinson was less concerned that his old teammate Dick Williams was close to winning a pennant as he was with Tom Yawkey losing one. "Because of Boston owner Tom Yawkey," Robinson said one night at a dinner in upstate New York, "I'd like to see them [the Red Sox] lose, because he is probably one of the most bigoted guys in baseball."

On August 20, 1967, five southerners voted against Thurgood Marshall's nomination for the Supreme Court, calling it a "disgrace to the country." An unrelated riot of black residents in New Haven, Connecticut, was quelled by police and a new "apathy gas" called "mace." At the same time, the Boston Red Sox swept a doubleheader against the California Angels that would define the season as one of destiny. After winning the first game, they came back from an 8–0 deficit to win the second game 9–8. That afternoon, a switch-hitting, emotional rookie center fielder hit two home runs in the first game and another in the second. The young outfielder, Reggie Smith, would be the first man in the history of the Boston Red Sox to homer from both sides of the plate in the same game.

Outside of Bill Russell, no black player would endure a more pronounced conflict with Boston than Reggie Smith. Smith would smolder about Boston, a city that for him represented the worst of class and racial struggles.

He would be the first exceptional black baseball player in Boston, the first to actually attract attention for his playing ability. He would dislike Boston. He would be one of the many black athletes who would come to the city able to achieve harmony with either the city or his club, but not both. He enjoyed playing for the Boston Red Sox and had warm if rather vague comments about Tom Yawkey. Where pain pierces the considerable constitution of Reggie Smith is precisely where Bill Russell felt it, within the daily life of living in the city.

As a Californian, Boston would be hard on him. He would never be comfortable with its primal racial discord, and he responded with anger. In future years, there would be players who believed Boston a suffocating environment and went on to enjoy productive careers in other cities. Reggie Smith was the first. Despite the arrival of Dick O'Connell, the grassroots levels of the Red Sox organization were still peppered with unfortunate racial customs, which left Smith and other black players with a real feeling of isolation. He was closest to Carl Yastrzemski, which he believed helped him come into his own as a player. Learning the major leagues was a chore within itself. He enjoyed the magic of that '67 team because of the previous depths of the franchise. It was an oasis.

He felt slighted in Boston for no other reason than being a black man in a city that was suffering a very real moral confusion on race. Reggie Smith was a highly intelligent player who was affected by the percolating troubles with the city's school system and convinced of an inevitable and ugly conclusion. Like Russell, race was a central part of the identity of Reggie Smith in a city that preferred to ignore the topic. If in future years blacks and whites would attempt racial détente by avoiding the subject, it was a subject that could not be avoided with Reggie Smith. Such a strategy, in a large sense, offended him, for understanding the very nature of what it meant to be black was the only way to understand him. There could be no ducking the subject.

It was a combination that would see no positive end. Reggie Smith did not attend Boston schools, nor did he have children who did, but the *feeling* of the times was something he could not escape. It was in the air. It was at the store, on the sidewalks, and in the stands at Fenway Park. In later years, as Boston's busing confrontations grew more violent, the hostility Smith recalled as barely under the surface emerged in a full-blown explosion. The worst place white Boston's anger lived was in his thoughts, thoughts that Boston's whites would soon make public:

> They parade on foot and they chant, "2–4–6–8–, we don't wanna integrate" or "Here we go, Southie, here we go," clap, clap. Adolescent high-school girls lead their mothers in song, "Over there, over there, oh the kids aren't going, the kids aren't going, the kids aren't going over there."
>
> Over there is the black man. Over there is everything they had fought to keep away.

As a player, Reggie Smith was as tough and intense as his personality, but Boston during those days was not yet ready for a black player to possess such outward ferocity. Joe Torre, the great manager of the New York Yankees, was always impressed by the passion Smith showed for the game. The two were teammates after Smith was traded to St. Louis in 1973, and as much as he enjoyed Smith, Torre sensed something distant and untrusting about him. Perhaps more than any black ballplayer who would play for the Red Sox, Reggie Smith was the player playing in a city before his time. Today, Smith would be hailed as a throwback, a tough guy. His old Dodger teammate Dusty Baker said in his colorful California vernacular, "Reggie's a foxhole dude. If it was war or a baseball game, there wouldn't be another person I'd want next to me."

Smith brought to the game a fierce, rugged playing style that, had he been white, would have been praised throughout baseball. He was a match, a strike away from ignition. Once, he and Detroit Tigers manager Billy Martin met underneath the Fenway Park grandstands to have it out after Martin ordered one of his pitchers to throw at Smith.

If Smith were white, he undoubtedly would have been called an RA, which stood for "red ass," a curt but laudatory term reserved for that type of hard-nosed player who owes his place in the major leagues as much to hunger as to talent. Those players possessed an intangible fuel that produced gritty, winning baseball. Pete Rose immediately comes to mind. Reggie Smith's fire did not elicit laurels, but misunderstandings. He was the angry black man, a stereotypical, thin term that minimized both his complexities as a person and the climate in which he was expected to do his job.

There was no question of his awesome ability. He could run, throw, and hit from both sides of the plate for both average and power—what today's game would label a "five-tool" player. Bill Lee, the left-hander who teamed with Luis Tiant to form the top of the Red Sox pitching staff in the 1970s, clashed with Smith on dozens of occasions. The two fought verbally and more than once physically. He still understood Smith's awesome ability:

> I am sure that he was the greatest piece of baseball machinery that I had ever seen. There wasn't anything a person could do on the playing field that Reggie couldn't do better than anybody. He could hit for power and average from both sides of the plate, run like a world-class sprinter and play centerfield as well as anybody in the league. He also came equipped with the greatest arm I had ever seen. Once, during a rain delay Yaz and Smith were sitting in the dugout discussing their arms. They decided to pass some time by having a contest to see who could throw the ball further. Yaz had a great gun. He jumped out of the dugout, took a running start and heaved the ball from the first base line to the base of the left field wall. A great throw. Reggie did not take a running start. Stepping out of the dugout, he walked over the spot Yaz had thrown from, reared back, and threw. We never saw that ball again. It cleared every-

thing. I could never get over the power and majesty of his toss. Reggie would get off a throw like that in a ballgame, and he'd just awe the opposition.

But Reggie Smith was young and black, from the predominately black city of Compton, California. He wasn't a "red ass" but approached the game with an intensity that intimidated whites, who saw him as difficult, angry. It was not at all an inaccurate portrayal; it was just that Smith roiled in Boston, made uncomfortable by the racial makeup of the city. Reggie Smith was nobody's fool. He was supersensitive, but he knew the game, and it was a stone-cold con. White players who ran hard, slid harder and took no shit were intense team guys, the ones every winning club needs. Black players who did the same were distant and moody. This wasn't just harmless perception, no way. It determined who got traded and who got traded for. It also affected the bottom line, come money time and even more threatening, when a player's playing days ended. The white player with scars on his knees was considered a future general, the black player an outcast.

The blacks who survived in the game after the bat was out of hits were the ones who smiled all the time, who made everyone feel at ease. That's why Bob Gibson, with all he had to offer to the game, couldn't stick in it. After a while, Reggie Smith got tired of it. He also came of age during a revolutionary time. In Boston, Bill Russell was the most outspoken athlete in Boston on the subject, and Smith gravitated toward Russell's special energy. It hurt Smith that despite their celebrity, blacks often faced difficulty in finding housing. Like Pumpsie Green, Smith was drawn into Boston's racial dilemma. Unlike Green, Reggie Smith would not accommodate, nor would he shy from the debate. He was of the new era of black player, one that did not necessarily make ridiculous statements to the press, but one that also was becoming increasingly aware of the special circumstance of being black in America, one that would not excuse America for its racial practices. Like Russell, Smith enjoyed a political growth that was off-putting—and more than a little intimidating to whites—but was part of his natural growth. There was no way, Smith thought, that he could not enter the fray. It was the life happening all around him.

By growing up in the Los Angeles area, Reggie Smith was immediately taken by the polarity of the city's racial groups. Nor was Smith a mere bystander in Boston. Smith found himself disappointed by another truth that would permeate his calloused exterior: the notion that the white fan base would always hold him at a distance, regardless of how well he played or how affable he might be. Smith responded with rage, justified but equally destructive. In a sense, his experience in Boston was similar to that of Russell. He was expected to produce winning baseball for the home fans, although some were the very people who sought to deny him rights as a person. He did not handle this conflict well, and he waged what at times was a constant war with the home fans at Fenway.

During his first call-up with the Red Sox, the young first baseman Cecil Cooper recalled the tempestuous relationship between Smith and the Red Sox fans. On one occasion, Cooper remembered Smith standing on the top of the Boston dugout in a heated exchange with the fans. It was an exchange that Cooper recalled was decidedly racial.

For a player such as Bill Lee, Boston was a dream. He also hailed from southern California, but he was white and was very much accepted by the Boston collegiate and counterculture scene. Lee was also irreverent, spoke loosely, and enjoyed a freedom of personality that because of the culture and the times was denied Reggie Smith. This cultural distance created enmity between the two men, causing fistfights in the clubhouse on more than one occasion. In a sense, perhaps even as revenge, Lee taunted Smith not only with his freedom but also with his awareness that he could benefit from a racial double standard in a way Smith could not.

> Smith had a lot of problems playing in Boston. He was a black man playing for an organization that, in a scouting report written in the late fifties, had called pitcher Earl Wilson "a nice colored boy." The Red Sox had also been the last organization in major-league baseball to break the color line. The racial philosophy of the club reflected the philosophy of a very large, vocal segment of the town's population. Reggie received some hate mail, the sort that started, "Dear Nigger," and then got nasty. The letters could only hurt his psyche. That wasn't enough for some crazies. They took to throwing hard objects at him in the outfield, forcing him to wear a batting helmet while he was out there.

Like Russell, Smith was stunned and frustrated by Boston. Unlike Russell, Reggie Smith played on a team that was just recently undergoing the process of integration. The Boston Celtics for years had fielded prominent black players, and thus Russell's isolation was tempered by the presence of great black stars, such as K. C. and Sam Jones. The Red Sox of the late 1960s were an integrated team, but the team culture represented a decidedly different story.

Smith said he had never seen a place where not only did the various races keep to their own neighborhoods, but the interaction of different racial groups was virtually nonexistent. Once, when he was asked by a reporter if he thought Boston was a racist city, Smith said, "Yes, I do."

With that one response, Reggie Smith believed his Boston career came to an end. On the field, the Red Sox were never completely happy with Smith. He was a solid player, but he was not Willie Mays, who would become the enduring unfair standard for black all-around players for generations to come.

Smith said, "Boston was clearly different from any place I ever played. It was the most divided city that I ever played in. In places like St. Louis, it wasn't like that. In Boston, you had to know the ground rules. There were places you could and places you couldn't go. It angered me, but it was the way it is. I dealt with it. There were probably some things I would have handled differently, but that's the way it went."

His rough-edged personality made him a malcontent in the eyes of Red Sox management. For black players of the day, being labeled trouble was a kiss of death. Smith knew what this meant. It meant that you must continue to produce at a peak level to survive. The first bad year he had or the first sign of decreased production, Smith often told himself, would be his last in Boston. When it happened, he was upset but not surprised. In 1973, the Red Sox finished in second place, eight games behind Baltimore. Smith was beset by nagging injuries, yet he still managed his best year of combined average and power. He hit .303 with twenty-one homers and a curiously low total of sixty-nine runs batted in.

More damning than his offensive totals, Smith only played 108 games in the outfield. In the eyes of management, Smith had suffered his first subpar season. In addition, there was talk of a young black slugger named Jim Rice and a center fielder named Fred Lynn who might be ready in 1974. Smith was traded to St. Louis for Bernie Carbo and pitcher Rick Wise. Both Carbo and Wise would be invaluable pieces to the powerhouse Red Sox teams of the 1970s, but moving a player of Smith's abilities was a reflection of the Red Sox and the city's effect on a young black player.

One teammate, Cecil Cooper, liked Smith immensely, held deep respect for his talent, and sympathized with him for being in an environment so different and so much more constraining than that in California. Lee believed Smith hated him. The two fought twice in 1972, causing Lee to take a few cruel swipes at him in his autobiography. Lee believed the Boston experience made Smith increasingly insecure. In Lee's words, Smith tried to emulate Yastrzemski in the futile hopes of reaching Yaz's social plateau in Boston, a plateau Lee says Boston would never have allowed Smith to attain. "After a while he earned himself a nickname: Carl Reggie Smith," Lee wrote.

Reggie Smith believes his being outspoken on race during a time of racial unrest and playing for a team that had suppressed any real stance on the racial issues of the day made him a prime target.

St. Louis was a different story. Smith became close with the great Bob Gibson, which to Joe Torre was proof in of itself that Smith had plenty to offer as a man. To attract the attention of a man as skeptical and demanding as Gibson meant you certainly possessed special qualities. Gibson had the rare ability to keep an entire clubhouse loose. He was not only black, but also a great pitcher and clubhouse leader. Gibson was a man to be listened to. He saw Smith's ferocity—much of which existed in himself—and tempered it with humor, as perhaps only Gibson could. Smith would rage, and Gibson would call him "Spike," in reference to the angry bulldog character on Bugs Bunny cartoons. The presence of Gibson and Lou Brock, thought Torre, was the most important thing for Reggie Smith in that first year in St. Louis. Torre knew what could happen to a ballclub that was racially volatile. He was a member of the Atlanta Braves teams of the 1960s and recalled the great racial rift that existed on those clubs. Brock and Gibson made sure that didn't happen to the Cardinals, long a special group. "Those two guys didn't shy from letting you know what it was to be black. That was important. On that team, it wasn't buried. It was out in the open, and that made it easier."

It was a special element of leadership that the Red Sox lacked, and would continue to lack until Luis Tiant emerged in the mid-1970s as the soul of the clubhouse, if not the franchise.

If there was a cordiality surrounding Pumpsie Green, one that allowed him to enjoy his place in history, there existed with Reggie Smith the feeling of lost opportunity. Peter Gammons, a young sportswriter for the Boston *Globe*, believed Smith to be the unhappiest player he ever saw play in thirty years following baseball in Boston. Smith was angry, both at the way he was treated by Boston fans and angry that it was not a better time upon which to reflect. Nineteen sixty-seven was the year everyone loved the Red Sox, but it was another of his years in Boston that Smith must look at evenly. There would be in him a wish to have enjoyed it more.

> I never felt welcome in Boston. I grew up on the West Coast, in Los Angeles. I knew it wasn't home, and it didn't feel like home. I remember after the Celtics won the world championship, someone asked me to respond to Bill Russell's feeling that Boston was a racist city. I made comments to the effect that it was, and I was immediately considered a troublemaker. I knew that the first bad year I had, my days were numbered.
>
> And I believed that it was a racist city. I looked at the ethnicity of the city and its divisions. South Boston was Irish. The North End was Italian. Out on the fringes in Brookline and Newton was predominately Jewish. And in the core of the city was Roxbury, where 90 percent of the blacks lived. There was nowhere you could move outside of that circle without feeling uncomfortable or in danger.
>
> Because you're an athlete, it's easy to put the blinders on. There are times when people afforded me goodwill. But it was because I was an athlete, because of what I was, not who I was. If I were just another black living up there, I would have gotten the shaft, too.

EIGHT

There are two distinct histories of the Boston Red Sox: the Red Sox as they existed before 1967, and the post Impossible Dream Red Sox. The latter is how the team is generally known, and that is why it is a franchise revered. One year rehabilitated just about every important trait of the franchise.

Tom Yawkey was now the benevolent owner who despite his best effort, *just couldn't win the big one.* He was no longer the disinterested owner frustrated by Boston politics, but the caretaker not only of the Red Sox, but of Boston baseball.

Fenway Park, once the biggest of Tom Yawkey's bunions, grew into the star attraction. Whole books would be written about the old yard, the same joint Yawkey would have bulldozed in his sleep one hundred times over. That dank mustiness, the leaks and creaks, now gave the place character. The grass was greener than ever. Fenway was a shrine and while Yawkey couldn't have known it at the time, the old boneyard would outlive him, his wife and the Yawkey sixty-nine year association with them.

The Red Sox would grow into the literary team, favored by the smart set above all others. There would be years, even, where the lineup of writers who lionized the Red Sox would prove more formidable than the Sox batting order.

Even Ted Williams, who didn't need anyone's help, would ride along. He was the greatest player in the history of the franchise, but the fact remains that only 10,453 fans showed up for his final game. After 1967, myth would take over, and *everyone* was there to see Ted hit that last home run, circle the bases that one last time, too proud to doff the cap. In future retellings, all of New England was sitting right next to John Updike, instead of the empty seats that constituted the truth.

This is how the Red Sox preferred to be remembered, and rightfully so, because considering the Yawkey regime previous to this flowering, without filter is to be unimpressed and more than a little disturbed by the racism and anti-Semitism, cronyism, alcoholism, and losing that defined the team.

Nothing diminished the shine of the Red Sox after the Summer of Love; not the Vietnam War and not the St. Louis Cardinals, who rode the brilliance of Bob Gibson to a seven-game victory. The Red Sox were no longer a baseball team. They were an institution that represented all of New England.

It was no small achievement. Never again would the Red Sox fail to draw near-capacity crowds at Fenway Park. Before, a frustrated Tom Yawkey even considered selling the team. He had tired of wrestling with Boston's politicians over the possibility of a new stadium, was weary of the losing, and, most importantly, was sick of losing money. If there existed a perception that Yawkey was the benevolent owner who didn't mind throwing away money as long as he could be a part of the game, it was, thought Clark Booth, a piece of popular fiction.

After 1967, he was not only silent on the ballpark issue, but Yawkey became something he hadn't been in more than a decade: attentive. The pennant race aroused him, as much as realizing two years earlier that the young talent around him was wasting under Pinky Higgins. Yawkey's ear was the ultimate silent victory for Dick O'Connell, a man who hadn't been and would never be close to Yawkey. Dick Johnson would note that O'Connell would serve Yawkey faithfully from 1946 until Yawkey's death in 1976 and never once did Yawkey come to O'Connell's home in Winthrop for even a cup of coffee. Nor was O'Connell invited to ever spend time at the plantation in South Carolina or even join Yawkey for a meal at Yawkey's suite at the Ritz-Carlton in Boston. He began his career with the Red Sox an outsider and he remained one. In a sense, being called an outsider from the Yawkey camp was a compliment. If Dan Shaughnessy believed O'Connell was the most underrated figure in Red Sox history in the past fifty years, Clark Booth couldn't have been in greater disagreement. Booth believed O'Connell was the most underrated figure in all of Red Sox history, for in no uncertain terms the man who saved Yawkey's franchise was Dick O'Connell.

The Red Sox were not, however, the only Boston establishment that over the course of the next decade would be transformed from mediocre to one of the most powerful and influential institutions in New England. As much as the Red Sox, the Boston *Globe* ascended to heights previously unreachable. The *Globe* was only known in sports circles for once owning the Red Sox and building Fenway Park in 1912. It was not dynamic and almost never broke news. Over the next decade, the *Globe* would undergo a remarkable transformation to include the best sports section not only in New England, but also in the country. At virtually the identical point in history as the Red Sox, the Boston *Globe* would soon become an institution of considerable reach and power.

For decades, the *Globe* was gray, slugging it out in fruitless competition with six other daily newspapers in Boston's sullying but unsatisfying circulation wars. The *Globe* did not distinguish itself in either direction. It was neither particularly sensational nor was it considered prestigious. If in later years the *Globe* would be known for its aggressive stances on progressive issues, the paper during the Robinson tryout in 1945 was virtually nonexistent. During those days, there was nothing that suggested it was destined for any level of greatness. The more sensational *Record*, which seemed to run a picture of a woman in a bikini on every other page, had Dave Egan, Ted Williams' antagonist but the most outspoken member of the press about racial issues. Egan was also one of the best educated sportswriters of his time. In the 1940s and early '50s, it was the *Record*—and the strong voices in the black press—that stood out in front of the race issue. It was Wendell Smith, Egan, and Izzy Muchnick who pushed Eddie Collins for the Robinson tryout.

In the early 1960s, four newspapers existed in Boston, but a shakeout would leave only two—the Boston *Globe* and the *Herald*—by 1972. The rest were gone, casualties of time and the growing television age. For a time, the *Globe* lagged behind in both circulation and energy. Bud Collins, a young *Boston Herald* reporter, represented the moral voice of the Boston sports pages when he arrived from Cleveland in 1954. Collins found himself frustrated constantly by being told by his *Herald* editors to avoid writing about racial issues, lest he bring embarrassment to the Red Sox as well as open discussion on a topic never eagerly broached. There was, Collins understood bitterly, a conflict of interest at work. The *Herald* owned the radio station WHDH, which broadcast Red Sox games. During the early 1960s, the *Record American*'s Larry Claflin took the lead in numerous racial issues, such as Pumpsie Green's call to the majors and the Red Sox's refusal to support Earl Wilson after being refused service at the Cloud Nine bar during spring training in 1966. The *Globe* was a below average and nondescript paper that generally avoided controversial issues, although it was Clif Keane's account of the Robinson tryout that gave it life. The *Globe* covered games with a bland workmanship and never stood in the way.

That changed in 1965 when Tom Winship took over the paper. Winship, who had replaced his father Laurence, sought to reshape the *Globe* with vigilance. It started with a youth movement that was doubly fortuitous, for it turned the *Globe* into a strong, readable paper and also put the paper on the same level with many of the cultural issues that simmered during the 1960s.

While the *Globe* rose to prominence with its coverage of Vietnam and politics, Winship applied the same vigor to revamping the sports department. In a sense, it was not unlike O'Connell taking over the Red Sox. Winship awoke the *Globe* from its slumber and found there was talent in his sports department. He supported that talent by hiring more. Bud Collins, who had worked at the *Herald*, joined the *Globe* in 1962 and in addition to becoming one of the more brilliant newspaper writers, grew to be an expert on tennis. Bob Ryan, an enthusiastic kid from New Jersey, was hired in 1967 and covered basketball with an energy that immediately separated him from his peers. Peter Gammons, who grew up in Groton, an hour outside of Boston, took over as a young baseball writer. Will McDonough, a determined, pugnacious reporter who grew up in South Boston, blocks from where the *Globe*'s Dorchester offices would later relocate, had been at the paper since 1959 and had begun to distinguish himself as a top football writer.

The result, thought Tom Mulvoy, was not unlike a ball club receiving a top pick in the draft each year. The youth movement paid off, and by the early 1970s, the *Globe* had engineered a complete reversal. It had gone from one of the worst newspapers to one of the best in the country. Mulvoy served as an assistant sports editor and over the course of a thirty-five-year career at the *Globe* rose to the ranks of managing editor. During those years, he saw the *Globe* doing something the rival *Herald* did not. It hired young people, and in a relatively quick space, the *Globe* was, especially for a vehicle of the mainstream, the more dynamic, youthful newspaper. As an example of the *Globe* as powerhouse, its high school reporters in 1975 and '76 included Dan Shaughnessy, who would later become a leading voice at the paper. Lesley Visser, who would later rise to prominence as a television journalist, was a pioneering reporter who was one of the first women to cover professional sports, which meant breaking down the concrete gender barriers that existed. Dave Smith, the influential sports editor of the *Globe* during those years, remembered spending as much time trying to obtain credentials for Visser to enter the team clubhouses as editing her copy. It was the *Globe* that was a leading voice in fighting for women's access into a sports world dominated by men. A pioneer, Visser would be an inspiration to thousands of young female journalists who chose to enter the foreboding environment of sports reporting.

Al Morganti and Kevin Paul Dupont would both become leading hockey reporters. Morganti, who would join the cable giant ESPN, and Dupont, who would build his reputation as a hockey writer at the *Herald* and later follow in the *Globe* tradition as a premier hockey writer, would become two of the best-respected hockey voices in the game.

The *Globe* had, in Mulvoy's words, "captured the moment." It was no longer gray. It was no longer boring. It would lead, not follow. In 1969, the paper was the second major newspaper to call for the unilateral withdrawal of troops in Vietnam and would become the first paper to call for Richard Nixon's resignation. It was, he thought, a wonderful and unprecedented time to be in the newspaper business.

The *Globe* sports section was no less special. The Red Sox were revived, but Boston had always been a hockey town, and this was the time of Bobby Orr, hockey's most revolutionary player. The Celtics were no longer a dynasty but were always formidable, and the New England Patriots, the football team, were always a colorful story. Under the direction of Ernie Roberts and Dave Smith, the editors of the evening and morning editions of the paper, the *Globe* sports section would become the premier writer's paper in the country. It expanded and soon the paper boasted an expert in the four major sports. Ryan became a renowned basketball writer, Francis Rosa wrote hockey, McDonough covered football, and Gammons covered baseball. In addition, Bud Collins was the leading tennis authority in the country.

The paper was well written. Gammons, Leigh Montville, and Ryan would be known as the "Young Turks" of the paper, and it was also revolutionary. Gammons received credit for introducing the "notes" columns, which would contain three-dot items of baseball gossip about trade possibilities, news, and other trends. Soon, the *Globe* would expand the formula for each sport every Sunday. The columns were gigantic, one full page of notes per sport. The paper, which was always heavily opinionated, spent money, too. Even if the local teams were not playing, the *Globe* did not rely often on wire copy for big stories, sending a staff reporter to the top sporting events. It was a departure from the days when Bud Collins first arrived in Boston and was surprised at how provincial the sports mindset was, that any event occurring outside of New England was not much of an event at all. On Roberts' suggestion, the paper turned Jack Craig from a copy editor to the nation's first sports media reporter. It was the first sports TV and radio beat in the nation.

It was a dramatic departure from how sports had generally been covered in the past and would be the template for how all sports would be approached in the future. The Sunday notes, thought Mulvoy, were "a chance for our writers to empty their notebooks," but it was more. It was another concrete example of just how far the *Globe* had come.

In a way, the innovation of the notes columns was emblematic of Boston as a town, for it was an insular city that thrived on back room intrigue. Boston had always been a place known for its insider behavior, and the popularity of the notes columns solidified the *Globe*'s desire to project a behind-the-scenes authority.

There were casualties of this reliance on insider information, the first being the traditional idea of objectivity. Beat writers were generally charged with writing the game and little else, but now they were sprinkling their copy with juicy tidbits of information, much of it credited anonymously. That left *Globe* reporters open to the charge of lessened credibility, pushing agendas of favorite sources, or, worse, fabricating items. The second casualty, thought Mulvoy, was the lack of something he cherished: The lengthy magazine-style feature stories would now be appearing even less in the *Globe*.

As the *Globe* grew in importance, so too did the prominence of its writers. Soon, the *Globe* became the place where other media outlets sought experts, and the paper was faced with the challenge of retaining such a talented staff. Earlier, in 1968, Bud Collins had begun working tennis broadcasts on Boston's PBS affiliate, and two years later, CBS called and offered Collins an opportunity to do color commentary for its U.S. Open broadcasts. It would be the beginning of a thirty-year television career.

Tom Mulvoy's brother Mark, too, looked to Boston for talent. Mark Mulvoy was the managing editor at *Sports Illustrated* and thus was born the roots of a *Globe–Sports Illustrated* nexus. If the Red Sox had become something of a national team after the miracle of 1967 and later a terrific World Series in

1975, the *Globe's* position as a springboard to both the national magazine scene and TV gave Boston writers a level of influence that surpassed even that of New York City's newspaper circles. Now everybody wanted to work for the *Globe*, because you could go places fast. It was viewed as the springboard for greater opportunities in sports, and if it didn't happen, then hey, the paper was at the top of the profession.

The 1975 Red Sox, Mulvoy thought, played an interesting role in raising the profile of both themselves and the *Globe*. Those were the days before the Internet and the dominance of cable television and twenty-four-hour sports stations. When a national event took place, the scores of reporters that covered the team relied on the local paper. During the Boston-Cincinnati World Series of 1975, the *Globe* was on prominent display for the nation's journalists.

The *Globe* was proud of its reputation as a writer's paper, but its sudden tentacles to even greater prestige increased its cachet. With Bud Collins starring as tennis' premier color commentator on television, television outlets looked to Boston again. Boston would be the place where television came looking for experts. Will McDonough parlayed his football acumen to a job with NBC in the early 1980s. Lesley Visser, who would be a pioneer for women in sports, would do the same with ABC and CBS. Peter Gammons would make the jump to *Sports Illustrated*, only to be misused as a hockey writer. Leigh Montville, Ian Thomsen, and Jackie MacMullen would all at different times move to *Sports Illustrated*. With connections to two coveted destinations—television and the industry's top sports magazine—it wasn't long before every writer in the country wanted to work for the *Globe*.

Over time, Mark Mulvoy's parochialism extended to the *Globe's* rival, the *Herald*. Gerry Callahan went to *Sports Illustrated* in the 1990s. Charles Pierce would write for the *Herald* as well as a stint at the short-lived *National Sports Daily* and later as a writer-at-large for *Esquire*.

Before Tom Winship's youth movement, Boston reporters were never considered on a fast track to national attention, but in a short span, the Boston *Globe*—and to a lesser extent the city of Boston itself—became the plum sports-writing destination paper in the country. Being in Boston opened up lucrative possibilities.

There would soon be another perk to being a Boston *Globe* writer. As the Red Sox and Boston Celtics grew in popularity—the next phase of their development into a nationally recognized team would be the caricature of the franchise as long-suffering and jinxed—the Red Sox opened up a door to the publishing world. Bob Ryan, Peter Gammons, and Dan Shaughnessy would all parlay their beat writing knowledge into book deals. If it was not financially lucrative—Shaughnessy after the Red Sox collapse in 1986 would build something of a cottage industry on the growing and fashionable notion of the Red Sox as a hexed, bewitched franchise—the added cache of a book deal raised the profile of these Young Turks even more, and by extension of the Red Sox franchise. If the *Globe* was slow to hold the Red Sox or another sports team accountable for its actions, the department would suffer charges that its writers were caught in the worst conflicts of interest, for it is difficult to vigorously cover the underside of a franchise with book deals pending.

Shaughnessy, who would over the years gain a reputation as one of the more cynical of the Boston writers, felt he was even more difficult on the Celtic and Red Sox teams he covered to compensate for any appearance of impropriety. "I think everyone knew when I stepped into the clubhouse it was all business. The meter was running."

The rise and influence of the Boston *Globe* were illustrated no better than in the rivalry of its two greatest writing stars, Will McDonough and Peter Gammons. Each in his own way reflected the city's strengths and weaknesses through his copy and approach to the job.

If there would be little doubt that the Boston *Globe* would outshine and overpower its competition in Boston during the 1970s, so too would Gammons and McDonough distance themselves from their peers to become the central figures in Boston sports journalism. They would compete bitterly with each other to be known as the influential voice in the city and would in their own way steer every important Red Sox story for three decades.

For its long-term effects on a city and its signature sports franchise, there would be no more lingering, important story in Boston baseball history than race, and more than any two reporters in the city's history, Gammons and McDonough would shape the parameters of the discussion. They would do this not only by what they wrote, but also by what they did not. In the truest testament to the power of both, McDonough and Gammons would spawn a generation of reporters that would emulate the two giants in both style and personality.

Both moved the market in their own way. McDonough did not believe the Red Sox were a racist franchise and thus would pay no future penalty for past decisions. He would not cover the story of race and the Red Sox as a story at all, but more as a fabrication created by people intent on damaging the legacy of Tom Yawkey and Joe Cronin, of whom McDonough was especially fond. More than any other reporter in the city, it would be McDonough who would deny the existence of race as a legitimate factor in assessing the club.

Gammons was different. Race was not a journalistic topic that particularly energized him, but he would never doubt the existence of a serious racial chasm inside the Red Sox organization. How the two men approached the story of the Red Sox and its racial dynamic would be as important to the story as the story itself.

They were both New Englanders. Gammons grew up in Groton. It was the same home town as that of Dan Shaughnessy, who would become a prominent *Globe* sports columnist in the 1980s. Gammons attended the University of North

Carolina before joining the *Globe* in 1969. Gammons was affected by the counterculture aspects of the baseball world around him in the late 1960s and early
'70s, but he would not stray far from the baseball and writing establishment.

Peter Gammons was an immense talent, and when he took over covering
the Red Sox in 1972, after three years as a backup for Clif Keane, he represented immediately a permanent break from the gray old *Globe*. He was similar
in age to the players he covered, itself a departure from the traditional beat
writer–player relationship in which writers were often twenty or thirty years the
players' senior. Gammons was part of an early group of reporters that included
Leigh Montville, George Kimball, and a young television reporter named Clark
Booth. In the early to mid-1970s, this group drank with the players and shared
a camaraderie that was a reflection of new times. In the beginning, Gammons
was not the star of the group. George Kimball, who was a true part of the
Kulturkampf of the 1970s, joined Gammons and the group. Kimball worked for
the alternative Boston *Phoenix*. He was a writer of fiction and of poetry, spending time in the New York beat scene of Greenwich Village and the lower east
side. He spent much of his time at the Lion's Head, the legendary New York
literary bar. He was a sportswriter who also counted George Plimpton and
Hunter S. Thompson as friends. Kimball lost his eye in a bar incident and, as a
play on words, named his column in the *Phoenix* "The Sporting Eye." He was
an energetic writer and an early mentor to a young student out of Boston
College who also worked at the *Phoenix*, named Mike Lupica, who himself
would become a nationally known reporter, author, and television personality.
Boston in those days was flourishing as a college town, despite the looming
racial crisis. There seemed to be, thought Glenn Stout, a freshness to the sports
writing that did not exist before or since.

What elevated Gammons above the rest of his peers would be with the
Sunday notes columns. Every Sunday, Gammon filled an entire page with
inside news of the game. Those pages were accompanied by very little art or
graphics, and the sight of a full page of gray type was a monument to his reporting. Gammons was a tireless reporter and would be credited with revolutioniz-
ing baseball beat coverage. He was constantly on the telephone and was
consistently one of the first reporters to arrive at the ballpark and the last to
leave. What made Gammons so remarkable, Shaughnessy thought, was that in
those years Gammons gathered all of his information himself. His work ethic
was incredible. "He made contacts with players, coaches, managers and general
managers," Shaughnessy said. "He didn't get his information from other
reporters or other accounts. He had his own sources. What you saw every
Sunday was original reporting." Soon, sports pages across the country emulated
the Gammons style. Each paper hired a writer in addition to the beat writer to
compile the nuggets of inside information that Gammons now made an integral part of baseball's coverage.

Peter Gammons would always be considered by his peers to be something of a climber. He gravitated toward power, and his ambition was rarely hidden. He enjoyed being a powerful player, especially in framing the game's current issues. By the mid-1970s, Gammons was the premier baseball writer in Boston, and the *Herald*—a workmanlike paper that because of its lack of a powerful columnist voice would always lack the *Globe*'s reach—could do little to curb his influence.

Will McDonough was different. He was every bit as ambitious as Gammons, and his zeal to be an insider was equal to that of Gammons. No sports department would ever boast a baseball and football writer that were more wired into their subjects than Will McDonough and Peter Gammons. Where the two differed was not so much in the end results, but in their personalities. Class would be a central issue. Not only had Gammons attended the Groton School, one of the elite prep schools in the nation, but his father served on the school's faculty.

McDonough was a tough Irish kid from South Boston. He was from the streets. He was an Irish Catholic in a city where being so was only a benefit because of hard struggle. Being tough mattered, especially being from Southie, where no one gave anyone anything. In fact, it was the opposite. Everyone in Southie saw the anchors of life they coveted being taken away. He attended Northeastern University and joined the *Globe* in 1959 at the bottom rung, as an intern. If Gammons climbed at the *Globe* from being deigned a star and taking full advantage of a great opportunity by outworking the competition, McDonough saw his own rise through nothing except grit, tireless sourcing, and connections.

Both would outwork their peers, but their class differences would be sharp and telling, for McDonough and Gammons would exemplify nothing more than the historical class struggle between the Irish and the Yankees, a battle that had been acting itself out for more than a century.

As a football writer, Will McDonough would grow to be a giant. He knew the game's power players and like Gammons, was as powerful a player in his coverage of the Patriots and the NFL as there was in the league. McDonough preferred the old school ways, when reporters and their subjects stood much closer. He enjoyed the insider's position, when the game was simple and a handshake could be trusted. There were no agents, no complications.

McDonough had his quirks. Over the years, McDonough would almost boast of his retentive abilities. He would write whole stories, with quotes, without having taken a single note. He was quick to ally himself with people in power; over the years there would be few journalists, if any, who would call an owner at home as readily and easily as Will McDonough.

He was combative. The most famous instance of his temper came when he grew tired of the media needling from Patriots cornerback Raymond Clayborn in 1977. When their argument heated, Clayborn inadvertently poked McDonough in the eye, and McDonough responded by sending Clayborn to the floor with the right cross. It would be one of the most famous moments in Boston sports journalism, the day a reporter knocked a player on to the canvas. Pugnacity didn't stop there. McDonough made enemies, and as his position as a reporting giant grew, he was not the person to cross. He could be cruel, using his column to protect his allies and destroy his enemies, no small hammer. To disagree with McDonough was to risk the wrath of a powerful and well-connected reporter who had a column each week that reached hundreds of thousands. Clark Booth marveled at how complete McDonough's enmity could be. "When he circled the wagons on you, you were finished. I never saw someone who could be so unforgiving of a person. And he was a giant, so you didn't want to get on the wrong side of him."

Given their powerful positions, it may have been inevitable, but the two men, Gammons and McDonough, would grow to despise each other, the result a rivalry that would be legendary at the *Globe*. Although collectively the two men would, along with Bob Ryan and Francis Rosa, elevate the *Globe* into elite status, they would never get along personally.

Part of the reason, thought Dave Smith, was their disparate backgrounds. McDonough was the tough, street savvy kid from Southie who, in the town of Harvard and MIT, attended Northeastern University, which back then was considered on a level far below the cream of Boston universities. His rise at the *Globe* was not as a part of Tom Winship's "youth movement," but as an irresistible force whose reporting skill could not be denied. For thirty years, McDonough would be bitter that Gammons enjoyed greater support at the *Globe*, while, in his view, he would never be handed anything. It was a perspective completely consistent with insecure Southie, a clannish place where its view of life was "us against them." Southie was such an insular place that its residents viewed fellow Bostonians from different neighborhoods as outsiders, with complete and total suspicion. Gammons, meanwhile, was a suburban kid who attended boarding school and seemed to have an easier time not only in his roots at the *Globe*, but also in life. Class set the two men apart from birth.

They were equally distant professionally. McDonough began his *Globe* career in 1959 and would work for more than a decade at the paper before rising out of the ranks into a prominent position. Gammons didn't do the early grunt work that McDonough endured. For Will McDonough, dues had to be paid, and in his mind Gammons didn't pay the toll. He left the University of North Carolina, was immediately chosen and, if not groomed for stardom, was given a golden opportunity to succeed. Although it was impossible to deny the end results, Will McDonough simply didn't believe Peter Gammons earned the chance in the first place.

In one sense, Will McDonough and Peter Gammons were alike. In their daily reporting, neither held the Red Sox very accountable in its culture and climate for minority players. Yet like the other areas of their relationship, it was for wholly disparate reasons. Peter Gammons did not seem to own much of a personal or moral passion for the race question, while McDonough simply did not believe that race in Boston was a story at all.

Gammons would never take on race as his personal cause, even though he would be one of the most astute and knowledgeable people in the game on the subject. There would be no person in Boston journalism who knew the Red Sox belief system from the bottom to the top of the organization better than Peter Gammons. He considered Eddie Collins to be one of the biggest reasons the Red Sox moved so slowly on race, and during his years on the beat he would interview old Boston scouts who told him of their frustration attempting to interest the Collins-Cronin front office in talented black players—such as Willie Mays—only to be rebuffed by management. Players, especially some Latino players, would confide in him about the difficulties of playing in a demanding city without the support of management.

As his column grew in importance, Gammons would hint at the simmering racial divide that tore at the organization, but would rarely pay lasting attention to the issue. When an issue exploded, Gammons would write. In later years, when as free agents players owned the freedom to choose which cities they would play in, Gammons would consistently mention the trepidation on the part of black players to come to Boston without explaining in much detail why. The reason for a player's possible discomfort in Boston or reluctance to play for the Red Sox was as a critical missing element in his reporting. It wasn't just a myth. Rarely, if ever, would Gammons reveal the cultural attitudes that existed deep within the organization, for doing so would be indicting specific individuals. Over the years, black players would explain to Gammons their hesitation and questions about Boston, but such revealing conversations rarely made print at the time. On separate occasions, Ellis Burks and Jim Rice would both tell Gammons privately how difficult it was for them to play in Boston.

It wasn't as if he weren't interested, for in informal settings Peter Gammons would talk at length about just how difficult the climate of the Red Sox could be for black players and about the team's reluctance toward having a black star as its signature player. When he did write, he was brilliant, for no one in the Boston press corps would have the reach of Gammons for so long a period. Gammons writing on the racial climate of the Red Sox gave the story instant credibility, as it did on February 1, 1976, when he discussed how the sport once unchallenged was now losing some of the best black talent to other sports:

> Do you get the feeling that if Willie Mays, Frank Robinson, Henry Aaron and Bob Gibson (all good enough for Baseball's Hall of Fame), were 20 years younger . . . Mays would be a running back, Gibson a linebacker, Aaron a free safety and Robinson a guard for the Kansas City Kings. . . . If the Red Sox farm system, which has no black

players on the horizon, is any indication, those percentages may drop even further in
the next five years.

By writing sparingly on race, Gammons would mirror Jim Rice, the first
black superstar in Boston, who allowed the team's attitudes to erode his spirit
for the city but never used his influence to institute real change.

When the *Globe* would be vigilant in facing race as a question in baseball,
it would be Larry Whiteside in the 1970s, Dan Shaughnessy and Michael
Madden in the 1980s, and a talented reporter from California named Steve
Fainaru in the late '80s and early '90s whose names would be out front on the
story. Undoubtedly, Gammons was the power behind the throne, a wealth of
knowledge and sophisticated detail about a city and a team to whose ascension
he contributed.

Part of the reason Gammons shied from racial issues, thought Glenn
Stout, was the same reason the entire Boston journalism community did: He
could. There was no competition to push them, no voice that forced a response
lest the *Globe* and Gammons fall behind on a most important topic. When it
chose to, the *Globe*, in Tom Mulvoy's words, "held the Red Sox's feet to the fire."
But it could also be maddeningly ambivalent toward race. There was never a
strong black journalistic legacy in Boston to begin with, which made it easy for
the *Globe* and *Herald* (which has never hired a black baseball writer for any
period of time) to avoid prickly issues. Doc Kountze was a loner. The national
black press that once existed in the 1940 and '50s to prod Eddie Collins and
Tom Yawkey went by the way of the Negro leagues. The talented black
reporters were assimilated into the mainstream, and an important piece of the
left disappeared into history. The only remaining piece of the black press in
Massachusetts was the decidedly weak *Bay State Banner*, which was more a
business journal than an alternative force in the city.

The alternative weekly papers, the *Phoenix* and the *Real Paper*, were slightly
more aggressive, but they lacked the reach of the *Globe*, which was the biggest
journalism force in New England. With such a lack of competition, a *Globe*
series on race relations in the city could seem progressive, but only because there
wasn't another outlet writing about the subject at all.

Boston journalism avoided race issues because Boston and its surrounding
regions were overwhelmingly white. There was not much clamor for sticky
racial issues that, if uncovered, would spoil the fun of following the Red Sox.
There was in the 1970s and '80s enough backlash from busing that it was a risky
gambit to harp on the Red Sox and their record on race.

But the biggest reason Peter Gammons avoided writing about race was his
personality itself. He was an insider, not a moral crusader. Race aside, he would
not be the type of reporter—after he became a giant name in the business—to
take unpopular stances or choose to dissect complicated, messy issues that devi-
ated from the game's power structure. He could be brilliant at it, as he was in

his underrated 1985 book *Beyond the Sixth Game,* a brief but entertaining and informative book on the dramatic way baseball—and the Red Sox in particular—had been affected by the advent of free agency. Gammons also chose to be a baseball insider, and to be a true insider it is unwise to take too many unpopular stances, lest sources view you with unwanted suspicion. There is no question that his journalistic legacy suffered from this choice, but his import and influence in the game rose tenfold. By 1990, after twenty years in the business, Gammons would be the most influential name in baseball journalism. He would also become a rich man. When he left the *Globe* for good in 1999, his multimedia contract with ESPN was worth an estimated $1.3 million.

Gammons, Clark Booth decided, wanted less to be known as a hard-hitting journalist than to be known as that very Boston of traits, an insider, a confidant. In the process of his ascension, Gammons would also suffer from charges that he conflicted himself by planting stories in his column that furthered the agendas of sources, especially in the areas of trades. More than once—in large degree because he would credit anonymously even the most innocuous of quotes—Gammons would be accused of making up items and quotes in his column. McDonough would attack him harshly on this point, and Gammons, choosing ice over fire, refused to engage.

Booth and Gammons came up in the business together, were part of the media group that drank with the players at the Eliot Lounge, the old Boston watering hole. Gammons, Booth thought, wanted nothing more than to be the journalist with the power to move the market. It would be reflected in his columns, for within each voluminous edition would be predictions of the next up-and-coming superstar, of the unknown front office force behind the latest winning team. Gammons would become the must-read in baseball. In this climate, it would not be surprising that Gammons did not compromise his stature by taking on a hard and potentially bloody topic as the Red Sox and the strains of racism that marred the organization.

"I like Peter. We came up together. We ran together during those first years in the business," said Booth. "But there is a weakness to Peter. In a way, he's something of a fan. He wanted so much to be acknowledged. You can't have that and take on serious topics at the same time. It just doesn't work. He's really a hits-runs-and-errors kind of guy."

Meanwhile, Will McDonough was not a social engineer, and did not see his position as responsible for cultural accommodation. He tended to view the world in simple, rhetorical terms. Life was what it was. It was not perfect, and you played with the hand life dealt you. His view of race relations was conservative, and like many a Boston Irish Catholic, he still saw himself at times as a hounded minority, although it had been nearly a century since the Irish in Boston won a political and popular majority. He was exasperated by the racial question in Boston, unable to empathize with the notion that it was a difficult, uneven city for blacks. For McDonough, because life was imperfect, you had to adapt to the culture; the culture didn't adapt to you. Thus, he grew short with social alchemies such as busing or black players pressing for rights. He preferred players who came to Boston, kept their heads down, and kept their mouths shut. This was especially true of black players, the more vocal ones having traditionally more trouble in Boston. Once, he received a letter from Mo Vaughn's father. Vaughn was involved in a bitter contract struggle and McDonough was slamming him mercilessly in his column. "I responded to his letter, father to father," McDonough said. "And I told him, 'I'm going to give you some advice for your kid. Tell him to be quiet and play ball. That's how you do it around here.'" It was a typical McDonough response: unapologetic, pointed, and impolitic.

The result was a conservative, angry voice that was reactionary in the face of a new generation of player, black and Latino, with different cultures and belief systems.

The times were what they were, and to Will McDonough, you accepted them. Thus, he did not believe that Tom Yawkey was a racist, nor did he hold Joe Cronin responsible for the team's inaction regarding signing black players in the 1950s. McDonough would revel in his friendship with Cronin over the years and refused to acknowledge in print any of Cronin's transgressions. Even Cronin's own admission in a 1979 *Globe* story by Larry Whiteside that he and the Red Sox front office believed it was better that "the two races have separate leagues" did not move McDonough from his position. "Joe Cronin was a friend of mine. I was the last person to interview Joe before he died. He didn't have a racist bone in his body. Joe and Tom Yawkey wanted to integrate, but they didn't out of sensitivity for black players. They couldn't have integrated like other teams, not when their farm systems were in Birmingham and Louisville. The Red Sox have never had a problem with black players. They've had a problem finding black players who could *play*." If McDonough took a position loyal to his friends and beliefs, it was nonetheless a perspective that severely weakened his credibility. He didn't defend Pinky Higgins because Higgins was indefensible. Higgins wasn't clever enough to cultivate sources in the press to protect his legacy, as were Yawkey and Cronin. Will McDonough protected that legacy.

Over the years, McDonough would be the chief defender not only of Tom Yawkey, but also of the Red Sox organization. McDonough's style created two camps in Boston journalism. One side believed that McDonough's vaunted Rolodex had turned his journalistic instincts on their head, that instead of using his power to expose the sports power structure and inform the public, he instead used the vast column space and influence to peddle their agendas. This was especially true in the case of the Red Sox, where McDonough had always been considered one of the most powerful journalistic insiders. The other camp believed that McDonough was simply, despite whatever ethical transgressions he may have committed or how behind the times he may have been, a journalistic giant. He owned the great sources, the best. He was close to every major player in the city, from Red Auerbach with the Celtics to the Delaware North Company with the Bruins to Joe Cronin and John Harrington with the Red Sox. The younger generation of reporters blanched at how obvious it would be in his column that he was carrying out the work of a powerful team owner, while his defenders would defy them to develop and exceed the contacts Will McDonough had built over a forty-year journalistic career. Ironically, in this vein both he and his bitter rival Gammons would suffer the same criticism.

McDonough saw race in Boston in clear and linear terms, but he also was looking from the lens of a great and powerful Boston majority, the Irish Catholics. He was part of the in crowd in Boston, the political power brokers in the city. McDonough privately enjoyed that a Southie kid like himself could himself become a power player in the city. William Bulger, a Southie son who would rise to be state's senate president, once hired McDonough as his first campaign manager. He grew impatient with talk of institutional and cultural racism, the type of insidious belief structures that permeate an entire organization but have no single culprit. To believe that the Red Sox could have developed a racist culture over a half-century, he wanted the guilty unmasked. "Everyone keeps talking about the Red Sox being a racist ball club. Well, who was it? Was it Tom Yawkey? Was it Joe Cronin? Was it Dick O'Connell? Who?" McDonough's temper was easily inflamed by race, an illustration of impatience with a difficult topic that belied his Boston roots. He wanted the smoking gun. To Will McDonough, if the cross wasn't burning on the lawn, racism didn't exist. Bud Collins, who considered himself a longtime admirer of McDonough as a journalist, separated with his old colleague in the area of race. "It was one of the many areas where Will and I disagree," Collins said. "But it might be the most important."

He would be an undisputed force, but in a world that was becoming increasingly nonlinear, Will McDonough could sound irrelevant, out of touch. His columns would be reactionary, thinly veiled salvos against a changing world where white men were no longer exclusively in power. Race was an element that ultimately needed to be confronted. It would not be uncommon for a McDonough column to rail against the new generation of sports, with each example containing some form of lament along racial lines. He would be a bulldog in representing his clannish, old-line values, even if those values seemed horribly out of date.

Clark Booth would not argue McDonough's place as a certified giant in Boston journalism, but "for a giant he has a lot of blind spots." In the arena of the Red Sox, many black players would leave Boston frustrated but unable to pinpoint exactly what was wrong; something, however, troubled them. In most cases during the 1970s and '80s when the Red Sox refused in large measure to deal with the residual strains of racism that lingered as a result of the Collins-Cronin-Higgins days as well as the tension in the streets of Boston, the culprit McDonough sought was the Red Sox franchise itself. It was everyone and no one simultaneously, a concept McDonough refused. Players who enjoyed good careers in Boston, Booth believed, may have had great careers if the organization took a greater interest in nurturing their talent. Peter Gammons would note that managers such as Ralph Houk and Joe Morgan couldn't relate to black and Latino players, and that it may have cost some young players, a young Red Sox infielder named Jackie Gutierrez, for instance, a better career. That meant until the organization rooted out its old-liners in the farm system and began to change its internal opinions toward black players as potential prospects, the cloud of racism would always be there.

"Will McDonough," thought Tom Mulvoy, "is the most elemental guy I know. He always believes he's right. Nuance isn't Willie McDonough. He makes his call and that's it. You're not going to get a philosophical treatise from him."

The growth of the *Globe's* sports department was, in comparison to the events in the rest of the *Globe* newsroom, the easy part. What was more difficult for men like Ernie Roberts, Dave Smith, and Tom Mulvoy was staking out a position on covering sports in Boston at a time when the city was exploding under the heat of a racial quagmire. In 1974, the state-mandated school desegregation plan went into effect, which effectively tore at what was an uneasy peace among Boston's ethnic factions. Inside of a year, there would no longer be any illusions about the state of race relations in Boston. The National Guard would be as familiar as the teachers in certain schools.

For a time, the belief existed among the *Globe's* editors that sports could be covered separately from the drama and violence that took place in the city's streets. They were isolated from the deep faultlines that were being exposed in both the city and in the *Globe's* own newsroom. Dave Smith arrived in 1970 from the Miami *News* and as a non–New Englander, he felt very much the outsider. The unspoken philosophy in the beginning was to keep race off of the sports pages. Sports were different. The teams were integrated and they were just that, games. The *Globe* discovered quickly, however, that there could be no escape from the great racial conflict. It tore Boston apart, and there would be no safe haven. The newspaper itself knew this, for not only was it charged with covering the busing story, but it was also part of it. Tom Mulvoy remembers those days in the mid-1970s when angry anti-busing factions fired shots into the *Globe* offices. He remembers one specific occasion where he was nearly hit by a stray bullet. In response, the *Globe* editors in consultation with the Boston Police Department placed snipers on the roof of the *Globe* building.

Newspapers traditionally are slower to change than the events they cover;

for all of Tom Winship's youth movements and innovations, in 1974 the *Globe* employed only a dozen blacks, and none had risen above the rank of reporter.

In its own way, the *Globe* had reflected Boston in a way it had not anticipated, or relished. Even today, the belief in the Boston black community is that to be successful, a black professional must leave town and begin a career elsewhere. Only after achieving success in another part of the country is it possible to return to Boston. The point is clear: Young black professionals are not given the opportunity to rise through the ranks in Boston. The entrenched level of institutional racism is simply too great to do anything except toil in lesser positions. The path is simple: Leave, and then return with a reputation. Maybe then—and it isn't a guarantee—a Boston company will offer an opportunity.

Like the rest of the city, the *Globe* was now forced to face itself. With busing as the catalyst, bitter clashes raged in the newsroom about the lack of black advancement while older white reporters bristled at what they perceived to be selfish behavior from the black staffers in the face of a bigger crisis for the newspaper. Now was not the time for self-interest. To the blacks at the *Globe*, now was precisely the time.

In the *Globe* sports department, the transition was not without its difficulties, but they were of a decidedly different nature. In the *Globe*'s history, they had previously hired but one black sports writer, and Mulvoy recalls him lasting only a few months in the early 1960s. Throughout the brunt of the civil rights movement in the 1960s, the Red Sox were in their own way more progressive than the papers that covered them. Neither the *Globe* nor the *Herald* sports sections employed a single black reporter on its staff. It would be reflective of a curious and damning trend that would be most pronounced in baseball. As the game grew increasingly black and Latino over the years, the baseball press corps would remain overwhelmingly white, thus creating a considerable and dangerous racial and cultural distance between the reporters who covered the teams and the players they covered.

In 1973, the *Globe* hired Larry Whiteside, a black sports reporter from Chicago who had covered the Milwaukee Braves for the Milwaukee *Journal* for the previous ten years. In his words, Whiteside joined the *Globe* because "they desperately needed a black." Being from Chicago, Whiteside had some trepidation about coming to Boston. He had heard of its poor reputation for blacks in terms of living arrangements as well as career advancement, but he was also impressed by the city's reputation for the arts as well as its high intellectual quotient. Boston was also the city of the Celtics, the integrated champions who were at the time at basketball's forefront of hiring black players and shattering the racial notions that permeated that sport. They had hired Bill Russell, the great star, to be the coach in 1967, the first black coach in the history of integrated American professional sports. Despite Russell's hardship in Boston, that made an impression on Larry Whiteside.

Moreover, Boston in the early 1970s still enjoyed a strong reputation among black circles for its wonderful entertainment. Slade's, the great jazz club and restaurant, along with the Wig-Wam and Hi-Hat, was still a respected name in black nightlife, and the great jazz musicians still made Boston a regular stop. Foggie's Barber Shop was where the sports world and black community connected.

Upon arriving in Boston, Larry Whiteside and his wife stayed at a black family's rooming house. A holdover from the days of segregation, it was the tradition in the black community in those days to offer living quarters to newcomers in the city. Eventually, Whiteside and his wife settled in affluent Newtonville, a close suburb of Boston. His wife was a public school guidance counselor, fortuitous because she found a job immediately in the Newton school system. A black family wanted to sell their home to another black family and the Whitesides were in a fortunate position. The asking price was $70,000. They bought the house for $62,000.

In general, Whiteside remembers his transition inside the *Globe*'s offices to be generally mild. Ernie Roberts, the sports editor, and Dave Smith were especially kind. Smith was a relative newcomer to Boston, having worked in Miami. That Smith took an interest in his success made his position as the only black in the department a tenable one.

Adjusting wasn't always smooth, for Whiteside's arrival signaled a cultural shift at the paper. Unlike the newsroom, there was only Larry Whiteside in a department that, Mulvoy remembers, still contained pockets of the old-line attitudes. One such person was Clif Keane, a veteran reporter who would cut an odd figure in Boston sports. Keane had a general reputation as a racist, if not in his heart then surely as a product of his generation. He was incorrect in his speech, frequently dropping racial slurs as a matter of habit. Like the old custom of bench jockeying on the field, such talk was common in the press box. The arrival of black reporters changed that. Once, Keane held court in the *Globe*'s offices and let his feelings about blacks be known into the conversation. "He was over there talking about niggers," Whiteside said. "I calmly went over and said, 'If I ever hear that word out of your mouth again, I'm going to knock the shit out of you.'" Keane retreated. It was reminiscent of the Del Baker-Pumpsie Green incident, where Baker had forgotten he was part of a new integrated world. Keane did not realize such talk was no longer acceptable in an integrated newsroom.

But Clif Keane was also one of the few reporters to pester the Red Sox on racial issues. If it was not a constant, Keane nevertheless needled the Red Sox in print. Harold Kaese, one of the respected veteran columnists at the paper, was at the very least indifferent to racial matters. Keane was more pugnacious. It was Keane who sat at the Robinson tryout in 1945 and heard a belligerent voice bark out, "Get those niggers off the field." Keane believed it to be Tom Yawkey, a viewpoint seconded by Clark Booth. Glenn Stout also believed the story to have merit for two reasons. First, the Red Sox were heading for New York for a road trip, and Yawkey frequently worked out at Fenway when the team was away, and second, it was likely that with World War II ending, Yawkey was spending more time in Boston to see the players who were returning from the war. Will McDonough flatly disagreed that it was Yawkey who said the words, arguing that Yawkey wasn't even at Fenway Park that day. McDonough, opinionated and combative, hated Keane and questioned whether Keane was even at the tryout at all.

But McDonough was not at the tryout, either, and his insistence that Cronin was not present was a complete contradiction of the reporting of the tryout as well as of Cronin's own statements in later years about Robinson and the event. Cronin said numerous times that he was present at the tryout.

For Clark Booth, however, it was Keane who was a significant figure in casting a light on the Red Sox as a racist franchise. "Without Clif Keane, no one is ever talking about that tryout with Jackie Robinson. He put a voice to it. I don't think Clif Keane was a racist. I think he was a nut, a weird guy. That sentence 'get those niggers off the field' is the scarlet 'A' on the Red Sox brow. Clif brought that out."

For Whiteside, the press box was a lonely place. He would be the only black in the press box and while camaraderie would soon come, there was clearly a distance between him and the gentry of white reporters. There were no women, only white men in suits. They were reporters, scouts, broken-down baseball men, and a lone black. As much as the ball clubs, the baseball press box was a racist place in itself, a reflection of the larger society. For the media, baseball was the most prestigious because of its traditions and history. Only in baseball did writers have so much invested in the game. They were the caretakers. They voted for the most coveted postseason awards, like the Cy Young and Most Valuable Player awards. Most importantly, it was the writers who decided which players gained induction to the Hall of Fame. To receive a Hall vote, a writer needed to belong to the Baseball Writers Association of America (BBWAA) for ten consecutive years. It was the most coveted of sportswriting perks. It, too, was largely prohibitive to blacks. When Larry Whiteside received his baseball writer's card in 1970, he was the first black beat writer to travel regularly with the club and the fourth African American in the storied history of baseball to receive a card. The first was Wendell Smith, who worked for the mainstream Chicago *American* in 1956. Sam Lacy was second, with the Baltimore *Afro-American* in 1958. Bob Teague with the New York *Times* was third in 1961. Wendell Smith would be elected to the writers' wing of Baseball Hall of Fame.*

---

* In later years, when Wendell Smith was elected to the Hall of Fame by winning the J. Taylor Spink Award for a lifetime of distinguished baseball writing, the combination

It was not a progressive time. The old press box, Whiteside recalls, would have made a great movie. There were cigars and alcohol, both before and after games, no women, and one black—him. He remembers the Boston media being a hard-drinking one, and he reflects on the attitudes and hostility that periodically surfaced from his presence. Ron Bergman, the longtime Oakland A's beat man for the Oakland *Tribune* and San Jose *Mercury News*, remembers the cynical and often cruel treatment of Whiteside in the press box. He remembered when the Red Sox would come to the West Coast on a road trip and different members of the press corps calling Whiteside "token" for being the only black in the room.

It was the loneliest of assignments, thought Mulvoy. On the one hand, he was selfishly pleased for the paper that Whiteside could, in effect, be an ambassador for the *Globe* with black athletes, for it was rare for a ballplayer to look into the banks of writers and see a black face. But conversely, he knew that Whiteside was often in an impossible position. There would be times when Whiteside and a black athlete would share a drink and compare tales of their similar, lonely roads. Journalistically, the details with which Whiteside would emerge made great copy, but he knew he ran the risk of breaking a confidence with a player. Because of this awkwardness, many a great story did not appear in the newspaper.

The worst part for Larry Whiteside, however, was subduing his anger at the words and sentiments that would be so casually tossed around during games. Men like Keane, men of that generation, made no secret of their dislike of blacks, their belief of inherit white superiority. Periodically, as with Keane, Whiteside would burst. Generally, he kept it all in. Dave Smith felt Whiteside was in a remarkably difficult position. He couldn't win, Smith felt. If he wrote hard stories on racism in the game, he would be accused of making excuses for black athletes. If he criticized blacks in print, they would recoil at the only black in the press box attacking them. That made him an "Uncle Tom." The worst part of it all, thought Smith, was that everyone was watching. He was the first black reporter of any substance or longevity in the press box, and like the black players on the field twenty years earlier, he knew that he was being scrutinized by his competitors, his coworkers, and most likely his bosses. Whiteside knew this. If he didn't make it, he believed, it might take another twenty years before another black received the same opportunity.

---

of Whiteside and Claire Smith—the first woman and first African-American to cover a major baseball beat—lobbied hard but unsuccessfully for Sam Lacy, not Smith, to be the Hall of Fame inductee, for Smith in 1948 had been on the payroll of the Brooklyn Dodgers for $50 per week to be Jackie Robinson's ghostwriter. Smith would be the first, but O'Connell believed it was Whiteside who was truly the groundbreaker for generations of black sportswriters.

"Wendell Smith's claim to fame was that he was Jackie Robinson's right hand man, that he was on Branch Rickey's payroll," O'Connell said. "But to do the job of being a beat man, around a club every day, it was Larry Whiteside. He took the shots that made it easier for everyone who followed him."

NINE

Everybody waited. They knew it was coming, and it was only a matter of how bad it would ultimately be. During the summer of 1975, the Red Sox streaked through the hottest months of the baseball season and did not wilt. They seemed to face each challenge only to emerge a stronger team. It did not contain the suddenness and blissfulness of the 1967 club, for they had already been rebuilt by Dick O'Connell and over the previous five years had been competitive but just flawed enough to lose. They always seemed to stumble at the end, as they did in 1972 and again in 1974, but there would be no such disappointment in 1975. The Red Sox were even doing something they hadn't done probably since 1946; they were winning even in a year when the Yankees were a good team. Beating New York head-to-head in itself was a cause for celebration.

Away from Fenway Park, there would be precious little joy in Boston that year, especially as the summer months faded and days got shorter. A large question loomed like a sunset. How the city would react to the citywide, court-ordered busing that was scheduled to take effect in September was the question to which no one truly wanted the answer.

By this point, how the city found itself at the precipice of civil war was immaterial to the fact that the day was coming, and quickly. That the Boston School Committee, a highly political and demagogic entity, had stalled for nine years, playing to the fears of the most conservative coterie of Boston's white neighborhoods instead of forging a workable school integration plan, was no longer relevant. That the idea of prolonged segregation in any city, never mind a city as well-read and politically viable as Boston, was absurd never found its way to the school committee. All that was clear was this: On September 7, white and black students would be bussed citywide to end the segregated school system in the very city that in 1855 was the first in the nation to integrate its schools.

There were opportunities to avoid the state imposing busing on the city, a solution that succeeded in offending everyone, even the black families whose inferior education was precisely what the plan sought to redress. Legendary columnist Jimmy Breslin was dispatched to Boston, hired by the *Globe* to observe the initial days. He did so with a bitter, lyrical eye. To him, the battle lines were clear, and the real fight wasn't black versus white as much as it was poor versus poor. The rich, the ones who could afford to leave the city, sat back in their comfortable seats in the suburbs, which, because they were outside of the voluntary state plan that bused a small number of minority students to participating suburban schools (METCO), were immune from busing. The poor, without options, were left to fight for the city's gristle:

> In the Battle Royal here in Boston, the victor is awarded the same prize as the loser—possession of a place like Charlestown High School. Maybe a quarter of the school's graduates get to a college. But on they fight. South Boston, Charlestown, Roxbury. And not once does anyone stop clawing for long enough to see that all they accomplished is to make things even easier for the eternal opponent—the people with money and power—who pull even farther and farther ahead each day.

It was all in the faces, what was going on in the city. It was in the newspapers every day. Twisted, contorted close-ups of hatred, is how the black people would see it. That talk about the special relationship, about how blacks and whites in Boston enjoyed an accommodation, well, that went out the window. The true face behind the mask was revealed now, and it was a nasty one. Burning into memory were those Southie housewives, jaws tightening, winding up for the spit that was to come was easy, because for a while it seemed like it happened every day. Even the moderate ones, the whites who didn't revel in the resistance came to grudging accommodation with integration that sounded very much like warfare. "I don't mind black people," they would say, "But I hate *niggers.*" Those faces were contorted every day, every morning, sharp and fierce. This was Boston, home of Shaw and Garrison, and Douglass. Even the black people who didn't buy into the hundred-year-old nonsense that Boston was different were shocked by the severity. *They really do hate us.* Then the bottles flew.

That brought opportunity. Once, while campaigning for the 1976 presidency, Alabama governor George Wallace arrived in Boston for a meeting with the editorial page editors of the *Globe.* While walking through the newspaper's offices, Wallace received a standing ovation from the paper's pressmen and mechanics, the very blue-collar Catholic sect that was the most vitriolic against busing. "I only hope to get as good a reception upstairs," Wallace said, to which a Globe pressman responded, "Don't count on it, George." But these two angles placed a disproportionate emphasis on only one segment of the debate. This, thought Boston historian Thomas O'Connor, represented one of the great blind spots in Boston history. The people throwing the rocks and bottles at the school buses had been well represented, while the voices of the black kids on the buses and the parents who put them there stood largely silent.

The truth, however, was that Boston's black community was at the most ambivalent about the prospect of sharing classroom space with whites. The city's history of a harmonic, although polarized, place was in real terms a myth. Boston survived within a delicate fabric that demanded each demographic remain inside its given boundaries. Thus black families fretted about safety, and what many truly wanted was more community control over the schools inside of the black community. There were benefits and disadvantages to METCO, a state-sponsored program that bussed minority students from the city to the better-funded and equipped suburban schools, but to many black parents in Boston, the existence of METCO presented the dangerous suggestion that black neighborhoods were inferior by virtue of being black. The only way to receive a quality education was to attend schools with whites. It was, thought Boston city activist Ruth Batson, a dangerous and poisonous concept to the self-esteem of a black student. There was another, more sinister belief among blacks that METCO existed as a way for suburban districts to receive additional state funding, like everything else, at the expense of the black community.

With no one content, the city burned. The events were sensational, constant, and bloody. Ted Landsmark, a black lawyer, was stabbed in the abdomen at City Hall with the staff of an American flag in 1976. A black student at Roxbury High stabbed a white student in the chest. White parents reacted with a constant force and rage that revealed the true face of Boston behind the abolitionist rhetoric. Yves Jean-Louis, a Haitian maintenance man, drove through South Boston on his way to pick up his wife. When whites on the street saw the black man in their neighborhood, they pulled the man out of his car at a red light and beat him mercilessly. His car windows smashed, he ran until the mob caught him and beat him with hockey sticks. Gleeful in their rage, they left Jean-Louis for dead. Finally, Jean-Louis was rescued by a police officer. Elvira "Pixie" Palladino, the bigoted East Boston anti-busing advocate, said of the Haitian, "I really believe, in the pit of my stomach, that he got exactly what he deserved. He had no business being there."

The most hardened Bostonians were surprised watching the city of abolition and liberty in flames. Writer J. Anthony Lukas illustrated a scene typical of the chaos and sentiment in Boston, a sentiment that could no longer be hidden:

An impish-looking sophomore named Jimmy Walsh had an idea. Together with a friend, he ran down the street to his family's apartment in the Bunker Hill project, pulled an old pair of jeans and a sweatshirt from a closet and stuffed them with wadded newspapers. Fashioning a head from a black plastic garbage bag, they hung a cardboard sign: "Nigger beware!" around its neck. Tying a rope around the effigy, they climbed to the project roof and flung it over the edge. "Look at the nigger!" Walsh shouted as the crowd below cheered.

On the first throw, the dummy caught in the limbs of a tree and dangled there for a few minutes. Soon the boys retrieved it and tossed it further out onto the street. The crowd in front of the Green Store broke and ran toward the dummy, kicking and

stomping it in a frenzy of release. "Let's burn it!" someone shouted. A match was produced. The dummy, doused with gasoline, erupted in flame. Prancing around the fiery
"corpse," the boys shouted, "Burn, nigger, burn."

The Boston *Globe* had been thrown into the middle of the fire. Journalistic
precepts notwithstanding, the *Globe* could not be objective on a story of such
personal magnitude. It did its best and wound up pleasing no one. Dave Smith
remembered the *Globe* spending some $500,000 replacing its windowpanes
with bulletproof glass. For sports, if there was an unspoken edict, it was simple:
Keep busing off the sports pages. Focus on sports, especially the surprisingly
dominant Red Sox pennant run. In the worst of the crisis, during the first
months of September and October, Kevin White, the mayor of Boston, would
say that he was convinced the city would burn to the ground, and the only event
that kept it from doing so was the glorious 1975 Red Sox playoff run. For Dave
Smith, the Ohioan who had arrived in Boston in 1970 just in time for busing,
it was a hyperbolic and scary thing for a mayor to say. What frightened Smith
more, he recalled, was that White was probably right.

The 1975 Red Sox were a dynamite baseball team. If the 1967 Impossible
Dream took New England by surprise, the 1975 team was the realization of just
what could be possible when money is spent smartly and attention is paid to the
development of good players, without heeding any agendas. The Red Sox were
a second windfall of the Dick O'Connell tenure. At the center of the team was
Carl Yastrzemski, then in his fifteenth season. He wasn't the dominant player
he was in 1967, but he was still the undisputed leader of the Red Sox. The third
baseman, Rico Petrocelli, was still there, the two holdovers from the '67 team.
A Cuban castaway named Luis Tiant was the pitcher who won every big game
and would represent the heart—and in many ways the hope—of the team in the
1970s. Bill Lee, a left-handed Californian, would beat the Yankees and become
an idol to the scraggly youth of the nation's biggest college town.

The catcher, Carlton Fisk, was a New Englander from New Hampshire
who exemplified the quirks and soul of a region. The two rookie outfielders, an
easygoing center fielder from Southern California named Fred Lynn and a
powerful young man from South Carolina named Jim Rice, would simply be
known as the Gold Dust Twins.

The team was young and it was integrated. The Red Sox had personalities
that played off of each other, and even during the height of the busing crisis in
the city, the Red Sox, perhaps for the first time in team history, possessed a team
whose youth and diversity would be their biggest assets.

They would not win the World Series, beaten this time in seven games by
the powerful Cincinnati Reds, one of the signature teams of the 1970s. But they
would capture the imagination of a city weary of civil war and a country in desperate need of diversion.

The 1975 World Series would produce a capital windfall. The exuberance of Lynn, the antics of Lee, and the gallantry of Tiant and Yastrzemski pushed the Red Sox as a franchise to the forefront of the major leagues. It was a continuation of the 1967 effect on the team. Plus, the Red Sox were so young, it would only be a matter of time before they were back in the World Series. The team gave a tense city for moment a feeling of levity, especially because in a city torn apart by racial animosities, the loudest cheers at Fenway were for Tiant, the black Cuban.

The Boston *Globe* elevated itself beyond its competition with yet another innovation, the extended special section. For the first time, a sports section ran special pages for each day of the event in addition to its regular sports pages. Normally, the custom had been to have a special section on the first day of the World Series or a day earlier to advance the event. The *Globe* had raised the bar once more.

But if Cincinnati was the biggest winner of the World Series, a very close second place had to be awarded to Peter Gammons. Nineteen seventy-five, thought Dave Smith, made Gammons in the business. After that series, he would find himself on the fast track to becoming a legitimate force in the baseball. The whole *Globe* concept was to create experts in each sport, and Gammons had become the standard. He had written well all year long and had developed a reputation for writing the most refreshing, imaginative game stories in years. During the World Series, Dan Shaughnessy thought, Gammons had done what all sports beat writers strive to accomplish but what few can do very well. He wrote big about big games on deadline. It is a skill most beat writers lack because of deadline demands and their closeness to a team for nine months. There was another bonus, Shaughnessy thought, and that was the rest of the sports world was watching Boston. Gammons shone when it counted the most. His reputation was sealed. He was a player.

For a brief moment in time, the mid-1970s represented the best the Red Sox had to offer in decades. It may have been bad luck to toss such lofty concepts around, but the Red Sox were considered destined to be the next baseball dynasty. The team was strong, and because Rice and Lynn were rookies, the team hadn't yet seen its best days. It was colorful. Tiant and Lynn, thought Peter Gammons, represented the Red Sox in a way that no one since Ted Williams had. In 1967, Red Sox fans came to the ballpark to witness a collective, improbable story as well as return from a long drought of losing. With Lee and Tiant, the Red Sox had personality. Coming to Fenway was now an *event*. Fisk not only was local, but he also shared a bitter rivalry with Yankees catcher Thurman Munson for the title of best catcher in the game. In addition to the success of the franchise the individual personalities of this team made it doubly interesting.

There was an added bonus. The Red Sox were not saddled by racial trou-

ble. In fact, it was an ironic twist that the race-torn city looked to the traditionally resistant Red Sox for a desperately needed sign of racial harmony.

The only problem was the health of Tom Yawkey. Yawkey had been ill for
more than a decade and it was widely believed throughout the organization that
at seventy-two, he would be fighting for each successive year. Yawkey was the
dominant figure of the franchise, and it became increasingly obvious after the
1975 World Series that he was in serious physical trouble.

During the O'Connell years, the Red Sox developed black and Latino talent, and for the most part, good players were promoted. Reggie Smith had been
traded to St. Louis, partly to make room for the arrival of Lynn, and also
because Smith never could agree with Boston. Clark Booth could not remember a more angry and unhappy player in Boston during those days. Smith was
traded to St. Louis following the 1973 season, but it wasn't in a giveaway. The
Red Sox received Bernie Carbo and Rick Wise, two players who would become
integral parts of the 1975 team.

It was a general staple of the O'Connell era. If a player was dealt, there usually had to be a baseball decision that went into the decision. The racial over-
tones that clouded the Red Sox judgment in player personnel matters in the
1940s, '50s, and into the mid-1960s and had made them laughingstocks
because of the team's won-loss record and how it was perceived were largely
forgotten under O'Connell.

It wasn't as if O'Connell was perfect. Trading Earl Wilson was a mistake,
and it would always remain unclear from the club's standpoint if the Cloud
Nine incident led to his dismissal from the club. Wilson would always believe
that. O'Connell traded budding relief pitcher Sparky Lyle to the Yankees for
Danny Cater. That was an unmitigated, colossal blunder. He was more often
right, however, than wrong, and for the first time in decades the Red Sox were
to be taken seriously as an organization that wanted to win and, at least at the
major league level, wouldn't let a player's color stand in the way of that goal.

At the major league level, much of the coaching staff was welcoming to the
players and there was surprisingly little infighting. For the first time in Red Sox
history, the unspoken quota of employing a low, even number of minority players disappeared over a number of years so that by the pennant-winning year
1975, the Red Sox hired six minority players on its roster.

For Tim McCarver, who knew of the Red Sox's lax reputation, it was a surprising moment. McCarver had been a member of those illuminating Cardinals
teams of the 1960s that had broken down so many racial barriers as a team. He
was at the end of his career and when Fisk was injured in the summer,
McCarver was signed until Fisk healed.

O'Connell may have changed the Red Sox culture, but to Tim McCarver,
the Red Sox was still run like a country club. It was an example of just how
deeply ingrained into the soul of the franchise the country club attitudes truly

were. He thought to himself, *if this is change, what could it have been like before?* The Boston clubhouse revolved around Yastrzemski. The star system was clear. Everyone knew the rules. Yastrzemski was Tom Yawkey's favorite, and the rest of the Red Sox deferred to him. For McCarver, who had been on a club with three future Hall of Famers—Bob Gibson, Lou Brock, and Orlando Cepeda—the attention Yastrzemski received in the Red Sox clubhouse was stunning. It was as if the Red Sox players doted on Yaz without him necessarily respecting them. It wasn't a two-way street. On the Cardinals, with those powerful personalities, everything went both ways.

On the minor league level, however, the deep remnants of the Red Sox culture were apparent. The minor leagues, because they lacked the sophistication, scrutiny, and money of the major leagues, would always be slower to change. Cecil Cooper was first called up to the Red Sox in 1971. He would spend five years in the Boston minor league system and only a powerful belief in himself kept him from quitting in the face of dealing with men and attitudes that weren't conducive to his success. In 1974, he arrived in the major leagues to stay. He was black, soft-spoken, and highly intelligent. A Texan, he was confident but kept to himself in Boston for much of the year, rarely venturing out into the city beyond his baseball boundaries. He was close to the two budding superstars, Jim Rice and Fred Lynn, and enjoyed soaking up the big league experience. The busing violence didn't affect Cooper directly. As a ballplayer, he was insulated by his status. He and his young wife did not have children and thus were not directly connected to the public school system.

Being with the big club was a joy to Cecil Cooper. As much as he marveled at Carl Yastrzemski's tireless work ethic, he was equally amazed at Fred Lynn's natural ability. When Cooper arrived to the big leagues, Yaz was already a big star. But Yastrzemski, the son of a potato farmer on Long Island and a person for whom baseball would always be a game of hard work, spent hours before a game taking extra hitting. He would return to the clubhouse with beads of sweat dripping from his face, immediately suggesting by example the amount of work needed not just to make the big leagues, but to stay there. Fred Lynn, on the other hand, did things on the baseball diamond that just seemed to come so easily. Cooper remembers Lynn arriving at the park just in time to hit, then putting on a clinic in batting practice. Where Yastrzemski grunted, Lynn glided. Where Jim Rice hit with a fierce intensity, Lynn flowed gracefully. Rice's ferocious swing once snapped a bat with a check swing. Lynn took his easy, left-handed stroke and hit ball after ball over the fence. "He never, ever," Cooper remembered, "looked like he was trying."

Cooper's quiet demeanor did not preclude him from drawing sharp opinions of his new city. He remembered Reggie Smith's misery. He remembers owning some trepidation about the city and the team. What, he thought to himself, could be going on here that built such fury inside of Smith? The hate mail Smith received from his supposed hometown fans gave Cooper a clue. Cooper had heard about the difficulties of the city and could read from the newspaper and television images every day that Boston was not a peaceful city. It was very different from Texas, even the big southern cities of Dallas and Houston, which had their own harrowing racial codes of conduct. On occasion, the busing violence seeped into the clubhouse from time to time. Even young Rice, the rookie phenomenon loathe to speak out on social issues, made comparisons to his home in Anderson, South Carolina, and what was happening in Boston. "The kids always worked everything out themselves. That was the big thing. The parents stayed out of it. Kids are able to adjust. If the parents had gotten all involved it would have been just as much trouble as up in Boston."

While both were faced with the realities of being black in Boston, Cecil Cooper's temperament could not have been more different than that of Reggie Smith. Smith angered quickly; Cooper was not easily riled. Furthermore, Cecil Cooper actually liked Boston. "Me, I didn't have any problems. I heard others say they encountered difficulties. I knew there were places you weren't supposed to go in Boston, but I considered myself a pretty young, naïve guy. Rice, Lynn, myself. We were all young and we hung out together." Busing existed only along the periphery of his consciousness. Unlike Smith, he was not the target of the type of hate mail that would turn him against his new city.

Cooper possessed a quiet certitude. He did not smolder. Peter Gammons believed that Cooper was well served in Boston by a certain level of sophistication. "He would have succeeded," Gammons said, "regardless of the environment."

It was in the minor leagues where Cecil Cooper first felt challenged. Being from Texas, he knew the frontal assault of segregation—family members often talked about the southern social and physical boundaries that became second nature to a black in Texas—as well as its subtleties. He may have never doubted his abilities as an offensive player—Cooper was one of the American League's most fearsome hitters in the late 1970s and early '80s—but in the lower minors with the Red Sox, he wondered if he would ever receive a legitimate chance to prove himself. One particularly tough man was Rac Slider. Slider was his minor league manager and immediately the two clashed. Slider thought Cooper would never be a major league player. Slider thought of Cooper as too slow and lazy to make the majors; his demeanor too laid back. Slider's impression, Cooper thought, was no doubt informed by the stereotype of southern blacks as indolent and undisciplined, a stereotype that persisted within the Red Sox organization. "He wanted to release me," Cooper said of Slider. "That opened my eyes."

Slider was also a tough, conservative throwback who collided with many of the newer players. One difficulty for a black player, thought Cooper, was the double standard. The eccentricities of white players were tolerated, he thought, but those of blacks were not. A white player, like Bill Lee for instance, could frustrate the old guard of baseball men such as Slider, but was still considered too talented to release. A black player could be equally talented, but the game's white management had little time or patience to accept a difficult black personality. It was a very real feeling that prevented blacks from asserting their personalities. A single misstep, so went the attitude, and everything a player had worked for could be taken away swiftly.

"Temperament was everything. Once you got a reputation, you couldn't live it down. The knock was that they didn't want to play," Cooper recalled. "I bet there were a lot of players, black kids, who were better than me. They never got the chance."

When he arrived in Boston, Cooper relied on the ignorance of his youth. No one asked him questions, and he didn't volunteer his opinions. He developed a certain skepticism toward the Boston media, even though he wasn't the focal point of the team, as he would be with the strong Milwaukee teams later in his career. This allowed him to assimilate into and discover the city without much notice. He recalls a feeling of relief that he could watch the city as a baseball-playing spectator. In truth, he and the other players enjoyed their elevated status as professional athletes. They were relatively well paid and thus didn't rely on the Boston public school system to educate their children, as would the city's black and white poor.

Tommy Harper, who played with the Red Sox in the early 1970s and would make Massachusetts his home, did not play on the 1975 team, but was in Boston in 1974 when the city began its initial busing phase. He played for California and Oakland in 1975, but as detached as he may have been from events, he still owned a home in the Boston area and felt a chill as the riots in South Boston and Charlestown intensified. It was impossible, thought Harper, to be black and not be at least peripherally aware of what was happening in the city at the time. Harper was a northern Californian, from the Oakland suburb of Alameda. He had seen it firsthand back home, where the result of violent confrontations with police created the Black Panther Party for Self-Defense. That was back in 1967. Now, in 1974, he walked through Boston with a measure of caution, understanding his elevated status as a baseball player, but also not wanting to be caught unawares in a city fraught with tension. "You were a ballplayer, yes," he said. "But that didn't stop you from being a man. You were still black in a city that during those times had a lot of hostility toward blacks. You still had to function. You had to buy groceries. You had to go to the store. You may have been detached from all that was happening, but you weren't immune. More than anything else, you just had to be careful. Mind your own business. Go to the ballpark and come on home."

If the Boston *Globe* preferred to keep race and sports off the front page, it was nevertheless a topic that would always be linked, for as much as the Red Sox were learning the process of dealing with a multicultural clubhouse, so too, were the writers who were covering the club. For younger writers such as Peter Gammons and George Kimball, race was a difficult topic, if only because the times were explosive and race was one of the great elements that distanced people. Cooper never believed that the writers covering the club understood him as a person or his background, nor did he feel particularly compelled to provide them with much insight. He was, by his own admission, reluctant to talk. He wanted to be left alone. It was a hard contrast to Reggie Smith, who was clearly affected by the times but also knew that speaking out on difficult, controversial issues made him a target. Harper, too, withheld much from the press for fear of reprisal from management.

The younger writers were forced to cross social hurdles, but for them dealing with black players did not create the type of culture shock that existed for some of the older Boston writers, writers who, like the club, were not accustomed to an integrated presence in the clubhouse. Men such as Clif Keane and Larry Claflin were in the 1970s considered completely out of touch, unable to relate to a black player who had survived the civil rights movement and emerged confident and less fearful of what anyone said. Clark Booth believed that black players never received much of a fair assessment in Boston, that the media never understood to a large degree this newer, liberated attitude. It created an interesting juxtaposition for a man like Claflin, who during the late 1950s and early '60s considered himself if not a champion of the cause, then at least a person morally aware of the societal discrepancies. In the 1970s, however, there were people who considered him to be an old racist. It was a description that deeply hurt him. The same could be said for Clif Keane, who would always be considered by a number of his peers to be locked into a different time.

Some of it, thought Jack O'Connell, was generational. Racial slurs were part of the press box. With some people, with men such as Keane, the use of racial language or off-color jokes in the presence of a black person was proof of a comfort level instead of an affront. "To some people, they could talk like that around a black person. That meant you were all right. They knew it wasn't going to cause a race war or something. But you had to be careful, because there were some people who didn't take kindly to that. Instead of it meaning we were all friends, it meant just the opposite. It meant that we had a long way to go."

The compromise was, for black players, a very bad one. "The writers never could handle serious black men," said Glenn Stout. "They didn't know how to deal with them. The black players who usually did well in this town were the ones who acquiesced in some way, to let everyone know they were nonthreatening." Under such a generality, Reggie Smith did not survive well with the Boston media, nor did Joe Foy, who played third base on the 1967 team.

The players who did survive were either easygoing or, worse, class clowns. In the center was Larry Whiteside, who became the sounding board for black players. It was a difficult dance for Whiteside, who skillfully had to use his position as the only black writer in the press box to gain a position of confidence, but also had to ensure that players still respected him as newsgathering member of the press. On the one hand, he enjoyed being in their confidence. Whiteside once went to the home of an unhappy Reggie Smith and wound up playing tennis with Smith, who was an accomplished player. On the other hand, he wasn't the player's shrink. He still needed them to talk to him on the record. He was a reporter who was to call what he saw, both positively and negatively.

One such example occurred when Larry Whiteside and Tommy Harper were sharing a conversation in spring training; Harper told him that a private club in the team's spring training town of Winter Haven, Florida, was offering free dinners and hospitality to players as a way to raise the club's profile and create contacts with the Red Sox. It was the local Elks Club, and it did not admit blacks. Harper was offended by the custom, which was carried out by a representative of the Elks leaving free passes in the lockers of the white players. When Harper asked Reggie Smith why he didn't receive a pass, Smith just laughed sarcastically and pointed to the skin on his forearm.

This was a major story, but Harper asked Whiteside not to write the story. Harper trusted Whiteside. The two knew each other a few years earlier, when Whiteside was a baseball writer for the Milwaukee *Sentinel* and Harper an outfielder with the Milwaukee Brewers. Harper's logic was simple. They were both fairly new in town. Harper was one of the only blacks on the team and knew of baseball's low tolerance if it considered someone a troublemaker. Whiteside was the only black in the press box. Neither needed the heat of a racial scandal.

Whiteside never wrote the story. That was 1973.

TEN

There was, during the worst days of busing, one place to go for a respite: Fenway Park. Baseball could do that, but what really made the game compelling in Boston was the pitcher on the mound. The guy at one point nobody in baseball wanted—washed up, they said he was—turned out to be exactly what the Red Sox needed.

If Jim Rice would be Boston's first dominant superstar, then Luis Tiant was the first player of color in the city's history to be so totally embraced that he would enter a space usually reserved for white stars. He captured the imagination of Boston fans in a way that seemed impossible, especially in the framework of what was happening on the front lines in Charlestown and Southie.

He arrived from the scrap heap, a washed-up pitcher that couldn't crack the roster of the Minnesota Twins or Atlanta Braves. His demise was especially curious because only two years earlier, in the pitcher's year of 1968, Tiant was a twenty-game winner with a staggering earned run average of 1.60. At the end of the 1970 season, he was nearly out of the game. Then Dick O'Connell struck again, signing Tiant to a minor league contract. Could he still pitch? Nobody knew. His age was listed as thirty, but he was Cuban and in the myth of Cuban baseball players, age would always be a flexible concept.

For a time, it was a disaster. Eddie Kasko, the Red Sox manager, defended Tiant's ability even though he saw little evidence that the portly pitcher could contribute to a Red Sox team that was competent but not nearly on the level of the surging Oakland A's or perennial Baltimore Orioles. He appeared in twenty-one games in 1971, winning only once and losing seven for a team that lacked the pitching to overcome the pitching-rich Orioles. The Boston crowd, one that would spur him to the greatest success of his career in the years to come, turned mercilessly on him. He would remember one particularly harsh fan who consistently sat directly behind the bullpen, waiting to pour abuse on to him. "I didn't think I had any future in Boston. I was finished. But Eddie Kasko protected me and as it turned out, Boston was the best time of my life."

Despite the beginning, to remember Luis Tiant in a Red Sox uniform is to think about the most sustained, hopeful period of recent Red Sox history, a time when the championships were only a season away and the future was a welcome sight. The current Red Sox aura as a star-crossed and cursed franchise did not then exist. Tiant dazzled the faithful with a dizzying delivery, a basket of different pitches, and a memory bank of clutch performances. Tiant was valiant, and there was sizzle to his steak, evidenced by his ninety-six wins in his first five full seasons with the Red Sox. He was, Yastrzemski said, "the heart and soul of this team." There are a million stories about what Luis Tiant meant to the Boston Red Sox during the 1970s, of how he kept the Red Sox loose and was the backbone of those exciting, perilously flawed teams. Tiant also knew how to keep a clubhouse loose. He remembers talking to Tommy Harper after Harper played a particularly bad game. After the game he consoled Harper. "Tommy, don't worry because you played like shit and looked like shit. You only smell like shit."

"I knew how to make you laugh," Tiant would say. "If you went 0 for 4 with four strikeouts, I'll still make you laugh. I try to find in everyone the weak spot."

Cecil Cooper remembered the first time he saw Tiant sitting in the whirlpool with the Fu Manchu mustache and a long cigar protruding from his mouth. He couldn't help but burst out in laughter. Dwight Evans would often walk by Tiant's locker and begin laughing. There are moments during the conversation when he starts talking about something or other and I find myself doing it, too.

"I don't know what it is," he said. "There is something about me that makes people laugh, even when I'm not trying to."

"One of a kind," Cecil Cooper said, laughing.

But Luis Tiant could easily be underestimated. He was a kind, good-humored man who made it a point to make everyone laugh, and he spoke in thick affecting, broken English. The consequence of his personality was to be taken for a clown. Tommy Harper recalled that Tiant knew exactly how to make people feel at just the right moment, but that no one was more focused toward victory in a big game. It would be this part of Tiant's personality that would be largely forgotten.

Underneath the humor was a concrete pride that drove Luis Tiant. His father, Luis Tiant, Sr., was a Cuban pitching legend who pitched in the Negro leagues and was for years at the highest levels of Cuban baseball. When Fidel Castro annexed foreign and domestic property under sweeping communist reform, Tiant knew it would not be long before Castro closed the country's borders. Thus, in 1962, under the wire he defected to the United States and signed with the Cleveland Indians. He would not see his family again until Tom Yawkey engineered a tearful reunion in 1975.

There would be in Tiant an invigorating burst for life. He knew of his good fortune of being a talented pitcher, and that each day forward would never be as difficult as those of his youth, of being in Cuba without future prospects beyond playing sports. "Being poor," he says, "was the worst. The only chance you had in Cuba was baseball. When you're poor, you've got no hope. Every human being should have a chance. For a lot of people life is being poor. Poor, broke, then you die."

Tiant was a solid pitcher in Cleveland, but it would be in Boston where he grew into a legend. Peter Gammons believes there to be no bigger money pitcher during his time than Luis Tiant. Some might argue for Jim Palmer, he says, but those people aren't from Boston. Tiant, like most athletes, would never forget the booing, and in no small part, the abuse motivated him to achieve even greater success. "People booed me. They booed me all the time. There was this one woman, I think she was the daughter of a Boston cop. She kept yelling at me, 'Go back to Cuba!' I told her, 'You go home and help your mother clean the house.' That shut her ass up."

Tiant won twenty games three times for the Red Sox and pitched well in virtually every big game. A 15–6, 1.91 ERA and a huge playoff push in 1972 made him the soul of the Red Sox for the remainder of the decade. Cecil Cooper offers a smile when remembering his timeless 163–pitch, 5–4 win in Game 4 of the '75 World Series. Even in defeat, Tiant was valiant. He gave up a long, exhausted homer to Cesar Geronimo in the eighth of Game 6 that gave Cincinnati a 6–3 lead and he departed to a standing ovation, at that moment needing a miracle to avoid the end of the season. During the comeback of the last week of 1978, when the Red Sox and Yankees interlocked in a pennant race for all times, Tiant said the Red Sox would lose the final game against Toronto "over my dead body." He pitched a 2–0, complete-game shutout. To be on the mound during the most pressurized-filled moments illuminated him.

Treat him like a clown, but call him for the big game to bail everyone out. That was the thing about sports, Tiant would say. If you can't motivate yourself for those moments, with it all on the line, then you've got a lot of problems. Tiant could. He was born for it. He would laugh at those big leaguers who said a pitcher couldn't be the leader of a team because he pitched only once every five days while the rest of the boys slugged it out daily. The whole game starts on the mound. That thought made Tiant smile, the Fu Manchu bordered a big, determined smile.

Tiant wasn't alone on the hill, either. He was being watched, if not on television back in Cuba, then in a more important place, in the mind and the spirit. At the Parque Central, the central plaza in downtown Havana, the thirst for baseball is never quenched, and every day at four P.M., the men would cluster at the stone benches and talk baseball. They've been doing it since before Castro came down from the Sierra Maestras to take his prize. Orlando Hernandez was just a boy in the late 1960s, but he knew of the great Tiant, as well as Tiant, Sr. the old Negro league pitcher and Cuban legend. He was ten years old when Tiant twisted, arched, and fired everything he had at Cincinnati in the Series, and when El Tiante and El Duque would meet years later, with the old master wearing a Red Sox uniform and the next in Yankee pinstripes, El Duque would grow sentimental with pride for Cuba, and the craft.

Tiant would always be conflicted about race; he was a leader on the mound but was savvy enough to avoid the incendiary statements to the press that could have turned a hot city against him. That didn't mean he was anybody's fool, he just tried not to swim in the hot water. That's how it would be in Boston, though. Tiant would spend the days downplaying the effects of the club's history of race and the city's maelstrom, yet couldn't give an interview without returning to how blacks and whites got along. Race never went away.

Peter Gammons believed Tiant built the cultural bridges in the Red Sox clubhouse, and it was—again, an example of treating Tiant as jester, not general—the something the pitcher never received the proper credit for. Even when the Boston chapter came to an end for him, and the racial tension inside of the organization began to simmer did no one think that maybe Tiant was more important than thought; that Yaz wasn't kidding when he called El Tiante the heart of the ball club.

Maybe he was the guilty conscience of the city, as had been often suggested. Even if people *didn't* cheer Tiant to ease themselves of the burden of citizenship in the city's larger picture, it sure was weird to hear those chants of "Loo-ee! Loo-ee!" one day—and they were loud—and then see Ted Landsmark's face covered in bandages after a mad group of white kids beat him down that day in Government Center.

Of course, it wasn't all that neat and form-fitting. The Red Sox were New England's team and the same people who cheered Tiant weren't the same people who stuck the staff of the American flag in Landsmark's chest.

Tiant himself would not be so vigilant. If the fans came to Fenway as an escape, then so be it, he said. He would grow frustrated that it so colored the best years of his life, and also the city where the good times occurred. As the years would pass, Tiant would take a more demure approach to race, hoping it would not always be as powerful a topic. But Tiant also understood that racism was not a figment of his imagination or of the black players who endured difficult times in Boston. He lamented about Reggie Smith. "Tough guy. He had a tough time, too." Then he simultaneously adored Tom Yawkey. "He was a good man. He took care of me. He loved me, *everyone* loved him."

For Tiant, race got in the way of some great years, but he was no clown and was not oblivious to the crushing power of racism. He is a black Cuban and while he talks about his father, Luis Tiant, Sr., he is reminded that his father was a great Negro League pitcher for the New York Cubans, but was not allowed to compete against whites in the major leagues. Like Cecil Cooper, he believes the diversity of races and personalities on those 1970s teams contributed greatly to the team's success but would be greatly troubled by the persistence of racial questions in Boston. His heart is heavy in this regard. "Boston gets a bad rap. I heard so many people say that Boston is racist. Everyplace is racist, even my own country of Cuba. Some people had problems there, and I do feel sorry for all the Afro-Americans there and what they went through. But what happened to me, I can't say a bad word about Boston."

The more he preferred not to discuss it, each pause returned Luis Tiant to race as the central topic of the Boston Red Sox.

Despite the humor, something important was missing inside Luis Tiant. He would be haunted by elements of the lonely and the unfinished. He was bitter with the way he ended his major league career. It ended with him pitching for the California Angels, beating the Red Sox in 1982 for his final win. He never wanted that, to beat the Red Sox. He never wanted to leave Boston in the first place. Leave Boston? No chance. Tiant's contract was up, but he knew what was out there, after 15 years in the big leagues, through seven years with Cleveland and through rock bottom with Atlanta and Minnesota. And he knew that for his career, there would be no place as satisfying as Boston. The best years were in Boston. The team was so close during the decade. They missed by a hair in '72 and '74, got beat by a Reds dynasty in '75, and lost out by a game in one of the greatest pennant races in baseball history. That year, 1978, Tiant wouldn't let them lose. More than the Yankees it was ego—illustrated by Don Zimmer and Bill Lee feuding at the price of a pennant—that buried the Red Sox, that made a one-game playoff possible in the first place.

No, his place was in Boston. Time was running out on this team's special window, and in 1979, the Red Sox were going to finish what they started.

Red Sox management didn't think so. Tom Yawkey was gone, and the gigantic void, filled by Haywood Sullivan and Buddy Le Roux didn't think Tiant to be so valuable after all. That was one part of it. The other was that Le Roux and Sullivan thought Tiant was just an old fool who could be intimidated into signing a contract for less than what he believed his market value to be.

And what was it, for numbers could not even begin to detail what Luis Tiant meant to the Red Sox. If the players—Yastrzemski, Rice, and Eckersley—could see how important Tiant was, why couldn't Le Roux? Tiant didn't believe he was asking for much, just a two-year contract. Tiant wasn't even haggling over money.

Le Roux insulted him, tried to back him into a corner. Tried to scare him, he did, by telling Tiant that his considerable reputation as a big-game pitcher wouldn't serve him in this new free agent game, where players forgave security to test their worth on the open market. The words Le Roux used were immortal.

"Luis," he said, "Think about your age."

None of this would have happened, thought Tiant, had Tom Yawkey lived.

He would have made sure his club was kept together, would have taken care of Tiant; he wouldn't have just let him walk.

Nearly a quarter century later, traces of the sting could still be found in Tiant's voice. "They didn't want to sign me. They offered me one year," Tiant said sourly. "Everyone got more than one year. They were good to me, but I repaid that and more. They weren't looking at the big picture, at what I did for that team."

Thinking of him as the court jester was the worst misjudgment they could have made about Tiant. He was all about heart, and Buddy Le Roux punched him, right in his pride.

George Steinbrenner was watching. He had just won his second straight World Series, beating the Red Sox in that classic one-gamer at Fenway. Steinbrenner, lurking, marveled at how the Boston management could be so cavalier with such a vital organ. Maybe Tiant was thirty-six and maybe he didn't have a whole lot left, but whatever Tiant brought to the Yankees would be that much more Steinbrenner would be taking from the Red Sox.

So it was done, and Boston took another one in the chops from New York. The Yankees signed Tiant to a two-year, $840,000 contract.

In the spring of 2002, George Steinbrenner would walk along the hallway of Legends Field with a fondness for Tiant that 22 years later would still be powerful. He would still be leveled by how the Red Sox couldn't see in the man what Steinbrenner thought was so plain.

"I loved Luis Tiant. I loved him as a person, that is very clear," Steinbrenner said. "But what I really loved about him was Luis Tiant, the competitor. He was one of those people whose will to compete was so sure. You could see it in him so obviously. He seemed to be saying 'give me the ball and get the hell out of my way.'"

The Red Sox wouldn't be a good team again for seven years. Yaz knew it right then and there. Lots of players have talent, but few have the guts to go with it. "When they let Luis go," Yaz lamented, "they tore out our heart and soul."

Then he was gone. If the first wave of baseball's integration would be on the field, the next—managerial, front office, and patronage jobs for blacks and Latinos—would be much harder to attain. It is here where Tiant would be severely damaged by being known more as a class clown than as a dominant, serious pitcher who happened to be funny. There were no jobs at the major league level and no offers in the minor leagues, nothing for a man who gave everything he had to baseball. For the next two decades, the Red Sox would never offer Tiant a job in the organization, and he would not find his way back into baseball until a decade after his 229th and final major league win. In the meantime, he worked for the Massachusetts Lottery, curious for a person whose most serious vice was gambling. There is more than a passing sentiment that Tiant's gambling made him too hot to the touch of skittish baseball owners.

Tiant would drift. He worked from 1992 to 1997 with the Los Angeles Dodgers before landing in Savannah. He was a borderline candidate for the Hall of Fame, but nothing would hurt him worse than being shut out of baseball. It was the most painful of slights watching pitching coaches around the majors who never accomplished get jobs while he would not.

Luis Tiant carried a genuine sadness after baseball. In 1998, he accepted the position of baseball coach at the Savannah College of Art and Design, an odd place for a man who once stood at the very top of baseball in Boston. More than the rest, Luis Tiant would be stricken by the profound emptiness that comes with no longer being on the biggest stage, with being average except for the memories.

A pair of pioneers: The disastrous 1945 tryout at Fenway Park was a bitter humiliation for
Jackie Robinson (left) and history would undermine the special role of Isadore H.Y.
Muchnick. What resulted, however, was a warm and lasting friendship between the two
men, standing on each side of Muchnick's son David in 1962. (From the collection of
David Muchnick)

A millionaire and his mentor: Tom Yawkey (left) purchased the Red Sox in 1933 and
immediately placed his franchise and trust into the hands of boyhood idol Eddie Collins.
With Yawkey's blessing, Collins would be responsible for a series of hires that would shape
the racial attitudes and culture of the Red Sox for decades. (Courtesy of the Sports
Museum of New England)

The face of a franchise: For years, Mike "Pinky" Higgins boasted "there would never be any niggers" playing for the Red Sox while he was manager of the club. A personal favorite of Tom Yawkey and Eddie Collins, his consistent promotion within the organization was the clearest symbol that the game may have changed, but the Red Sox would not. (Courtesy of the Sports Museum of New England)

The accidental pioneer: It could have been Jackie Robinson or Willie Mays who integrated the Red Sox, but Pumpsie Green would be the first black player to play for them. While other black players would be vocal about the difficulties playing in Boston, Green kept all of his silent frustrations inside. When Green arrived in 1959, a call from Robinson completed baseball's integration. (Courtesy of the Sports Museum of New England)

There would be no player more uncomfortable with the jagged racial dynamics of the city and the Red Sox than Reggie Smith (right). Smith's time in Boston was emblematic of the difficulties a young black player faced playing for a team that had yet to confront its racial culture in a turbulent city. Only a friendship with Carl Yastrzemski (left) was worth savoring. (Courtesy of the Sports Museum of New England)

Two for the show: Reggie Smith holds a signed baseball marking a two-homer game during the Impossible Dream year of 1967. The first Red Sox player to homer from each side of the plate in a game, Smith found his immense talent to be more burden than blessing, as he would never fulfill unfair expectations. (Courtesy of the Sports Museum of New England)

Cecil Cooper congratu-
lates Jim Rice after
another Rice home run.
Cooper was a gifted hit-
ter who would become
an exceptional player,
but only after he left
Boston. A reserved per-
sonality, Cooper would
never endure racial
hardship in Boston, but
would be frustrated by
the lack of opportunities
in baseball's upper man-
agement once his play-
ing days ended.
(Courtesy of the Sports
Museum of New
England)

Unending ironies:
Harper slides back to
first in an April 1974
game against the Kansas
City Royals. Notice
Harper wearing the
number 4, which
belonged to Sox legend
Joe Cronin, who passed
on Willie Mays and
Jackie Robinson
because, in his words,
"We all thought it was
better to have separate
leagues." Cronin's num-
ber was retired in 1984.
(Courtesy of the Sports
Museum of New
England)

Ferguson Jenkins (right) came to the Red Sox with a glowing reputation and seven 20-win seasons, but once in Boston never came close to that type of success. He would be one of many black players to arrive in Boston as one man, and leave town very much another. (Boston Herald).

George Scott (below) played for the Red Sox on two separate occasions and would be one of their most colorful players ever. Scott, however, would not be taken very seriously and would grow bitter at the lack of opportunities in the game once his playing days ended. (Boston Herald).

The best of moments
(right): For Dennis "Oil Can"
Boyd a championship
moment was one to savor, for
the majority of his eight years
in Boston would be memo-
rable only for their tumult.
(Courtesy of the Sports
Museum of New England)

The power that defined an
era (below): Jim Rice epito-
mized the offensive powerhouse Red Sox teams of the
mid-to-late 1970s. Rice was
proud that he was not only
the most feared power hitter
in the American League,
but consistently hit over
.300. His magnificent numbers could not thaw an
uneasy relationship with the
city. (Courtesy of the Sports
Museum of New England)

A lonely centerfielder: Ellis Burks was supposed to be the next great Red Sox outfielder, but he would be stifled by unfair expectations and racial isolation. Like Jim Rice a decade before him, Burks would be the only black player on the Boston roster in 1990 and part of 1991. (Boston Herald)

The simmering feud between Vaughn and team GM Dan Duquette culminated in Vaughn's eventual departure from the Red Sox. Neither would benefit from the separation. Vaughn would never be the dominant player he was in Boston, and Duquette would be vilified for allowing such a productive and critical member of the team to leave. (Photo by Bill Chapman)

Above: Jim Rice (left) would have no greater ally in baseball than Don Zimmer (center). While Rice would clash with the media and be uncomfortable with the organization's reluctance to sign star black free agents, he would always be Zimmer's favorite player. Wearing warring hats, the two share a pre-game moment along with Tony Cloninger. (Photo by Bill Chapman)

The future (right): The wondrous Pedro Martinez (pitching) and shortstop Nomar Garciaparra now lead the Red Sox into the millennium with less conflict than the past. (Photo by Bill Chapman)

ELEVEN

When Tom Yawkey died of leukemia on July 9, 1976, forty-three years of stewardship over the Red Sox ended. It was an era during which neither his supporters nor his detractors ever knew enough about him. There would, however, be no doubting the scope of his power. Yawkey was the vice president of the American League for years, saw Joe Cronin elected to the presidency of the league largely as a monument to his standing, and, although posthumously, would be the first owner ever to be inducted into the Baseball Hall of Fame.

How much responsibility for the moral direction of the Red Sox belonged to Tom Yawkey would be a topic worthy of hot debate for decades; but only in Boston. Outside of the city's parochial walls, Yawkey posed no mystery. To David Halberstam, the great overseer of the American century, Yawkey was clearly a racist, a man who accepted the social order and embraced its benefits. To Leonard Koppett, the Hall of Fame reporter, Yawkey could have changed the rigid culture of the franchise if not with a single stroke then with consistent vigilance. Bob Ryan, the influential columnist for the Boston Globe who would be elected into the basketball Hall of Fame for his coverage of the Celtics, believed Yawkey to be an unremarkable, charitable man, who viewed race with little priority. "He was a man," Ryan said, "who was very comfortable with the way things were."

The most prominent members of the black press—men such as Wendell Smith and Sam Lacy who covered the groundbreaking era of desegregation saw Yawkey the way they saw many powerful white men: disinterested in racial change because it didn't affect them.

They didn't, thought Clark Booth, call the Yawkey Red Sox "the plantation" for nothing. Nor was Marty Nolan, the noted *Globe* political columnist call the Red Sox "the klavern." At the top of it stood Thomas A. Yawkey, the seminal figure in the history of the team. If Yawkey was not inflammatory in the way of a George Weiss he nonetheless enabled the Red Sox to possess the air of a southern, redneck franchise. How long would Pinky Higgins have lasted had Yawkey not wanted him, and promoted him again and again? That was where the support of Yawkey suffered its mortal blow.

Everyone in baseball knew the Red Sox way. Doc Kountze knew it, how Yawkey would seem so charming, like when they met that day in Fenway Park.

Yawkey would be so engaging, *really open to suggestion*. Then, he'd do nothing. Even that was incorrect. He wouldn't do *nothing*, but something. He'd give Higgins a raise and more power. Buck O'Neil spent a lifetime in the Negro leagues, with the Kansas City Monarchs, sealed off from being a major leaguer by smiling, charming men like Yawkey, men who told him how good he would be in the big leagues, if *only times were different*, as if the times were created all by themselves. A half-century later, O'Neil would not speak easily of Yawkey or the rest of the men who kept him out, at least until his youth was all gone. "Give us the chance," O'Neil said, "and we'll do the rest." For too many years, Buck O'Neil believed Tom Yawkey's Red Sox never gave black players a chance. O'Neil would have to live with that, but so would Yawkey, for by letting men like Higgins, Cronin, and Collins define the racial attitudes of the Red Sox, those attitudes wound up defining him.

He may have died in 1976, but the specter of Yawkey would dominate the franchise for another quarter century after his death. Within the city, its press would deal with Tom Yawkey as an institution instead of as a man. As a man, Tom Yawkey was a total mystery, even to those subordinates who worked closest under him. His name would be symbolic with Boston, but in forty-three years of owning the Red Sox, he never took up residence in the city, preferring a suite at the Ritz-Carlton Hotel across the street from the Boston Common and Public Garden. Only in the final few years of the ownership of the Red Sox under the Yawkey name did any real examination of Tom Yawkey come, and it was not initiated by the city's print media, but by writers Richard A. Johnson and Glenn Stout. Only then, after a sweeping history of the team was published in 1999, did the Boston media feel it safe to begin to examine the most important figure in Red Sox history. There would be no sweeping Yawkey biography, as there are of most figures that tower over institutions of influence in a place as learned and powerful as Boston.

Outside of Will McDonough's withering attacks on anyone who dared question Yawkey or especially Joe Cronin, there would be no real discussion of Yawkey that could formulate a sketch of the man by the Boston newspaper people who knew him best. Such an omission represented a powerful indictment of the Boston press, for it was a media that built itself a reputation as insiders. Yet for the previous six and a half decades of Yawkey control and influence over the Red Sox, he would stand beloved by some, held responsible for the team's racial transgressions by others, and unknown to all. Dick O'Connell, one of Yawkey's most loyal soldiers, never even knew he had a daughter.

Yawkey's death was the first of a series of critical events that would bring the most prosperous and hopeful time in postwar Red Sox history to a painful and bitter close.

Now Yawkey was dead, but major league baseball wasn't quite ready for any other name to stand at the top of Red Sox stationery. The Yawkey imprimatur was essential, for Boston was an American League flagship. That meant there could be no way that Haywood Sullivan or Buddy Le Roux would be allowed to succeed the towering Yawkey. Yawkey himself never left a blueprint for the Red Sox after his death, so Bowie Kuhn, the stiff commissioner of baseball made an executive request: he wanted Jean Yawkey, the widow, to take over the franchise. A request from the commissioner of baseball is in fact an order, so after some hard political wrangling, Jean Yawkey purchased the Red Sox and the Yawkey name remained after all.

So did the Tom Yawkey cronyism. The first thing Mrs. Yawkey did was fire Dick O'Connell, the best general manager in Red Sox history. His firing wasn't because he screwed up the Earl Wilson trade, or the Cecil Cooper deal, or the fact that he gave Sparky Lyle away to the Yankees. No, Dick O'Connell was fired because Jean Yawkey didn't like him. She had her reasons.

If his firing would be a bitter blow to O'Connell, who had served Tom Yawkey faithfully since 1946; his removal would have deeper and more devastating repercussions on the franchise. Making a business decision based on personal taste was the first sign that the Red Sox had fallen back into the old habits and proof that Mrs. Yawkey as an owner would in practice not stray far from her husband. O'Connell's removal would prove to be a critical mistake, for an untested Sullivan ran the Red Sox during baseball's most volatile period of labor unrest and enormous change. Free agency was in its infancy and its arrival was immediately changing the balance of power in baseball. O'Connell was never fully accepted under Tom Yawkey, and he had certainly made enemies within Red Sox hierarchy, most notably with Jean Yawkey. The animosity that existed between O'Connell and Jean Yawkey dated back decades and Red Sox insiders knew there would be no place for Dick O'Connell in the new Red Sox organization. In a sense, O'Connell's firing and Sullivan's ascension were reminiscent of the Red Sox under Tom Yawkey, for there was nothing professionally that warranted the move. O'Connell was successful at the time of his dismissal; his successor, Sullivan, would preside over the dismantling of a franchise.

O'Connell's influence on the Red Sox, in those dozen years, did more to create the modern Red Sox organization than did the previous three decades. He had built a farm system that was the core of two pennant-winning teams. He had taken a flyer on the wondrous Tiant, who rewarded him by becoming one of the great Red Sox pitchers of all time. When he made mistakes, they were grand, having traded Sparky Lyle, Reggie Smith, and Cecil Cooper, all players who went on to have much better than average careers. When he left the Red Sox, Smith became an above-average player in St. Louis and won a World Championship with the Los Angeles Dodgers in 1981. But Dick O'Connell brought respectability to Red Sox management. He did this by not being as political as his predecessors. He was not, thought Clark Booth, by any means a racial pioneer or progressive, but he made sure he did not miss on signing talented players regardless of race. Too often, thought Booth, people expected change to occur only under the hand of a racial crusader. This was incorrect. Change took place when winning became the primary agenda, and, for the first thirty-two years under Tom Yawkey, the primary agenda in Boston had been cronyism. No team in baseball history would spend so much and produce so little in terms of victories and championships as the Tom Yawkey Red Sox. To this end, O'Connell was different. "Just give me the best players," O'Connell would often spout as a motto. It would seem simple enough, but during the history of the Red Sox it would become the most difficult task for the franchise.

The New Englander who turned the Red Sox from a laughingstock to an institution would never work inside of baseball again, and certainly not for the Red Sox while Jean Yawkey ran the club. Years later, in 1983, O'Connell would suffer the embarrassment of being part of a famed takeover attempt of the Red Sox on the part of Buddy Le Roux, a former basketball trainer for the Celtics and a limited partner of the team. Le Roux sought to wrest control of the team from Yawkey and re-install O'Connell as general manager. The worst piece of the entire takeover disaster—dubbed "Coup Le Roux" by the clever Boston press—was that Le Roux staged his assault on the night the Red Sox were honoring Tony Conigliaro, one of the more tragic figures in Red Sox history. Conigliaro, whose career was derailed when he was beaned by a Jack Hamilton pitch in the summer of 1967, had suffered a debilitating stroke. The bickering came hours before a fundraiser on his behalf. That afternoon would represent the lowest point of the franchise.

With O'Connell gone, the Country Club was open for business once more, in many ways more damaging to the Red Sox reputation than ever before. In the old days, the Red Sox franchise may have been the ultimate house that sat atop the hill—Yawkey's millions went unrivaled for years—but in spirit and attitude Boston was no different than the rest of baseball. Even the teams that integrated first were still in many ways products of their generation. Even Branch Rickey, baseball's great emancipator, held back Roy Campanella and Don Newcombe from joining the Dodgers at first because he didn't want his club to be *too* black. When he joined the Pittsburgh Pirates, Rickey didn't take his groundbreaking spirit with him, for the Pirates would own a mediocre record on developing nonwhite players in the 1950s.

What solidified the Red Sox as the chief plantation in baseball was what occurred as the 1980s approached. The game, and the country had progressed enough that all the talk about racism was a history lesson, or so went the rhetoric.

The Red Sox actually regressed. The air of discomfort sat on the franchise like a morning fog. Even black players who were established felt the effects. This wasn't supposed to be, for the piece of folklore that existed among black circles in Boston was that a black person who came to Boston with a reputation would generally be accepted. It was receiving the opportunity to climb through the ranks of a given industry in Boston—and yes, baseball was an industry—where blacks were thought to have experienced the most resistance.

Yet Ferguson Jenkins arrived in Boston with a strong reputation before arriving in Boston—he was a future Hall of Famer with seven twenty-win seasons with the lowly Chicago Cubs—languished on powerful Red Sox teams. Jenkins got in bad with manager Don Zimmer and the clash of egos—and the fact that Jenkins was chummy with Zimmer arch-enemy Bill Lee—ruined any chance of success in Boston.

Bob Watson, a slugging first baseman who would later become the first black general manager in baseball, arrived in Boston in a trade in 1979. He hit .337 in just 84 games before leaving town as a free agent.

Then the Red Sox hit rock bottom. When Watson walked, that left Jim Rice as the only black player on the club. In 1979! This did not go unnoticed in baseball, nor would it be considered a coincidence that Rice was isolated in a city embroiled in racial discord for the better part of that decade. If it were a one-year aberration, maybe Rice as the only black face on the Red Sox would have been a short-term story, but it wasn't. In 2000, the Oakland A's broke spring camp without a single African American on its roster, but those numbers would not totally reflect the internal policies of the team. The following year, the A's fielded four black players—Ron Gant, Jermaine Dye, Terrence Long, and Billy McMillon, as well as three black Dominicans—Miguel Tejada, Jose Ortiz, and Luis Vizcaino.

The Red Sox were different. Rice remained the only black on the club for nearly four years. Between 1979 and 1984, the Red Sox roster contained just two black everyday players. For contrast, the Pinky Higgins Sox of 1961 employed more black position players than the Haywood Sullivan Sox of 1983.

That alone raised eyebrows, returning blacks in the game to that old refrain, "What's going on up there?"

How a team that had enjoyed racial camaraderie in the 1970s in the face of busing—led by the ebullient, nation-building Tiant—could become known once more as The Plantation was not just the result of a quiet but constant racism but bigger, dangerous forces the Red Sox were painfully slow to recognize.

The first was a severe talent drain within the organization. Under Haywood Sullivan, a southerner who played football for Bear Bryant at Alabama, youth aged without replacement. A succession of drafts no longer brought harvest, but humor; between 1976 and 1980 the Red Sox farm system would produce weak prospects, while Lynn, Fisk, Burleson, and Tiant would all be gone by 1980 and Yastrzemski would enter his forties. The result was first seen in the standings. The Red Sox of the early 1980s, thought Peter Gammons, were not only the least interesting Red Sox team in more than a decade, but mediocrity following such high expectations threatened to squander the successes that revived the franchise.

The second was Sullivan's natural conservatism. The club became unimaginative in both the construction of the team and men hired to lead it. The success of the home run–hitting clubs of the late 1970s led the Red Sox to romance lead-footed, right-handed sluggers. The O'Connell teams were the most balanced in Red Sox history, a challenge to a Red Sox culture that would traditionally sacrifice speed, defense, and pitching for power. Sullivan's would lack chemistry, too, evidenced by the famous "twenty-five players, twenty-five cabs" description of the Red Sox.

When Zimmer flamed out and was ultimately fired after the 1980 season, Sullivan hired Ralph Houk, the old Yankee who managed the great 1961 and 1962 World Series championship teams. Houk was from a different generation. He came into the game in 1947 and as a manager would be known for having difficulty with the modern player. Houk was reared in the old Yankee system that in the 1940s and '50s notoriously avoided nonwhite prospects. Instead of finding a dynamic new manager, Sullivan lured Houk, who in his previous eight years of managing hadn't finished higher than fourth, out of a three-year retirement.

Houk alienated black and especially Latino players during the early 1980s. Few blacks, because of the biases in the game, sat on the bench. This policy was in itself insidious, for the white marginal player who spent his time learning on the bench was usually the type of player who would one day be considered a manager. Without similar black players, the pool for black managers would always be small. It was another example of how different the Red Sox were without O'Connell. If O'Connell's managers were difficult, they were also largely nondiscriminatory in their harshness toward players. Plus, all of them had played their careers completely in the integrated era. Dick Williams, Eddie Kasko, Darrell Johnson, and Don Zimmer were all managers under whom integrated teams played well. Zimmer and Williams were teammates of Jackie Robinson. Zimmer would take young Jim Rice under his wing. Eddie Kasko pleaded with management to have patience with Tiant. Cecil Cooper remembered Johnson from the minors being one of the first individuals in the Red Sox system with whom he would be himself without the feeling of fighting some racial stereotype.

Houk not only came up in the Yankee system as manager, which did not move quickly on integration, but he also moved from the Yankees to the Tigers, which like the Yankees would rarely develop gifted black players.

To Peter Gammons, Houk's generational tendencies were best illustrated through his relationship with a black utility player named Chico Walker. In the case of Walker, Gammons thought, there was always a white utility player who would play ahead of him. There was always a reason Walker never received a real opportunity to win a job.

"Chico Walker was a bright, intelligent player who could have had a much better career," Gammons said. "He had a lot to offer. But for some reason, and I think Houk was the reason, there was never a place for him in Boston. He went on to Chicago and had some productive years."

The Red Sox were plagued by a total mismanagement and the club's refusal to accept and exploit free agency. Sullivan's conservatism gave him an almost spiteful view of free agency, and he would become one of many owners who spent more time angry at its existence than dealing with a new economic reality. His inbred economic beliefs—widely considered extensions of the frugality of Jean Yawkey—were so flinty that they eroded the club's core. Tiant was let go in a nonsensical move that was the by-product only of Sullivan's unwillingness to give him more than a one-year contract. Under the reserve clause, Tiant noted, he would have stayed with the Red Sox, but they may have forced him to take a pay cut. Soon, Fisk, Lynn, and Burleson were gone, all because of the club's financial stinginess and inside jealousies. Good players left town, but few arrived in return.

It would be no coincidence that the owners who most quickly exploited free agency would be the mavericks instead of the institutional men. It was reflected in their franchises. While not always successful, men such as George Steinbrenner of the Yankees and Ted Turner of Atlanta embraced the new system and often clashed with the old guard of ownership, while as an owner, Tom Yawkey could always be counted on to maintain the game's status quo. Hence, Yawkey held firm to the game's color line, even when it was clear segregation was an outdated notion, and his loyalty to the game's past would hurt its present and future. Yawkey could always be expected to vote on the side of the league and the commissioner, even though his habit of overpaying players stood as something of a walking contradiction. Free agency would be no different, and the Red Sox would follow this trend in Yawkey's death.

If he was a giving owner, he did so on his own terms. He didn't like having to negotiate with ballplayers. In this sense, Sullivan followed the Yawkey path. He was clearly uncomfortable with the new baseball landscape, one where the players now used agents when negotiating contracts. The confrontation during the early days of this new world intensified when it became clear that the Red Sox at one point employed the most players in the league who used agents. When Curt Flood first challenged baseball's reserve system in 1969 and '70, it was Carl Yastrzemski who publicly denounced Flood for allowing his runaway greed to threaten baseball's salary structure. Years later, when the battle for player rights had been won and, because of him, players were enjoying salaries in the tens of millions of dollars, Flood would never forget Yastrzemski's rebuke of him. "He was one of the fortunate ones. He got to spend all of Tom Yawkey's money. I wasn't an owner's favorite."

Instead of being creative, he resisted. Sullivan may have been a former player, but Haywood Sullivan would not easily negotiate contracts with players.

Dan Shaughnessy thought of Sullivan as a petty and jealous man who could never quite escape from the truth that he was not a very good player and now had to pay more gifted players salaries he himself could never attain. Shaughnessy believed this failure on the part of Sullivan to be the first significant crack in the complete dismantling of the Red Sox.

Had O'Connell remained general manager a few years longer, thought Peter Gammons, racism would have been an unfortunate but distant part of its past, no different than the days when the St. Louis Cardinals and New York Yankees were considered just as racially resistant as the Red Sox. Now, the club's racism was alive, not just some remnant of the old days, and the Red Sox as an organization countered not with action, but denial. Red Sox were something they had never been: racially diverse, harmonious, and good. By the time Sullivan stepped down as general manager in 1984, the great deeds of Dick O'Connell would become a mere footnote, forgotten by everyone except the most perceptive followers of the franchise.

Dealing with race, especially the racial composition of the club, thought Glenn Stout, was something that had to be dealt with proactively. Failing this, it would be too easy to sink back into predictable patterns. If the Red Sox were not employing racist policies under Sullivan, they nonetheless were victims of a conservatism that exposed the club to charges of racism. Sullivan, thought Larry Whiteside, was not a racist in the sense of a Pinky Higgins, but was more defensive by nature, not prone to taking chances in personnel.

Then the power structure changed, too. For one hundred years, teams held the strings. You didn't want to play for your team? Fine, you could retire. Think you deserve a pay raise? Here's a pay cut for your trouble. What could you do? Play, or go become a plumber. Or go sell washing machines. Lady Kenmores were a fine choice.

With free agency, players could now test the market, make a pitch—or have their agents do it—to a team where they wanted to play. Reggie Jackson sought out New York and the feeling was mutual. They could also do something else, something new and not to be underestimated. Players could now decide who they *didn't* want to play for. For blacks, that often meant Boston. Baseball is a small business, and for thirty years, word had spread around the campfire. *Don't go there. Bad place for the brothers. City and team.* The whispers had always been there, but now players could voice their opinions freely, because they had power over their careers.

Racism had now affected the bottom line: winning. It always had, of course, but difference was the club was now paying the price for its transgressions. If the Red Sox needed a speedy leadoff hitter—say, a Tim Raines—it could only happen in a trade, because Raines often said he'd never play in Boston. Even a trade could be unlikely, because players with ten years of service and five with the same team could veto any trade. It was no small thing, because for the Red Sox, the past was the present, and players were only becoming more powerful.

This was all too bad for Lou Gorman, the new general manager, because Gorman came to Boston with the reputation for being a fair man. Whether Gorman knew it or not, he was always negotiating with black free agents with two strikes against him. What he walked into, though, was much bigger than his rep.

Players were available on the open market for all teams to bid upon, some of them the very top talent in the game. The teams that made vigorous efforts to sign these elite players were sending the message that racial characteristics were less important than fielding a championship team. They were also saying to their public—because in most cases a free agent signing would likely be the highest-paid player on a club—that they were unconcerned having a black or Latino player being the signature player of the franchise. It was, thought Peter Gammons, a real challenge to a team such as the Red Sox that had never had a black player be the signature player of the franchise. During his best years, Jim Rice may have been the best player on the team, but the Red Sox belonged in spirit and thrust to Yastrzemski. When Yastrzemski retired and Rice was the most visible member of the team, the Red Sox did not surround Rice with other high-priced black players, but instead isolated him, proof that faultlines still existed within the franchise. There was a feeling among blacks in the game that the Red Sox were reluctant—in a city that had suffered through busing—to tilt the racial balance of the team toward blacks and Latinos for fear that the city would not in those years embrace a largely minority team.

During the 1980s, the Celtics were the most successful team in the city, winning championships and appearing in the NBA finals five times in the decade. They were the Celtics of the Big Three. The trio of Larry Bird, Robert Parish, and Kevin McHale is still regarded as the greatest frontcourt in the history of the game.

For what it's worth, the Boston Celtics did break the color line in basketball and were the first team to crush many early taboos of the game. As history would have it, however, the Celtics' pioneering beginnings would be long forgotten, replaced with a reputation—like the Red Sox—as basketball's most racist team. The case of the Celtics is curious—made more curious by the ever-lurking specter of the city itself—and is perhaps at times even more perplexing than that of the Red Sox. They were the first team to hire a black player, Chuck Cooper, in 1950, three years after Jackie Robinson integrated baseball and nine full years before the Red Sox fielded a black. The Celtics were the first team to hire a black coach, Bill Russell. More significantly, the Celtics were the first to end perhaps the most damning of unspoken Jim Crow rules, the so-called "three-fifths" rule that said a white majority must always take the court.

Yet for all of the pioneering, the championships have embodied white basketball. It would be reputation both merited and unfair. The damning of the

Celtics—in the eyes of the African American—begins with the logo. The leprechaun represents all things Irish, which immediately suggests animus toward
blacks. In Boston, with its neighborhoods polarized along racial borders, the
Celtic leprechaun is of itself a strict line of demarcation. During the championship days, Boston blacks identified not with the winning Celtics but with
hated rival Philadelphia 76ers, Los Angeles Lakers, and later the Detroit
Pistons.

The great controversy, of course, stemmed from the racial makeup of the
Celtics. Jo Jo White, the high-scoring Celtic guard of the 1970s, felt that Red
Auerbach demanded—even as the league's demographics shifted overwhelmingly to a black majority—that the Celtics always be as racially balanced as possible. "Red was always smart enough to understand racism is there. That's why
Red always tried to keep it even—six whites, six blacks, maybe seven-five," he
said. "No matter what they'd say for the record, it was always assumed there had
to be a certain amount of whites on the team. You'd start with the blacks you
knew would make it and figure everyone else would be white."

The result was the Boston basketball team leading the league in white
guys. It's been a running joke for years: white plus height equals a job with the
Boston Celtics. The white guy will always find a home in a Boston jersey. If it
wasn't Jerry Sichting, it was Scott Wedman, or Greg Kite, Mark Acre, Jim
Paxson, or Fred Roberts.

Much truth exists within these jokes, but none of them were very funny. Jo
Jo White believed that Auerbach, in the words of Al Capone, was merely
responding to the will of the people. Boston, he believed, wouldn't support a
majority black team, even if it were successful. Cedric Maxwell, the irreverent
forward who played on two championship teams, voiced a similar theory: "If
you conformed your personality, if you became less threatening, you could be
embraced as one of the family. But if you maintained your blackness, if you
spoke out on an issue not relating to basketball, they got uneasy. Isn't that
ironic? The Celtics were at the forefront of bringing blacks into the league, but
now they are a team built through bias. They were selling to a particular audience, no question."

In any case, the Celtics—and Bird especially—were considered the white
man's lone NBA outpost. The Utah Jazz would periodically receive a similar
criticism. The racial underpinnings of the Celtics-Lakers epics of the decade
were obvious, especially in the 1987 finals, when the Celtics were the only team
in the NBA capable of fielding five white players on the court at the same time.
That the only team to be able to do this was located in Boston was not lost on
African Americans. It was virtually impossible not to be caught up in the unfortunate racial sideshow that took place. In *The Selling of the Green: The Financial
Rise and Moral Decline of the Boston Celtics,* an edgy, vengeful book intent on
exposing the Celtics, authors Filip Bondy and Harvey Araton wrote:

The Celtics' pattern is painfully obvious: whenever they have had enough strength among their top eight players to contend for a championship, they have stacked the back end of their roster with token whites. When they've struggled . . . they have brought in some black reserves to take a look at them in more active roles. From 1958 to 1965, the Celtics had only one black who might be classified as a little-used reserve: John Thompson. As times got tougher in the late sixties and seventies, this changed. From 1984 through 1987, at the peak of the Bird years and leading up to the stock sale and overall expansion plans, Carlisle and Kite, both white, received free glory rides to two championships from the end of the bench. At one historic juncture in 1986, ten of the 14 players on the Celtic roster were white.

Bird, the great player, was white. Just like Havlicek and Cowens before him. After Russell, no championship Celtic team has been led by a black player. And while Russell, the moody superstar, was respected, it was Cousy and Heinsohn who were beloved.

Meanwhile, Magic Johnson, Kareem Abdul-Jabbar, and James Worthy led the L.A. Lakers. There was no question which team black America would be pulling for. The Celtics, having finally bested the fast-improving Pistons in a raucous, exhausting seven-game series, saw Isaiah Thomas announce that if Bird were black, he would only be just one of many very good players instead of one of the game's immortals.

Thomas, facing the wrath of the NBA and its public relations machine, retreated quickly with a forced public apology. But Thomas only said what many black people had felt for years. It was what they felt when a white colleague rose quickly through the ranks in the office or when white players received more lucrative offers for endorsements. And this preference, this desire to consistently elevate white achievement, was the reason many blacks on the Red Sox never believed they would ever feel welcome in the city or the clubhouse.

For what it was worth, Bird, the superstar, was but a pawn himself, the generally innocent flashpoint for larger, muddier problems. In the end, the whole sorry story was unfortunate, for basketball in the 1980s was compelling enough without the enactment of a larger racial drama. Bob Ryan recalled the depressing feeling of covering the Celtics at Boston Garden with the knowledge that regardless of how well Bird played, the truly raucous applause always came when Kevin McHale, the white power forward, blocked the shot of a superstar black player. "I didn't necessarily want to think about it, but I knew the reason why."

The early 1980s saw total lethargy within the franchise, and likely set it back a generation. The Red Sox would constantly deny the existence of such a torpor. To Larry Whiteside, the only black member of the regular Boston baseball corps, this reversal under Sullivan's watch was not the result of his policies or a reflection of his personality. Whiteside liked Sullivan personally and would be one of the few members of the press that believed—without much concurrence—that Sullivan deserved nearly as much credit for the Red Sox development of black and Latino players during the late 1960s and early '70s as Dick O'Connell. Whiteside believed that Sullivan was simply the unsuspecting victim of forces beyond his control. He did not handle player movement or their newfound freedom very well, nor did he anticipate the effects of his frugality on Rice. While handicapped by his roots as a Deep Southerner, Sullivan was not, Whiteside believed, as much old fashioned racially as he was economically, but he was now paying the price because of perception. Nor was Sullivan the type of general manager who paid much attention to the racial makeup of his club, even though it would continue to be an issue with the team, especially in a city like Boston, which was still enduring the wrenching consequences of busing. In another time, such aloofness might be considered an asset. In Boston following O'Connell, it was an indictment.

For years, Sullivan and the Red Sox would respond to the mounting perception of the franchise with a wounded innocence. Perception was not reality. If there existed an unqualified belief that the lack of black players in the post-O'Connell regime was the by-product of a deeper, unresolved strain of racism within the Red Sox, proof would appear on a sunny spring morning in mid-March 1985.

TWELVE

Tommy Harper returned to the Red Sox as a coach in 1980. He had played fifteen seasons for seven different teams. He was not unlike many athletes who come through Boston, find they like it, and decide to stay. He bought a house in the Boston suburb of Sharon and felt at home.

The first year back in spring training told him little had changed. The players were certainly younger and he had aged, but when he walked into the clubhouse, the invitations were there. The Elks Club still invited the white Red Sox players, but not the blacks. It was the same old story he asked Larry Whiteside not to write in 1973.

For five more years, Tommy Harper seethed. He had gone to Red Sox management years earlier. He left the organization and came back only to find that nothing had changed. Back in 1972, he approached Haywood Sullivan, warning him that the Red Sox faced potential embarrassment. Sullivan listened, nodded attentively, and then adjourned the meeting. It lasted less than five minutes.

In the spring of 1985, enough was enough. In March, Michael Madden of the *Globe* broke the story:

WINTER HAVEN, Fla. - Sitting on the bar of the Elks Club, dead center in the middle as if it had been measured, was a large glass container. Scrawled on its side was the handwritten plea to support the restorations of the Statue of Liberty, a noble cause for which "The Elks have pledged $1 million." The jar was half full with paper money of all denominations.

A middle-aged man with glasses and a florid face who gave his name as Bill Carter was sitting on a barstool directly in front of the Liberty container. Amid the chaos and shouts that had erupted, this man was explaining why no blacks from the Boston Red Sox ever had been inside the Winter Haven Elks Lodge.

"Simple," he said. "Because we don't allow any niggers in here."

The Red Sox response, as Madden wrote in his exclusive, was one of edgy denial. Madden was writing a nonstory. Haywood Sullivan said Harper was merely stirring up trouble and, refusing to be part of such unimportant business, declined comment. Will McDonough would be dismissive of both Harper and his paper's scoop. "That place wasn't popular. Nobody even went in there. Nobody cared about that place. We made something out of nothing." Lou Gorman, the team's new general manager, said that the entire situation with the Elks Lodge was one that everyone on the Red Sox "kidded each other about."

Tommy Harper knew retribution would come in some way. He knew it too well, for he had been in the league too long to believe otherwise. He told Madden the same thing he told his wife Bonnie the night before he decided to talk about it: He was going to get fired. The game was too entrenched, too used to proceeding unchallenged, to accept such a breach of protocol. Talking about the ball club to the media carried a price. Being black and speaking out about the racial practices within the game was nothing less than career suicide. Nineteen years earlier, during spring training, Earl Wilson told the press of being refused service at the Cloud Nine bar and the Red Sox's subsequent refusal to back their own player. For his honesty, he received a one-way ticket to Detroit.

Tommy Harper knew the team's reputation was deserved. Reggie Smith knew it, too. Smith was one of the more unhappy players in Boston; before he was dealt to St. Louis he became increasingly more vocal about a double standard for white and black players.

Encouraging white players, coaches, and media to patronize a segregated establishment also damaged feelings within the clubhouse. If Tim McCarver and Curt Flood believed crossing the difficult racial boundaries of the 1960s together as a team made the St. Louis Cardinals more formidable in pressure situations on the field, it is doubtful the Red Sox—segregated with the blessing of management—ever possessed as much faith in each other.

When Madden wrote the story in 1985, the only surprise was that someone finally published what everyone around the ball club already knew. In 1979, Peter Gammons walked into the Red Sox offices and requested a sit down with public relations men Bill Crowley and Dick Bresciani. Jim Rice, then at the height of his power as a player, told Gammons that the Red Sox were issuing passes to the segregated Elks Lodge to the white players. Rice said he didn't care, but the practice was emblematic of the undercurrent that was afflicting the team as a whole. This, thought Gammons, could turn into an ugly, very embarrassing situation. The Red Sox were now in a competitive market for players; practices such as this would not make Boston the most attractive city for blacks, and the Red Sox already had the burden of trying to live down past sins. If the Red Sox couldn't figure out why black people looked upon them with such suspicion, Gammons thought, here is the proof.

Gammons recalled both Bresciani and Crowley recoiling at first, then assuring him that the Red Sox organization had ceased the practice of issuing cards to its players, coaches, and staff. Satisfied, Gammons never wrote the story, but in retrospect, he believes that taking the Red Sox at their word was one of the most questionable journalistic decisions he would ever make.

Gammons didn't feel duped by Bresciani or by Crowley. He believed that the Red Sox no longer encouraged the Elks Club. Gammons could have written the story without warning and embarrassed the Red Sox. In other cities, perhaps this is what precisely would have occurred. Gammons, however, gave the Red Sox an opportunity to clean its dirty laundry in-house.

What the club didn't do, Gammons felt, was sever ties with the Elks, officially and publicly. By the 1980s, the Red Sox and Elks Club maintained such close relations that many Red Sox players didn't need to consult public relations for a pass. They could call directly to Sullivan or the Elks Club and drop the Red Sox's name.

Larry Whiteside, too, knew of the Elks Club practices, for twelve years earlier, Harper had turned him on to the story. In retrospect, Whiteside echoed Gammons. He should have never let the Red Sox get away with it.

For the Red Sox to continue a relationship with a racist organization for two decades was another example of the team's lack of initiative or sensitivity to its own political position. The Red Sox simply weren't interested enough in considering the ramifications of patronizing the Elks Club. Haywood Sullivan was not a Pinky Higgins or Walter Briggs, thought Larry Whiteside, but more a man who simply could not recognize the speed of a changing world.

Considering the mediocrity of the previous four seasons, the 1985 Red Sox finished the season a hopeful 81–81. That was still, because they had won four more games the year before, considered a disappointment. Their two best pitchers were kids named Dennis "Oil Can" Boyd and Roger Clemens. The 1985 team wasn't good enough to contend with Detroit and Toronto, but it was better than the woeful squad of the previous season. The Kansas City Royals won the World Series that October by shocking the St. Louis Cardinals, and the Boston Celtics began at the end of 1985 what would be their last championship run.

After the winter meetings, December is a quiet time in baseball. Five days before Christmas, Tommy Harper received a letter from the Red Sox notifying him of his dismissal from the ballclub. There was no reason in the letter. He didn't need one.

The Boston *Herald* broke the story. Harper was out. The Red Sox maintained that a change was being made because of poor performance. The real reason, he knew, was that March day in Winter Haven when he told Mike Madden that the Red Sox were condoning racist practices and had been for nearly two decades. The outcome he predicted had come to pass.

Peter Gammons was not surprised. Gammons believed Harper angered Haywood Sullivan, who had been promoted to the team's chief executive officer. Gammons believed that Sullivan, a southerner who enjoyed long ties to the Elks Club, had been embarrassed by the bad publicity and reacted accordingly.

His rival, Will McDonough, believed Harper to be fired for aligning himself with Buddy Le Roux, who tried years earlier to wrest the team from Sullivan and Yawkey and had recently been ousted himself.

Harper violated the rules and paid the price. In baseball, you don't speak out. It was reminiscent of Carl Furillo, the old Brooklyn/L.A. Dodger who was released after winning the 1959 World Series with the club. Furillo was a casualty of change. The Dodgers had moved West, and it was time to begin a new history. Furillo maintained he was injured, and according to the rules of the major league player contract a player cannot be released when hurt. He has the right to his full salary. A dozen years earlier, Roger Kahn wrote about Furillo:

> The wine has soured. There are not going to be any more hurrahs for Carl Furillo, and those that he remembers if he truly remembers any, are walled from him by harsher, newer memories. His career ended in anger, lawsuits, frustration. He speaks of one prominent baseball official as "that prick." Another is a "lying bastard." One of his lawyers "ended up buddies with the guy I paid him 5,000 bucks to sue."
>
> When I found Carl Furillo, he was a laborer, installing Otis elevator doors of the World Trade Center, rising bright, massive, inhuman at the foot of Manhattan Island. We sat in a basement shack, beneath incalculable tons of metal and cement, and talked across ham sandwiches at lunch. Furillo seemed to enjoy being interviewed. He wanted to hear about some of his teammates, Carl Erskine and Preacher Roe. But mostly he wanted to spit rage. He believes that he has been cheated.

Furillo sued and he won, but the cost would be his career in baseball. The game has a way of silent retaliation. Furillo still had some baseball left in him, but suddenly he couldn't find a job in the majors. No one would hire him to even pinch-hit. There were no coaching jobs in the majors or minor league systems. He won his settlement but lost his future.

Officially, the Red Sox said Harper was fired for poor performance. In a particularly haughty moment, Gorman redirected any discussion of race as a motive in the firing by asking why no one wrote about the other coaches in the organization who were also reassigned. Between the lines, he questioned Harper's loyalty to the organization. The Boston newspapers chastised the Red Sox for both cowardice and retaliation.

Tommy Harper became Carl Furillo. He spoke out against the power and lost his job. The phone would not ring. *"Speak up and get bounced out?"* Luis Tiant's question echoed. Harper did, and was out of a job.

Tommy Harper would not want to talk about the days between Christmas and the first week of 1986. For him, the facts spoke for themselves. The meritocracy he thought existed in baseball was a lie. He had always thought of himself as a part of the game, but in truth he was an outsider, a figure foreign and distant to the men who have always run Major League Baseball. They were the ones who made the rules, signed the checks, and possessed the power. He would choose to downplay the subsequent events of his firing, but those days produced hard introspection and resolution. He could not let the Red Sox get away with this.

In January 1986, Tommy Harper filed a discrimination lawsuit with the Massachusetts Commission Against Discrimination, the same MCAD that felt the need to pressure the Red Sox to integrate with Pumpsie Green back in 1959. He charged that the firing was an act of retaliation by the Red Sox for his revelations about the Elks Club and the team. The suit was filed jointly with the federal Equal Employment Opportunity Commission (EEOC), which in 1986 was headed up by one Clarence Thomas.

Reminiscent of Eddie Collins' letter to Isadore Muchnick forty years earlier, the Red Sox issued a release about Harper's firing and the team's relationship with the Elks Lodge. It was a statement of condescension and denial, a complete repudiation of the experience that virtually every black player over the years had encountered with the Red Sox:

> Red Sox management abhors racism in any form and will never lend its name to racist practices, attitudes or institutions. Anyone who knows Red Sox management personally knows that that attitude prevails in their personal and public lives. The Red Sox's goal as an organization is to field a winning team and to bring Boston a World Championship. Racial bigotry has not played and will not play any role in the fulfillment of that goal.
>
> The Boston Red Sox have never had any official or unofficial relationship with the Elks Club of Winter Haven. The Red Sox have never solicited or procured passes to that club, do not subsidize or encourage in any way memberships in that organization by any employee, and have in fact actively discouraged employees from accepting gratuities from or patronizing that organization which maintains a racially discriminatory or restrictive policy. The Red Sox Baseball Club has not and will not take any action against any employee to discourage an employee's opposition to racism in any form.

The Boston press—Madden and Whiteside at the *Globe*, Joe Giuliotti of the *Herald*—tore at the Red Sox for insensitivity. Spring training approached and Harper remained jobless. The regular season revealed a powerful Red Sox squad that had matured into a first-place team. There would be no regret on the part of Harper. He followed his principles. There was no denying, however, that it had cost him his job.

No one on the Red Sox publicly backed him. Perhaps they were in the impossible position of being outraged but powerless, but more likely they saw no personal advantage in doing so. Jim Rice, the team's best player and elder statesman, was aloof. Young, fiery Oil Can Boyd declined comment, but was waging a racially tinged war with the team that would soon become very public. The recently acquired Don Baylor said the Red Sox had been a first-class organization. This was the public face. In private, Baylor seethed. He would feel the brunt of the Red Sox hesitation to make overtures toward blacks when years later he would be frustrated by the team's failure to interview him for a managerial position.

The Red Sox approached the All-Star break in first place. Roger Clemens was the best pitcher in baseball. On July 1, EEOC found in favor of Harper. The Red Sox fired Harper in retaliation for him exposing the Elks Club story, the report said, and went a major step further, claiming the Red Sox fostered a climate of antipathy toward minority employees. The Red Sox disputed the findings of the commission, but eventually settled out of court.

So Harper had won, but like Furillo twenty-five years before him, he was out of the game. The EEOC and MCAD may have vindicated him, but his victory did not translate into job opportunities. In fact, there were no jobs for Tommy Harper. Not with the Red Sox, or any major league club. The 1986 Red Sox went to the World Series without him. It was one of the most devastating times of his life. Tommy Harper found work as a mechanic on Brookline Avenue, so close to Fenway he could practically hear the cheers.

While Harper lived in exile outside of baseball, the black network inside of baseball filed another claim against the Red Sox. As sensational as the Harper situation was, Boyd exploded a week after the verdict when he wasn't chosen for the All-Star team, trashing the home clubhouse at Fenway and jumping the team. It was the culmination of a tense existence in Boston for the emotional Boyd. He disappeared for three days in a pennant race and even after returning would define the difficulties of a young black player in Boston.

Ron Washington, who played for six organizations, was also such a player. He was not a star. Indeed, he was a career utility man who needed to rely on guile and a hard-work ethic to remain in a manager's good graces. He recalled his early days with the Los Angeles Dodgers and Minnesota Twins and the great contrasts between the two organizations. The Dodgers, with their long integrated tradition, never gave Washington the feeling that his situation was predicated much on race. In Los Angeles, the best players generally played. If you played poorly in L.A., Washington recalled, "there were so many no. 1 draft picks up there breathing down your neck you wouldn't be around long."

Minnesota was different. Like the Red Sox, the Twins—and predecessors Washington Senators—had long earned a reputation for being a difficult organization for black players. Washington never felt comfortable there. He felt that he was never just a player, but a *black* player. This feeling gnawed on frail nerves. One error surely led to another. Mistakes were compounded by stern, often condescending lectures and the looming possibility of demotion. Relaxing and playing ball—perhaps the most important ingredient to major league success—were rarely possible.

It was this intangible feeling—the feeling of being different—that permeated the Red Sox clubhouse in the 1980s. It was a vibe first given off by Houk, defended by Sullivan, and later accepted by Lou Gorman, the Red Sox general manager from 1984 to 1993.

"I remember Boston," Washington said. "I never played up there, but you always knew what other brothers said about it. They said that it was a tough, tough place if you weren't a star. If you weren't a superstar, a guy whose talent couldn't be denied, you weren't going to get much of a chance."

The Red Sox did little to encourage black free agents to the team. During the 1980s, the Red Sox would field the fewest number of blacks of any major league team and would not sign a single black free agent. The organization was slow in general to embrace the new system, another of Leonard Koppett's examples that even outside of racial issues, the Red Sox have been a step behind change as a franchise. If the Red Sox's failure to sign black players contributed to the belief throughout the game that the team didn't want them, the Tommy Harper incident cemented that mindset.

By the end of the 1980s, racism and the Red Sox were inseparable topics. Lou Gorman was not the architect of the team's slide following the 1978 playoff game, but was now in control of the team's future. Gorman had come from the New York Mets, a team that historically would have its own trouble cultivating black players but in the mid-1980s had struck gold with Darryl Strawberry and Dwight Gooden. Gorman would forge a reputation as a tough contract negotiator and an unremarkable, if not dynamic, baseball man. He traded for Dave Henderson, the outfielder from the Seattle Mariners who became a playoff hero, as well as for Calvin Schiraldi, who became a playoff goat. He would become most famous for trading away a young prospect named Jeff Bagwell to Houston for journeyman pitcher Larry Andersen and by uttering the legendary sentence, "the sun will rise, the sun will set, and I'll have lunch," in reaction to a 1987 spring training contract dispute with Roger Clemens. Gorman was not considered by his peers or the media that covered him to harbor any real biases toward black players, but he would quickly find himself trapped by the tendency to sign right-handed sluggers to play in Fenway Park. Like Sullivan, the end result would also be the same. Black players simply did not fit into management's construction of its team.

It was a difficult issue, one that needed articulation but was delicate in nature. The Boston press would rarely cover race with nuance. After Harper, two episodes brought the subject back to the front burner. The first was that 1987 represented the fortieth anniversary of Jackie Robinson's major league debut. The second was Al Campanis' infamous television appearance. Campanis was the Los Angeles Dodgers executive who, when asked why there had been such little black advancement into baseball management, responded that blacks not only were not interested in managing or joining the front office, but also lacked the "necessities" to succeed.

Now a national issue, the Boston media focused more closely on the Red Sox as an organization. This, thought Glenn Stout, was precisely the problem with the Boston media's handling of racial issues. Race was covered as an *event*, no different than a fire or a big game, when it needed to be handled more as a constant, living part of the franchise. Racism in the game, he believed, was a cancer, and cancer must be monitored at all times. When ignored, it would spread. Stout also saw something more disconcerting in the press. By covering race in this fashion, the media would always be surprised at the existence of a racial divide, or explosive issue, and thus ill-equipped to report in any way other than with a reactionary tone.

On the Red Sox, the issue of the team's existing *culture* would give Stout's concern considerable weight. Where the Harper episode was an embarrassing, revealing moment, the true racial tension that existed within the framework of the Red Sox would be in the team's atmosphere, always a more difficult problem to corral. Racism in the organization existed more by feel than by pointing to a demagogue. Rice felt it, and the tension between blacks and the players such as third baseman Wade Boggs created a riff that ran through the clubhouse of some fairly successful teams. On the Red Sox of the 1980s, there was no unifying force such as a Luis Tiant that brought the natural cliques of a team together. Boyd struggled under the weight of being a young, emotional black player in Boston. The feeling would be similar to the wind; you can't see it, but you know it's there. Dave Henderson, who would be phased out in 1987 by Gorman to make room for a twenty-two-year-old black center fielder named Ellis Burks, left the Red Sox bitter and sympathetic to Rice's dilemma. Like Rice, for two seasons Burks would be the only black on the club; his isolation would be even more pronounced than that of Rice, for it was 1990 and the Red Sox were still hounded by a lingering racial dilemma. The dilemma would frustrate Gorman and the players, as well as the media covering the team.

If the press did not cover the overt racism that existed throughout the 1950s and '60s because of a generational divide and an overall lack of interest, the Boston press in the 1980s flailed at the issue. Here the landscape was more complex. There was no man like Pinky Higgins around. Black players as well as white were well paid, and with the exception of Harper, there were few clean examples—outside of the organization's consistent avoidance of free agents—that the organization was acting with malice toward black players.

Yet the issue persisted. Overall, the *Globe* would write about racial issues more apologetically, trumpeting the hire of a black player or the arrival of a player such as Burks. In a way, it spoke to the moral and strategic confusion in the paper's coverage.

The city's dueling giants, McDonough and Gammons, took different approaches to the story. McDonough wrote about race in April 1986, two and half months before the Harper verdict, by defending Tom Yawkey, who had been dead for a decade. "They smear the man and his memory with the legacy of Pumpsie Green and the presence of Tommy Harper," McDonough wrote, adding:

> I knew Tom Yawkey, the man to whom they trace all of his alleged racist history. I never thought he was racist. But I wasn't as close to him as Joe Cronin and Dick O'Connell were. These two former Sox general managers knew him as well as anyone in Boston. Over the years, I asked both if Yawkey ever suggested they do anything racist. The answer was no.

Peter Gammons believed the existing racial tensions on the club were apparent to anyone in the clubhouse on a daily basis, but were increasingly difficult to cover because the team's best player, Rice, refused to speak out in any way. His silence on the biggest off-field issue that faced the club would be a staple of his enigmatic career. Had Jim Rice taken an active role in voicing his thoughts on his only ball club, Gammons thought, history would have taken a dramatic turn.

THIRTEEN

On a hot, sticky spring day in March 2002, the Red Sox and New York Yankees played a meaningless exhibition game at Legends Field, the Yankees' pristine spring training home in Tampa, Florida. There would be many events of the day—the game itself, for one—that would be completely forgettable. The memorable moment occurred not during the game, but before it, when Jim Rice, the first and greatest black star in Boston baseball history, sat in the visitors' dugout, signed a few autographs, and then broke what was nearly 30 years of silence about what it meant to be the signature—and for some years the only—black baseball player in Boston.

He spoke not only with speed and passion, but with the urgency of a man who had much to say but little time in which to say it. The sudden urgency would in some way explain the Jim Rice of today, a man who during his years in Boston much preferred to let his bat—and the numbers he compiled with it—represent him at all times.

If the words had been there during all these years of grudging silence, Rice chose to keep them buried deep inside of himself, as protection for a man who in his playing days stood at such a distance from the rest that he cut a figure that would be at all times intriguing, menacing, and irritating.

The Jim Rice of this day was forty-nine years old, far removed from the tumult and confrontation of being young, powerful, and central to the fate of the franchise, yet he still carried a powerful presence. He is a coach in the club's minor league system, and he is in the process of engineering a new and interesting course for himself as he settles into the other side of middle age. He is not a new person, reinvented and affable, but the window into his considerable experience no longer seems fastened by dead bolt.

The hair is still black. The build is solid and intimidating, but softer. His midsection, once cast iron, now sags and presses slightly against a tight uniform. Trails of gray touch his facial hair, yet he is still formidable. The forearms bulge, thick and sinewy, making it easier to drift back to that day in Detroit when Rice snapped a bat in two trying to check a swing.

Perhaps more than any other baseball player in Boston's history, Jim Rice represents the key to many questions. He is the bridge that has spanned virtually all of the post-1967 eras. He was there for Tom Yawkey and Oil Can Boyd. He was there before free agency and for many years was the highest-paid member of the club during it. He wore the Red Sox uniform during the darkest hours of racial chaos within the team and its city. His career began with busing and ended a few weeks before a man named Charles Stuart put the city once again on the brink of tearing itself apart.

For this, much would be demanded of him, for everyone wanted a piece of Jim Rice, the important part, in order to better mold him into what they needed him to be that day, that year.

"I had a job to do. I wanted to do my job and go home. That's it. I didn't want to be the highlight. Reggie Jackson enjoyed it. I didn't. The Boston Red Sox were my team. I wasn't going to go out there and draw attention to myself all the time because I didn't enjoy that. But if you asked me a question about what I did or how we did, I would answer it. But I didn't kiss anyone's butt. I got mad when you asked me stupid questions. I wouldn't answer stupid questions. I *won't* answer stupid questions."

With Rice, as with so many others in the city before and after him, it would always come back to race, to knowing what he knows. In the late 1970s and early '80s, black players came to Fenway Park sympathizing with Rice about his difficult lot; being a black athlete in a city suffering in a racial maelstrom. When he became a superstar, the best player in the American League, and talk began of his one day ascending to the Hall of Fame and baseball immortality, another unwanted request also came: candor about race. He would respond to the demands with a fierce independence. He would fight stubbornly and bitterly to maintain his privacy and his sense of identity, refusing to be characterized always as black first and Jim Rice second. This is his right, he says.

Race would always be the flashpoint. Jim Rice knew it, for the heavy racial cloud that sat just above the franchise from the time he was an infant made just playing baseball and enjoying his gifts impossible. The more he resisted being defined by race, the more his silence amplified his blackness. It was a decades-old dance that made all partners equal parts weary and angry.

Avoiding race would be impossible, and the result would be a bitter clash between those who wanted to know him and his desire not to be known, or even understood. Clark Booth believed Rice to be more complex and elusive than the usual assessment that Rice was simply difficult for no reason. To Booth, Rice's 16 seasons represented something of a lost opportunity, that there would be no telling what Rice could have accomplished in an environment that wasn't so totally dominated by race.

In a sense, Jim Rice was Ted Williams, fighting futilely against race the way Williams fought the shift, believing at some basic level that instead of relenting—once, just once—he could somehow overcome a world that was so much larger than he, by sheer stubbornness. Fate put him in that position, and Jim

Rice would spend his whole career and the better part of three decades in Boston fighting his fate of being the only person in the world who could explain what it meant to be the greatest black baseball player the city of Boston would ever see.

Everyone, it seems, owns a strong reaction to Jim Rice. He is a man who does not elicit neutrality. Don Zimmer, his former manager, would call Rice his "favorite ballplayer," one he "loves like a son." Ken "Hawk" Harrelson, his old Red Sox teammate and golfing buddy, would chew on a toothpick during an A's-White Sox broadcast in 2000, offering only three words to define Rice: "Hall of Famer." Ellis Burks, who was a young center fielder during Rice's final playing days, credits Rice with being one of the greatest influences on his baseball playing, and he would only speak with reverence of the secret side of Jim Rice, the man who counseled young black players about their more difficult road in Boston, of the special challenges that came with being black in a city in the throes of confronting its most difficult social dilemma.

His rivals praised him. To a man, his New York Yankee foes offer the type of reverence worthy of a dangerous opponent. Lou Piniella, the Seattle Mariners manager, called Rice "fearsome." Chris Chambliss shook his head, nodding with the respect reserved for an old adversary. Willie Randolph would speak with deference to Rice's tremendous strength. Reggie Jackson called Rice "the most destructive hitter in the American League." Roger Clemens, a teammate in Boston in the 1980s, called Rice a "hero, someone who taught me how to be a big-leaguer." Don Baylor, his teammate on the 1986 World Series team, engaged in heated battles with Rice over what he considered to be Rice's lack of leadership and selfishness. Yet Baylor possessed deep respect for Jim Rice the player. "He did a lot for that town. He was the guy on that team you never let beat you," Baylor said. Nineteen eighty-six hero Dave Henderson offers the most colorful of compliments. "Jimmy," Henderson says, "was a bad motherfucker."

This is how baseball people talk about Rice. They focus solely on his craft. They talk about the strength, that he never lifted weights yet was one of the top strongmen of his era. They talk about the time Matt Keough hit him in the back with a fastball in Yankee Stadium and Rice responded with a home run that seared through the air as if it were a meteor. They talk about the check swing that night in Detroit and that he did it *again* in Baltimore.

This is the simplest way, for to expand beyond is to plunge into the other side of Jim Rice, the Rice of legend whom more than one reporter would mercilessly call a "complete asshole." Rice—in breaking the ironclad code of solidarity between blacks in the game—was considered "the wrong kind of brother" who "never cared about anything or anybody but himself." He would be the Jim Rice above casual courtesy or concern, distant and beyond reach.

Talking about Jim Rice's talents on a baseball diamond left little room for debate. If you were there, you saw it: the home runs, the power, and the awesome ability. If you weren't, ask someone who was, and they'll tell you that quite simply, Jim Rice was the most fearsome hitter of his time. Bob Ryan, who would be as powerful a journalistic figure in Boston as Will McDonough and Peter Gammons but used his influence to write lively, enjoyable columns about the events on the field instead of as an industry insider, consistently voted for Rice for the Hall of Fame. He did this despite the contention that Rice has not been immortalized because he could be so difficult with the writers that they are serving him eternal payback for years of slights.

In Boston, Jim Rice resembled Paul Bunyan, a character more fit for myth than for reality, someone who did things that simply weren't possible. Carl Yastrzemski was revered, but few people tell stories about Yaz the way they talk about Rice. Unprovoked in a circle of writers at the winter meetings in Dallas in 2000, Peter Gammons mentions a towering Rice home run. A few weeks later, Gammons retells the famous Leigh Montville story in the *Globe* of how Rice grew up in the segregated city of Anderson, South Carolina. When Rice was a teenager, the city planners redrew the district lines in order for Rice to attend the local white high school, and thus exploit his phenomenal athletic talents. When Rice graduated, the lines were redrawn back to their original specifications to uphold the previous patterns of segregation. When Rice was a rookie with the Red Sox in 1975, Montville went to his home in Anderson, S.C., and wrote a flattering portrait of Rice, his family, and of course his superhuman strength. Harrelson would laugh in the television booth in Oakland about the time he bet a younger Arnold Palmer their comparative paychecks that Rice could out-drive Palmer on a golf course in Florida. Palmer watched Rice hit a golf ball and demurred.

Reporters, in a curious blend of bitterness and awe, would describe the difficulty and fear that came with interviewing him. Bill Madden, the venerable baseball columnist for the New York *Daily News*, still hasn't forgotten a Rice slight from 20 years ago. Clark Booth believed Rice to be the one athlete in Boston with whom he wished a better relationship had been formed. Everyone, it seems, would have a story.

Recalling the exploits would be the easy part of Rice. To step beyond the game, into the part of Jim Rice he doesn't want known, is to plunge into a deeper, murkier space.

In the spring of 1975, Jim Rice began a rookie campaign that offered only a glimpse of his marvelous capabilities, and suggested that he might be one of the greatest power hitters who ever played the game. Rice possessed tremendous ability. He was unusually strong, stood six-foot-two, and weighed 200 pounds.

Hank Aaron once said that if anyone would break his home run record, he thought it would be Rice. He hit .309, drove in 102 runs, and hit 22 home runs. His manager in the high minors was Joe Morgan, who once said Rice was the best baseball player he had ever seen. Rarely had a player possessed such raw power and acute hitting ability. For Rice, hitting was in the wrists. He choked up on the bat, a rarity in a power hitter.

Then a Vern Ruhle fastball late in the 1975 season broke Rice's wrist and kept him out of the playoffs and the World Series. It would be one of the most profound disappointments of his career.

Zimmer was a coach on the 1975 team and would soon be Rice's manager. In Zimmer's eyes, Rice was the ultimate ballplayer who did everything an old-school baseball man wanted. Zimmer played with Jackie Robinson for the Dodgers in the 1950s, and the thought of the tough professionalism of those Brooklyn teams reminded him of Rice's work ethic. He came to the ballpark on time and never argued with coaches. He was, in Zimmer's estimation, the rarest of creatures: a modern ballplayer with old-fashioned values. He played hurt and didn't give his manager any lip. He wanted to improve as a ballplayer and in time became a solid left fielder. Jim Rice *worked.* Zimmer most liked his respect for authority, a quality in lesser supply in players and society after the 1960s. There was much incentive for this, as Rice was the third in a dynasty of Boston left fielders. For 50 years spanning World War II to the fall of the Berlin Wall, the Red Sox fielded only three: Ted Williams, Carl Yastrzemski, and Jim Rice.

To understand Rice is to sweat, to believe in a work ethic that was almost Puritan in nature. There would be no greater honor to him than to play in pain; he saw no greater weakness in others than those who did not. Life was easy, Rice believed, when a person was healthy, but a man's character could only be realized when he competed when less than healthy. It would be an inflexible barometer he set for himself and his teammates.

"What does being in the lineup mean to your teammates? Everything." Rice would be animated, for durability was the ultimate badge. "Playing hurt, showing that you are taking the responsibility to help your team, that it matters to you that you want to be the person to at least try to drive in those runs when your team needs them. And what happens if you don't? Then you stand up for that. But the other guys are there, and they see you playing through it."

For a time, playing in Boston did not appear to affect Rice. He was at times proud that at home in the South, the cities had already dealt in large degree with the racial issues that were percolating in Boston. "I never did see the toughness that came with playing in Boston. I know other guys heard it. Nigger this, nigger that. I never got any of that. That was never my experience. I know it was for guys like Reggie Smith. But it wasn't like that for me. When I came to Boston, I saw that it wasn't only black and white, but everybody was so separated. The Irish didn't get along with the Italians, and they didn't get along with the Jews, and they didn't get along with the blacks. And inside, the blacks from the Caribbean didn't get along with the blacks from the South. And I thought to myself, 'Oh, no! What is this place?'"

But as his position with the team grew more important, Rice found himself constantly in the position of spokesman on racial issues. If Reggie Smith could never find comfort in Boston because of its sharp racial divisions, Rice would rely on the team and his insulation as a player. While some blacks would always sense uneasiness about the city, Rice would protest that during his entire career the Red Sox treated him well and created an environment that made him feel welcome. He remembered Tom Yawkey fondly, as a man of warmth, though by the time Rice arrived at the major leagues in 1975 Yawkey was dying of leukemia. He was a product of the Red Sox farm system, the first home-grown black player that possessed superstar quality. Being a player insulated Rice from the busing violence that marred the city during those years.

The 1975 club under Dick O'Connell was integrated beyond mere numbers. It was one thing to have black players on a club, quite another for them to be signature, contributing members. Tiant, thought Peter Gammons, was the pivotal figure, for his gregariousness and personality brought difficult personalities closer together. He wasn't a clubhouse lawyer or a person like Bill Lee, who volunteered controversial opinions to the world outside of the game, angering players who saw his act as merely a way to get his name in the paper on days he wasn't pitching.

Almost from the start, Rice was an intimidating figure. His worth to the team was immediate and great, and like other great players on winning teams, he was thrust into a position of spokesman. Yet Rice was different, for 1970s Boston, there was no escaping the racial dynamic that was being played out in the city. Nor could he avoid the past history of the Red Sox, no matter how much he wanted. He may have been treated well by the Red Sox, but the specter of Reggie Smith and Bill Russell, black men who did not warm to city, hung over him. Furthermore, Rice was a test case of sorts for a media that was undergoing the sharp change of learning how to deal with black athletes. There would be no escape from the racial divide. Rice could see it, for it was happening in the contrasting styles of himself and Fred Lynn.

There would exist a rivalry between the two young outfielders, enhanced by Rice's injury that kept him out of the World Series, and Lynn's winning of both the 1975 Most Valuable Player and Rookie of the Year awards, one of which likely would have gone to Rice had he not been injured.

As the seasons progressed, there would be little question that Rice was the superior player. He was stronger, and after winning the MVP award in 1978, vindicated. Lynn was consistently beset by injuries, a weakness in Rice's eyes.

Lynn, however, was the more glamorous player, and deep down, in the private spaces of his heart, Rice was angered by the perceived double standard that the person who was clearly the fulcrum of the team did not receive the adulation that was usually reserved for white players. Lynn played center field, the sexier position, and he possessed a dramatic flair that the Boston media gravitated toward. Plus, Lynn was white and Boston had never embraced a black player as it would a white.

A disturbing racial drama was being played out between the two men, one that embittered Rice. Rice had done what was asked of him. He came to the ballpark, was in the lineup every day, and produced.

What it really came down to was this: Jim Rice understood the hero game, and he didn't like it. He wasn't an idiot. White players would always get the credit, the accolades, the warmth. Those fans may want their kids to grow up with my skills, thought Rice, but did they want them to be *me?* How much do they know what I am?

Black ballplayers could be respected, even idolized, but if there was a white player who could do anything a black player could do, he would be elevated high up and above the rest. He would be supernatural. Look at Mantle. He was fast, but was he faster than *any* player who ever lived? No, that wasn't it. It was that Mantle could run like a black man, in that class. That made him a god in the eyes of the hype machine. That was the hero machine at work, and you had to be white for that kind of send-off. Had Rice been white, he would have been lauded as a modern-day Gil Hodges: strong, silent, important. Being black, though, meant Rice was moody, arrogant, and distant.

"Here I am coming into a situation. They had Freddy Lynn. He was supposed to be the Golden Child. Mr. Everything. And then here comes this nigger from South Carolina who was every bit as good, and was one of the top five players in the American League, and it was a different story. It didn't work out the way everyone thought it would. They didn't know what to do. I wasn't white. I wasn't Irish and I wasn't from Boston. But I knew the rules. I wasn't going to do or say anything that was going put what I had in jeopardy."

To a person such as Jim Rice, there could be no greater affront to his idea of professionalism. Dan Shaughnessy of the *Globe* was a first-year reporter, covering New England high schools in 1975. He and Rice would always have a contentious relationship. To him, it was not race that kept Rice away from greater acceptance, but Rice's own difficult personality. Sean McAdam covered the Red Sox for the *Providence Journal* in Rice's final season. He believed Rice chafed at not receiving his due. "Maybe it was convenient to play them off as polar opposites," McAdam said. "If Lynn was the carefree Californian, Rice was naturally opposite, the sullen black guy. I always thought his bark was bigger than his bite, but at times he almost seemed to conform to the perception. He never let people see he was having fun. He still harbors a lot of bitterness."

Yet much of what Rice endured was no different than the common experience of being black in American society. How to navigate the harsh waters of a white world that was largely uncomfortable with an independent black presence would be the challenge not only for the Reggie Smiths and Jim Rices of the world, but for any black person trying to find a living space in the larger culture.

Many reporters who covered the team thought Rice tried too hard to assimilate into the Red Sox culture, a culture that certainly did not place much of a premium on accentuating one's blackness. To some observers, he went so far that he seemed to shun virtually any aspect of baseball life where it would be an asset to be black. He never publicly questioned the country club atmosphere of the team, even as he saw many black players leave the Red Sox embittered. He never spent much time cultivating inner-city programs—outside of donating money—and lived in the suburbs for his entire career. Some people in the game would say the most offensive thing that could be said about a black person, that Rice "wanted to be white." Reporters said it. Even Margo Adams, Wade Boggs's scandalous mistress, said it about Rice, reminiscent of when Bill Lee said the same thing about Reggie Smith.

"Reggie did his best to act like a white man trapped in a black man's body. It was a strange and sad thing to watch." Lee, one of the most divisive players on the team, recalled that Yastrzemski "had become an institution in Boston, a status Reggie wanted but one he knew he could never reach." Of course, Lee's cruelty was matched only by his ego. He rode Smith, saying that Smith mimicked Yaz so much that people would call him "Carl Reggie Smith." Lee said this seemingly without the knowledge that Smith's first name was Carl. His middle name was Reginald.

It would be on these points where Rice would draw inward, justified and angry to be corralled into a city's—and a culture's—obscene fascination with race. If that's how it was going to be, Rice wasn't going to cooperate. Just leave him the hell alone and save the racial commentary for the psychologists.

Rarely, thought Clark Booth, was there enough introspection, on the part of both whites and blacks, to understand all that was being asked of a twenty-five-year old kid from South Carolina. The result would be an inevitable clash.

"The only thing he had going for him was that he was the first black, homegrown superstar," Booth said of Rice. "And that's not enough. You can't make a person a leader. Leadership has very little to do with experience, and Rice had little world experience outside of baseball. It had nothing to do with temperament or endowment in terms of ability, and when you think about it, it was all patently unfair."

Rice's response would be varied, but always hot. He would collide with the media, or he would say nothing. Years later, before the Red Sox and Yankees took the field in Tampa, Rice was incredulous.

"Why was it up to me? Look at the odds. Was there a racial problem in Boston before I got there? There was and there was one during, and there was one after. I was employed by the Boston Red Sox. If there is a problem with race on the Boston Red Sox, and you need someone to address that, the Red Sox need to do that part. I needed to take care of myself and my family first. Those problems existed long before me, and the people who wanted me to be the one to talk about didn't need me to. Why do you need me to explain something you already know exists?"

What Rice wanted, thought Luis Tiant, was what most people wanted, and that was to enjoy the freedom to live. Rice didn't want the burden of responsibility of speaking for his race on political issues, nor did he enjoy being expected— simply because he was black—to connect with blacks from the inner city. "It is very difficult," said Peter Gammons, "for blacks to be emotional in this town." Rice did not want to be labeled, but in a place as racially charged as Boston and playing for a team that had little to no experience in dealing with black players as individuals, it was inevitable that he'd be stereotyped. Rice loved to play golf, yet instead of it being one man's passion, the game itself was proof in some quarters that he had lost his way as a black man. He lived in the suburbs, as do millions of people. For Rice, though, it was another example that he was distant from his people, that he wasn't from the North or, for that matter, from the inner city.

He was young, athletically gifted, and rich, and he seemed to have wanted to carve out an identity for himself instead of a prearranged destiny. Perhaps Tiant would say it best: "He didn't want to be anyone or anything but Jim Rice."

Rice had already been at war with the Boston media. Clark Booth believed the first, irreparable cracks came after Leigh Montville, the Boston *Globe* columnist, went down to Rice's hometown in Anderson, South Carolina, during Rice's rookie year of 1975. It was September, and the Red Sox were streaking toward their first pennant in nearly a decade behind Rice and Fred Lynn, two rookies who were expected to play a lifetime in Boston.

The story appeared, coincidentally, during the same week as the city's busing crisis entered its early violence. Though it was a glowing portrait of a budding superstar, Rice hated the story, convinced that a prying media had no right to speak to his family or friends. "He was absolutely infuriated that Leigh went to his home and talked to his family," Booth said. "And it was a great piece that made him look terrific. To him, though, it was a clear and unforgivable invasion of his privacy. He just didn't understand how it all worked."

Rice himself leans back on the dugout bench. The back of his neck is quickly developing glistening beads of sweat on a sweltering day. The first affront came from Clif Keane and Larry Claflin, two veteran reporters who hosted a radio show titled *Clif-n-Claf.* Keane was waiting to interview Rice, who was apparently out shagging fly balls. When Rice returned, he found an annoyed Keane, who told him, in so many words, not to get too high.

"It was Clif Keane. He looked at me and said to me 'I can make you and I can break you,' and I looked him right in the eye and I told him, 'You can't do anything to me.' That was it. That was the beginning."

For a short time, Rice had been cordial with the media, a departure from his future reputation as a formidable interview. Then, after the confrontation with Keane, Zimmer saw a harsh change in Rice's demeanor. "He put his head down after that," Zimmer said. "He wasn't going to give anyone a break."

From that day forward, Rice found himself embattled with the news media. Zimmer remembers trying to offer Rice advice on how to deal with the media, whose members had long memories and held one trump card over difficult, talented players: the Hall of Fame. The Baseball Writers Association of America voted for the Hall of Fame, and if Rice wasn't careful, Zimmer told him, "some of those vindictive bastards will get you back."

The strategy was simple, Zimmer told Rice. Treat the good ones well and, in his words, "fuck the rest." On the whole, Zimmer told him, the reporters weren't bad people, but Zimmer recalled being frustrated that Rice appeared to retrench further. "If I have to kiss their asses," he told Zimmer, "I don't want to get in." It would be a stalemate that would never be resolved.

During the latter half of the 1970s, Rice put up monstrous offensive seasons while the Red Sox, lacking in pitching depth as always, fell short of the postseason. Rice won the MVP in 1978 with one of the great seasons in the game's history, but the Red Sox faltered at the end to the Yankees in a most memorable one-game playoff. Peter Gammons always wondered how after that season—one of the greatest in baseball history—Rice still could never seduce, and win the public.

To Rice, the reason was that Gammons simply didn't get it. Rice wasn't going to be a clown for the media and for white fans who could only relate to a smiling black face. He remembered Yaz brooding, but never paying a price for the moodiness. Sure, it wasn't all racial, but race was a big part of Boston life.

Rice would always be a difficult personality. Cecil Cooper did not envy the media, whose job it was to speak to Jim Rice every day with news-producing questions. "Jimmy was my boy," Cooper said. "But he was not an easy man to know. He was one of those hard-to-get-to-know guys." He withdrew, answering questions with only the most terse of responses, offering little more. Luis Tiant felt he and Rice got along, which is to say they didn't clash. He remembered no colorful anecdotes about Rice, during the high times of success or even the relaxed moments of major league life. Like the media that covered him and his peers, Tiant would describe Rice by returning to his strength. "He hit the ball so hard you'd be afraid he'd kill someone," Tiant said. "So strong."

Inside of Rice, thought Clark Booth, was a fierce racial pride that was completely misunderstood in Boston. Rice, Booth believed, did not want to alter his personality in order to be seen favorably by a Boston press that traditionally had a difficult time understanding the great cultural distances that often existed between black players and the media. He had seen it with other players during his career with the Red Sox, where blacks acted in the most stereotypical of ways to be looked upon favorably by whites. Booth recalled a particularly embarrassing moment when George Scott, the boisterous Red Sox slugger, appeared on Keane and Claflin's radio show once during the late 1970s. The interview disintegrated into slapstick, and Keane and Claflin both made derogatory comments about blacks eating watermelon and fried chicken, laughing and joking the whole time. If it was a risky, humorous bit, it also suggested the dangerous and outdated attitudes toward blacks and the sort of minstrel behavior that black players were often forced to assume to gain acceptance. When Scott played along with the bit, Rice grew even more upset.

When Booth reported the story for television, it was a painful moment for Larry Claflin, who was deeply hurt that Booth had portrayed him as a racist. For Claflin never saw himself in that way. Professionally, he was one of the only reporters in Boston writing about race as a real topic in regard to the Red Sox during the 1960s. Claflin was the old *Herald* writer who wrote of Earl Wilson's trouble in spring training. When Claflin once asked manager Pinky Higgins why Pumpsie Green hadn't made the team out of spring training way back in '59, Higgins called him a "nigger lover" and spit tobacco juice on him. Claflin thought of himself as the one reporter back in those days that was unafraid to confront the Red Sox on racial issues.

To Booth, Claflin had insulted an entire race by reviving the ugly stereotypes that prevailed in a previous era. He had crossed a line that in a new and changing world was no longer funny. Claflin may have believed the radio show with Scott was harmless humor, but it also illustrated how deeply rooted stereotypes were in the mind of some white journalists. Claflin, humiliated and angry, wrote a piece in the Boston *Herald* defending his record as one of the few racial champions in the city. More than that, Claflin was devastated. As a result of the incident, the two would not speak again.

It seemed there would be a natural alliance between Larry Whiteside and Jim Rice, for Rice was the only black on the Red Sox during many years and Whiteside the only black in the Boston press corps, but Rice's closest ally was the *Boston Herald*'s Joe Giuliotti. Rice and Giuliotti on the surface would appear to be an unnatural alliance, for Giuliotti was an Italian from the blue-collar neighborhood of East Boston. East Boston in the mid-1970s represented one of the most resistant neighborhoods to school integration, and Giuliotti was no strident left-winger politically, but he understood the world in class terms. Yet the two had more in common, for both Rice and Giuliotti tended by nature to avoid the spotlight, and they were suspicious of those who sought it. For these two men, the work itself, not the trappings of stardom, were the reward.

For a time, Whiteside and Jim Rice got along well. With other black players, Whiteside enjoyed a better relationship than his white counterparts, for
they could also commiserate about their common difficulties. In this regard,
Rice would be different. Whiteside would enjoy no special favor with Rice.
Indeed, the opposite would often occur.

Their relationship would change after a famous clash in Baltimore.
Whiteside wrote a story about how Jim Rice called himself "Jim Ed" to some
people and "Jim" to others.

In Whiteside's retelling, the story appeared to be fairly innocuous. When
he arrived at the ballpark, however, Whiteside found Rice furious. What
resulted was a shouting match between the two, with each telling the other, "Go
fuck yourself." Whiteside saw Rice by the batting cage, and he left the
Baltimore dugout and sidled up to Rice. They were the only two blacks around,
Rice on the roster and Whiteside in the press box, he reasoned. Therefore, he
told Rice, they really shouldn't be carrying on with such animosity. It was bad
for both. Rice responded by giving Whiteside an earful. He didn't need to patch
anything up with anyone, especially with a meaningless reporter like Whiteside.
Whiteside responded with a ferocious broadside, "I don't need this from you. I
don't take any shit off the white boys and I'm not going to take any off a lowlife
nigger like you," and walked away.

After the game, Rice stormed at Whiteside, all five-foot-eight of him,
grabbed him by the collar, and lifted him off the ground. Joe Giuliotti, the beat
man at the *Herald*, stepped in the way of Rice and needed help from center
fielder Tony Armas to pry Rice off of Whiteside. "I saw my life flash before my
eyes," Whiteside remembered. "We used to be closer, but things were different
after that."

Days later, Rice made an attempt at an apology. During a game, Rice
instructed Tommy Harper to call up to the press box and clear the air.
Whiteside would have none of it. If Rice wanted to apologize, he should make
the phone call himself. "Larry's position was 'let him get on the phone and do
it himself,'" Giuliotti recalled. "He wanted Rice to be a man about it."

Rice's inherently difficult demeanor didn't help. Jeff Horrigan, a young
reporter for the *Union Leader* of Manchester, New Hampshire, remembered Rice's
contempt for those reporters who covered the team every day. He acted, Horrigan
remembered, as if he didn't care about what was said or what was written about
him, yet always knew how each paper had covered him. Horrigan hated Rice's
annoying habit of making snide comments to each reporter about the day's stories.
Ironically, Horrigan was one of Rice's biggest supporters, yet that carried no weight
with Rice. The people who respected his skills were enraged by his arrogance.

Rice would be known by the national media as the most difficult baseball
player to deal with. As with his enormous strength, everyone has a story along
these lines. In 1979, Tom Boswell, the respected reporter for the *Washington*

Post, watched Rice break up an argument between Rick Burleson and an umpire in Baltimore, and in the process of being a peacemaker, Rice inadvertently knocked the umpire to the ground. After the game, Boswell asked Rice how it felt for the reigning MVP to knock an umpire to the dirt, to which Rice replied along the lines of, "If someone asks me another stupid question like that, I'm going to pick them up and throw them into the garbage." The result was Boswell writing a story that said Rice threatened his life and he had never been so scared. To Rice, the affair was another example that he could not trust the media to retell a story, that he would always be portrayed unfairly.

He rarely helped himself, as illustrated in perhaps the most famous clash with a writer of Rice's career. Steve Fainaru was a twenty-four-year old reporter for the Hartford *Courant*, and at that age, covering the Red Sox was a heady assignment. The team had lost a close game to the A's, and the writers were surrounding catcher Marc Sullivan. Rice dressed next to Sullivan, and Fainaru recalls spillage around Rice's locker. Rice responded, in Fainaru's words, with the "usual shit." While reporters interviewed Sullivan, Rice chirped in the direction of the media pack. They were scum. They were maggots. At that moment, Rice and Fainaru met eyes, and Rice was offended by the look on Fainaru's face. "I must have had a look of total disdain," he said. Rice went on the offensive.

"You got a problem with me?" he asked.

Fainaru replied, "No."

Rice went to the shower. Fainaru was humiliated and angry. Why, he asked himself, did Rice have to treat him in this way? And why, he wanted to know, was he expected to accept this humiliation when he wouldn't in a normal situation? Like most of the reporters, he was as sick of Rice as Rice was of them. When Rice returned from the shower, Fainaru approached him and explained that if he was going to harass people, he should expect it in return. At that instant, Rice grabbed Fainaru, ripping his shirt. Two players, Dwight Evans and Mike Greenwell, intervened. Greenwell escorted Fainaru out of the clubhouse, advising him to leave, lest he risk being killed by Rice. Neither man ever apologized to the other.

"People say he apologized to me, but he didn't," Fainaru said. "And I certainly didn't apologize to him. I never felt I had a reason to apologize at all."

As much as Rice may have tried to give the appearance of invulnerability, playing in Boston had a profound effect on him. Some of the turbulence was a by-product of the special dynamics of the city, the belief that Boston would never embrace a black star. Rice also received no protection from the Red Sox organization. He stood out in left field and endured taunts from the home crowd at Fenway, the worst being the epithet "Uncle Ben," in derogatory reference to the black caricature and the name of a rice product. Yet Rice said nothing.

Clark Booth believed that while Rice would forge a career that would make him a near Hall of Famer, a better, more encouraging environment could have pushed Rice to even greater accomplishments. In Rice, Booth simply saw a man who held in so much of himself in order to cope with a harsh situation. There would be so much both the city and Rice as a man would lose by this constant tension. Peter Gammons agreed. In Boston, he thought, there would always be an inherent suspicion of black players. Few would believe it, but Gammons was one of the few people in the press who felt there was another side of Rice's personality that Boston never saw.

In the dugout at Legends Field, Rice heard these stories of the past, and the stoic facial expression did not change. Rice sat there, sifting through the memories and reflecting without anger. Then he pounced, frustrated by his own isolation.

"What was I supposed to say? What was I supposed to do? You talk and talk and now you're a troublemaker, somebody with a big mouth. My rule was to be quiet and when you have something to say, say it. But it wasn't my way; it wasn't my personality to always have something to talk about. I'm not Charles Barkley. He can get away with that. Think about the personalities involved."

For a time, Rice was insulated from the larger question of race. Part of the reason was that, during the mid-1970s, race was not a pressing issue for the Red Sox. Then, during the mid-1980s, his protections began to disintegrate. More than any other individual player, Rice would be adversely affected by the firing of Dick O'Connell, for it sent the Red Sox into a lethargy, an organization-wide slumber that created a massive regression from the progress made under O'Connell. In the shortest of spans, Rice found himself the only black player on the Red Sox.

In private, Rice would express his bitterness about both the lack of black players on the Red Sox as well as the club's seeming disinterest in them. When a prominent black free agent would sign with a rival—such as Dave Winfield and the Yankees—Rice would ask Gammons if the Red Sox had made a bid on him. He would always refuse to be quoted, which diminished the urgency for writers to take up the issue.

But the incident that revealed Rice's true character on racial issues was Tommy Harper's lawsuit in 1986. Before Harper, Rice drew sympathy for playing for an organization that did not seem interested in creating a better environment for its best player. After, Rice solidified a reputation as a man who would not help anyone, friends and teammates included.

When Harper won his discrimination case against the Red Sox, it seemed to be the perfect opportunity to begin the healing process. Everyone close to the Red Sox—players, management, media—knew the team had deep troubles with race, but far too infrequently was the club's racial dynamic discussed frankly and constructively. "The truth is," thought Larry Whiteside, "that few of us ever had the guts to write about it."

Harper stood up to the Red Sox, revealed the organization's transgressions, and was vindicated in court. He had the guts, and he was left out in the cold by his teammate to shoulder the weight by himself. The other blacks on the team were in no position to help Harper; Oil Can Boyd and Rey Quinones had around a year or two worth of service time and as such lacked the experience and cachet to confront management. Don Baylor had only just joined the team that year. But Rice was a Boston institution. He was on a Hall of Fame track and was keenly aware of the difficulty black players suffered in Boston. He always said he didn't care, but it was Rice who told Peter Gammons about the Elks Club affair in 1979, six years before Harper went public.

In print, Rice sounded aloof about the whole affair. "I'd have to wait till I hear both sides. There might be some things Tommy says that I agree with and some that I don't," Rice told the Boston *Globe*. "What can I say? I've been here 12 years in this organization and I've been treated first class since I've been here."

Rice's comments were the clearest illustration not only of his disregard for others, but of selling out a friend, for Tommy Harper wasn't just a stranger on the sidewalk. Harper may have been working in an auto body shop, but Rice was making $840,000 a year at the time and did not stick his neck out, though a person in his position could have had much influence on the direction of the franchise. Of the media, Joe Giuliotti enjoyed the best relationship with Rice, but this was a most unforgivable act. "I know he and Rice were close and it makes sense that they fell out over Rice not backing him. If Rice spoke out, used his influence, the whole story could have been different. But that was Rice. He's not going to get involved in something as political as that. Can you fault him? Yes, because you're supposed to back up your people, you're supposed to back up your friends in a situation like that."

Other black players around the league would not make public statements, yet privately they were deeply disappointed by Rice. Don Baylor was not one to stay quiet. He took on Rice in public. Baylor had just joined the Red Sox in 1986 and was immediately put off by Rice's lack of activism. "Jim, who was Tommy's friend, said nothing," Baylor wrote in his autobiography. "Team captains, guys with Hall of Fame numbers who carry some weight, should speak up in those situations, not crawl into a shell."

In both a micro and macro sense, Peter Gammons was conflicted. He knew Rice hung Harper out to dry and also missed perhaps the greatest opportunity in the history of the franchise not only to promote change, but to completely alter its moral direction. Had Rice used his clout, his name, to take on the issue, perhaps Red Sox management would have listened and saved itself much embarrassment. Rice personally would have satisfied the tenets of leadership and deflected charges of being distanced from an issue that affected so much of his career.

Yet secondarily, Gammons felt it unfair to fault a person for not being a leader. It simply wasn't part of the personality of Jim Rice. Gammons saw something else in Rice: Rice had been around Boston long enough to understand the rhythms of the city and that he may have paid a high price for being outspoken. Rice knew too well that black athletes who spoke out were often vilified in the press and by the fans. "The people here," said Gammons, "want you to speak out and then again, they don't. It would have been a lose-lose situation. Rice knew that."

Steve Fainaru was struck by the courage of Harper and unsurprised by all that Rice did not do. "You're supposed to take a stand for your friend. . . . There's been a lot of interpretation and attempted psychoanalysis about why Jim Rice is the way he is, but the inescapable truth is that the guy is an asshole. Don't get me wrong, he's a Hall of Famer, an unbelievable ballplayer, but he's still an asshole." Once great friends, it would take years before Rice and Harper again grew close.

Rice would be disappointed by the characterizations of those years and after more than a quarter century, he began to unburden himself.

"Peter Gammons and all these other guys had all this information and held so much of it back. There was so much out there that you would never know about. Why did he need me to talk about what he knew? If he knew it, say it."

What Rice wanted was courage, the same courage he brought to the plate against a hard-throwing pitcher. He would not then, and would not on this day, shoulder what he considered to be an undue amount of the load. He knows, he says, that he is right, and this is the burden of Jim Rice.

"Everybody wanted more from me about things I didn't have firsthand knowledge on. Why didn't more blacks come out to the game? I don't know. You have to go out and find that out. Don't ask me, because I don't know. Do I have opinions? That doesn't matter because I don't know why. You say black people used to say, 'Why go to Fenway just to get beat up?' Well, why did they feel that way? They felt that way for a reason. But I can't speak to that because it didn't happen to me. You have to go out and ask the people why they feel that way."

Few people would ever see the human, elder statesman side of Jim Rice, but he immediately took Ellis Burks on as a protégé. When Burks was called up in 1987, Rice told Red Sox clubhouse man Vince Orlando to put Burks's locker next to Rice's. Like Bill Russell and Pumpsie Green 30 years earlier, Rice took Burks around the city, gave him primers on the various climates of the organization. With Burks, Rice was everything he had long been accused of not being—a leader.

If Jim Rice would not speak to anyone in public about the racial climate of the team or the city, he privately expressed concerns with Ellis Burks. The organization, he said, was a decent one. Lou Gorman, the Red Sox general manager, was a good man. They were skittish about race throughout the organization, but Gorman treated him well. Rice was wary of Red Sox management for years, both Sullivan and Gorman, because of the simple fact that the club appeared to have no interest in black free agents. It was clear to Ellis Burks that the years Rice spent as the only black on the club, years that were supposed to be his prime, were lonely and difficult ones.

Rice never spoke out, but he gave Ellis Burks a telling piece of advice that provided important insight into Rice's feelings about Boston and his years with the Red Sox. They were words Burks would never forget. "Get your six years in," Rice told Burks, "and then get the hell out of Boston."

Rice would never again be the hitter he was during his first seven seasons in Boston, but he was still one of the more feared hitters in baseball. Nineteen eighty-six would be the last great year of his career, and fault was found with that year, for Rice hit 20 home runs, a figure low for him. When the decade came to a close, Jim Rice found himself at his most vulnerable. His great skills began to erode, and his enemies, the ones with long memories of the days when he looked down his nose at them from the mountaintop, lined up for payback.

"Such giants," wrote Harold Kaese in the Boston Globe with élan in 1959, "are not easily brushed aside." He was talking about an aging Ted Williams who was nearing the end, but he certainly could have been talking about Jim Rice in 1988. When the previous generation discusses the painful disintegration of a player—of hanging on too long—it usually focuses on Willie Mays. To listen to people of that generation, watching Willie Mays missing fastballs by a foot, dropping fly balls, and being merely human in the outfield remains the ultimate example of seeing an undignified fall from Olympus.

Retirement itself is not a difficult topic to discuss in baseball compared with the question of whether a player *should* retire. The whispers surrounded Jim Rice in 1988 like a condemned man. John McNamara, the Red Sox manager for part of 1988 who was considered as fair a manager as the Red Sox have had, compared Rice's sudden decline to that of Mays: "Willie Mays is the only one I ever saw lose it overnight."

How truly incredible the decline would be for a man known for his forearms snapping a bat in half with a check swing, remembered for his eyes, those same eyes that years later would burn in that Tampa dugout. When Rice failed, it was not only at home plate but also in the outfield. The fly balls he snatched with practiced ease now tortured and mocked him. One day he showed up with glasses, the next he was finished as a left fielder. Exposed, he could not even rely on years of goodwill compensation, for there were none.

"Is there any other superstar in America who would be treated with such fury for failure?" wrote Leigh Montville of the *Globe*. "Never an easy guy to know, sometimes a flat-out churl, Jim Rice always has let his numbers and his bat talk. They were the only public relations experts he ever thought he needed. What does he do now that they have gone on strike? He has wanted to be alone in the past, so he is alone now. He has been defined by the way he hit a baseball. He has made a fortune by hitting a baseball. What does he do now? It is as if he is some mythological character, caught in heavy chains."

The power was gone. It had declined for much of the 1980s, and in short order after 1986—Rice's last great season and the Red Sox's most recent appearance in the World Series—Jim Rice became an angry singles hitter. The Red Sox in 1988 bounced manager John MacNamara on Bastille Day and hired Joe Morgan, the career minor league manager who 14 years earlier was Rice's triple-A skipper at Pawtucket. Morgan, a weathered New Englander from nearby Walpole, now had every New Englander's dream. He was managing the Red Sox. And the first thing he was going to do was get tough. He was going to take Jim Rice down.

The Red Sox were riding high, winners under a flummoxing spell called Morgan Magic, and on July 20, 1988, Rice's Red Sox career essentially came to a close. The Red Sox were leading Minnesota 5-4 in the eighth inning when Morgan sent infielder Spike Owen to pinch-hit for Rice.

It was an embarrassing moment for a man who had worn only one uniform his whole career. Needing to establish himself as manager, Morgan upstaged Rice, purposely embarrassing one of the greatest, proudest players ever to play for the Red Sox. Rice and Morgan, the fifty-seven-year old manager who happened to be a career .191 hitter in 88 career big league games, engaged in a shoving match in the dugout, for which Rice was later suspended for three games. In the past, Rice rarely if ever protected his teammates, and in turn, they did not, in large measure, protect him. In an example of how much comeuppance awaited Rice, even embattled Oil Can Boyd—who considered the Red Sox, and Morgan in particular, racially insensitive—sided for the most part with Morgan.

Ellis Burks was disheartened by the entire affair. It was an example, both he and Boyd agreed, of the ego that dominates the game, and more importantly the fractious relationship of man. Rice deserved a measure of respect for his achievement. But Morgan saw a golden opportunity to take on a declining star and establish himself as an authority figure as manager.

Rice was the leader of the Red Sox for 16 years, and now a guy who had never before managed a big league team and was never a regular in the big leagues pinch-hit a weak hitter like Spike Owen for him without telling him.

As many enemies as Rice may have made, there is a code in the game that says you don't embarrass anyone, never mind a player who deserves to be in the Hall of Fame. But Jim Rice was not the first person in baseball to be sent such a caustic message. Casey Stengel had embarrassed Joe DiMaggio by sending a defensive replacement to center field during the 1951 World Series. The message was the same, only 37 years earlier.

Jim Rice's departure would be one of messier in Red Sox history, without dignity or John Updike. With Rice, Morgan first embarrassed him, and then enraged him. The Red Sox took action against Rice, and the media, forks and knives sharpened to repay Rice for years of hostility, lined up behind Morgan, who uttered his immortal line, "I'm the manager of this nine."

"Jimmy had put too much time in this game to be treated like that," Burks said. "I know he didn't get along with a lot of people, but who do you remember more, Joe Morgan or Jim Rice?"

The press, energized, hailed Morgan for standing up to Rice, the declining and tainted slugger. It was all an unfortunate show, brought to the fore by 16 years of welling animosity. Instead of a tearful, melancholy good-bye, the end of Jim Rice's career represented the perfect time to get even. The *Globe's* Will McDonough fired the first shot:

> There should be just one thing left in Boston for Jim Rice. The road out. It says here the three-day suspension the Red Sox gave their former slugger is a joke. A copout. If they call that supporting their manager, I wouldn't want to be Joe Morgan. As soon as Rice put his hands on Morgan Wednesday night, he should have been gone permanently. In Rice's words, his actions were inexcusable. In my words, they should not be excused. The fact is, Jim Rice can't play baseball anymore, and he knows it. The skills that made him one of the most feared power hitters in the game are gone. Five things make up a great player: the ability to run, to throw, to field, to hit and to hit with power. Rice can't run, throw or field. Never could. He has four home runs this year. The power is gone. The lights are out.
>
> He can no longer contribute to this team as a player. He has never contributed to it as a leader. Wednesday night was typical of Jim Rice. When things didn't go his way, he turned into a bully. An intimidator. This is his history. He shoved Sox publicist Bill Crowley, some 30 years his senior, a few years ago. He tore the shirt off a sportswriter last year. Now he tackles 57-year-old Joe Morgan and pulls him into the dugout runway in front of the entire team. What could be more demeaning to a manager?

A dizzyingly quick playoff lost to Oakland—led by Sox castaways Dave Henderson, Dennis Eckersley, and Carney Lansford—finished the 1988 season and Morgan Magic. Rice came to camp in 1989 determined to prove he was still the deadly power hitter of past reputation, but at thirty-six Rice's skills had abandoned him. His rhetoric about his numbers—the precious numbers that he said should be his only judge—was turned against him at the worst possible moment.

"Even when healthy, how much of an asset is Rice, when almost three-quarters of his hits are singles?" asked *Globe* columnist Dan Shaughnessy.

> Since the start of the 1987 season, Rice has 278 hits, and 204 are singles (73 percent). When Rice was cranking, less than 60 percent of his hits were singles. In his three monster seasons of 1977–79, Rice had 620 hits and only 59 percent (367) were singles. . . . [Mike] Schmidt was hitting .203 with 6 homers when he quit. He was 39 years old and in the final year of a $500,000 contract. In 148 at-bats, Schmidt struck out 17 times. Rice has fanned 32 times in 160 at-bats. Schmidt's slugging percentage was .372. Rice's is .358. Schmidt had twice as many homers as Rice and more RBIs in fewer at-bats. Which man should have retired?
>
> "I no longer have the skills needed to make adjustments at the plate to hit or make some plays in the field and run the bases."
>
> Schmidt made the preceding statement, but at this hour it applies to Rice.

With a week left in a lost season of 1989, Jim Rice was released. He refused a job with the front office. He still wanted to play. He, in fact, expected to play baseball in 1990. He had hit 382 home runs, hit .298 lifetime, and personified an era in Boston baseball history.

The phone didn't ring. There were no offers to pinch-hit or make a club out of spring training. The Paul Bunyan figure disappeared quietly and anonymously. Joe Giuliotti broke the stories. Rich in irony for a person who rarely seemed concerned with how he treated anyone, Jim Rice expressed disappointment and anger in how he was treated at the end by the Red Sox.

Yet the lowest point came immediately following his release. The mutual wounds were given time to heal and Rice received a phone call from Lou Gorman, the Red Sox general manager. Rice didn't go out the way a superstar, potential Hall of Famer should, Gorman said. Therefore, the Red Sox were calling to invite him to a day in his honor.

But there was a catch. They wanted him to share the spotlight with relief pitcher Bob Stanley, who had retired that same week. This was the same Bob Stanley who uncorked the wild pitch to tie Game 6 of the 1986 Series and later the grounder to Mookie Wilson to lose the game. It was the Bob Stanley who despite being a reliable but unspectacular big league pitcher remains one of the all-time scapegoats in Red Sox history. Jim Rice was mortified. The Red Sox said it was a misunderstanding. John Harrington said the Red Sox desired to honor him in some way, but that Rice never told the team what his wishes were. Thirteen years after Rice's release, that day has still never come.

Shrugging, Rice waves his hand dismissively about the prospect of closure, of a retirement ceremony. "I played the game because I had a gift. I don't want anyone to give me anything if they don't think I deserve it. Do I deserve it? That's not for me to decide. That's for others to decide. Let's put it this way. I know what I did out there."

His proponents say playing in Boston was more difficult than he ever revealed. Don Baylor thinks that if Boston could have embraced a black star, Rice would have been as popular as Yastrzemski, and perhaps even Ted Williams. Ellis Burks believed that Rice would have enjoyed multimillion-dollar endorsements, but the combination of Rice's volatility and the city's racial climate made this scenario virtually impossible. The endorsements he did receive after his wondrous 1978 season dried up amid complaints that Rice was too difficult to work with. His detractors may acknowledge Boston's racial confusion, but most point directly to Rice himself, his standoffish attitude and unwillingness to treat people with even the most cursory moments of dignity. He was a man unto himself, and the price he paid for that was to receive little adoration outside of his abilities in the batter's box. To them, Jim Rice is not a beloved figure in Boston or anywhere completely and totally because of Jim Rice, not because of playing in the shadow of Yastrzemski or Williams and certainly not because he was a black man playing in a city that during his time was embroiled in a serious racial crisis. He was not friendly to anyone for any length of time. He wanted to be judged only on his numbers. But when there were none to post, Jim Rice the man carried little value. Rice had treated so many people with such contempt over the decade that when he fell, a long line of people waited for him on the way down.

Reggie Jackson considered Jim Rice to be the most dangerous hitter in the league, himself included. "He was the most feared hitter in our league, the most destructive. He was the guy in the league who could do the most damage. His situation up in Boston was tough, but he had the ultimate weapon. He had that whip in his hand, and that shut a lot of people up."

Then the whip lost it crack, and the man who had no use for the world was suddenly the one who now needed it the most.

With Rice, reflection would never be easy, but he was also a black man born in 1953 America, and no one can understand what that means in its fullness.

He would wear only the Red Sox uniform in his professional career, yet Rice never was completely at home in Boston. The number 14 never was retired, but the Red Sox haven't issued it to another player, either. The day of adoration and healing never came. The curtain never closed as much as the show was abruptly canceled.

In Tampa, Rice sat on the bench until it was nearly time to go. Tim Wakefield, the knuckleballer, was 20 minutes away from facing Mike Mussina in front of ten thousand fans who would never miss a Red Sox-Yankees joust, even if the score didn't count. Three decades without catharsis is too long a time to so easily let the clock have its way.

"Time to go?" Jim Rice said. "Aw, shit. I was just getting started."

FOURTEEN

At home in Texas, Ellis Burks prepared for the 1990 season. As the weeks approached, he began hearing news of the off-season in Boston and seriously began to wonder what kind of city he was playing in. Burks was a quiet, sensitive, and talented young man who was already bothered by his previous two years in Boston. He was uncomfortable by the way Jim Rice had been let go the previous September. Watching a player who gave his entire career to the organization being showed the door so coldly was bitter lesson for a young player. Nevertheless, Ellis Burks would eventually have to learn about life in Major League Baseball: There is little room for sympathy in business.

Rice was only the start. The Tommy Harper affair was still fresh in the minds of the black players not only on the team, but in the league. Burks did not understand the particulars, for he was still a young player with much about his own future to concern himself with, but he began to notice a curious, disconcerting trend. Black players would leave Boston tainted and bitter. Burks saw it with Rice, and to a lesser extent with Don Baylor. Dave Henderson, who was traded to the San Francisco Giants in large degree to make room for Burks, would wear a T-shirt underneath his playing jersey that read simply, "Boston sucks."

The player whose career most concerned Burks was Oil Can Boyd. Over the winter of 1989, Boyd signed a free agent contract with the Montreal Expos, putting to an end a tumultuous seven years. The Red Sox did not sign any black free agents over the winter, and with Rice and Boyd now gone, there was another possibility that concerned Ellis Burks: He could enter the regular season as the only black on the roster.

Burks was not the stereotypical ballplayer unconcerned with the larger world around him. He was a thoughtful young man who was troubled by how 1989 ended, both with the team and with Rice. If he was concerned about the direction of his team, the weeks before spring training 1990 made him wonder about the city, too. He asked himself if Boston had ever enjoyed even a short period of racial peace.

Gary McLaughlin had been working as a dispatcher for the Massachusetts state police for fourteen years. At 8:30 P.M. on the night of October 23, 1989, a call came in that would be, in his words, the most arduous call of his life.

There was no time to waste. The emergency distress call came from a cellular telephone. The man on the other end was nearly hysterical. He and his wife had been robbed. The robber took the couple's belongings and shot the man's pregnant wife in the head. The man told McLaughlin to hurry, for he too had been shot in the abdomen and was quickly losing consciousness.

The caller blacked out from the pain, but the cellular telephone was still connected. McLaughlin contacted the city police and directed them to the site of the car and the wounded couple by cleverly listening to the sound of the police sirens through the cellular phone connection. The differing clarity of sounds told him which of the police cruisers was closest in proximity to the couple.

Police brought the couple to the emergency room of Brigham and Women's Hospital. Doctors feverishly performed an emergency cesarean section on the young woman, Carol Stuart, and saved the life of Christopher Stuart, premature by eight weeks. The next day, Carol Stuart died. Her husband, Charles Stuart, shot in the stomach, lived thanks to the resourcefulness of state dispatcher McLaughlin. It was an act of quick thinking that, for a time, made Gary McLaughlin a hero.

When he came to, Charles Stuart told police of the brutal assault. At a stoplight, a black man jumped into the back seat of the couple's 1987 Toyota Cressida and demanded the couple's valuables. Charles Stuart gave a detailed description of the assailant as a six-foot-tall bearded black male wearing a black sweatsuit. The assailant asked for Stuart's wallet. Stuart replied that he was not carrying one. Believing Stuart to be a police officer, the assailant took out a silver .38 caliber revolver and shot Carol Stuart in the head and Charles in the abdomen before fleeing into the black Mission Hill section of town.

The shootings brought numerous pertinent social questions and revived the racial suspicions that had marred the 1970s. Was the city so unsafe, so violent that a young family could not even be saved by the city's prestigious hospitals? Was this what Boston had become? Almost immediately, Boston's racial instincts flared. The mayor, Raymond Flynn, a former basketball star who was elected in 1983 with the goal of engineering a healing in the city, vowed a manhunt of the black Mission Hill neighborhood, dispatching every available detective to find the suspect. The state's legislature sprung into action, calling a special session asking to reinstitute the death penalty—long since abolished in Massachusetts—in anticipation of the killer's capture. Francis X. Bellotti, a former state attorney general and candidate for governor, said if the electric chair would be instituted, he'd personally pull the lever on Carol Stuart's killer. A group of anonymous local businessman offered a $15,000 reward for any information that would lead to the arrest and conviction of the person who committed the murder.

The depth of the tragedy reached across each section of Boston, eliciting an outpouring of grief and despair. More than eight hundred people attended Carol Stuart's funeral in the suburban town of Medford. Both Governor Michael Dukakis and Mayor Flynn watched a twenty-six-year-old expectant mother buried long before her time. Charles Stuart, still recovering, did not attend his wife's funeral. He wrote a letter that was read aloud at the funeral. The letter urged forgiveness for the killer.

The next seven weeks represented another example of Boston's intractable racial problem. The Boston police combed the city's black neighborhoods. Blockades and checkpoints were established. Within Boston's black community there was a mixed but largely silent reaction. It was a horrible tragedy. A pregnant woman shot in the head was a vicious, heinous crime. But within such sentiments existed a deeper conflict. While the police swept through the neighborhood in pursuit of a killer, where, they asked, was similar attention when a black person was killed? In a black community disproportionately affected by violent crime, there were no manhunts when innocent people were killed, only the grief of the living. Nor were there thundering proclamations of justice or much introspection about the sanctity of human life. Certainly, mayors and governors didn't attend the funerals. It was just another illustration, in the minds of African Americans in Boston, of the double standard that came with being black, that a white life carried so much more value. A city was enveloped in a dragnet and the highest political dignitaries attended the funeral of an average person, yet the streets took black lives every day with barely a single mention in the newspaper. It was a frustration that mounted, spilling into daily conversation. Clearly, the intention was not to minimize the seriousness of this crime, but was Carol Stuart's murder so much more heinous than the crimes that were committed daily in Mattapan, Roxbury, and Dorchester? Sandra Williams, a black resident, lived near Franklin Park in the black section of Dorchester. Boston *Globe* columnist Eileen McNamara, who would later win a Pulitzer Prize with the Boston *Globe*, captured Williams in a moment of grief for her murdered boyfriend, speaking for virtually the entire black community:

> There were no cameras clicking, no minicams rolling at the city morgue when Sandra Williams identified the body of the man who shared her apartment near Franklin Park. James Moody, 29, was shot to death only a few hours after a robber attacked Charles and Carol Stuart outside Brigham and Women's Hospital. But no calls were heard at the State House for tougher sentencing practices. No news conferences were convened to mark a lone black man's passing.
>
> "And no mayor called about my loss," Williams said.

It was a difficult position to articulate, and so the black community remained largely silent. Any suggestion outside of outrage would be looked on unfavorably by public opinion, for it smacked of political opportunism and insensitivity. Therefore, it was impossible, and out of line, to use these shootings to attract attention to the murders that took place almost daily in the black community.

Seventeen days into the world, Christopher Stuart died on November 9, 1989. He would be buried in a private ceremony eleven days later, a ceremony his father Charles would again be too weak to attend. Police detectives leaked leads to the news media about possible suspects, in the hopes of both forcing the suspect into making a mistake and alleviating the pressure of having no real leads nearly three weeks after the murder.

Two days after young Christopher Stuart died, the police arrested William Bennett, a thirty-nine-year-old paroled career criminal, presumably for the double murder of Carol and Christopher Stuart. But instead of being charged with murder, Bennett was arrested in the suburb of Burlington on a motor vehicle violation. While in jail in Burlington, he was arraigned on an armed robbery charge involving a Brookline video store. Still not charged for the Stuart murders, Bennett was held nonetheless while police attempted to build a case. They had their man.

Police visited Charles Stuart in his bed at Boston City Hospital, accompanied almost daily with mug shots of potential suspects. On November 21, he exhibited a "strong, physical reaction" to a mug of Bennett. Stuart did not positively identify Bennett, but his reaction by itself fueled media coverage that Bennett was the killer.

Bennett, in the ultimate display of street bravado, helped the state's case. He was arrested in the first place because of his own mouth. While the police were sweeping Mission Hill with roadblocks and door-to-door searches, neighbors told officers that Bennett had loosely bragged to confidants that he shot the Stuarts. It wasn't long before he was picked up in Burlington.

Crime was all that William Bennett knew. When he was arrested, the Boston *Globe* reported it to be the sixtieth time in his life that he had been pinched. The first time was when he was fourteen. In 1973, he shot a cab driver he was robbing for not having enough money. When he told the cabbie to hand over his shoes, Bennett shot the man for not moving fast enough. It turned out, cynical Boston *Globe* columnist Mike Barnicle wrote acerbically, that the cab driver was a double amputee.

So in a perverse way, being known as the person who shot Charles and a pregnant Carol Stuart carried with it an impressive street value, especially with the case dominating headlines and news shows all during the winter.

Three days after Christmas, Charles Stuart, having been released from the hospital earlier in the month, singled out Bennett as the man who looked "most like" his attacker.

Matthew Stuart was conflicted. He had heard that his brother Charles picked Bennett out of a lineup, but instead of feeling even the smallest measure of relief, he grew uneasy. Over the course of the next few days, he consulted a member of the family who was a lawyer, then was instructed by close friends to retain his own. With Bennett now selected out of a lineup, it appeared only a matter of time before he was arrested and charged with one of the most sensational double murders in the city's history. It was with this that Matthew Stuart fell victim to his conscience. What followed were stunning details: He recounted to his lawyers that he met Charles at his car on the night of the shootings. Charles handed his brother a Gucci bag and told him to take it to suburban Revere. It wasn't until later, when he looked in the bag, that he saw the contents: a diamond engagement ring and a silver, snub-nosed revolver, the same one Charles Stuart told police his black attacker had used on him. Matthew Stuart's lawyers ordered him to retell the exact story to police.

A week into 1990, the police encircled Charles Stuart. Matthew had turned state's evidence against his brother, and—over the New Year's holiday—the stunning facts of the case spilled from Matthew Stuart's embattled conscience. It was a remarkable reversal. Charles Stuart, his brother said, shot and killed his pregnant wife and, as a cover, shot himself in the stomach. He then called Matthew, who later said he had no idea that while he acted Carol Stuart lay dying in the car. He took the murder weapon and the jewelry in the Gucci bag from the scene. Matthew told police he threw the bag into the Pines River in nearby Revere. Charles Stuart then got on his cell phone and called Gary McLaughlin at the state police dispatch for help.

Charles Stuart killed his wife, and the motive was money. He was the sole benefactor of a series of life insurance policies on Carol Stuart that totaled nearly $600,000. Two weeks before the murder, Charles took out a $10,000 insurance policy on his wife. Just after Christmas, Charles Stuart took a cashier's check for $10,000, the value of the Cressida, and bought a 1990 Nissan Maxima. Before the holidays, Stuart collected $83,000 of another $100,000 policy.

Not only was Stuart the killer, Matthew Stuart told police, but he had also conspired to kill his wife in their own home, but aborted the plan. According to the plan, Matthew was to break into his brother's house to give the appearance that Carol Stuart had startled a burglar. At that moment, Charles would murder his wife. Charles even told Matthew to wear shoes two sizes too small to avoid suspicion. The night of the aborted plan, Matthew Stuart hid in the bathroom and managed to escape unseen. Matthew Stuart told these details to police on January 3.

The morning of January 4, authorities began the manhunt for Charles Stuart. At approximately 7 A.M., the police and prosecution closing in on him, Stuart drove the Maxima to the lower deck of the Tobin Bridge's double-deck span, the bridge named for old Boston Mayor Maurice Tobin. He scrawled a note that said, "I love my family . . . the last four months have been real hell. . . . All the allegations have taken all my strength." He then leaped from the bridge to his death into the icy January waters of the Mystic River. The police listed the death as a suicide. Hours later, police announced that William Bennett was no longer a suspect.

It was the most chilling, ruthlessly brilliant example of a man who exploited a city's—indeed, an entire culture's—racial neuroses and nearly got away with murder. As the case receded into the past, numerous holes in Stuart's story that had existed from the beginning were examined. But the Boston police, the public, the politicians, and the media were too preoccupied with the outrage of a white life taken by black hands and all of the implications that came with it to notice. Charles Stuart knew this.

Psychologist Dr. Alvin Poussaint said Charles Stuart employed a racist strategy "that he knew would work, i.e. that people would be only too willing to believe a story that pinned the blame on the black community." Wrote the *Globe*'s Ed Siegel, "There's no doubt Poussaint is right. . . . In this case, we were all too quick to believe the worst of the black community, and the only way for the media to atone for that is with improved coverage of what's happening within all of Boston's communities."

The black community, shrill in its vindication, demanded an apology from what it saw as an overzealous police force. Indeed, the quiet realization that the full force of the city's law enforcement resources was turned on an innocent black community left residents both vindicated but resentful. It showed them what they already knew: Justice was not administered equally. Worse was the belief in the black community that what created the fervor wasn't just a white person being killed, but a white being killed by a black, which returned many blacks back to the unequal justice system of decades before.

Bennett, too, wanted to talk. He demanded an apology. He claimed his life had been ruined by the newspapers, television, and general publicity. It was one of the more unfortunate by-products of the entire affair. Bennett had essentially confessed to the shootings, and, to further inflame matters, the black community and its leaders used, as an example of white oppression, a man who had been arrested sixty times, who had robbed and shot black people over a twenty-five-year criminal career.

For a time, the white establishment stood firm. They could not be faulted for acting in that manner. Charles Stuart had nearly killed himself in his hoax, which had eliminated him for the time being as suspicious. He gave a detailed account and description of the night, which included the sound of the attacker's voice. The police even found the keys of Stuart's car in the Mission Hill neighborhood where he was attacked. Later, in an act of healing that appeared cynical to many, Mayor Flynn offered an apology to the Mission Hill neighborhood and to the career-criminal Bennett, who spent almost two months in jail.

Black leaders were largely unmoved. They wanted more, and tensions increased. Mike Barnicle of the *Globe*, who would later be caught in scandal himself and fired, attacked the black leadership for opportunism.

> Naturally, a pack of publicity hounds in the black community—a few ministers and headline-hunting politicians now passing themselves off as skilled homicide investigators—jumped on Bennett's arrest as proof of a racist plot by the white power structure to make every black man, woman and child in Boston out as ruthless, bloodthirsty criminals. I guess they are upset that because nobody thought to beat the truth out of Stuart that night in the hospital after he had shot and very nearly killed himself. It is strange that none of them conducted a press conference Oct. 24 when sweeps were actually being conducted in the Mission Hill project. But that's not a surprise because the many, many times that dead black bodies have been found on street corners and in homes—victims of the gunfire, drugs and gangs that plague that community more than most—not many members of the clergy or government show up. Just cops, ambulance attendants and mothers crying over corpses.

When he had heard that Charles Stuart had committed suicide and why, the dispatcher Gary McLaughlin was sullen, morose. He was a hero whose diligence saved an alleged murderer's life.

"I feel empty," he said.

The Red Sox were not insulated from the Stuart case. Ellis Burks arrived at spring training incredulous about the latest episode of unrest in the city. To Burks the case revealed just how little had changed between the races and, moreover, how Boston stood apart from the rest of his experiences. Burks was from the South, but nothing there prepared him for the deep animosities that existed in Boston. It was as if, he thought, the people in Boston truly wanted to believe the worst about each other. "It always made me wonder," he said years later, "just what the hell was going on up there. Anyone who knows anything about the streets couldn't have fallen for that. I mean, isn't the man always a suspect first, especially if he lived and she died? When a man attacks someone, he's going to take the man out first, not shoot a pregnant woman in the head. Chances are, he wouldn't have even bothered her at all because she wasn't a threat. But when you throw black into it, oh boy. What a city."

Burks began to wonder what the effects of the Stuart case could have on his own situation. He had a great deal of respect for Lou Gorman, a man Burks considered honorable; but the club hadn't signed any black free agents over the winter and the team's other black, relief pitcher Lee Smith, was terribly unhappy in Boston. Smith would be one of the best relief pitchers of his generation and in time would save more games than any pitcher in history. In Boston, he was considered lazy—always a dangerous rap for a black person—and the fit simply did not work. Burks' fear was that black players, already wary of the city's reputation, wouldn't come play for the Red Sox even if the team had offered them the moon, plus millions of dollars. Already, players around the league were asking Burks about the playing conditions on the Red Sox and the living conditions in Boston. Mel Hall, a black outfielder playing for the Yankees, would always be wary of Boston. "I don't know how the black athletes deal with it, but it's got to be uncomfortable for them," he said. "I think it's part of the whole situation there in Boston, like that thing where that lady got shot and they blamed it on a black guy when it was really her husband who did it. It's like, 'The guy's black, we want him dead.'"

When the 1990 season opened, Ellis Burks' worse nightmare was realized. He was the only African-American position regular on the team. Like Rice, his isolation became complete when, after eleven appearances, Gorman traded Lee Smith to St. Louis for slugger Tom Brunansky. Like Rice ten years earlier, Burks was now the only black on the roster.

Ellis Burks was born on September 11, 1964, in Vicksburg, Mississippi. He grew up in Fort Worth, Texas, and was signed at nineteen by Boston scout Danny Doyle. Yet to hear him tell it, he never really even wanted to play baseball. "My mother wanted me to play more than I did," he said. "It was all a ploy to keep me out of the house. She wouldn't have her kid in the house on a hot day." When Burks first came up to Boston in 1987, he was already in the middle of a storm. Rice was in the midst of a rapid decline, and the Red Sox had coldly dumped 1986 World Series hero Dave Henderson to make room for him in center field. Henderson and Burks would be close, and while Henderson would be a hero again with Oakland, he held a certain bitterness toward the Red Sox that lasted years.

Burks had his own problems in Boston, the biggest one being his potential. Not since the Reggie Smith, Tommy Harper, and Fred Lynn days had the Red Sox seen such a complete player. Burks was faster than Lynn and Smith, a better hitter with more power than Harper, and a defensive player comparable to Lynn.

He was a gifted, graceful athlete. Six-foot-two and a lithe 180 pounds, his ability was apparent. But Burks began his third full season with the Red Sox with an uncomfortable mixture of great promise and resignation. The expectations for him were high, but he had suffered injury problems, and the worst tag a player could have was to be called fragile.

Parts of his troubles were racial. He was lonely in a clubhouse where he was the only black, and for Burks it was important to have some form of racial camaraderie. Rice, his private mentor, was gone, and the team was dominated by personalities such as Wade Boggs and Mike Greenwell, two southerners that Burks got along with by maintaining little social contact with them.

His real difficulty came from the expectation of being great. It was a pressure that in no small degree came from being black. Around baseball, black players like to refer to it as the Curse of Willie Mays, which is to say any young, black center fielder who has speed and power will always be compared to the great Mays. A compliment, but also a sure recipe for failure, for Mays is considered the greatest, most complete baseball player who ever lived. The Curse was not in the compliment, but in its inverse: Any player who did not live up to these unrealistic expectations would be considered a failure. Once, during a heroic streak in 1988 that would turn the Sox into division winners, Minnesota Twins manager Tom Kelley proclaimed, "When is Ellis Burks going to be MVP? This year, next year? When?"

Later in his career, during an Oakland A's–San Francisco Giants game, Dusty Baker, Orlando Cepeda, and Burks talked with A's coaches Ron Washington and Thad Bosley. Cepeda, tired of the hip-hop music blaring over the loudspeaker, did a hilarious impression of a rap artist. With his thick Dominican accent, he began to curse in song, "Yeah, bitch. I'm a-gonna kill you and your mama, too. Fuck this, fuck that. Yeah." With the circle howling with laughter, Cepeda said incredulously, "And all the kids buy it."

Then the group got serious. Baker, who played eighteen years in the majors, mentioned Eric Davis as an example of the Mays Curse. "No one would just let him play. He had to be Mays, but he wasn't. Well, who the hell *is* Mays? Hit .350, fifty homers, drive in 130?" Burks gave an icy laugh. Boston would be his most bitter experience. Management, with little experience with black players as a whole, simply could not understand why Burks wasn't Superman. "They just never left me alone up there. I was supposed to be the next this or the next that. I was never just Ellis. I was also young, and didn't know how this game worked. I found out in Boston."

In his worst moments, he turned to Jim Rice, who was in the throes of his own decline. That Rice could suffer so much in fighting for his professional life and still take the time and interest to mentor a young player made him all the more special a person to Ellis Burks. There was something, clearly, about Burks that Rice saw in himself. He constantly tried to impart the importance of playing hurt to Burks, not only as a way to gain the respect of his teammates, but to impart to Burks that statistics aside, this element of his game would make him a complete player. There was another element to Rice's logic. He also understood too well the stereotypes that existed in the game that blacks were less inclined to play in pain. It was, Rice believed, less important for whites to show a high pain threshold than for blacks. Rice knew Burks would be held to a different standard, for that was true of black life in general. What he did not want, however, was for Burks to be unprepared for it.

Burks was supposed to be the team's savior, and when he proved to be a good player instead of a transcendent one, Burks found his relationship with his manager, Joe Morgan, to be a cool one. Morgan had replaced John McNamara in 1988. He was never a regular major league player and had toiled in the minor leagues as a manager for decades. He was from nearby Walpole; it was refreshing to the provincial New Englanders to have one of their own as a manager, and he immediately scored points with many writers—especially Will McDonough—for taking a stand on Jim Rice. Morgan enjoyed the attention of the writers, for in managing the Red Sox he was living a dream job.

But Ellis Burks did not trust Joe Morgan. Part of it was his treatment of Rice, but the other reason for his distance was what he saw to be Morgan's consistent attacks of him to the Boston writers. Morgan would tell writers that Burks was too injury prone and would not have a long career and, most disturbing, often questioned Burks' commitment. Morgan seemed confounded that Burks was injured so often and, in ballplayer verbiage, wondered if Burks was "jaking it," a euphemism for faking it on the job.

On the field, Burks didn't feel much support. Nineteen-ninety would be his most productive year in Boston. He hit .296 with twenty-one home runs and eighty-nine runs batted in, and the Red Sox qualified for the postseason for the second time in his three seasons. But his efforts never seemed quite good enough. There was, in those days, always an emphasis on what he couldn't do. Burks also saw it as another reflection of the Willie Mays Curse. "Of course, if I'm black, fast and play the outfield, I should be hitting .400 with 50 homers, right?"

Burks could never find comfort with the city's polarized structure. Some teammates had warned Burks about the city's social climate. It was Boyd who first told Burks about avoiding South Boston, the busing hot zone. "Oil Can told me to stay out of there, if I valued my life. I didn't believe it, that you would drive through there and have various names hurled at you and rocks thrown at your car. It never happened to me, because I didn't go out there." He knew the team had suffered from a poor rapport with black fans and resolved to make inroads with the city's black community. It was a concept that held little interest for Rice, but Burks was energized.

He went to Foggie's Barber Shop on Tremont Street, the epicenter of the Boston black community. Burks recalls frequently appearing on WILD, the city's lone black radio station, appealing for fan support. He was shrewd in his requests. Instead of creating a possible racial firestorm by asking black fans directly over the air to come support the team, he knew WILD's constituency was predominately black. "I used to say, 'let's have some WILD listeners come on out to the ballpark.' I was too smart to say it the other way. But hell, there was no response. I learned that early in my time in Boston. Black people don't go to Red Sox games. No matter what we did. We tried giving those tickets away. Couldn't do it."

The pace and the character of the city at times unnerved Burks. Peter Gammons would drive to Fenway with Burks one day when the two stopped at a red light. People yelled at each other during the forty-five seconds between light changes. Bostonians gunned their engines as fast as they could in between stop lights.

"You know how in New York people hit the horn the second the light turns green?" Gammons told Burks. "Well, in Boston, they hit the horn while it's still red."

Still, despite the differences in the culture, much of what troubled Burks about Boston was the presence of Morgan, who many close observers believed harbored resentment toward blacks. If he grew tired of Rice, it was nonetheless seen by blacks to have a racial tinge to it. Would a rookie manager disregard a white star in the same manner? Burks asked. Boyd and Morgan clashed equally. Boyd, ever combustible, was in the midst of career-threatening blood clot problems. Boyd would always draw attention; and it was widely rumored that, even if not directly involved in drugs, he had made the acquaintance of numerous drug dealers in a neighboring, notorious Chelsea. While Boyd recovered from his injuries, Morgan told reporters that Boyd would never live to see his thirtieth birthday. "He'll either be dead or in jail," Morgan said.

Morgan's shortcomings in this regard were clouded by both the team's winning streak and the amour that existed between him and the press. "He reeled everyone in with homespun, everyman stories," Gammons said. "Then you look it up in the baseball encyclopedia and you see he hit .190 for his career." Gammons knew that black players on the team clashed with Morgan, but couldn't understand exactly why. He and Morgan shared a good relationship. Boyd believed that Morgan possessed an old strain of the Boston Irish dislike of blacks. Larry Whiteside agreed, offering up the bitter old joke about black-Irish relations in Boston. "It wasn't that the Irish are racist," Whiteside said. "It's just that if you happen to be black, they don't want you around."

The culmination of tension for Burks came one day when Morgan called him into his office before a game. The two men sat in the manager's office at Fenway Park. At first, Morgan said nothing. Then, with that slow, salty New England accent, he began. The conversation was a rambling one. Burks said nothing while Morgan talked about what bad form it would be for Burks to get into trouble so early in his career.

It was then that Morgan offered what Burks considered one of the more priceless lines he'd heard in his life.

"Just be careful," Morgan warned. "I hear you've been chasing that cat, that white cat a little bit too hard lately."

At first, Burks was stunned. He and Morgan could have been from different planets, and at times it may have seemed as if they were. But here they were speaking the same ballplayer language. Burks knew what the "cat" was. It was the euphemism for women. Morgan was sending Burks a message through strong-armed channels. In an instant Burks understood. He had been seen at a Boston nightclub with a white woman, otherwise know as the white cat.

Burks was incredulous. "Can you beat that shit? I was a young professional ballplayer and he says that to me. I thought he was going to say something about my performance on the field. I was producing. At the time, I remember I was even hitting over .300, so I remember being surprised I was in his office in the first place. But he was talking about something else. And that was how I found out he and the Red Sox had their spies out on me."

"Morgan Magic," Burks said, bitterly.

Perhaps more than any other player, Dennis "Oil Can" Boyd would represent the difficulties that came with being a black ballplayer in Boston. If a self-confident and sophisticated Ellis Burks couldn't navigate Boston's difficult corridors, then Oil Can Boyd was in a sense doomed from the start. He was emotional, a southerner, and completely ill prepared for dealing with the Boston baseball culture. Boyd was talented, enigmatic, and immature. From 1984 to 1986, Boyd won forty-three games, but would only win seventy-eight in his ten-year career. As much as he broiled emotionally and wrestled with his own self-control, his own steep emotional requirements, combined with the difficult environment of both Boston and the Red Sox, set the stage for nearly a decade of volatility. Jim Rice, a guide to Ellis Burks, tended to have little time for Boyd. When Boyd first arrived from the minors, he exemplified the kind of youthful enthusiasm that came with being in the major leagues. Clark Booth thought Rice was turned off by what he thought to be Boyd's extensive clowning to appeal to a media he himself could not brook. It was a reminder to the fiercely proud Rice how whites sought to project black athletes as less focused than whites. The last thing a black player should do, Rice surmised, was encourage them. Peter Gammons remembers visiting Boyd's family in Meridian, Mississippi, and being taken by the family's baseball lineage. "Oil Can loved to play baseball," Gammons said. "He didn't handle this city well. It was a little much for him, but he loved the game."

Oil Can Boyd clashed with the Red Sox establishment three times before the famous All-Star snub outburst in 1986 that led to a three-day walkout/suspension and a mandatory psychiatric evaluation. The Red Sox were convinced that Boyd was using drugs, a damaging, reckless contention that was speculated on publicly by the media and the ball club but would never be proven publicly. The very mention of Boyd and his alleged involvement with drugs was enough to damage an already fragile relationship.

To those around him, there existed a bipolarity to Boyd's personality. He grew up poor, in the southern Delta town of Meridian, Mississippi, about two hours from Vicksburg, Ellis Burks' birthplace. The expectations of Boyd were immediate, both what he expected from himself and what was expected of him. He was of a baseball-playing tradition in Meridian. His father regaled the young Boyd with the stories of the great black teams that barnstormed through

Meridian; Dennis Boyd's pitching hero was the legendary Leroy "Satchel" Paige, who had pitched in his prime thirty-five years before Boyd's birth.

There was to Oil Can Boyd a sense of hot desperation. He was at times a brilliant pitcher, as he was in the pennant-clinching game in 1986 against Toronto. He reportedly spent his money quickly, and one reason for his tirade after failing to make the All-Star team was the loss of the $25,000 bonus that came with it. He pitched poorly in the playoffs and was crushed when he was not chosen to pitch Game 7 of the 1986 World Series, although it was his turn to pitch. When television cameras turned to Boyd at the end of Game 7, Boyd's tears seemed generated more by his being on the bench than by the team's losing.

Boyd, thought Boston *Herald* writer Charlie Pierce, was everything the Red Sox feared about dealing with black players. But he was not crazy. Curiously, Boyd's self-centered personality may have been precisely what the Red Sox needed. After the depression following Game 6, Boyd was perhaps the only person in the Red Sox clubhouse happy the season was still alive. He wanted more than anything to be the hero. He left a poor community with the expectation not just of making the major leagues, but also of being great. The 1990 census reported in the city of Meridian that 27.3 percent of the city's households earned less than $10,000 annually. Boyd was the successful one; he was *the one who made it*. He reacted to events in Boston as if he were being cheated out of his one chance at success. When the pressure began to mount and the Red Sox failed to protect him, race crept steadily into the debate. Boyd came to view the Red Sox as racist along with the city.

Ellis Burks believed Boyd received harsh treatment in Boston that was emblematic of Boyd's personality. A minor event became major. On more than one occasion, the Red Sox forced Boyd to undergo psychiatric evaluation. He once failed to return some pornographic videos during spring training, which became a huge and embarrassing story in Boston. He grew frustrated when he contrasted how he was treated with the treatment of the great hitter Wade Boggs, who was embroiled in an adultery scandal that tainted both his teammates and the organization worse than anything Boyd would ever do. When Boggs told the media, during the height of his Margo Adams scandal, that he once willed himself invisible, Boyd was quick to comment. "Who," he asked, "needs the psychiatrist now?"

The Red Sox would never publicly recant the widespread assumption that Boyd had taken drugs, nor would the media confirm or deny the team's internal whispering. Instead the accusations sat in the public eye, adding to the intriguing figure cut by Oil Can Boyd.

Steve Lyons, the former Red Sox outfielder whose outlandish personality made him something of a name in baseball, thought Boyd's problems stemmed more from the stifling nature of the organization than from the city. He believed the fans of Boston responded to Boyd in a way that the organization did not. "Boyd was great. He could pitch and the fans loved him," Lyons said. "He ran into trouble when the organization kept trying to make him something other than Oil Can. They kept trying to change him, to make him less emotional, less colorful. What they didn't realize was that the more emotional he was, those were the times when he pitched the best."

Boyd's own outbursts gave the impression he was emotionally out of control. Burks felt it unfair that Boyd was expected to undergo psychiatric evaluation, which of itself became a public spectacle.

Dan Shaughnessy believes that the one player he misread over the years was Boyd. "I was certainly hard on him at times," he said. "I wrote tough things about him, but what I think everyone forgets about Oil Can was how much he loved to pitch. He was from that great Negro League tradition. That side of him got lost in all the other shenanigans."

What finished Boyd in Boston were injuries. The organization in the late 1980s had clearly lost patience with him, and, more importantly to them, they were not sure that with his recurring circulation problems he would ever pitch effectively again in the big leagues. When Boyd left, it was to go to Montreal, where he was reunited with Tommy Harper, who after a year and a half out of the game was hired as a coach by the Expos.

Steve Fainaru, who when he joined the *Globe* would write some of the best stories about the team, believed Boyd to be a victim of a confluence of factors, the first being the city's racial climate clashing with Boyd's personality. Fainaru also believed Boyd to be ill served by the Red Sox as an organization. "The race thing in Boston was so overwhelming that it was so much bigger than Oil Can. The longer he stayed in Boston, the worse it got. After a time, it just swallowed him up."

If the Stuart case provided the sensational headlines, so much that it spilled into the isolated world of Major League Baseball, then the steady undercurrent of hostility that kept Boston segregated also still remained. For more than a decade, the two largest housing projects in South Boston were segregated. Neither the Mary Ellen McCormack nor the Old Colony Housing projects housed a single minority family. It was a reflection of the deep-rooted segregation that existed in Boston and also a strong sign of the powerful resistance of South Boston in particular to any form of racial integration. Fifteen years after Arthur Garrity ruled that South Boston high would be 50 percent nonwhite, it was time, so said a mandate from the federal Housing and Urban Development office, that South Boston's housing projects must be integrated as well.

While Ellis Burks was wondering if the city of Boston would ever enjoy a moment of peace from its continuing racial divide, here was yet another crack in the city's fragile foundation. The relationship between blacks and whites in Boston became at one point so intractable that years earlier the leaders of

Roxbury, one of the poorer, mostly black sections of Boston, attempted to secede from the city and form a new, separate municipality called Mandela.

Unlike the busing situation, in which the Boston School Committee's refusal to recognize segregation in the city's schools exacerbated simmering tensions, the Boston Housing Authority (BHA) admitted that neither the Old Colony nor the Mary Ellen McCormack contained nonwhite residents. For years, the federal government had pushed a reluctant BHA to settle the imbalance, but the authority—fearing another racial catastrophe—purposely steered nonwhite applicants to public housing in different parts of the city. South Boston was and remains the city's most virulent symbol of white resistance. It had been that way in the early 1970s with busing, and more than a decade did not change that fact.

But public housing belonged—so went the federal argument—to each member of the city, regardless of neighborhood and race. That included South Boston, clearly one of the most explosive neighborhoods in the country and, because of busing, the nation's most infamous.

"What's absolutely outrageous," white South Boston city councilor James M. Kelly said in a perverse appropriation of civil rights rhetoric, "is that because of the color of their skin, South Boston residents are not allowed to live in South Boston developments." Furious, too, were many of his constituents in South Boston. In their eyes, it was happening again. The federal government was interloping, forcing South Boston's housing projects to be integrated.

Kelly's political spin, the grandstanding, came with a demonizing intent. They forced us to go to school with them, his words said between the lines, and now they're forcing us to live with them, too?

Who wanted to deal with this again? Not Mayor Ray Flynn, himself already singed from an enraged black community over the Stuart case. Not either the residents of South Boston, and certainly not the sacrificial blacks who would be slated in 1988 to begin the long overdue process of integrating the housing projects.

South Boston whites were forced to share schools with the blacks. Now the government was saying the blacks had the right to move next door. In 1990, South Boston was 97 percent white.

In his blood, Flynn was one of them. He grew up in South Boston, was one of the final cuts of the Celtics after graduating from Providence College, and for a time was something of a local hero when he was elected mayor in 1983. Southie had one of its own in charge, and many Southie residents remember Flynn on the front lines of the anti-busing movement. That changed during his first term in office. Flynn quickly earned a reputation in South Boston as sympathetic to the city's blacks, which was a politically dangerous tag to carry.

Part of what moved Flynn, thought longtime political columnist Marty Nolan, was the fight over busing. Flynn was embarrassed by the old news footage that showed him wearing a plaid suit, arms interlocked with anti-busing forces defying the federal order. He did not want to become, like a George Wallace, an old symbol of the resistance to an inevitable new world. He considered himself an urban populist, and when campaign irregularities chased the incumbent, Kevin White, from seeking a fifth term, Flynn ran for mayor.

Flynn, Nolan thought, also benefited to a lesser extent from his athletic background. He very nearly made the Celtics roster in the 1960s and from his basketball days was used to an integrated setting. In the election, he ran against black activist Mel King, whom he played against in high school. During the campaign there was a surprisingly low level of racial animosity.

When Flynn defeated King—whose candidacy was largely symbolic—he immediately set out to support his campaign rhetoric and represent all neighborhoods. Flynn did this knowing there could very well be a serious backlash from the South Boston and Charlestown constituencies, neighborhoods that believed he betrayed them. As a symbolic gesture, Flynn made a point of jogging through predominately black neighborhoods as a show of unity.

If Flynn was fearful that South Boston would not forget his support of the black community, he was right. When he won a bitter reelection in 1987, he failed to carry his old Southie neighborhood.

A black woman named Mary Bullock moved her family into the Old Colony project in October 1989. She was the first black person to move into the South Boston projects in over a decade. Days after arriving, locals welcomed her to South Boston by pumping the Bullocks' front door and kitchen with gunfire.

It was the type of response that made the city, trying to distance itself from its past and to encourage all races to enjoy Boston, cringe. Even now, almost a decade removed from the city's worst chapter, racial peace in the city seemed hopeless. By December, the Bullock family moved out.

FIFTEEN

After Mary Bullock moved out of the Old Colony project, black, Asian, and Latino families gradually moved into South Boston. Over the next four years, the housing projects in South Boston that once were the focus of palpable hostility would be integrated without much notice. Occasionally, there would be racial skirmishes, but the prediction that integrating Southie housing projects would become the next explosive chapter in the city, the sequel to busing and the Stuart case, went largely unfounded. This relative quietude represented a first sign of hope that the climate of the city was changing to some degree. If resistant Southie could integrate—even at a trickle—maybe a possibility for healing in the city existed after all.

There were early signs of quiet change. When Mary Bullock's apartment was ripped by sniper fire—that October week when Charles Stuart began hatching his murderous scheme—members of the South Boston community responded immediately. Mary Bullock recalled white neighbors offering their sorrow and condolences. Others offered support and even shared a cup of coffee with their beleaguered new tenant, a simple level of physical interaction that even in 1990 was a gigantic breakthrough. Even minor support for a black person was long unthinkable in South Boston, but when she moved, Mary Bullock herself believed, maybe for the first time in her life, that the violent attitude against people of color in South Boston was becoming a minority opinion.

That a black Bostonian felt strongly for Southie was as revealing as the neighborhood responding to her. To Michael Patrick McDonald, it was as if collectively the community was saying that it didn't want to be known as the racist hub of the city. McDonald had lived in the Old Colony projects for much of his life. He had always lived in South Boston and was a child of the streets during the worst days of busing in the mid-1970s. McDonald remembered when the Bullock family moved into Old Colony and the muted, then growing, response of the community. South Boston may never welcome large numbers of blacks into its enclave, but they weren't stoning their new neighbors, either. For a long time, McDonald felt it impossible for whites and blacks to coexist in Southie. Too much had happened. Now, at the beginning of the last decade of the century, he had begun to sense a healing.

Years later, McDonald would write *All Souls*, a searing, despairing memoir of life in Southie, both under the specter of busing and the fearsome control of the gangster Whitey Bulger. The integration of the housing projects in South Boston was a significant, underreported event, McDonald thought, because it represented the first crack in the rigid segregation that existed for decades in the city. Much of what people believed they knew about different groups came second or third hand. The slow dissipation of residential segregation would foster a new day in Boston.

Adrian Walker was a young black reporter from Miami who came to the Boston *Globe* in 1989. One of his first assignments was to cover the Stuart case. It was an immediate entry into the Boston psyche. While covering the Stuart murders, Walker also watched with great interest the integration of the South Boston projects. He was new to the *Globe* newsroom, and the few friends he had in Boston had told him to beware of the city. His friends outside of Boston couldn't understand why he was moving to Boston in the first place. It was a common response from black professionals. If black athletes were wary of coming to Boston to play, so too were black professionals who faced opportunities to work in the city. Walker saw the *Globe* gravitating toward the difficult position of incorporating race into the discussion of covering the news not as a single, isolated event, but as a constant element in a city that was finally taking the grudging steps of change. It was a heady decision, for as the Massachusetts economy developed into a high-tech epicenter, the retention and recruitment of black professionals would become as important a story in the city as the Red Sox's inability to attract free agents.

Still, Adrian Walker persisted. Like Cecil Cooper, Larry Whiteside, and Luis Tiant, he was attracted to Boston, and the *Globe* in particular. A certain type of energy existed in Boston, a metropolitan feel and potential that he gravitated toward. Plus, Walker loved the inner workings of politics, and there were few better places than Boston to receive an up-close education in big-city machine politics.

Over the years, Walker began to see important changes. Being from Florida, he did not have the institutional memory of some of his colleagues, but his vantage point as an outsider provided an important perspective. Where the Stuart case—according to the conventional wisdom—was supposed to be the springboard to another decade of racial strife, Adrian Walker saw just the opposite. Like Michael Patrick McDonald, Walker sensed a collective weariness among Boston's residents from the decades of civil war. It was, he believed, as if Bostonians—even those who hadn't necessarily been champions of racial harmony—were embarrassed. Walker believed the Stuart case pushed Boston to a collective moment of introspection. Were these events going to continue to define Boston as a city of deep, insuperable racial divisions with a curious alter ego of high intellectual standards? Or was enough, finally and mercifully, enough?

Part of the reason for the city's slow revival was the gentrification of some of the city's most entrenched neighborhoods. The city was simply running out of prime real estate. Roxbury, the heart of the black community, sat very near the South End and Back Bay, two attractive locations for development. Roxbury stood very near the city's downtown office and convention center space. It also bordered parts of Northeastern University, the growing private institution that would begin expanding. The result was the transformation of neighborhoods that had owned specific and rigid characteristics for decades.

The same began to occur in the entrenched white enclaves such as South Boston, Jamaica Plain, and parts of Dorchester.

There was another new element, thought Marty Nolan, and that was Ray Flynn, the mayor. He had staked his political clout on bringing warring sections of the city together and to a large degree succeeded. Nolan believed that Flynn simply never received the proper credit for fostering a newer, more accessible attitude in Boston. Flynn was, thought Adrian Walker, the invisible hand that nudged the city in a more positive direction. This was significant, especially after his predecessor, Kevin White, presided over Boston during the busing years and had emerged with a clear pessimism about the future of the city's neighborhoods.

Deeper problems still existed within the city. Boston's black community, mired in a decades-old political malaise, still lacked the power of a cohesive voting bloc that would allow it greater clout in city government. It was still a fragmented, curiously aloof electorate. In 2001, some thirty-six years after his death, Adrian Walker would echo a Malcolm X sentiment from the 1940s and '50s in lamenting the apparent passivity of Boston's black electorate. Outside of Tom Atkins in 1967, and Mel King in 1983, the city would not boast a serious black mayoral candidate in its history. Perhaps more importantly, Walker felt Boston's black community lacked what it truly needed: the black power broker who could navigate the city's winding political corridors. Boston would never enjoy a signature black politician like Adam Clayton Powell, in Harlem who knew how to get things done. Although he was never mayor, Bill Dawson in Chicago was legendary in this crucial role. Izzy Muchnick had it years ago in Boston for his Jewish constituency. In basketball, they would call it the *go-to guy*. One of the great disadvantages of the Boston black citizenry, Walker felt, was that black Bostonians traditionally would rely on white politicians to do their politicking for them, an echo of Malcolm X's half-century-old judgment. The greatest disadvantage, however, was the meager size of the city's black population. Until the early 1960s, blacks made up only about 4 percent of the city's residents. There was no go-to guy in the city because there was little to be gained by appeasing the black population. Before World War II, Dr. Silas F. (Shag) Taylor was as close to a black power broker as the city would see. He and his brother, Bal Taylor, however, lacked votes to deliver the Irish political machine that a Dawson could deliver to a Richard Daley. Alan Lupo characterized Taylor's difficult position:

> Bal Taylor, in later years, once told a black reporter, "This area needed a voice, and we've tried to supply it, by George: it's worth our while to see that the people are taken care of." So, on a smaller scale than Lomansey and old Pat Kennedy, the Taylors wheeled and dealed, and if it was a smaller potatoes, that was not due to any lack of abilities of the Taylor family, but instead to the small numbers of blacks and the even smaller of black voters. In the 1930s, the forties and fifties, the local black pols—the Taylors never ran for public office; others occasionally ran and often lost—were the focus of what little power existed in the black community. They and the clergy were the leaders. Shag and Bal Taylor worked closely with Curley; they served in the high councils of local and state Democratic politics. They were the house niggers, but they traded in on that for jobs, housings, or anything they could get.

As the black migration swelled, the new clans of blacks didn't quite get along, anyway. Being unable to set aside differences in class and culture to mobilize politically was a critical failure on the part of black community, but in the 1990s, as the city grew to a nonwhite majority, being able to do so was crucial to a new Boston, one where the entrenched establishment began to share, Walker thought. It would be a critical element necessary for the city to attain its full potential. Moreover, the changes taking place in Boston—with city residents of all races moving into decades-old ethnic strongholds such as Southie, Charlestown, and Roxbury—would only be cosmetic unless buttressed by real and diverse political power.

Adrian Walker saw the early 1990s as an opportunity not only for healing a damaged city but also for newer possibilities. It would be true in his own case, for being a prominent columnist for the *Globe* was a position not without power. Before being fired in a plagiarism scandal, Mike Barnicle had used that space to shape opinion for years. He was a powerful force. Now Adrian Walker had the same opportunity.

An obvious consequence of the busing aftermath—white flight—left for black and minority Bostonians a rare opportunity to seize power. In 1960, Boston's blacks comprised 4 percent of the population. By 1995, the city's minority population represented nearly half of its total.

Yet the result would not be a new activism on the part of the city's blacks. Indeed, an old busing nemesis seized power in the city. Jimmy Kelly, the pugnacious city councilor from South Boston who vehemently fought busing and even did jail time, won the presidency of the City Council. Michael McDonald knew the feared Jimmy Kelly. Everyone from Southie knew the man just as much as did everyone in Roxbury, Mattapan, and Dorchester. This was the same Jimmy Kelly who early during the Stuart case said of the black community, "A major problem is, let's face it, the instability of the black family. A total dependency on government. Too many black people are looking to government to be their savior." McDonald remembered a beaming Kelly when he met George Wallace back in 1976. "Ma brought her guitar and accordion up to the Lith Club and took the stage to do her own antibusing anthems, and she said she never saw Jimmy Kelly so excited as when he finally got to meet George Wallace."

The *Globe*, also energized editorially, wondered in print how a divisive politician like Kelly could engineer a successful power grab when the city's minorities could have made an unprecedented statement of voter power, not unlike when the Irish stunned the Brahmins at the turn of the nineteenth century. In a way, Kelly's ascension mirrored the Red Sox—over time, everything about the city and team mirrored each other. For Kelly personified an era that the city wanted to rid itself—busing—yet with Kelly at the front of a "new Boston," it looked very much like the old one. How reminiscent it was to the old days of the Red Sox, when Pumpsie Green was there, as was Earl Wilson and what did Yawkey do? He gave Pinky Higgins a promotion.

Adrian Walker believed he knew the answer. Part would be a function of the political topography—the city's voting districts fragmented minority neighborhoods, essentially stripping them of a mandate. The other reason would be more telling and damning: A lack of real political activism on the part of the city's repressed minorities kept it from building powerful coalitions. The *Globe* covered the story:

> In front of the audience at the City Hall ceremony, Kelly addresses the concerns of all of Boston's middle-class residents, whatever their race. When, for example, he declaims on the need "to end the insanity of this slow-motion civil war we have going on in certain neighborhoods, kids killing kids over nothing," he is seeking to keep middle-class minorities in the city by fighting crime in their neighborhoods.
>
> But during interviews, it's clear that Kelly's priority as City Council president is somewhat different. "My main objective is to stabilize the city, to maintain a white middle class," he says. It's also clear that Kelly is willing to help minority residents only as long as they are willing to remain in the neighborhoods where they currently reside. Asked if he considers himself a separatist, Kelly replies, "If people want to associate with people most like themselves, let them."

There are moments where Kelly's South Boston neighborhood reminds Adrian Walker of its past. In November 1992, Donald Williams, a black man, was severely beaten in South Boston. The heart of the city would not change overnight, for South Boston still owned a lingering antagonism toward the city's minorities. During the 1990s, Walker did what was long the unthinkable for a black person in Boston. He didn't move to South Boston, but to Savin Hill, a section of Dorchester reserved for whites and as close to Southie as one could be without actually making the perilous crossover.

The initial steps toward a healing of the city's fractious nature would be incremental. "It never will go away completely," Walker said. He would be ultimately positive, even in hopeless cynicism. If Ray Flynn did not receive his proper credit, the major change in the city is that Boston is no longer Boston in the traditional sense. As the city prospered from the high-tech boom of the 1990s and rental prices rose sharply, entire families who had lived in Roxbury or Southie for generations moved out. The hope for the city, Michael Patrick McDonald would say acidly, is when everyone who didn't get along can no longer afford to live in Boston. Like virtually every other neighborhood in the city, gentrification threatened South Boston's traditional demographics, with generations of poor, isolationist Irish giving way to Boston's more polished and upwardly mobile residents. People like Adrian Walker.

If the 1990s began a healing of sorts for Boston, Ellis Burks would not be around to witness it or its effect on the Boston Red Sox. For the first time in his professional career, he entered the winter of 1992 with uncertainty. He had completed his sixth season in the major leagues, which meant he was eligible for free agency. The Boston years had been difficult; he hit just .254 in 1991 and .251 in 1992. He could not avoid injury, and it was affecting every part of his game. Once the best stolen base threat the Red Sox had seen since Tommy Harper twenty years before, Burks would be thrown out on the base paths more often than he would succeed. His power had diminished and criticism of him increased. More often, he would remember Jim Rice's advice: *Get your six years and get the hell out of Boston.*

But Ellis Burks knew something the Red Sox did not. For the first time in years, he felt completely healthy. The bulging disk in his back, which he injured by foolishly trying to transform himself from the solid, all-around player into the prototypical Boston slugger, had finally healed. He had high hopes for 1993, which was the first year since his All-Star season in 1989 that he expected to enter the season at 100 percent.

It never happened. Management, exasperated, decided that he was physically unreliable, too injury-prone to be a consistent contributor to the team. Burks, General Manager Lou Gorman decided, would not have a long career. He couldn't play a week without getting hurt. The Red Sox did the unthinkable for a player of Burks' talent and the investment the team made in him. They declined to offer Burks a contract. His Red Sox career was over.

It was a painful moment. The Red Sox were the only organization he had known. They signed him in 1983, the same year as Roger Clemens, and Burks had invested himself emotionally into being a member of the Red Sox. The last few years, indeed, had been hard ones: In addition to his mounting anger that nothing he did on a baseball field would satisfy expectations, Burks was frustrated that management seemed to have little interest in the special needs of black players. They in fact didn't seem to have any interest in black players at all. Burks had endured what Jim Rice had endured before him, being the only black position player in a twenty-five-man clubhouse. It was a lonely feeling, and while Burks possessed the type of personality that allowed him to navigate through the various cliques on the team, he also felt a special type of isolation. He liked Mike Greenwell. He enjoyed Oil Can Boyd. He missed Jim Rice. Burks reflected on Boyd's explosive career with the Red Sox with empathy. "It made my time there look easy."

Once, Mike Marshall, a white outfielder, asked Burks what it was like to be the only black in the Red Sox clubhouse. Marshall had come over from the Los Angeles Dodgers and seemed convinced that it had no real significance. For a moment, Burks was stunned. Then he asked Marshall to try to imagine being the only white in the room, including managers, coaches, and ownership. Burks then asked Marshall to also imagine enjoying different movies, different food, different places to hang out, and a different view of life than everyone in the room. Marshall quickly dropped the subject; Burks felt Marshall simply could not fathom being that alone.

Whether or not it was intentional, Burks echoed a common theme among blacks when they would discuss their "time" in Boston. It would commonly sound like a jail sentence. Years later, after he had moved on, Burks noted that he always would ask fellow black players who came through Boston out of curiosity if times had changed, but the responses were often similar to his own. Inside the team or out in the city, there would be no black support of the team, as Burks' unheeded radio pleadings had demonstrated to him.

The Red Sox qualified for the postseason in two of his six seasons, yet Burks was visibly unhappy. Like most ballplayers, there existed in his mind a belief that he and the Red Sox could work out their differences and become a winning ballclub. "I really thought I would spend my whole career with the Red Sox," he said. "Maybe it was me being naïve because it was my first organization, but I didn't do anything to not be offered a contract. I thought I would finish my career in Boston. I learned that I wouldn't the hard way."

Burks looked forward to 1993 for another reason. Joe Morgan was gone. He had been fired after the 1992 season. This was a positive sign for Burks, as Morgan consistently burned Burks by leaking stories to the press that Burks was always healthy enough to play and was just goldbricking it, in baseball lingo. The old third baseman Butch Hobson—he of the bone chips and forty-four errors in '78—was named the manager.

After six years in Boston, not being offered a contract was a bitter disappointment. The final insult for Ellis Burks came during his final days, when only Lou Gorman acknowledged him and thanked him for his effort as a member of the Red Sox. "Lou was a good man. He was the only person who called or said anything. He thanked me for my time in the organization. He showed class, but he was the only one. I never heard from anyone else. Not even a 'good luck, Ellis.'"

So Burks went into the winter looking for a job. He found one with the Chicago White Sox, signing a one-year deal. Immediately, baseball was fun again. The White Sox possessed a healthy mix of veteran and young talent, a club close to breaking through. Chicago hadn't won a pennant since 1983 and were in worse shape in the championship department than the Red Sox. The Chicago White Sox hadn't won a World Series title since 1917, and the 1919 Black Sox scandal symbolized the ultimate in baseball corruption.

Most interesting for Burks was the Chicago clubhouse. He had never played for another organization and was immediately struck by the black presence. He found himself surrounded by black clubhouse leaders. Frank Thomas, Tim Raines, Lance Johnson, and Bo Jackson, as well as Latino players such as Ozzie Guillen and Roberto Hernandez, were the lead players, along with Robin Ventura and Jack McDowell. There were proven people of color who took leadership roles on a winning club, a foreign concept to Burks. Until Pedro Martinez and Mo Vaughn in 1998—ninety-seven years into the team's history—the Red Sox would not field a team with minority players out front. Rice and Tiant were keys to the teams of the 1970s, but those teams truly belonged to Yastrzemski and Fisk.

"That team was special, really special," Burks said. "We had Frank and a bunch of guys who knew how to win. It was so different from Boston because there was always so much pressure. It wasn't just pressure about being black and not fitting in—although there was that—but pressure about winning, period. Everyone up there is so gloom and doom. You lose today, and oh, man, we're going to see stories about Babe Ruth, the curse and what not. On that Chicago team, if we lost today, we'd win tomorrow."

The city was different. Burks was now playing in a city with a sizable black population and with a tremendous black culture. Ellis Burks had never experienced such an environment. It was a complete departure from Boston. Granted, Chicago had its share of racial trouble; its Cabrini Green and Robert Taylor housing projects on the city's South Side were some of the most dangerous living quarters in the world, and—for blacks—life under the Richard Daley machine could be harsh. For decades, the thousands of blacks entering the city were channeled into the ghettoes. Chicago was not a promised land for blacks, but Ellis Burks sensed a different energy among Chicago blacks than he felt from blacks in Boston. Part of the reason, he believed, was the confidence Chicago blacks seemed to have. Chicago's blacks were politically active; the city contained a sizable black population, and its black residents enjoyed some political successes. Harold Washington won the city's mayoralty in 1987, and Eugene Sawyer replaced him after Washington's sudden death. Adrian Walker always believed it possible for blacks in Boston to duplicate the political successes of blacks in other cities. The problem, Walker felt, was the blacks themselves, who in Boston had never been politically active enough to wrest power from the Irish bosses who have controlled the city for a century.

To Burks and the great majority of black professionals, virtually everything about Boston carried with it a racial element, which was unfortunate to him because he actually liked his employers, the Red Sox. In Boston, the shadow of race always tainted the discussion. Boyd had his troubles, but outside of Joe Morgan, Ellis Burks enjoyed his teammates and the energy of Fenway Park.

Chicago was different. At that time, Michael Jordan was the star of the city, and almost all of the weight he felt in Boston—of being black in a racially uneasy town, of not being Willie Mays, and of being stuck with the fragile label—disappeared. Burks was able to play his game, fit quietly into the team structure. The result was a solid comeback season and a contribution to the team's playoff berth.

The press approached the team differently. The Chicago newspapers maintained a perspective about the game that Ellis Burks found refreshing. They covered the team, but it wasn't so *personal,* as it was in Boston. Burks saw this media proprietorship of the Red Sox more clearly in the case of Jim Rice.

"The power of the pen is a hell of a thing," he said. "They control so much about how you are viewed. Jimmy had problems with Dan Shaughnessy and he had problems with Steve Fainaru. You know what they say, the media can make or break you."

Chicago was a vindication for Ellis Burks. The White Sox, as baseball would have it, broke up the 1993 division-winning team after losing to eventual World Series–winner Toronto in six games. Burks moved on to Colorado after the 1993 season, where he would be reunited with Don Baylor and enjoy a productive four-year run with the Rockies. The highlight was 1996, when he burst out with a .340 average and forty home runs and a second-place finish in the National League MVP balloting. Colorado made the playoffs in 1995, the fourth time Burks would qualify for the postseason. He wound up in the playoffs again in 2000 with the San Francisco Giants, playing for Dusty Baker, and again with Cleveland in 2001.

Ellis Burks would grow into a solid major leaguer and would forge an above average career. Of the Red Sox of the 1980s, only two would play into the twenty-first century. Roger Clemens is still pitching with the New York Yankees, and Ellis Burks is the only position player left, the very player Walpole Joe Morgan and Lou Gorman said would never have a long career.

SIXTEEN

By 1993, the Red Sox malaise was complete. The team had squeezed every ounce from their diminished resources, and the result was consecutive losing seasons for the first time since 1965 and '66. The firing of Joe Morgan at the end of the 1992 season may have seemed like a new beginning, but it would be only in a cosmetic sense, for dumping the manager could not forestall what would be three straight years of losing baseball, something that hadn't happened in Boston since Pinky Higgins poured beef Stroganov in the lap of Bud Collins and spit tobacco juice on Larry Claflin.

If the city was beginning to chart a new path for itself in the years following the Stuart case, the Red Sox as an organization were still confounded by race. To the annoyance and frustration of Lou Gorman, the team's general manager, time only intensified the feeling that Boston was the worst place for a black player to play. For someone as dignified and tranquil as Ellis Burks to be so unhappy in Boston was a telling sign, as was his rebirth as a member of the Chicago White Sox. Like Earl Wilson, Reggie Smith, and Cecil Cooper before him, Burks' talent flourished away from Fenway Park.

Gorman was paralyzed. In the truest sense, he was a victim of the past sins of the franchise. He preferred to be judged by his peers on his personal record as a baseball administrator; although he was no trailblazer for racial change, Gorman would be tainted more for his stubbornness as a contract negotiator than any type of racial troubles. He had been in charge of the Red Sox since 1984 and had acquired players he believed would help the club. Like Haywood Sullivan before him, Gorman would not sign a black free agent in the 1980s, which fed into the ugly stereotype that the Red Sox, even as the 1990s approached, were still uninterested in signing black players.

But Lou Gorman was no racist, either. He stood up to the constant charges against the Red Sox by leaning on his record. Whatever happened in the past, Gorman believed, was just that. It was old news, and in a perfect world should have been no reflection upon the current actions of the franchise. This, thought Ellis Burks, was a colossal mistake, for it was certainly not a perfect world and the past transgressions were exactly what the Red Sox were paying for now. More important than the reality, the Red Sox were now fighting something far more dangerous and complicated to combat: history and perception. By doing nothing to remedy, or at the very least acknowledge, the past, Gorman was unwittingly contributing to the pessimism around him.

A year earlier, Jean Yawkey died at age eighty-two, ending fifty-nine years of a Yawkey overseeing the club. Unlike her husband, Jean Yawkey would not be known as the generous-to-a-fault owner who grudgingly oversaw the ball club. As an owner, she would be remembered more for the in-house fight first with Buddy Le Roux and later with Haywood Sullivan and for her control over the team than for shaping a franchise. Politically, the widow would never stray far from the husband, remaining in close alliance with the American League and rarely, if ever, taking a bold position. Like her husband, under her watch the Red Sox would not sign a black free agent, and a cloud of moral confusion would continue to hover over the team.

The Yawkey name would continue on. The Red Sox official ownership status, in 1992, was an estate called the Yawkey Trust. The man now in control of the franchise was John Harrington, a Boston native who had started back in Joe Cronin's American League office back in the 1960s. Harrington's position was to be the caretaker of the trust until a suitable buyer could be found for the Red Sox. Harrington, however, soon would discover that he enjoyed being a major league owner, and his control of the Red Sox would definitely be permanent.

A community of people in the press and with the Red Sox believed that for the first time in the history of the franchise, the Red Sox now possessed in Harrington an owner who recognized the racial stigma that plagued the franchise and pledged action. Harrington would be a mystery in a way different from Yawkey, but as the decade moved forward, there would be enough mixed signals to suggest that Harrington would cut a complex figure. He was completely a Boston product, from the eclectic neighborhood of Jamaica Plain and Boston College. There would be times Harrington would exhibit a moral frustration about the team's racial makeup and perceptions, others when it appeared he was no different than the Yawkey family.

Larry Whiteside, who had now been in Boston for twenty years, was equally frustrated. Like Haywood Sullivan, he personally liked Lou Gorman and saw subtle but important changes taking place within the organization. Harrington's appointment was one of them; Whiteside believed the Red Sox would always be considered a racist franchise as long as the Yawkey name controlled the club. It was not a position he voiced frequently; although he was, along with McDonough, the *Globe* baseball man with the most continuous tenure at the newspaper, he was still the only black regular in the press corps. It was a reality that forced him to move carefully. Still, Whiteside saw the Red Sox now attempting to reach out to the black community with ticket programs and youth sponsorship programs, but the team was met by the city's blacks with almost total apathy. The team hired an African-American woman, Leslie

Sterling, to succeed legendary public address announcer Sherm Feller. Elaine Weddington Steward, another African American, had been installed in the front office as a vice president and assistant general manager. For the first time in the team's history, it appeared that the Red Sox were beginning to take the arduous steps toward substantial change. With so many years of perceived slights, what existed between the club and the city's blacks was nothing short of a cold war.

Gorman, frustrated by the lack of response to his inroads by a bitter black community, threw up his hands in despair, convinced that even his best efforts would be fruitless. For years, the Red Sox were attacked for ignoring the black community. Now, when the club attempted to create a bond in minority neighborhoods, they were rebuffed with distrust. What, Gorman wondered, was he supposed to do? It was one thing to be aware of one's own actions and treat people accordingly, quite another to change the entire culture and perception of a team, which had been in place since the turn of the century.

There were legitimate reasons for this retrenchment. The first was the lack of tangible results. Despite positive talk, little about the Red Sox organization had changed publicly. The second reason was even more severe: The consequence of the team's history finally seemed to have caught up with it. Black players, who because of free agency now could control to a great degree which teams they played for, now did not want to play for the Red Sox. And they were voicing it.

It was one of the great unforeseen consequences of the free agent era. Saddled with the blemishes of the past, the Red Sox now found themselves at a severe competitive disadvantage. The price the Red Sox would pay for Eddie Collins, Joe Cronin, and Pinky Higgins would not completely be paid during that era, but now in the free agent era, in which players could decide not only what teams they wanted to play for but also which ones they did not. Hall of Famer Dave Winfield once said he would never play for the Red Sox for any amount of money, thanks to an ugly incident during the mid-1980s where a bottle was thrown at him from a moving car while he took a morning jog. Joe Carter, the great outfielder, would always be wary of Boston's reputation. Tim Raines, the longtime Montreal Expos great, was bitter toward Boston because of a day at Logan Airport when police detained him and his wife while connecting through Boston to a vacation in the Bahamas. The authorities said Raines fit the description of a wanted cocaine dealer. To Raines, it was an example of the mistreatment that came with being black.

In addition to free agents choosing to avoid Boston, players with tenured status in the game chose another strategy that indicted the Red Sox: They would include language in their contracts to prevent them from being traded to the Red Sox. Two high-level black stars, Marquis Grissom and David Justice, inserted language into their contracts that prevented them from ever being traded to the Red Sox. While the real reason for the clause was a personal animosity between the agent for both players and new Red Sox general manager Dan Duquette, the very idea of a black player refusing to play in Boston aroused old feelings. When he was to become a free agent in 2000, Peter Gammons told Ken Griffey, Jr., that he should consider Boston. A player of Griffey's immense talent along with an effervescent playing style would be revered in Boston, Gammons reasoned. Griffey's response was cool and incredulous. He would never consider Boston, the racist city, the place where he could get lynched. "I told him he would own the city if he came here," Gammons said. "He looked at me like I was nuts. The city still has a racist label. It's very sad."

During his worst days, Harrington would sink in racial quicksand. He would lament to *Sports Illustrated* that it would take "fifty years" before "this thing" goes away. Black fans were coming to Fenway at a trickle, which was a trend that was no different in ballparks across the country, yet in Boston was emblematic of a larger problem. Harrington would give periodic interviews with such despair that he sounded like a victim.

What could Harrington do? For starters, he could act. The network of black players believed the worst about the franchise, and only actions could change that. At the end of the 1992 season, Harrington made his first bold move as owner.

He went after free agent Kirby Puckett, the great Minnesota Twins star. It was the first time in the sixteen-year history of free agency that the Red Sox would aggressively pursue a black player. This was a high-stakes move, for Harrington was a product of a Red Sox organization that had ventured clumsily into the free agent market. Regardless of race, the Red Sox had been badly burned in the market, overpaying for bad players, missing completely on the chance to sign others. As his first move as owner, Harrington clearly did not want to blow this opportunity, for it would not only give the Red Sox a victory both in signing a great player and dilute the race question but would also signal his own arrival as a powerful owner in the game.

The Boston traditions greatly interested Puckett. He played a marvelous centerfield for nearly a decade in Minnesota and was the fulcrum of two World Series title teams. Now, he was a free agent and the frugal Twins management would not match his salary demand of $27 million over five years. Puckett—a true student of the game—very much desired his name to be attached to a historically rich team like the Red Sox. To be included with the great Red Sox players like Williams, Rice, and Yastrzemski—and perhaps to be the man to bring a championship to a thirsty city—would leave a wonderful legacy. Puckett was on a Hall of Fame pace, and legends are made, he reasoned, in century-old baseball towns like Boston and New York. Those cities not only owned great baseball traditions, but also were powerful media centers. It was no secret in the baseball world that big-league cities were not equal. Reggie Jackson knew that playing in New York raised his profile like no other city, even though he was arguably a better player in Oakland. Dave Winfield and Don Mattingly both knew this. Puckett was a splendid player in Minnesota, but there would be no telling how much more exposure he could have attained in a better media market.

Puckett was well known as one of baseball's great and most beloved, affable players, perhaps the game's best ambassador since Ernie Banks of the 1950s and '60s. If Oil Can Boyd, Reggie Smith, and Jim Rice couldn't quite acclimate themselves to Boston because of the pungency of their personalities, then Kirby Puckett possessed the innate ability to ease the tension in any room. There were other attractions. Fenway Park, with its short left field fence and thirty-seven-and-a-half-foot wall was an inviting target, for Puckett was one of the most dangerous right-handed hitters of his generation.

The Sox pursued Puckett with class and style. He and his wife were given a suite at the Four Seasons Hotel. At once, Puckett was impressed with the city's historical elegance. As a city, Puckett thought, Boston possessed a rare toughness, a similar edge that he felt he brought to the baseball diamond. And Puckett knew from the dozens of times he played in Boston as a visitor that the fans, often brutal to visiting players, were nevertheless knowledgeable about the game.

Puckett was wary. He and his wife enjoyed lunch with John Harrington and a couple of other Red Sox officials, but there was an unspoken undercurrent during the lunch. Harrington seemed somewhat fixated on Puckett's views of race relations. It was clear, Puckett thought, that Harrington was trying too hard to gauge Puckett's view of Boston. Puckett told Harrington that he was concerned about another sensational racial issue that occurred in Boston in 1990, when Boston Celtics rookie sensation Dee Brown was rousted at gunpoint by the local police in the affluent area of Wellesley. Puckett told Harrington and the Red Sox the sight of Brown facedown on the pavement with guns pointed at him concerned him. Brown himself downplayed the incident, and the protectionist Boston press praised him for not crucifying the city. Harrington did not duck the issue, and he assured Puckett that the Brown affair was a horrible mistake and that the city was becoming a better, more inclusive place.

Other than this preoccupation, Puckett was impressed with the Boston proposal. He enjoyed Boston as a city and was pleasantly surprised to see Elaine Weddington Steward at the lunch. That the Red Sox had hired a thoughtful, and intellectual African-American female attorney to handle contractual issues instead of being an affirmative action showpiece carried weight with him. This was especially true because Harrington's presentation was a total departure from everything he had heard about Boston's unwelcoming reputation. The Red Sox made a hard offer, $38 million over five years, which was some $11 million over the Twins' offer.

Ultimately, Puckett stayed in Minnesota. The Twins offered him $5 million less than the Red Sox offer, but Kirby Puckett merely wanted Minnesota only to increase its offer, not match Boston's. Also, Puckett's wife liked Minnesota and was not particularly keen on relocating. A few months before he was enshrined into the Hall of Fame, Puckett said race was not the deal-breaking factor in his staying with the Twins, but more his commitment to an organization that treated him well.

Signing Kirby Puckett would have gone a long way to continue the healing process that had begun with the calm integration of the South Boston housing projects and the finality of the Stuart case. Puckett also would have been the first black free agent signed by the Red Sox.

John Harrington frequently would use the Puckett anecdote as an example that the Red Sox have made efforts to undo the past or at least create a new future, but years of past history had destroyed any hope at detente.

Peter Gammons believed that Puckett was never sincere about coming to Boston, that he was merely using the Red Sox and other teams as leverage to broker a better deal with the Twins. Newly inducted into the Hall of Fame in 2001, Puckett would disagree with this notion. "I was real close to going to Boston," he said. "As close as you can put your thumb and finger without touching them, that's how close I came to playing for the Red Sox." Shane Mack, who at the end of his career played briefly with the Red Sox, said Puckett relayed the story to him and he explained to Puckett his understanding of Boston's historical relationship with black players. Puckett said he was aware of Boston's past, but was truly eager to play for the Red Sox, a sentiment rarely if ever uttered by a black player.

"I wouldn't have had any problems playing in Boston. I do my thing. If people like me, that's fine. I live and let live. I love people, so it wouldn't have been a big thing for me. But on the other hand, a different personality, a guy like Jimmy Rice or Oil Can, well, I can see why they had problems."

The Red Sox failed to land Puckett, but for one of the few times in the franchise's history, the talk of change was no longer an abstract notion but a very real one.

If John Harrington was wondering how to engineer a new legacy for the Red Sox, he had his answer.

The top two voices on the sports pages, though, hadn't changed outside of age. In the early 1970s, they were just making their way, but in the 1990s, Peter Gammons and Will McDonough were established giants. Both had made the national scene: McDonough had a go-round on television as a sideline reporter for NBC; Gammons was back at the Globe after two tours at *Sports Illustrated*.

Both were still rivals at the Globe and the biggest sports writing names in the city. By 1992, Gammons had struck the big time. He was the leading baseball voice in the country, and if he had revolutionized baseball coverage with his perfection—if not invention—of the notes column, he had taken the next fateful step: television. ESPN, the twenty-four-hour sports cable monster, signed Gammons as their chief baseball analyst. He was big before, but in New England and among the knowledgeable industry insiders. Now, Gammons was huge, the biggest reporting name of the grand old game, and on the cutting edge of new media. It would not be long before the Gammons name—thanks to the marketing muscle of ESPN—would become its own multimedia brand, baseball's Good Housekeeping seal. His position grew stronger still, because he still maintained his Sunday notes column at the *Globe*, which gave him an important print outlet to move the baseball market.

There would be professional jealousies and outright anger toward Gammons, for many print reporters felt his marriage to television was a traitorous move, for TV continued to diminish the importance of print media.

Worse for Gammons was the uncomfortable question raised that Gammons was now *too* big, and had lost his way as a reporter. He would consistently suffer charges that he no longer wrote for the fan, but for the executives in the game who vied for his attention and credit. Gammons always believed he stood on the right side of this conflict. "I've always considered myself the eyes and the ears of the fan," he said. In his view, he was the fan's entrée into a complex world; he was always a fan at heart and thought that the game should be fun.

Ultimately, what was good for Gammons was good for the Red Sox, for just like in the 1970s, the two ascended together. The Red Sox of the 1990s were as powerful as ever. John Harrington had parlayed an old friendship with Bud Selig to become one of the most influential owners in the game. Selig could count on Harrington to back whatever play he needed, which was reminiscent of the past. Understanding the power structure of the game was a move right out of Tom Yawkey's playbook.

Gammons may have made the jump to national prominence, but he maintained a decidedly Boston motif. He often filmed his live broadcasts from Fenway Park, with the Green Monster looming in the background. An aesthetic touch, but it also suggested that the Red Sox stood closer to the game's most powerful reporter than other teams. Such a relationship in of itself benefited the Red Sox cosmetically, for as an organization the Red Sox would always seem to be at the forefront of the game, even if other teams were more successful and more dynamic.

Gammons followed the clannish impulses of his New England roots in his work. He would throw his weight behind local executives and prospects. Receiving a mention in his column—especially during the late 1990s when he could be seen in the *Globe*, *Baseball America*, on his own section of the ESPN internet site as well as nightly on television—could turn a rank-and-file executive into a leading job candidate.

Unlike rival national columnists—virtually all of which made their reputations by covering teams on the baseball beat—Gammons never distanced himself from his soil and his team, the Red Sox. Trends in the game would be written through the lens of the Red Sox, all of which raised the profile of the Red Sox.

It wasn't just Gammons, however, who elevated the Red Sox into a stratosphere that would never be commensurate to the club's won-loss record. The early 1990s were watershed years for the baseball image, as the game was still—despite, or perhaps because of constant labor trouble—riding the crest of a boom in the game's popularity. And the Red Sox were popular, and the marketers knew it. Baseball books were plentiful, and the Red Sox—with New England being a literary capital—stood at the forefront. Ken Burns, the noted documentary filmmaker, ambitiously set out to chronicle the great history of the game, and the Red Sox were the most featured team in the nine-part series. To that point, the Yankees had won twenty-two World Series titles, the Cardinals were baseball to America's heartland, and the Dodgers were as influential to the course of the sport as any team, but were overshadowed by Boston. The Red Sox were by no means the best team in baseball, but they were the most visible. The result was the inflated importance of the Red Sox as a franchise.

The thing of it was, the Red Sox made money. For the literati, it was cool to be a Red Sox fan. Tragedy and loss made for better copy than sitting back in the easy chair and watching the Yankees stomp the rest of the league. The fan base was literate and insatiable. Only the Yankees—and possibly the Dodgers—were a more recognizable name brand, and the suits knew it. Sean McAdam, who would cover the Red Sox for the *Providence Journal* but would freelance a national column for the ESPN internet site, had his marching orders: The column may be national, but McAdam was to write the Red Sox as much as possible. Market research showed that the Sox were what fans wanted to read about.

The Sox were also a great story, especially with their newfound identity as hexed losers, who fought not only their opponent on the field, but the fates and history. That drew the people in, especially after the collapses of 1978 and '86, both to those hated New York teams. For the reporters who were around the team every day, that created opportunity.

Dan Shaughnessy, who had just begun his career in the mid-1970s, would by the 1990s be an established columnist at the *Globe*. After working in Washington and Baltimore, Shaughnessy returned to the *Globe* in 1982 and covered the Celtics and later the Red Sox. He would over time gain a reputation as being something of the staff cynic, especially after being made a columnist in 1992.

Where Shaughnessy made his mark was with the 1988 book *The Curse of the Bambino*, which chronicled three quarters of a century of Red Sox failures, all tied to one sin: the selling of Babe Ruth in 1920. The book, which originated in a *New York Times* column written by George Vecsey that told of the Red Sox team's fortunes wilting after Ruth's sale to the Yankees, made Shaughnessy a power player in Boston journalism and, like Gammons, raised the profile of the Red Sox. Shaughnessy, too, would hold considerable influence over the *Globe*. He wrote with a sardonic and hyperbolic approach, referring to Red Sox fans as "Red Sox Nation." An example of his reach would be the appearance of his phrases in the stories of other writers, as if Shaughnessy's pet prose was becoming a part of the newspaper's style.

If the *Globe* and the Red Sox rose to prominence together in the years following the 1967 pennant race and the escalation of the Vietnam conflict the two were fully established as unchallenged pillars of New England by the 1990s. Both the *Globe* and the Red Sox benefited from the relationship. The Big Four of the *Globe*'s sports section—McDonough, Gammons, Bob Ryan, and Shaughnessy—would all sign book contracts as a result of their years covering the city's high-profile teams; *The Curse of the Bambino* was the best example of this. And the Red Sox, thanks to an obsession with the team by some of the country's best-known writers, were pushed to a level of importance that was not commensurate with their success. The perception of the Red Sox follower as long-suffering and fatalistic—characteristics that have defined both the team and its followers—did not become vogue until the 1986 season and Shaughnessy's book. Before then, the Red Sox were hopeful, especially in defeat.

Throughout the rhapsody, race stood right there, at the heart of the franchise, but it was a topic that spoiled the fun. Couldn't write about the splendor at Fenway and think about Joe Morgan chastising Ellis Burks for hanging out with a white girl. Gazing at the Green Monster lost its luster when Jim Rice stood at the base of the Wall, advising Burks to "get his six years, and get the hell out of Boston." No, that didn't work, yet the duality would illustrate both Boston and the Red Sox.

As much as the Red Sox, the Boston press was conflicted. The Stuart case, along with the integration of the housing projects in Southie propelled race once more into the hot issue in Boston journalism. The Red Sox were next. It was the 1990s, but so little seemed to have changed from those ugly days of busing. No wonder Boston couldn't shake free of its past. Part of that was just Boston; it loved its past, but here—the constant bombardment of racial episodes—was an example where the city collectively wanted to just shoo the topic away.

That wouldn't be so easy, for a new generation of reporters began covering the team with a different eye. It would create a fascinating degree of tension inside of the two Boston newsrooms, for in the Boston sporting press, change came at a trickle.

When the writers did turn over, the new breed of Red Sox reporter was younger and more willing to write about race not only as a blemish on the club's image but as a factor in how the team made its decisions. The newer writers had grown up post-busing and thus enjoyed no illusion about any special bonds between blacks and whites.

They were more aggressive as well. Tony Massarotti was an intrepid reporter who gave the *Herald* a strong baseball voice, which served notice that the Red Sox would no longer be the private dominion of the *Globe*. Sean McAdam of the *Providence Journal* brought a keen insight to his paper's baseball coverage.

This new group of New England writers understoood that race was a defining issue, and if they were not always completely willing to tackle the more sensitive of team topics—Yawkey, for instance—they were nevertheless less fearful than their predecessors.

In August 1991, the *Globe* published a three-part series on race in Boston. The writer was Steve Fainaru, the reporter who had scuffled with Jim Rice in Oakland three years earlier. In a sense, Fainaru was the perfect one to tackle the story, for he was a tough reporter who covered sports because it was a topic interesting and newsworthy, not because he was a failed athlete who wrote about sports to remain influential in the game. A tendency existed in some sports writers to subconsciously consider themselves extensions of a given team, and the deadly consequence would often be that, given enough time on a beat, a writer kept more news out of the paper than went in. Steve Fainaru determined not to fall into that trap.

Fainaru was a generation younger than Gammons, Will McDonough, and Larry Whiteside, which made him less fearful of race as an issue. For him, a post–civil rights child, race was never an issue to be buried, but one that produced some of the most powerful journalism. Indeed, this zeal to dissect real issues in a realm that would have less and less of a connection to the everyday world served him well.

The greatest advantage for Steve Fainaru, however, was that he was not from New England, and thus would not be conflicted about approaching the stickier subject of racism in Boston. As a New Englander, to do so would be at some level a self-indictment. Fainaru grew up in the northern California city of San Rafael and was not shaped by the edgy, polarized racial politics of the East Coast. He would look at Boston with a critical, detached eye instead of a parochial and protective one.

Fainaru was young, and to be an outsider tackling Boston's most difficult subject was a heady assignment that brought more than its share of doubt. But he was also in a strong position, having been hired by Don Skwar, the *Globe*'s demanding sports editor.

The series, uncomfortable and revealing, spoke for the first time what black people in Boston already knew. Black fans felt uncomfortable at Fenway. They had viewed the team with suspicion and ballpark as unsafe. Racial slurs sullied the Fenway experience—they used to call Jim Rice "Uncle Ben" from the bleachers—which made for an awkward experience. What Fainaru's reporting did was it put a face to the feel of Fenway Park. Older blacks still harbored animosity for past insults. The Jackie Robinson tryout and the club's whiteness of the 1950s weren't only pieces of history but issues the team needed to bridge.

Then there were the players. Free agency was as dangerous as Tom Yawkey and Haywood Sullivan feared because yes, black players didn't want to come to Boston. They looked at Jim Rice and Ellis Burks and their lonely situation, but more importantly, they feared the atmosphere of Boston, a place where race was always at issue. Rice couldn't avoid it, so players around the league would naturally, by refusing to play there. How could the team move forward if these issues were never confronted? When the Red Sox brought up a rookie named Mo Vaughn, the team only had two blacks—he and Ellis Burks—on the squad. Thirty-two years after Pumpsie Green made the front page with his recall to the majors, Vaughn's arrival was also front-page news. The series asked pointed questions and praised the Red Sox for making strides since the Tommy Harper imbroglio. Lou Gorman voiced increasing frustration. "Of course you're bothered by the perception. I know it's out there, but I really don't know what you can do about it. It would be one thing if the situation was clearly blatant and there was obvious racism in the front office. If there was I would jump all over it, but I don't know one person who's a racist in this organization. We just have to deal with the perception now."

Outside of the *Globe* offices, the series was regarded as a strong piece of work. Fainaru recalls the response being, for the most part, positive. He also especially remembered black people in the city being grateful for giving their collective voice a forum to be heard, which would be another example of a community that clearly felt stifled. Fainaru also understood that he had challenged the city's conventional wisdom.

What Fainaru did not expect was the reaction from inside the paper. He had inflamed the paper's muscle, metro columnist Mike Barnicle and Will McDonough. Fainaru was surprised—and as a kid just starting out in the business more than a little shaken that two Boston giants dropped the hammer on him—but his old nemesis, Jim Rice, was not. This is what happened when you talked about race. In a way, he was vindicated, because he knew the vibe of the city. There was no way he was going to be on the firing line because if Barnicle and McDonough would charbroil one of their own white colleagues, what would they do to somebody black?

In class terms, Barnicle and McDonough were similar, and while Barnicle possessed a tough understanding of the deep class divisions in the city, he was nonetheless exasperated by the series:

Say 2,356 blacks were at the game the other night. Would that be cause for civic celebration? A lot of self-congratulatory pats on the back from do-gooders who look for
the racial angle in absolutely everything that comes down the turnpike?

Say there were none. Would it mean we lived in the American equivalent of
Johannesburg? That Boston is the most segregated city in the United States? That the
Red Sox don't like blacks and their fans make blacks feel uncomfortable and unwanted?

Look, the truth is, this is not the most racially affectionate city in America. It's
not the worst, but it's far from the best.

There's too much agitation here over black versus white. Too much attention paid
to silly numbers that are meaningless. Too much preoccupation with race at the
expense of the deeper culprits: class, money and zip code.

Blacks are a distinct minority in Boston. They have pathetic political leadership,
lousy access to decent schools, live in the most victimized neighborhoods, get trimmed
on services and are geographically and economically segregated by an isolated white
power structure that ignores things more out of insensitivity than out of ugly racial
design.

Barnicle showed a slight if cynical compassion, although he would be challenged heavily for the statement that "ugly racial design" did not play much of
a role in the segregation of the city's blacks. McDonough, whose journalistic
credibility—because his close relationship with high-ranking members of
Boston's sports establishment—frequently sparked debate in Boston sports-
writing circles, employed no such diplomacy:

After reading most of this paper's three-part series on the Red Sox and racism this
past week, I came to this conclusion. The series had about as many holes in it as the
Sox defense these days. . . . Let's get to the main issue of the series: Racism and the
Red Sox. The discussion has become almost an annual event. Yet never, including in
this series, have I seen one person named as the "racist" who dictates these policies and
instructs members of the organization to carry them out.

Was it the late owner Tom Yawkey, or his widow, Jean, who now controls the
organization? Was it a series of general managers—Joe Cronin, Pinky Higgins, Dick
O'Connell and Lou Gorman? Are we to believe it is the scouting department, responsible for scouting and drafting players?

Once again, no names. Joe Cronin was a friend of mine. I was the last one to do
a story with him before he died, visiting his home in Osterville when he knew his
time was short because of cancer. Stopping by his summer home had almost been a
ritual for the decade before that. We talked baseball. I asked him several times if he
was ever told and directed toward not having blacks on the team by Yawkey, and the
answer was that the situation was the opposite. Yawkey was so sensitive to the Jackie
Robinson issue and criticism of the Sox' lack of blacks that he wanted them on his
team. Ditto for O'Connell, who said the same things about Yawkey.

Fainaru got roughed up, but his work would stand out, for the series represented the rare courageous attempt to explain what the Red Sox had danced around for decades. The responses of two of the city's biggest columnists were not only insulting to the experience of being black and dealing with the Red Sox—something neither McDonough nor Barnicle could ever know—but they also served as proof of just how completely out of touch the two men were with the thinking of the black community.

There was something else. Fainaru wasn't even from Boston. What did he know? For starters, he knew plenty because he went into the Roxbury neighborhood for his reporting, a place McDonough would not have dared to tread. One thing was clear, though, going up against conventional wisdom in Boston meant running afoul of Will McDonough, and that would not be an easy decision.

It didn't matter that by the 1990s, McDonough was being pushed to the right of center by a new generation of reporters. Like Gammons, McDonough was a powerhouse, more so in the mid-1990s than in the 1970s, when he was building his reputation. McDonough now stood enshrined in the writers' wing of the Pro Football Hall of Fame and—now that Gammons had gone national—was probably the most powerful columnist in Boston. His Rolodex made it so. He grew defiant at pieces such as Fainaru's because he did not believe that racism was much of a story, but also because such reporting was an implicit renouncement of Joe Cronin, Tom Yawkey, and, to a real extent, his own reporting. Any real research of the Red Sox beyond the anecdotal would result in a total repudiation of Cronin and a Red Sox organization he would defend in his columns for years. Thus, he would bristle at the amount of time and newspaper space the *Globe* would devote to racial issues, and as a result McDonough's columns would become increasingly reactionary.

McDonough was an institution to himself, and he would use his great influence to defend men whose actions would not be treated well by history. Invariably, this meant Yawkey and Cronin. In a different era, the two were often lauded as great men, but during the nineties, both would suffer severe hits to their reputation.

The new book, "Red Sox Century" by Glenn Stout and Richard A. Johnson, puts forth the theory that the Sox have not been more successful because of their alleged racist leanings, filtering down from the late Tom Yawkey, who owned the team from 1933 until his death in 1976.

"Nothing could be further from the truth," said current Sox boss John Harrington, who was close to both Yawkey and his wife, Jean. "They keep talking about Yawkey being from South Carolina. He was not. He was born in Michigan and raised in New York. He went to Yale. He didn't go to South Carolina until later in life. But supposedly because he was from South Carolina he was therefore a redneck and a racist. Not true, but that story has a life of its own." Harrington broke into baseball working for the late Joe Cronin, when Cronin was president of the American League with his office in Boston. Cronin was the manager of the Sox in 1945. "I spoke with Joe about the [Jackie] Robinson thing and he told me the big reason the Sox didn't sign him then, and were slow to sign black ballplayers in that era, was because their top farmclubs were in Louisville and New Orleans. It could also be Birmingham. But they were in the deep South and, in those days, blacks were not allowed to play with whites in those states." In 1945, on the same weekend that Franklin Delano Roosevelt died, Robinson and two other black players came to Fenway Park to work out. They were scheduled to perform for the Sox brass after a Sunday game in Fenway Park between the Sox and Boston Braves.

The spin over the years is that the Sox didn't sign a black player until Pumpsie Green in the late '50s. Not true. They signed Piper Davis, a Hall of Famer in the Negro Leagues, and took him to spring training in 1950. They also gave him a $5,000 bonus, which was huge in those days. Davis was a second baseman, but he couldn't beat out Bobby Doerr so the Sox sent him to Scranton, Pa., which was their No. 3 minor league club, where he would be allowed to play. Piper played a few weeks, hit better than .300, but decided he would be better off back in the Negro Leagues. He was good for Scranton, but in the Sox's eyes, not good enough to beat out Doerr, who is now in the Baseball Hall of Fame in Cooperstown, N.Y. To say that the Sox's failure to win a world championship in the 1950s was due to not signing black players is a tough sell. The Yankees dominated that era, winning the World Series almost every year, and they had one black player on their roster, Elston Howard. Ellie, a wonderful class guy who helped the Sox win the pennant in 1967, must go down as the greatest player in the history of the game if he was the one responsible, because of his color, for winning all those championships for the Yankees.

The reason for McDonough's looseness with the facts was an important one. Reporters, journalists, and historians were now focusing on a story largely ignored, and history was closing in on Yawkey and Cronin.

As research on integration and the early days of baseball increased, the role of the Red Sox drew greater attention. Much of the reason for this new research was that the Negro leagues, once long forgotten, would now be fashionable. The players from those leagues were now late in age, and it would only be a matter of time before each living link to the past would be gone. Examining the nascent days of integration would ultimately lead to a treatise on the Red Sox, for they had been the last team to integrate and Yawkey and Cronin were the power behind the franchise. For years, McDonough had been able to deflect criticism with the anecdotal evidence that came with being friends with men such as Joe Cronin. That he had covered to some extent Tom Yawkey and Pinky Higgins ended much of the debate. That and the fact that McDonough swung a considerable cudgel in the form of an influential column in the region's biggest newspaper tended to curb potential dissent.

Peter Gammons, often detached from racial issues in print, began to weigh in on the Red Sox history. Even when he sought to diffuse the racial element to a story, it was virtually impossible, as race would be such an explosive and lingering issue in Boston. Its prominence in a given piece lent proof to the dissatisfaction of men such as Reggie Smith, as well as a tacit indictment of Tom Yawkey and the Red Sox way:

> The decision was made in March, the announcement came on May 31, and on July 1, Erwin Bryant moved into the Red Sox office. His official title was "administrative assistant to player development," which basically meant that Bryant was assistant farm director, with the additional duties of coordinating the scouting department. There was little notice, little attention. After he moved from Connecticut to the Yawkey Way office, only one writer asked to do a story on Bryant, which he declined. "I'm a low-key person, I just don't want to draw attention on myself because I don't consider myself or my situation unusual or special," says the 34–year-old from Lexington, Ky. So seven months into his job as the fourth-ranking baseball official in the Red Sox organization after Lou Gorman, Eddie Kasko and Ed Kenney Jr., Erwin Bryant remains in the background. Since he also happens to be the highest-ranking black baseball talent person in the organization, Erwin Bryant represents progress.
>
> The release never mentioned race. He hasn't been "a story." He is simply a rising baseball executive who happens to be black. . . . If our society is truly civilized, then the 24 million people in this country whose ancestors came over on the Mayflower appreciate that that ship was no different than a boat from Haiti. And when baseball is civilized, we won't have to be told what rising executive is black, white, Kurd, Serb, Lebanese or Pakistani, only that he is a person, like Erwin Bryant.
>
> We all realize that the Red Sox have made a conscientious effort to rid the franchise of its Mike Higgins perception as a racist club. In area communities, it is the most active local franchise and was honored by the esteemed Action for Boston Community Development for more grass-roots efforts than the other three sports organizations combined. It funds and runs inner-city youth baseball programs, without releases, publicity or attention, another sign of civilized progress.
>
> "I have very strong feelings about the Red Sox," says Bryant. "They have always treated me as a person, not a black man. They have always been honest; heck, the fact that I didn't make the majors wasn't racist, the fact that they kept me around so many years was the opposite, because they kept me because of what someone said I happened to be as a person."
>
> We have dwelled in the past long enough. Erwin Bryant, 34, bright, thoughtful and ambitious, is the fourth-ranking baseball person in the Red Sox organization, not the Xth-ranking black anything. Hopefully, he is the future.

The *Globe* series introduced Mo Vaughn as a potential new force in Boston. He was black, prep school and college educated, and a New Englander. The Red Sox had other black prospects in their system over the years, but none since Rice and Burks were so promising.

There was, from the start, a sense that Vaughn posed a special opportunity for both the Red Sox and the black community. Both on and off the field, he was expected to be the savior of the franchise. He was drafted in Rice's last year in 1989 and had the potential to provide the offensive power of Rice. But more importantly, Mo Vaughn was supposed to be the black player who could thrive and enjoy playing in Boston, the key to a new future.

Vaughn was cocky, for he relished the role of healer. It would be an integral part of his personality to accept pressure. He was not a Reggie Smith, a Californian made uncomfortable by Boston's sharp polarization, or a southerner like Rice, Burks, or Boyd, attempting to assimilate to the city's jagged ways. Mo Vaughn was a New Englander. He was from Norwalk, Connecticut, had family and friends in Massachusetts, and visited Boston numerous times growing up. He walked the city's streets with the self-confidence of a man who belonged.

It was as if his special purpose was to play in Boston. As a prospect in the minor leagues, Vaughn commented on Boston's deep racial divisions, the checkered history of the Red Sox. He knew the history. The ill-fated Robinson tryout was of special importance to Vaughn. He was born in 1967, five years before Robinson's death, yet was captivated by the Robinson legend. His mother once worked with Robinson's widow, Rachel. He would wear number 42 for his career in homage to the great Robinson. From the start, thought the media members who covered the team, there was something refreshing about Vaughn. He knew the Red Sox history and confronted it directly. Where black players before him suppressed their beliefs and personality for fear of reprisal or greater discomfort, Vaughn never shied from the special burden of being black in a city where blacks endured difficulty. He would survive or fail on his terms. His road would be different, he said, because of the unique black struggle, and there simply was no hiding that, just as there could be no hiding Boston's racial history. If there was a noble tendency among the races to attempt to ignore race when understanding a person, then Mo Vaughn *wanted* race to be a factor in considering him. He was a black man, and it was nothing to be ashamed of. The way to overcome these issues, Vaughn said, was to face them.

There was, Glenn Stout thought, always the freight train of race in Boston. Where Rice chose to lie on the tracks, let it run over him, and give the impression he was not affected by it, Vaughn was different. He would often say he might have been the best person to begin the transformation of Boston's image because of his standing as a New Englander. Unlike Rice, Smith, or any other black player to ever wear a Red Sox uniform, he understood his historical significance. He wanted that challenge, but there would be resistance.

Vaughn's confronting race in Boston angered Will McDonough. While taking another swipe at Steve Fainaru, McDonough attacked Vaughn for being forthright about his place as a symbol of racial peace in a city known for unrest.

Instead of considering race, McDonough wrote, Vaughn should simply play baseball. "My answer to that is, Mo Vaughn better spend all his time trying to bring together his bat and the baseball on a more consistent basis or they might be writing the same stories about him in Pawtucket."

Almost immediately, Mo Vaughn captured the hearts of the tough, expectant Boston fans. Part of the reason was his New England roots. There was no culture shock and no period of adjustment for Vaughn. He came through the Red Sox system and was the first local star since Carlton Fisk. He was a powerful player who, like Fred Lynn years before him, would learn to use the dimensions of Fenway Park to his advantage. He was a dead-pull left-handed hitter, like Ted Williams, but Fenway possessed one of the deepest right field porches in baseball. Unlike Williams, Vaughn began to hit outside pitches to left field, thus using the wall and raising his batting average.

For a time, Vaughn struggled. He spent the majority of 1991 in the minor leagues. Too aggressive, he struck out often and was sent back down to Pawtucket in 1992 by Joe Morgan. After Butch Hobson, Vaughn's triple-A manager in Pawtucket, was installed as manager, Vaughn played well in 1993, grew into a star in 1994, and, although Hobson was long gone, a superstar in 1995, winning the Most Valuable Player award. The Red Sox returned to the playoffs and had become Mo Vaughn's team.

Like Rice, he hit for power and average. In Vaughn's six seasons in Boston, his typical season produced a batting average of .315, thirty-six home runs, and 110 RBI. He enjoyed the superstar's role with clutch hits and big plays. Vaughn worked on his game as a first baseman, improving, if never being known for his glove. Joe Giuliotti of the *Herald* believed the biggest difference between Rice and Mo Vaughn was Vaughn's willingness to represent his teammates. The key to being a superstar, Giuliotti felt, was being able to work a room. Vaughn could talk with the writers. "He knew what you wanted. After a game you have to have 10 minutes to walk some of the reporters around the block," Giuliotti recalled. "You needed to have a few minutes to bullshit, even if you didn't want to. With Rice, all he wanted was to be left alone and play ball."

To understand completely the sea change Mo Vaughn's presence represented in Boston Red Sox history, one only need return to the edgy confrontations of black players and the media. Jim Rice ripping Steve Fainaru's shirt to pieces or threatening Larry Whiteside. Reggie Smith raging a war of words with hostile white fans in his home ballpark. Tommy Harper taking the Red Sox to court. Virtually all of Oil Can Boyd's career in Boston.

Vaughn immediately used his celebrity to try to incorporate black Bostonians into the Fenway mainstream. He headed numerous charitable organizations in the city and became a visible ambassador. His foundations sponsored cultural activities for disadvantaged kids as well as opportunities to come to Fenway and watch the Red Sox. He enjoyed not only being a star, but its responsibilities as well. "All I can be is me. And that should be enough," Vaughn said. "I don't know about being the bridge between the races and all that. What I do know is what I can do for other people. I'm in a position where I can help."

As a player, Vaughn possessed a flair for the dramatic. He would win games late. He wanted to be the person who succeeded under the pressure, who grasped the opportunity to be a hero, to carry a team.

For the first time since Rice, the Red Sox had a homegrown power hitter who was among the most feared hitters in the game. It was a staple of the Red Sox franchise that had been missing in recent years. In 1995, Vaughn firmly established himself as one of the great young players in the game.

The media enjoyed dealing with Vaughn. He was straight with reporters and often honest to a fault. Unlike Red Sox stars of the past, Vaughn accepted the responsibility of being a team leader. Giuliotti was impressed with his integrity, Tony Massarotti with his candor. Mike Stanley, a teammate, believed that Vaughn's presence deflected criticism from other players. He spoke for his teammates and took the heat that accompanied poor performances.

Massarotti, a beat writer for the *Boston Herald,* saw Vaughn not merely as refreshing, but as the seminal figure in a new chapter in Red Sox history. Because of Vaughn, Massarotti felt, the Red Sox could not only distance themselves from their history, but could create a new one.

As such, the gap between the city and its black population began to close. The city accepted Mo Vaughn as a man. His outward appearance was menacing. He was dark-skinned, bald, and a hulking six-foot-one and 260 pounds. He wore his blackness unabashed and was not afraid to embrace elements of black culture that might make whites feel uncomfortable. Sean McAdam, who covered the Red Sox for the Providence *Journal,* was struck by the contrast of Vaughn to men such as Jim Rice, who seemed to distance himself from any cultural staples of the black community. Rice golfed, lived in the suburbs, and avoided conversations that contained any racial undertone. Being black was an undeniable component of Vaughn's personality. He did not alter his personality to assimilate to a predominately white Red Sox culture, and no one could ever accuse Vaughn of trying to "act white," unfair criticism that stung both Reggie Smith and Rice. Yet through the force of his charisma, Vaughn began to transcend the issue of race in the city. Where Ellis Burks had failed to connect with the black community in large measure, Vaughn succeeded to a greater degree. If Will McDonough doubted Vaughn's ability to be a bridge between the races in Boston, Vaughn quickly trumped the newspaperman's words with actions that produced results. He belonged.

In turn, black players in the game began a slow reexamination of the Red Sox and the city. When Andre Dawson retired, he said playing in Boston was a high point in a career full of them. Dawson played for the Red Sox at the tail end of his career. Billy Hatcher, the hero of the 1990 World Series, was in 1992 the first black free agent the Red Sox signed. That came sixteen years after the start of free agency. Things were changing in Boston, and Mo Vaughn was one part of a giant difference. Dan Duquette would be the other.

When Dan Duquette replaced Lou Gorman as the general manager of the Boston Red Sox, it was, thought Tony Massarotti, with the intention of cleaning house both in terms of personnel and in the organization's culture. These orders apparently came from John Harrington. Harrington had long watched the Red Sox throughout the years, and from being part of the organization for thirty years, there were two staples of Red Sox culture he immediately wanted corrected. The first was the star system, where the team's best players essentially controlled the clubhouse. The other was the long-held perception that the Red Sox were a racist ball club. Both would have far-reaching consequences for Mo Vaughn.

Duquette, like Red Sox pitcher Jeff Reardon, grew up in the small Western Massachusetts town of Dalton. The two played together on American Legion teams and while Duquette did not possess the skills for a run at a major league career, he knew from the start that he desired to be part of the game. Cecil Cooper, the old Red Sox first baseman who became a star in Milwaukee, remembers a young, ambitious Danny Duquette with the Brewers organization in the early 1980s. "Even then," Cooper recalled with only partial kindness, "he was a climber."

Duquette did climb, and quickly. His first job in the major leagues was with Baltimore, and he quickly rose through the ranks. In a short span, he became the game's youngest general manager when he took the reins of the Montreal Expos in 1991 at age thirty-five. He immediately gained a reputation as a shrewd talent evaluator and developer of the farm system. He gained acclaim in the game as the Expos, cash-strapped as they might have been, developed such talents as Marquis Grissom, Larry Walker, Delino Deshields, and Jeff Fassero. Duquette's ultimate career goal was always to run the Red Sox, a dream come true for any New England kid. In 1994, he landed the dream job.

Duquette, thought Joe Giuliotti, had always been adept at cultivating minority players, especially those from the Dominican Republic and later, Asia. Teams with limited resources, like the Expos, required aggressive scouting in foreign countries to remain competitive. Latin countries such as the talent-rich Dominican Republic are not covered by the amateur draft, allowing teams to sign players at far below market costs. The Oakland A's paid close to $3 million for top draft pick Mark Mulder in 1998. For their wonderful shortstop Miguel Tejada, the A's paid out the grand sum of $2,000. Duquette would offend the hard-line baseball men who believed a general manager should at least have major league experience. How, they asked, could a person who never played the game consistently make baseball decisions?

In Duquette's second season, the Red Sox won their first division title since being bounced by Oakland in 1990. In three quick games, the Red Sox were eliminated by a resurgent Cleveland Indians team that had won one hundred games in the regular season and would head to the World Series. Mo Vaughn's first playoff appearance would be a total disaster. He and Jose Canseco combined for an 0 for 27 mark in a forgettable series. The Red Sox were out, but after tasting the postseason for the first time in five years, there were few complaints.

After the horrible playoff showing against Cleveland, Vaughn found out that there would be a reward for treating people, reporters that is, with dignity. It was something Jim Rice would never accept. In a controversial vote, Vaughn won the American League Most Valuable Player award, even though Cleveland's Albert Belle was statistically superior, as was his team. But Belle had been a churlish character in the game, and when it came down to a close vote, Belle would never win points for affability.

It was a new era. The Red Sox were winners, led by a black New Englander who was never diminished, never defeated by racial questions. Vaughn was a superstar, a Most Valuable Player who represented Boston, who certainly knew better than the rest that he stood for everyone in the city. Tony Massarotti believed that Vaughn was the most popular Red Sox player in a generation. What no one could have guessed was that 1995, supposedly the beginning of a new era of winning baseball and improved race relations, would be Mo Vaughn's high point in Boston.

SEVENTEEN

For most of 1998, Mo Vaughn would fight for his survival as a member of the Boston Red Sox. His contract expired at the end of the season and, despite his developing place in Red Sox history, there had been signs, both subtle and obvious, from John Harrington and Dan Duquette that Vaughn was no longer part of the future of the Red Sox. For the reporters who covered the team, its resurgent fan base, and a surprised American League, it was a bewildering, ongoing soap opera that began in January. Vaughn had produced gigantic offensive numbers for the Red Sox. As much as any member of the Red Sox, with the possible exception of Roger Clemens, Vaughn's name was synonymous with the team's. The confluence of three dangerous forces—money, ego, and pride—brought tensions between Vaughn and the Red Sox to a yearlong boil.

He had shattered barriers that had stood in Boston for decades, most importantly the notion of what it meant for a black athlete to play in Boston. In an era that saw rampant player movement and a real and disturbing detachment between players and the uniforms they wore, Mo Vaughn was the rare athlete who identified with being a member of one team. Joe Giuliotti, who worked as a reporter and columnist for the Boston *Herald* for forty-eight years and covered every important member of the Red Sox, from Williams to Tiant to Pedro Martinez, was impressed by Vaughn's professionalism. Vaughn would often tell Giuliotti of his goal to be remembered as the last of the great Red Sox. That meant he wanted to be known in the same category of Williams and Rice and Yaz, as a player who was developed in the Red Sox system, played his whole career in Fenway Park, and retired knowing only one uniform. Bitter at the contradictions and hypocrisies put forth by management, players of the late 1990s largely played for themselves and for money, but Mo Vaughn would be one of the last baseball players who believed his greater legacy should also be tied to a *team*. He lived in Massachusetts year-round, and his charity work was a staple of his investment to Boston. Vaughn did something else that was telling in an age where players were so distant from their public. Instead of throwing money at causes, Vaughn donated his time.

That Vaughn thought about his baseball legacy in terms greater than salary and individual numbers impressed Giuliotti, who believed that neither players nor

owners drew much pride from or attached any importance to loyalty, to finishing
the job you started. There was in Vaughn a healthy measure of old-fashioned values that was not often found in the game. Players such as Tony Gwynn, the great
hitter with the San Diego Padres, and Cal Ripken, Jr., who played with Baltimore,
may have stayed on with the same team, but they were players who arrived to the
majors inside of the first decade of free agency. They entered the game before col-
lusion and before it became commonplace to trade eventual free agents in order to
receive players in return. Vaughn, whose rookie year was 1992, was a child of the
free agent era, and very few players that began their careers in the 1990s expected
to remain with the same team. Mo Vaughn did not want to be known as a baseball hired gun, but as a lifelong member of the Boston Red Sox.

Doing so would be difficult to achieve, for the game simply no longer func-
tioned in that way. Vaughn knew this firsthand; he had seen the way the great
Clemens was summarily discarded by the Red Sox, even though he was
arguably the greatest pitcher in the history of the franchise. There would always
be memorable quotations from Red Sox management regarding Clemens. Lou
Gorman's response to Clemens' 1987 contract holdout—"The sun will rise, the
sun will set and I'll have lunch"—stood unmatched for almost a decade.
Duquette outdid Gorman in 1996. when deciding to allow Clemens to walk
away as a free agent, Duquette claimed that Clemens was "in the twilight of his
career." They would become famous last words. Stung, Clemens would win
consecutive Cy Young awards with Toronto in 1997 and '98 followed by consecutive World Series championships with the New York Yankees in 1999 and
2000. As a thirty-nine-year-old, Clemens would at one point during the 2001
season compile a record of 20-1 on the way to a third Cy Young award away
from the Red Sox and a record sixth overall.

Witnessing this, and the vitriol that followed Clemens' departure, served as
a lesson for Mo Vaughn; he saw in this a coldness, an adversity between players
and their teams that essentially guaranteed that most players would change teams.
Mo was no fool, but in a way he fell under the baseball spell that seduces so many
players into thinking the game will treat them differently than the rest. That's the
romance of the game talking, the sweet song whose lyrics sway you when the reality is as cold as cement. Vaughn saw examples all around him, of men of character who got sent out of town. He saw the way Ellis Burks was sent out of Boston,
back before the MVP trophy. There was Mike Easler, the former Red Sox desig-
nated hitter, who served as Vaughn's mentor and hitting coach, that is until the
strike of 1994 and he was later fired for not wanting to coach strikebreaking players. Then there was Clemens. Vaughn also knew that disputes in the game had
existed for years, despite the sheen that was always put on the "Golden Age" of
baseball. Hell, it was a Golden Age for the owners, he thought. The players had
no choice but to shut up and play ball. What kind of Golden Age was that?

Vaughn knew intellectually that the game would treat him no differently than the rest, but where Duquette was involved, it was Vaughn's passion that took over. *How could a guy who never played the game run a legend out of town?* Part of this was the nature of baseball, and another part was simply the personality of Dan Duquette. Vaughn's contract year would be no different; during 1998 an animus existed between Vaughn and the Red Sox that would grow very personal and destructive.

It would feel as if it were a season-long divorce. Vaughn and the Red Sox came to Oakland on Opening Day. As Vaughn took his first batting practice of the season, unleashing low liners and towering drives to all fields, chatter centered around Vaughn's cloudy future with the Red Sox. The left-handed crouch was his signature, a Boston baseball symbol no different than the Yastrzemski lean over the plate or the Tiant corkscrew delivery. He wafted three consecutive home runs into the right field bleachers of the Oakland Coliseum, and in a mixture of respect and admiration was then greeted by a few members of the Oakland A's. Vaughn shook hands with Oakland third base coach Ron Washington, then a third-year first baseman named Jason Giambi. Giambi would look up to Vaughn as not only a marquee player in the game but as an example of how Giambi would hope to impart leadership to his own young team.

No one would speak directly to Vaughn about the obvious topic, his contract. He was to be a free agent at the end of the season, and he still didn't have a contract. Frank Blackman, a longtime newsman with the afternoon San Francisco *Examiner*, soon approached Vaughn. Blackman first began covering professional sports in 1969. He began in a different era of newspapering. He was a gruff, difficult New Yorker who had grown increasingly bitter at the state of baseball.

Blackman, a talented writer, was hurt by life. After the tragic double murders of San Francisco Mayor George Moscone and City Supervisor Harvey Milk, the San Francisco 49ers were scheduled to play a Monday night football game against Pittsburgh. In the face of one of the city's greatest tragedies, the NFL refused the request to cancel the game. Blackman was at the game:

> They played a football game last night at Candlestick Park. The 49ers and the Pittsburgh Steelers. Big deal.
>
> There are times when watching grown men running around and falling down becomes much, much less than just a silly, pleasant pastime. Sometimes it is just plain stupid. Yesterday, after the Mayor of San Francisco was gunned down in his office, it felt almost as obscene trying to deal with something as meaningless and ephemeral as a football game.
>
> Sports is full of metaphors about life and death struggles, doing or dying. How grotesque these clichés seem in the aftermath of this tragedy. The final gun sounded, the final out recorded, athletes leave the field, take a shower, *and go on living*. There is, almost always, another game, another opportunity to win one for the Gipper.

Real life isn't that tidy or romantic. Real people bleed. Even die. Too soon. Way too soon. . . .

They played the game last night anyway. The Park and Rec Commission wired the 49er owner and the National Football League Commissioner Pete Rozelle asking that it be postponed 24 hours. The league said no way. There was no chance because it was a Monday night national TV game and beer and deodorant companies had spent a lot of money on commercials. Big bucks were at stake. Plus, the folks in Toledo and Nashville were ready for fun and games. It was a tough break for that Mayor what's-his-name, but life goes on. The game goes on.

I think I'm going to be sick.

The Blackman piece was excerpted in his memoir of Willie Mays. Once, after seeing the excerpt, Blackman leaned back in his chair, shifted his weight, and said solemnly, "I wrote that at a time when I really, really thought I was going be something special in this business. Seeing this now only makes everything all the more depressing." He then got up and walked away.

Blackman resented not only the hundreds of millions of dollars that were now part of the game, which made instant millionaires out of many unproven athletes, but also that such wealth created a distance that diminished the game.

Today's ballplayers, because of the wealth and the lack of real intensity created by the money, were just plain lazy, Blackman thought. If ballplayers dating back to the original roster of the Cincinnati Red Stockings—baseball's first professional team in 1869—were greedy, at least they played the game right. That professionalism, felt Blackman, had since been destroyed by the gravy train of guaranteed contracts, salary arbitration, and the easy satisfactions of enormous wealth.

Nor did today's ballplayers have to maintain a particular work ethic. In the past, players—both stars and scrubs—ran out routine ground balls and took pride in being complete players. Left-handed hitters, if they were worth the spit in their gloves, faced the tough, left-handed pitchers of the game instead of conveniently asking for a day off.

But perhaps worst of all, athletes today were less accountable for their actions, felt Blackman. This was a by-product of both the decline of the newspaper's influence in American society and the rising juggernaut of television, particularly sports television such as ESPN. Players didn't have to speak to the reporters who covered them, much less treat them with any level of professional respect, courtesy, or honesty. They could skip the daily beat reporters in favor of television interviews. Unlike the old days, today's athlete no longer needed the writer.

In this vein Blackman felt Vaughn was different, and a curious, almost endearing symmetry existed between them. Vaughn played a hard, workmanlike first base every day. Even during 1995, when he won the American League Most Valuable Player award, Vaughn set an example as a team-oriented leader. He was consistently professional with reporters, and he produced big numbers for his club. He ducked neither difficult questions nor fearsome left-handers such as Randy Johnson and prided himself, even in the days of one-dimensional sluggers, on becoming a good defensive first baseman. Vaughn would lament publicly the very aspects of modern baseball that ate at Blackman in the press box daily; he would complain that few pitchers pitched inside effectively, one of the few major weapons of intimidation they could use against hitters leaning out over the plate to gain greater advantage. Vaughn himself was notorious for crowding the plate, with his thick elbow pads serving as modern-day gladiatorial armor. As such, he never charged the mound whenever he was plunked in the hip or elbow with a fastball; he thought the game lost a great deal of its appeal when his contemporaries rushed a pitcher without real cause. He played a rugged, old-style brand of baseball and considered himself a throwback to those hardscrabble days, and Blackman, a tough, often coarse reporter himself, respected that.

The pre-game chatter intensified. Sox hitting coach Jim Rice back with the club lavished praise on the formidable talents of Boston's emerging young shortstop, Nomar Garciaparra ("I've seen my share, and I did my share, too," Rice said, speaking in quick, breathless tones that suggested that the notoriously brooding Rice was actually enjoying himself. "But *that* kid might be better than us all.") While Boston fans raced to the visitor's bullpen to watch the night's starting pitcher, Pedro Martinez, warm up for his Red Sox debut, Frank Blackman sidled up to Vaughn.

"Mo, this is off the record," Blackman started, nodding toward the Red Sox dugout. "But I just have to ask you a question. What the *fuck* are they doing with you over there? Are they fucking crazy?" Vaughn offered a vindicated smile. He seemed charmed by Blackman's curtness, that a reporter for a San Francisco paper was aware of his situation. If the Red Sox did not, baseball people knew Mo Vaughn's value. Around the league, Vaughn's feud with Red Sox management was well known, but few understood how the Red Sox would risk losing a valuable leader like Vaughn, probably one of the top five hitters in club history. To the left of the batting cage, Oakland A's Manager Art Howe looked at his young, bare-bones team, then watched Vaughn chatting with a few of his players and said, "If Boston doesn't want Mo, we'll sure as hell take him."

The primary players in the drama were Vaughn and Dan Duquette. If Dick O'Connell in 1977 would be the first general manager to radically alter the complexion and culture of the Red Sox, then Duquette would be the last. His arrival to the Red Sox in 1994 would be almost as significant as Vaughn's, for Duquette was the first general manager to confront the team's racial perceptions. Past regimes might be confounded by it, but Duquette set out to eliminate perceived bias as a characteristic of the franchise.

Duquette would not want to be known, and his curt manners would frustrate and anger the reporters who covered him as well as the executives around the league who attempted to negotiate trades with him. There would be general managers who tended to avoid dealing with Duquette, believing that he lacked the basic but key ability to be jocular in the atmosphere of baseball's old-boy's club, which is so often a prerequisite to making a deal. Duquette embodied the new style of baseball administrator, who evaluated players based on number crunching and cared little about building personal relationships with other baseball people. Recognizing this in himself, Duquette hired Lee Thomas as an assistant. A baseball man for forty years, as an assistant, Thomas satisfied the social requirements necessary to do business in the major leagues.

But in the area of wresting the decades-old racial notions from the Red Sox character, Dan Duquette, like Mo Vaughn and Dick O'Connell, would be a seminal figure in the franchise. Duquette did not shrink. He would stand where Tom Yawkey, Eddie Collins, and Joe Cronin never stood, at the forefront of the franchise's most central issue. If Yawkey and generations of Red Sox executives were exasperated by the persistent race question, Duquette did something about it. In his own way, he would show courage similar to that of Mo Vaughn.

Duquette could be charming. When discussing race and the Red Sox, Dan Duquette did not shy from the topic. Unlike his predecessors, he would not say the club's reputation was mere myth, as so many others had. Nor would he suggest that the racism that ran through the club was no longer an issue that needed to be dealt with. He did not refute the history, as if loud denial or blustery indignation would change the life experiences of Tommy Harper or Earl Wilson. He cited the positive steps the Red Sox had made under his administration with a mechanical precision.

The Dan Duquette years would transform the Red Sox from a team of predominately white players to a modern club with a diversity of the United Nations. Before his arrival in 1994, the Red Sox had hired the fewest number of blacks of any team that had been in existence since Robinson's debut in 1947. But Duquette signed players from all over the world.

Mo Vaughn would never be the only black player under Duquette. He acquired black pitchers such as Tom Gordon and Heathcliff Slocumb and everyday players such as Troy O'Leary, Darren Lewis, Damon Buford, and, later, Carl Everett. At numerous points in the Duquette era, the Red Sox fielded a majority of players of color at the same time. Duquette also surprised blacks in the game by retaining black utility players, which rarely was the case in the major leagues. It was a positive sign that the game was finally changing.

For all the other criticisms of Duquette's personality and style, racial profiling could never be a charge levied against him. Compared to the history of the Red Sox, this enlightened approach isn't talked about enough with regard to Duquette. "But," Tony Massarotti added nimbly, "I don't know if we should give him too much credit for something everyone should be practicing." The fact remains, however, that before Duquette's arrival, the Red Sox had signed exactly two black free agents, Andre Dawson and Billy Hatcher, both in 1993. In the forty-seven years of integrated baseball, the Red Sox before Duquette counted only two pitchers, Earl Wilson and Oil Can Boyd, and five black position players—George Scott, Reggie Smith, Jim Rice, Ellis Burks, and Vaughn—who held starting positions for at least four consecutive years in the club's history.

Duquette remedied some of the great sins of the franchise. The fired Tommy Harper was brought back as a coach. Dave Henderson and Reggie Smith were inducted into the Red Sox Hall of Fame. Carlton Fisk, who never wanted to leave in the first place, was hired on as a consultant. Fisk symbolized the intensity of the Yankees-Red Sox rivalry in the 1970s and when the two teams met in 1999 for the first time in playoff history, it was Fisk who threw out the first pitch. Jim Rice, who disappeared after the bitter end of his career, came back first as a minor league hitting instructor, then as the team's hitting coach. During the fiftieth anniversary celebration of Jackie Robinson's major league debut in 1997, Pumpsie Green remembered being treated with dignity and class by Lou Gorman and Dan Duquette.

These gestures seemed light-years from the Red Sox under Joe Cronin, who failed to sign Robinson in 1945. Wendell Smith, who with Izzy Muchnick arranged the tryout, said acerbically afterward, "We'll hear from the Red Sox like we'll hear from Adolf Hitler." Cronin, who was the American League president in 1972, refused to appear with Robinson as Robinson gave his final speech. Hall of Famer Monte Irvin, who worked in the commissioner's office, recalled Cronin eating a hot dog under the bleachers that day in Cincinnati instead of appearing on the field for the ceremony. Robinson died nine days later.

Outside of Duquette's activism, few people in the game would speak well of him. As much attention as Duquette would receive for rehabilitating the team's image in the area of discrimination, he would suffer heavy criticism in the other areas of the job. He would anger rival executives for being difficult to deal with; many believed that Duquette was never an honorable trade partner. He overpaid for marginal players and would never be forgiven for signing Jose Offerman to a four-year, $24 million contract in 1998 when the next closest offer was four years at $16 million.

Duquette demanded unquestioned loyalty from everyone who worked for him. He sought to control the information about his club, creating a tangible bitterness between himself and the demanding Boston press. An interview with Duquette could quickly turn ugly, which, thought Gordon Edes, was unnecessary because Duquette could be a good and intelligent interview when he wanted to. He would complement his impersonal style by eliminating the public face of the franchise. News would often be announced through the Red Sox Internet site instead of through any type of rapport with the Boston press.

He frustrated those who worked under him. His employees—coaches and managers at all minor league levels—were instructed to clear all interview requests with the Red Sox public relations department. Ken Macha, bench coach for the Oakland A's, recalled a Duquette edict when he managed the Red Sox double-A affiliate in Trenton and in the triple-A in Pawtucket. It was a mortifying experience for Macha, an intelligent, forthright career baseball man who desired greatly to be a manager. "What was I supposed to do?" he said. "A reporter would call me up and ask about a prospect and I wasn't allowed to speak about a player I was watching every day? I mean, I felt like an idiot."

Duquette placed his own needs above helping his staff climb up baseball's difficult and thorny ranks. "He had an inner circle," Macha recalled. "If you weren't part of that inner circle, you really didn't matter." Gerald Perry played thirteen years in the majors, worked in the Red Sox minor league system, and was Lou Piniella's first choice to be Piniella's hitting coach. Perry never received the chance to impress Piniella. Apparently, Duquette told the Mariners that Perry "wasn't yet ready." It was a humiliating blow to Perry and a potentially serious obstacle to his career advancement. If his own organization didn't think he was capable, what chance would Perry have of reaching the major leagues as a coach or even a manager? Eventually, Piniella did hire Perry.

The players were equally harsh on Duquette, partly because he never played in the majors. In the eyes of many baseball players, having the power to make baseball decisions while never having stepped in against a major league hitter or pitcher is unforgivable. Beyond this, Duquette's distant style continued to be a singular issue. "He was the kind of person," said Matt Stairs, who played for Duquette in Boston and the Montreal system, "who measured body fat over heart." Sean McAdam went one step farther than Stairs. "He measured on-base percentage over heart." Tony Massarotti believed that Duquette's obsession with numbers— the *Globe's* Gordon Edes once broke a story about his reliance on a sycophantic number-cruncher who wound up on the Red Sox payroll—was his defining characteristic. "All he cares about is if a guy can play, which is one of his greatest assets and at the same time maybe his greatest flaw. He's all about business."

Duquette had, thought Joe Giuliotti, an inability to brook debate. A Dan Duquette player did not speak, even when spoken to. He did not criticize the team—a sure sign of disloyalty—or the manner in which it was being handled. There was no debating this. To say in passing, "We need more pitching," could be considered a fatal affront to Duquette's authority. His intolerance of debate drew sharp criticism in the newspapers. Giuliotti roasted him in the *Herald,* referring to him as "Dictator Dan." The *Globe's* Bob Ryan asked if Duquette would prefer if robots, instead of human beings, played the game.

The side battle between Duquette and Vaughn amounted to nothing less than a battle for control. When Duquette was named general manager, he desperately sought, as most executives do, to shape the Red Sox into his image. Yet there was a problem: Key, influential players predated his arrival. Clemens was one, Vaughn another. They weren't just veterans, but historical figures in Red Sox history. Creating a new and lasting legacy for himself and the Red Sox would be impossible with the legendary Clemens and the formidable Vaughn in the clubhouse, both competing with Duquette as focal point of the franchise. Because Vaughn predated Duquette, it would be impossible for Duquette to claim any portion of Vaughn's success. Both men, it seemed, were establishing their place in the Red Sox hierarchy. Vaughn was an American League MVP, the emerging new superstar in the tradition of Williams, Yastrzemski, Rice, and Clemens. As both asserted themselves, neither would retrench.

Vaughn spoke his mind and backed it up. He was impolitic. He was not a clubhouse lawyer, whispering vitriol behind the scenes or off the record. Vaughn took the leader's position. If he disagreed with management's course of action for the ballclub, he said so. It was a sizable crack in the foundation between the two men. Vaughn was secure enough in his personality to open virtually all issues up for dialogue. Duquette clearly did not want to be questioned, especially publicly.

"Mo did what Rice didn't do. Mo spoke about the injustices he felt," Giuliotti said. "At the time it wasn't racial, it was about the construction of the ballclub. And he got his ass just about booted out because of it. That's why I nicknamed him [Duquette] 'Dictator Dan.' If you spoke up against him you were gone. Clemens, gone. Mike Greenwell, gone. Mike Stanley, gone."

Within a short time, a line was being drawn through the Red Sox clubhouse between players who were brought to the organization by Duquette and those who predated him. Almost to a man, those who preceded his arrival quickly found themselves in poor standing.

For Tony Massarotti, Duquette's putsch came on the order of Harrington. The Red Sox of the 1980s had been badly burned by a clubhouse that for years appeared out of control. The Harper lawsuit charred the image of the franchise. Wade Boggs made it worse. The Wade Boggs-Margo Adams affair scandalized the team and led to, among other things, the firing of John McNamara. Duquette's predecessor, Lou Gorman, was considered a fair and generally hands-off administrator who allowed disparate personalities to coexist. The Red Sox had long been known as a country club where star players were allowed great latitude. Tony Massarotti believes Harrington hired Duquette to summarily change this aspect of the clubhouse culture. "Before, the inmates ran the asylum," Massarotti said. "Dan Duquette put a stop to that."

After the 1995 playoff loss to Cleveland, Vaughn signed a three-year contract extension that ran through the 1998 season. He was the reigning MVP, and despite the poor playoff, optimism was high that the Red Sox would again taste the postseason. But during the negotiations of the contract, Joe Giuliotti noticed that there seemed to be a higher level of tension between Vaughn and

Duquette. Part of the reason was the belief that Vaughn's personal life was beginning to spin somewhat out of control. Vaughn had been involved in a fight earlier in the season in a Boston nightclub. The former boyfriend of a woman he was dating confronted him, and the man and his entourage beat Vaughn to the ground, closing his eye and bloodying his mouth. The group was a collection of local gang members who hung out with one of the city's emerging rap groups. Years later, that same group would be implicated in the brutal stabbing of Celtics star forward Paul Pierce.

The incident marked the first blemish on Vaughn's record as a player in Boston, and many people close to the team believed it to be first episode in a slow deterioration between him and the Boston front office. His clashes with management grew more pronounced. In 1997, he injured his knee and underwent arthroscopic surgery. Under normal circumstances, the surgery would have been considered routine, but in a tense environment, accusations flew. Duquette privately, and periodically publicly, blamed the knee problem on Vaughn's weight.

When Vaughn allegedly punched a customer at the Foxy Lady, a Rhode Island gentlemen's club, management grew wary of and angry at their star. That the team's most recognizable star frequented strip clubs was, thought Sean McAdam of the Providence *Journal*, taken as a personal affront to John Harrington. McAdam believed that Harrington possessed an intolerant streak for certain transgressions, and this was one of them. It was an organizational holdover from the 1980s, when another Boston star, Wade Boggs, brought embarrassment upon the organization when his adultery made national headlines. Sexual transgressions happened to be a vice Jean Yawkey could not tolerate, and Harrington, McAdam thought, was cut from a similar cloth.

"It personally rubbed Harrington the wrong way," McAdam said. "Here was the high-priced, high-profile face of the franchise whose most identifiable nightspot was a strip joint."

Another, more serious event strained Vaughn's relationship with the Red Sox. In early 1998, Vaughn sideswiped a row of cars before toppling his own. He would be arrested for driving under the influence. Vaughn was at first ashamed and later wounded by the reaction of the club. When Vaughn arrived in court for his DUI arraignment, not a single member of the Red Sox appeared on his behalf. This deeply wounded a person as proud as Vaughn. The year before, when Wil Cordero was arrested for beating his wife in a sensational case, a half-dozen or so members of the Red Sox front office appeared in court to support their embattled player.

Vaughn considered himself someone who gave both to the Red Sox and to the Boston community in a way no player had before. Now he had endured personal difficulties and his organization did not support him.

As early as 1997, the Red Sox sent clear messages as to the club's direction and Vaughn's future. With Clemens winning the Cy Young in Toronto, the Red Sox traded for National League Cy Young winner Martinez to replace him, and then signed Martinez to a six-year, $75 million contract, then the biggest pitching contract in the game's history. Nomar Garciaparra, who won the 1997 Rookie of the Year, now had security and a big contract, receiving a five-year, $45 million contract. Vaughn, who represented both the heart of the team and the power of the batting order, still had nothing. A silent message was being sent. Duquette, first by dumping Clemens, was reshaping the team to match his vision, and Vaughn wasn't part of it: The Red Sox's future and his would soon take different paths.*

Peter Gammons believed there was hope. He also believed that Duquette was taking a public flogging for what was in truth John Harrington's desire to be rid of Vaughn. His logic was consistent with an important part of Duquette's reputation. He was a man who evaluated largely by numbers. At that point in Vaughn's career, Gammons did not believe that Duquette would casually discard a player with such impressive offensive numbers.

Gammons also had inside information. He checked in with both Vaughn and Duquette around the All-Star break in the summer of 1998 and believed that the two men agreed on a four-year contract for around $42 million. The two men, Gammons recalled, felt they could live with those numbers. It was, Gammons thought, a done deal. The sniping would be over. Vaughn and Duquette had overcome their differences for the good of the franchise.

Then something went terribly wrong. When the Red Sox presented the offer to Vaughn, it was not for four years at $42 million, but two years and $17 million. It was a bizarre reversal that Gammons knew Vaughn would never accept. From that point forward, Gammons thought, the relationship between Vaughn and Boston was over.

The next step for the franchise was to win over the public, which was done through the powerful voice of the *Globe* and Will McDonough. Joe Giuliotti believed the Red Sox orchestrated a smear campaign through the Boston press to destroy Vaughn's once-golden reputation in Boston. McDonough, a known

---

* Joe Giuliotti's belief that the Red Sox organized a smear campaign to ruin Vaughn's reputation was supported by a great number of people in the baseball establishment. His contention was further buttressed by the club's Soviet-style retaliation after Mo Vaughn left. To commemorate the team's centennial, the Red Sox published a glossy coffee-table book called *The Boston Red Sox, 100 Years: The Official Retrospective.* Chapter Two begins a section called "The New Englanders," and from pages 28 to 51 the book pays homage to New Englanders who played for the Red Sox. Carlton Fisk, Jerry Remy, Mike Ryan, Bill Monboquette, Lou Merloni, Jeff Reardon, Tony Conigliaro, Rich Gedman, and the manager Joe Morgan are all featured in a graphic called "The Pride of New England."

    Mo Vaughn—fifth on the all-time Red Sox home run list, a .304 hitter in his six-year career with the Red Sox, during which he qualified for the postseason twice, and raised in the New England town of Norwalk, Connecticut—was omitted by the Red Sox from the list. It would be impossible to view this as an innocent oversight.

ally of Harrington, engineered a relentless attack on Vaughn. "The plan," Giuliotti believed, "was to turn the people against him and in a way, it worked. They said he was fat, out of shape." In print, McDonough would refer to Vaughn as "Mo Money." Once, Vaughn's father contacted McDonough asking why the columnist attacked his son so vigorously. "I talked to him, father to father," McDonough said. "And I told him I would give him a piece of advice. I told him to tell his son to keep his mouth shut and play ball."

Vaughn angered McDonough. He believed Vaughn to be too outspoken, too opinionated. When Vaughn would threaten to leave at the end of the 1998 season as a free agent, it further inflamed the columnist. There was something about Vaughn that tended to incite McDonough to an almost personal degree. Between Vaughn and Roger Clemens, few athletes would receive harsher treatment from Will McDonough. "All he did was talk," McDonough said. "You listen to him and he made it sound like he was on a chain gang in this town, like he was busting rocks. He made a lot of money, and he was treated right. His family was treated like royalty around here."

Race inevitably crept into the debate, even though it would become clear that mutual dislike between Vaughn and management would be the principal factor in this drama. Around the league, whispers of racism began to pepper the discussion. Sean McAdam believed that even at the turn of a new century, many white men in power still felt uncomfortable with a player of Vaughn's physical and cultural blackness. He was a large presence, big, black, bald, and wore earrings. He personified the hip-hop culture and socialized with rappers such as Notorious B.I.G. There was also a feeling that management was not comfortable with a black athlete being so outspoken, a sentiment that fans would grow to share. "It's a tricky thing," felt Peter Gammons. "People want you to speak out, to be a leader, until they don't."

Black players believed that the Red Sox would have reached some form of compromise with a white player and found a way to agree on a contract. But even if they earned tens of millions, black players were still treated differently, as commodities and not members of a baseball family. The Red Sox would never have let Yaz go, went the argument. Blacks were different. They were commodities, while great white players were members of a family. Dave Winfield, the Hall of Famer, played for six teams. Rickey Henderson, the greatest leadoff hitter the game has known, played for the Oakland A's on three different occasions, for the San Diego Padres twice, and for the New York Mets and Yankees, the Toronto Blue Jays, the Anaheim Angels, and the Seattle Mariners. The ageless Henderson, a sure Hall of Famer, believed in a certain double standard. "Come on," he said. "You might want to be fair, but don't be naïve, now. No way do they treat Mo that way if he was Cal Ripken or some other guy. He's too good for that. Put up too many numbers." Ironically, Henderson would play for Boston in 2002.

Vaughn and Duquette would fight all season, through the media and in negotiations that were, in truth, half-hearted in effort. A concern always seemed to surface during 1998 that stalled negotiations. The two sides were close until the DUI arrest. Vaughn's weight was a concern. On some days, Vaughn said he wanted to finish his career in Boston. On others, he intimated that he wanted to join Clemens in Toronto. On the worst days, his frustration would froth. Once, it erupted. "The Red Sox think I'm fucking around. They don't understand I'll leave this motherfucker in a heartbeat."

Vaughn contended that his problem with negotiations was not about money, but the respect of the franchise. They had taken care of Pedro Martinez and Garciaparra, but not him. When the Red Sox promoted the 1999 All-Star game, which was to be played in Boston, they made a point of omitting Vaughn's name in all literature and interviews, as if the organization knew well in advance that Vaughn would not be part of the club.

Yet Vaughn's rejection of Red Sox's multiyear, multimillion-dollar offers would infuriate fans living from paycheck to paycheck. They could not believe Vaughn, who felt the Red Sox were trying to run him out of town by poisoning the fans against him. Nor could they believe the Red Sox, who waited until the eleventh hour to begin serious talks with a player who defined them for the decade. Tony Massarotti felt differently. "People would say that Mo changed. That he lied or changed his stories. I don't think that is true at all. I think Mo is such an emotional guy, he said exactly what he felt *at that time*. He never ducked. If a few days later, he realized that he said something that he didn't exactly mean, that's not lying. We're human beings and human beings change their minds. He was always a stand up guy."

The real truth was that at that point, Vaughn was never going to remain in Boston. "Neither one really wanted it to happen the way it happened," Peter Gammons said on ESPN. "But with the two personalities involved, it really wasn't going to work any other way. To this day, I have no idea what really happened. Maybe we'll never know. I still thought that day in '98 that Vaughn and Duquette had come to an agreement."

Vaughn kept hitting. He came within two points of winning the American League batting title, and with a .337 batting average had a year comparable to his MVP year of 1995. The powerful trio of Vaughn, Martinez, and Garciaparra led the Red Sox to the postseason before suffering another bitter playoff loss to Cleveland, where Vaughn's final at-bat in a Red Sox uniform was a double off the Wall in Fenway to keep a fading season alive.

Once the Sox were eliminated from the playoffs, the only question was whether Duquette and Vaughn would find détente, or if Mo would walk in the same footsteps as Luis Tiant, Fisk, Lynn, and Clemens.

In October there still was no deal, and it became increasingly clear that Vaughn would leave Boston. By November, *Globe* Columnist Dan Shaughnessy wrote:

> This stinks. Vaughn put together six consecutive monster seasons for the Red Sox. He was a leader on and off the field—wildly respected by players all over baseball.

Moreover, he was a black athlete who said good things about working and living in
Boston. He's done legitimate community service and is an absolute kid magnet. His is
a huge loss, worse than the departures of Roger Clemens and Carlton Fisk.

On November 25, 1998, Mo Vaughn signed a six-year, $80-million con-
tract with the Anaheim Angels. It was over. Giuliotti blamed Duquette for
allowing Vaughn to leave. Gammons would always be conflicted, for
Harrington's hand could never be underestimated. Vaughn would harbor an
opinion he would never articulate.

Giuliotti believed that Duquette's cold style led to bitter breaks with
invaluable members of Red Sox history. "These two guys, Mo and Clemens,
should have been preserved. They should have received much better treatment.
They earned it. But they had a mind of their own. If you have a mind of your
own, I don't recommend playing for the Red Sox."

Tony Massarotti saw Vaughn not merely as refreshing, but as the seminal
figure in a new chapter in Red Sox history. Because of Vaughn, Massarotti felt,
the Red Sox could finally begin to distance themselves from their history.

"When he walked into the clubhouse, Ellis Burks was the only black person he saw. By the time he left, it was totally different," said Massarotti. "To me,
Mo is the barrier breaker in Boston. There are guys who paved the way for
everyone else. Mo is one of them. I look at him as the swivel point, from when
Boston changed as a team. He was the first to be completely embraced. He was
a real outspoken leader. During Mo's prime, he was the most beloved black athlete of any sport this city has ever known."

It should have never ended that way. Mo Vaughn came to Boston with more
expected of him than any Red Sox player in the franchise's history. He represented
not only the hope for a championship but also something much more important.
He was expected to eliminate the cloud that has hovered over this franchise since
that April morning in 1945. Others expected to carry the special burden of proving that a black person could thrive in Boston, but he also carried this weight for
himself. His pride could never have allowed him to voice reconciliation or regret,
for that would be in his mind the ultimate form of weakness. But there is no question that Mo Vaughn did not want to leave Boston or the Boston Red Sox. The
Red Sox, however, seemed determined to prove to Vaughn the one notion that has
defined them during the free agent era: The franchise is always bigger than the
player. The Red Sox wanted to prove this more than they wanted to bridge the
racial divide that has haunted them for more than half a century and more than
they wanted to win a championship. As such, Mo Vaughn left as they all have—
without champagne toasts, parades or the elusive World Series title that has
thwarted all Red Sox superstars since Babe Ruth's famous curse. He always wanted
to be known as the Last of the Great Red Sox, but by the end of his final, acidic
days with the team, few of the great things once forecast ever came to pass.

EPILOGUE

In the summer of 2000, Larry Whiteside would come to an unshakable conclusion about the Boston Red Sox. The image of the club as a racist organization could never completely be eradicated as long as the Yawkey name cast its enormous shadow over the franchise. No matter what John Harrington said, or Dan Duquette did, the Yawkey legacy had left too giant a scar. Too many years had passed, too many feelings hurt, and attitudes had become so hardened that even sincere gestures of change were met cynically. It would be impossible, he believed, to paint over the old canvas, for the creases and outlines of the years would forever find their way into the future.

On February 22, 2002, the Boston Red Sox would be officially sold to the ownership group led by John Henry, Tom Werner and Larry Lucchino. The Yawkey era, which owned the Red Sox in deed and attitude since 1933, was over. With the passing of the franchise by John Harrington to the new owners, a new history could finally begin.

Frustrated by the interminable length of time he believed it would require before the Red Sox could be rehabilitated from their past, John Harrington sounded fatalistic. "I don't know how you do it," he said. "I've been told it will take fifty years, generations before this thing is gone. I won't be around and you won't be around. It's impossible." He spoke as if the Red Sox were the unlucky sufferers of a malignant growth from within the organization. This, however, could not be further from the truth, and in many ways it is a sour reflection of the pessimism that so many Americans feel toward race relations. There was no one moment, no original sin that earned for the Red Sox the difficult burden they now own, but decades of conscious decision making. Over a fifty-five-year period, the Red Sox crafted their current situation, and they have paid a lingering price for it, one that they cannot merely wish away. To consider the club's image to be perception or the individuals who maintain control over the franchise as helpless is to trivialize what is truly at issue.

The new ownership now has an opportunity if not to rewrite the history of the Red Sox, then to create a new history, beginning with the first day of their purchase.

What began with the tryout of Jackie Robinson was fortified by twelve years of segregation and was reinforced by ugly and public episodes of prejudice. It is a history created by the choices of fallible, bigoted men that can be remedied in the same way by the better choices of more honorable ones. The method with which to counter decades of indicting history is not to wait for time to pass but to proactively engineer a series of successes. The sharp, impressive changes brought forth by Dan Duquette are the best example of this.

Creating a new history is indeed a daunting prospect. In the face of such a huge undertaking it is much easier either to consider the problem impenetrable or to accuse anyone who attempts to create dialogue on the subject—as Steve Fainaru did in his 1991 series in the *Boston Globe*—as an outsider or a troublemaker. This tactic, however, only hardens attitudes and creates apathy on the part of the Red Sox and a black community that so desperately would accept a sustained gesture of détente from the team. It also misses the very important point that change is completely and entirely possible. Few people in the nation in 1959—the year Pumpsie Green first arrived in Boston—ever expected cities like Atlanta and Houston to be considered prime centers of black commerce, yet they are the two cities where many African Americans see the most hope to gain a toehold in corporate America. When Kirby Puckett came to Minnesota as a rookie in 1982, the Twins suffered a reputation among black players no different than that of the Red Sox. Old Twins owner Calvin Griffith was one of the game's worst racists, and his club usually reflected Griffith's views. When he retired, Kirby Puckett became a vice president with the club and the Twins now boast the most talented, young black prospects in the American League.

The finest example of the possibility for change is none other than the New York Yankees, a franchise that was as virulently racist as the Red Sox during the 1950s. During their championship run of the late 1990s, the Yankees became a primarily minority ball club with mass appeal across the most diverse city in America. While there may still be internal feelings of racism that still exist inside of the organization, their best players follow no racial pattern. Jason Giambi is Italian American. Bernie Williams is Puerto Rican. Derek Jeter is of mixed race. Roger Clemens is a white Texan. Their best postseason starting pitcher, Orlando "El Duque" Hernandez, is a black Cuban. Mariano Rivera, the great reliever, is Panamanian. The manager, Joe Torre, is a throwback from those multicultural Cardinals teams of early 1970s and one of his very best friends is Bob Gibson.

During the spring of 2002, George Steinbrenner, the principal owner of the Yankees, leans on the bullpen rail at Legends Field, the Yankees spring training facility. He is talking about the history of the New York Yankees and how his team has conscientiously distanced itself from its past. "There comes a point in time where you have to give people a chance to perform, to have an opportunity to show what they are capable of. There are many, many things that have occurred in this society, with this franchise even, that we cannot always be proud of. But while you are here, you have the chance set whatever course you choose. You do this by being fair, by judging people on what they do, on how they perform. But you have to give them the chance to do it."

New York has endured loud and polarizing incidents, as surely as Boston. The Howard Beach incident in 1986 and the recent Abner Louima verdict and reversal are clear examples that New York is always an incident away from becoming a racial tinderbox, yet the city moves forward while Boston still fights the quarter-century stigma of busing. "But," *New York Post* reporter George King says, "There is a difference. Through it all, New York had problems, but it was never considered a racist city. Boston has to get past that. And that's not easy."

The Yankees still have, structurally, some of the same hard-line attitudes in 2002 as they did in 1961. Like the Red Sox, the team has never hired a black field manager and the unspoken belief within the team is that it would be a significant and surprise move for it to happen. On the field, where it counts, however, the Yankees sign only the best players. In the fifty years the Red Sox have struggled with their racial identity, the Yankees have essentially eliminated racism as a defining characteristic of their franchise. The difference, thinks David Halberstam, is that the Yankees, with George Steinbrenner, simply spend whatever is necessary to buy a championship. "In an odd sense, they outspent their racism. They became the standard for ruthless capitalism. There is little place for racial profiling in that type of structure."

Why, then, is it not possible for the Red Sox to do the same? As in the case of the city, a sustained will on the part of the Red Sox is imperative, lest the team enjoy the racial oases of 1967 and 1975. In both cases, the progressive, integrated teams of Dick O'Connell were followed by backlash, indicating that nothing truly changed in organizational mindset or in the perception of the city. Joe Giuliotti of the *Herald*, retired in 2000 after forty-eight years at the paper, believes in hope.

"The Red Sox have always reflected the city, and they always will," he says. "We got idiots like Louise Day Hicks. Those things happened at a time when blacks in the city had no political strength. Forced busing was the worst thing for everyone. Things have changed in Boston, obviously for the better. People have changed. I think we're a smarter, more intelligent city."

As the seventy-year specter of the Yawkey reign no longer dictates the team's future, but fades into history, there is no reason why the John Henry Red Sox cannot engineer a similar transition to the Yankees and other organizations. The hiring of the proper personnel—the franchise's biggest weakness over its history, largely due to the cronyism of Tom Yawkey—is the first key step.* Dan Duquette's approach, impersonal and cold, would cost him his job one week into the new regime. Although his dismissal would be not be mourned by many, especially by those whom Duquette treated so callously, Duquette should still in time be treated by history as a seminal figure in Red Sox history, for race would never be a principal factor in his hiring policies, as was the case with so many earlier Red Sox executives. Duquette completed what Lou Gorman started, and by the end of the 2001 season, the Red Sox would suffer in reputation only, not in its efforts to promote diversity.

Pumpsie Green doesn't know why there had to be men like Pinky Higgins. If he sounds naïve, he is merely thinking aloud in his retracing the difficult steps of his own personal path. "Sometimes when I think of the things people like me had to go through," he says, "it just sounds so unnecessary. When you think about it, it is almost silly, how much time and energy was wasted hating." His is the outsider's story of life in a very insular city.

In the spring of 2000, forty-one years after that first spring training in Scottsdale, Pumpsie Green is sitting in his easy chair at his home in the Oakland suburb of El Cerrito, California. He thinks about how he handled the segregated housing in Phoenix, the racial troubles in Boston and the life of a baseball player with limited abilities. He is proud of being the first black player in Boston Red Sox history. He wasn't a militant, because being provocative could mean danger, even death. He had seen it, when boisterous and proud black men would be forcibly rebuked for challenging the day's social customs.

"It is interesting when kids today listen to me or the stories of those days and say that they couldn't have ever lived through those times. Oh, you would

---

* There would be one final tarnishing of the Yawkey legacy, a disturbing revelation from a courthouse in Bartow, Florida. On May 16, 2002, Donald Fitzpatrick, seventy-two, a retired clubhouse manager and a favorite of Tom Yawkey, was convicted of sexual misconduct with African-American children he had hired to work in the Red Sox clubhouse during spring trainings in Winter Haven, Fla., and at Fenway Park over the period from 1975 to 1989. Fitzpatrick, who pleaded guilty to four counts of attempted sexual battery and had been linked to 13 previous victims—aged four to nineteen— agreed to pay each of the four plaintiffs in the case $10,000 each. He avoided jail time by agreeing to a plea bargain with a ten-year suspended sentence.

The current Red Sox ownership has denied any knowledge of Fitzpatrick's activities, as did various lieutenants of the Yawkey regime, but numerous sources summarily discount the denial on the part of the Yawkey ownership, convinced the Red Sox chose to ignore rather than confront a serious and disturbing problem.

The Fitzpatrick story represented not only the seamiest underside of the club, but also the culture of denial and cronyism at all costs that existed within the organization. The *Boston Globe*'s Bob Hohler reported that one of Fitzpatrick's victims, aged seventeen, came forward and told his story to a member of Red Sox management in 1971. The Red Sox responded not by reprimanding or dismissing Fitzpatrick, but by firing the victim who spoke up.

have adapted well, trust me," he says of the 1950s, of his time. "Especially being in a situation where you could lose your life."

At home, Green eases himself into his recliner. Sitting is a relief. Hip replacement surgery makes walking an unwelcome chore. At once, he may be looking out into the gray-blue haze cast over the San Francisco Bay, but his mind is one million frames distant, shuffling and sorting the images of a difficult, complicated past. He is wearing a blue shirt, tan trousers, slippers and, proudly, a Boston Red Sox baseball cap.

The pictures, he says, have been on the walls for years, but for him they still provide an adequate time machine. One is a framed picture of him playing shortstop in a Red Sox uniform, leaping over a forced runner at second and concentrating to fire a relay back to first. The dust is swirling and the old Fenway Park scoreboard, the one with both American and National League scores, sits in the background. He is young again, and it makes him smile.

His eyes dart around the room at the photos, the framed magazine covers. His even expression doesn't change, except when talking about spinning a double play, a favorite act. He sees himself and once more, he is an acrobat, an athlete. He talks specifically about the Red Sox and offers an ironic little smile when he considers history's role for him. He laughs bitterly that the Red Sox humiliated Jackie Robinson, that it slept when it could have acquired Willie Mays, and that these twists of fate left it to unassuming Pumpsie Green to integrate the Red Sox. It is a fact that he is proud of, even if during those days he wanted little to do with the attention that came with being at the epicenter of a moral drama within a franchise and a city. He harbors no bitterness toward the Red Sox or the city of Boston for any reason. He wanted an opportunity to play baseball and they gave him that chance. If he does not rage at being set apart from the Red Sox in those early Scottsdale days, it is this personality that allows him also not to be devoured by the past, and that makes him healthier today. It is, he says evenly, what healing is all about. He sits in the easy chair in his TV room, and the Red Sox cap fits him well.

"I still pay attention to the Red Sox. When I see them on the news or hear about them, because I was a Red Sox. In 1997, they asked me to come back for opening day and throw out the first pitch. Lou Gorman was very friendly. They brought a limousine for me and my wife. We had a hell of a time."

During a June hot streak that sent the San Francisco Giants into first place during the summer of 2000, Ellis Burks hears his name surface in the percolating trade rumor circuit. Before an interleague game against the Oakland A's, Burks takes a seat in Dusty Baker's office and asks his manager just how much truth there is to the rumors, particularly the one that has him returning to Boston in a trade with the Red Sox. When he leaves Baker's office, the Boston years he thought he'd left behind eight years previous resurface in his mind. "I decided that if I was traded back to Boston, I would announce my retirement," Burks says. "I just didn't want to go back there and go through all that again. I don't feel bad about being there and I'm glad people say it's a little different now. It just wasn't for me."

Jim Rice found détente and then healing with the Red Sox. In his first year as general manager, Dan Duquette offered Rice a job in the organization as a roving minor league hitting instructor. On balance, Rice's return represented a positive sign. He would never wear another team logo and reappearing in Boston signaled a healing between the star and his team. No one was more surprised by this than Ellis Burks. When Rice left after being released in 1989, he told Burks he would never again set foot in Fenway Park. Rice rose quickly and by 1998 was the hitting coach of the Red Sox before being fired after the 2000 season. He was retained by the new ownership and in the company masthead, under the title "instructor," and next to Theodore S. Williams and Carl M. Yastrzemski is his name, James E. Rice.

Rice is still waiting to enter the Hall of Fame. He inches closer each year but is still considerably short of the 75 percent of the vote a player must attain for enshrinement. In 2001, he received fewer votes than in the previous year, evidence that his window may have closed. The voters, of course, are the media members with whom Rice enjoyed a grudging relationship. Based on his performance as a player, Sean McAdam does not believe Rice is worthy of the Hall. Jeff Horrigan does, as do Gammons and Dan Shaughnessy. Neither believes Rice is being punished for his brusqueness as a player. Don Zimmer, his favorite manager, disagrees. "There has to be a little bit of that in the back of people's mind. He's a Hall of Famer as sure as anyone else is. But people don't forget how you treat 'em. If he was more cordial, he'd have a plaque by now."

During the first weeks of the new regime, Jim Rice would sit in the visitor's dugout of Legends Field before a spring game with the New York Yankees. Rickey Henderson is sitting next to him, incredibly, wearing a Red Sox uniform. Henderson says he was always intrigued by the Red Sox because of the club's history, but like other African-American players, knew of the club's reputation. "They shoulda got me 10 years ago," he says, slipping into diplomacy. "But they didn't. Times, I guess times were different back then."

Rice is hopeful for the future of Boston and the Red Sox, issuing a common theme. "With the new owners, it will be a new era. There will be a new opportunity. There will be all colors at the ballpark. Look at Rickey Henderson. Rickey will get black people to come to the ballpark. It is family entertainment. You have to go down to the neighborhoods, because it's all about family entertainment and convince people that this is a place for everyone."

Sam Jethroe died on June 16, 2001, and another link to the Jackie Robinson tryout is gone. Jethroe, like Pumpsie Green, is often recognized more for who he wasn't than the person he was. Robinson should have been the first black major leaguer in Boston, but it was Jethroe with the Boston Braves. Over the years, he would reappear briefly, usually when the subject of race and the Red Sox would be rediscovered. But Sam Jethroe spent his remaining years under the celebrity radar, as a bartender in Erie, Pennsylvania. A few days after his death, he is eulogized well by Martin Nolan, who said goodbye to a childhood hero in a well-written tribute to "The Jet," smiling at the happy memories.

Cecil Cooper would grow pessimistic about the next stage of black integration in baseball, the boardroom. He would always be considered one of the smartest, most respected of baseball men and when his playing career ended in 1987, Cooper resolved to make the arduous climb into baseball management. While others, such as Dan Duquette, never played the game yet found themselves rising rapidly in the game's hierarchy, Cooper was disappointed to find that there was little room for him. He would be named farm director of the Milwaukee Brewers—working for Milwaukee owner Bud Selig—a position he would hold in the 1990s before leaving before the 2001 season, but he never felt there was ample opportunity for him to become a general manager. On occasion, he would be invited to sit in on developmental meetings and also attended some league-sponsored training programs for minorities, but he never felt comfortable. Most disappointing to Cooper was his feeling of inadequacy. Not only would he feel ignored in meetings, as if he was in the room only to satisfy the appearance of racial progress, but he also believed white executives thought the same. Cooper's feelings were an example of the most insidious by-product of institutional racism. Perhaps his instincts were correct, but there was always the chance he had brought the feeling on himself. He would never know, and so would look bitterly upon his lack of advancement. He never believed that his opinion was valued. "That was it for me," Cooper said. "Let's just put it this way. I'll leave the rest to the younger guys."

Reggie Smith spent eighteen seasons as a player in the major leagues. Of the switch-hitting players in the game's history, only a handful—Chipper Jones, Bernie Williams, Eddie Murray, and Mickey Mantle—would hit consistently for more power. Joe Torre would be surprised at how Smith would fade from view. "When you think about established switch-hitters, his name isn't mentioned much. I thought he would have had more recognition. He was a better player, too intense a guy, to just kind of fade away." In 1997, he was the batting coach for the Los Angeles Dodgers. He wasn't a big man, but his presence brought to a conversation nothing short of confrontation. He was stocky, direct, owned a passing amount of gray hair, and a gray mustache all accompanied by a bowlegged limp. It is impossible to ignore the presence of Reggie Smith, for he moves with a studied intensity. He approaches all subjects with force, not humor or indifference. He has something to say, and he wants you to listen.

Boston was a bad place for him. It angered him and he thrived when he left. He was affected by a city that had not confronted itself, and even reflection is hard.

"When you start thinking about it, New England and Boston being the cradle of liberty and democracy, it's a little bit confusing that the city has that kind of image," he says to me. "But the image exists for a reason, there's something wrong up there."

For a moment, he talks about Jackie Robinson. The year is nineteen ninety-seven, the fiftieth anniversary of Robinson's debut and far from enjoying the league-wide ceremonies, Smith is more interested in using this as a marking point on the black progress in baseball.

While chomping on a Tootsie Roll, he is demanding, "What good is all the attention to the event if there is nothing behind it? Don't let his deeds get lost in the celebration. Getting to where we are today took a number of years. He was at the forefront of the changes that were taking place. Because of him, change occurred at a faster pace than society wanted to allow."

Internally, progress was still too slow in baseball for him. He starts to rattle off in quick succession all that baseball hasn't done. The game still acted without urgency in regards to hiring black managers or personnel in the upper reaches of management. At that time, there was only one black manager in the game and seven in the twenty-two years since Frank Robinson became the first black skipper with Cleveland in 1975 (By 2001, there would be five). In its 127–year history, baseball hired but one black general manager, Bob Watson of the Yankees (Kenny Williams' appointment to run the Chicago White Sox in 2001 and Omar Mineya's acceptance of the in-receivership Montreal Expos in 2002 tripled the number). Black ownership of a major league franchise was a far-off fantasy, although Donald Watkins, a billionaire from Alabama began 2002 seeking to purchase the Minnesota Twins. A fired black manager gets a second chance slowly or not at all. At that time, only one black manager, Frank Robinson, had been fired by one club and rehired by another. In Robinson's case, he managed in Cleveland, San Francisco, Baltimore and in 2002, the Montreal Expos. Update: Don Baylor, Hal McRae, and Dusty Baker have also received second managerial opportunities. By contrast, Phil Garner has managed the Milwaukee Brewers to seven straight losing seasons from 1993 to 1999. He was fired at the end of the 1999 season and immediately hired by Detroit, where in his first two seasons in 2000 and 2001 the Tigers lost eighty-three and ninety-six games, respectively.

Reggie Smith glares impatiently. This is exactly his point. He brings heat to the conversation and it is clear there is little that is casual about him. When Reggie Smith talks about progress in baseball, he is not comparing statistics, but more the various stations of his life, what he lived during those times and what life has done to him. There may be progress, but hardly enough to satisfy him.

Luis Tiant coached the baseball team of the Savannah College of Art and Design. It would be an odd position for a man who had won 229 games in the major leagues. Tiant, however, loved baseball and the major leagues would not respond to his repeated requests for a pitching coach position at any level in any organization. He would be bitter at being shut out of the game, but would never hold the Red Sox in anything other than high regard. Being a baseball player would never mean so much as it did when he pitched for the Red Sox. During the annual winter meeting in 2001, a short, balding black man wearing a snowy white Fu Manchu moustache walked across the lobby of the Sheraton Boston. It was Luis Tiant, and he headed to Dan Duquette's suite to discuss a job opportunity. When he returned to the lobby, the Red Sox had named him pitching coach of the club's Class A team in Lowell, Massachusetts. At the City of Palms Park in the spring of 2002 was Tiant, hitting fungoes to the new generation of Red Sox. "I'm so happy," Tiant says, "that they brought me home."

Larry Whiteside, felled by chronic back trouble and later by a stroke, stays at home for spring training 2001. It is the first spring training he has missed in more than thirty-five years. He is on long-term disability leave from the Boston *Globe*, and won't appear in spring training in 2002, either. His optimism about the Red Sox's relationship with African Americans is curbed by a learned journalistic reflex. He has seen the team slip back into its old ways after minor successes too often. He is not, these days, as concerned about the Boston Red Sox as he is about his own profession. He was the trailblazer who integrated the Boston baseball press corps and nearly thirty years later, he is still the only black reporter to cover the Red Sox on a daily basis in the city's history. He is disappointed that for all his trailblazing spirit, there are exactly two full-time black beat writers in the major leagues. It is a disappointing admission, proof that there are many more mountains to climb. As the century changes, even the Tom Yawkey legacy has been discussed by mainstream outlets that long feared the hot button of challenging the Red Sox's most famous owner. There are pockets of resistance. Influential *Globe* sports columnist Will McDonough sees race in Boston as a media creation, a topic alive only because the Red Sox haven't won a championship. It is a viewpoint that is immediately offensive because he is not black and thus cannot relate to the tremendous emotional distance that African Americans have felt from Boston.

The *Globe* and to a lesser extent the *Herald* have both placed the spotlight on the difficult experiences many black people have had in Boston, but the legacy of the black baseball writer, he believes, appears in peril. Whiteside is the link to the old black press and the assimilation of the modern black reporter into the mainstream. Before Larry Whiteside, the only regular, sustained black baseball writers were from the black press, Sam Lacy of the *Baltimore Afro-American* and Wendell Smith of the *Pittsburgh Courier*. Whiteside brought the two worlds together. Of the group of stars that comprised the *Boston Globe* staff in the 1970s, it would be Larry Whiteside who did not ascend as the others did. He will not explain why. In 1999, the *Globe* promoted Michael Holley to the position of columnist. He is the first black sports columnist in the paper's 130–year history.

Al Skinner, the black basketball coach at Boston College, speaks at once of the wonderful college environment of Boston and how his recruitment efforts are hampered because black parents still have the images of the racial strife of the 1970s ingrained in their memories. Long memories build trepidation in African Americans about sending their children to Boston. In late 1999, the city officially ended busing as a matter of public policy, closing the book on the city's worst chapter.

The city is softening, and creeping toward its stated seventeenth and eigh-teenth century goals of egalitarianism. To achieve these small but important steps, the Boston political and business establishments made efforts through recruitment, education, and sheer will to face the problem of race head-on, instead with the classic Boston style of denial. Michael Patrick McDonald, the South Boston writer, is pondering a question about the hope for Boston. At least in the eyes of the politicians, he says, the hope is to get rid of the hardened attitudes not by education and coalition but by gentrification. With higher housing costs, the poor of each race who fought each other for Boston's soul in 1970s will no longer be able to afford housing in the city. "And Southie and Roxbury," he says, "will be better places in their eyes, with less tensions, but they will no longer be the Southie and Roxbury we remember." The soul of the city is the true issue here, and in our own ways, each racial and ethnic group in Boston is trying to own a piece of it. The divisions are still considerable.

"Often, as in Southie or Roxbury, these neighborhoods were ruined not only by outside hostility and oppression (and racism in Roxbury's case), but by inside manipulation by powerful individuals (gangsters, politicians, and other corrupt "community leaders") with selfish goals rather than communal goals," McDonald says. "But the neighborhoods of Boston didn't *have* to be dysfunc-tional. . . . Today's city is increasingly made up of dot-commers, all facing a com-puter screen, believing in the individual over the community, and whose goals are more around individual acquisitions, real estate investment, and toys from Brookstone. This will make for incredibly unhealthy and lonely cities, as well as promote crime in the long run, as the distance increases between the haves and have-nots."

After *All Souls* was published, McDonald sought to heal the old wounds of busing by organizing a reunion with all the various combatants from those dark days. Call it a triumph of survival, perhaps. Fearful of a renewal of past pain, Boston mayor Tom Menino nixed the idea. "He thought it was just best to leave it all in the past. But he doesn't understand those days are with us every day."

On a meaningless September day in 1999, Mo Vaughn taped his ankles in the air-conditioned cool of Edison Field, the home stadium of the Anaheim

Angels. In Boston, there would be much commotion during the final month of the baseball season. The Red Sox would try in vain to catch the New York Yankees for the division title while staving off upstart Oakland for the wild card. Why Vaughn would no longer be a part of such action was a question no one in Boston could answer easily. In Boston, Vaughn stood at the center of an important team. In Anaheim, he wouldn't play a meaningful game all season.

There would be much regret in his face and in his mannerisms. Vaughn doesn't want to talk about the details of how it happened, of how he walked away from what he felt was his calling and how the Red Sox were happy to see him go. He doesn't want to talk about the slights that hurt him deeply or the embarrassing events in his personal life that gave the Red Sox the ammunition to mount a public campaign against him to justify their private souring. The waters were so dirtied between him and the team that everyone, it now seemed, had forgotten that there once had been years of smiles.

At first, he won't talk about John Harrington or Dan Duquette, the two men who told him he no longer had a future in Boston. It reveals a telling piece of his personality, past details being secondary to current reality. Nothing will change the fact that after six seasons, two playoff appearances and one MVP award that he is no longer a part of Boston, so he sees little point in an analysis of how it all happened. After nearly a decade of goodwill, he now sits three thousand miles away, in the hazy backdrop of southern California, where cabernet sauvignon is available at the ballpark by the bottle. Mo Vaughn looks lost, completely out of place. He looks as if he is in exile.

Few people who know him believed he would ever be truly content in California, a sunny place devoid of an East Coast thirst for baseball. Sean McAdam wasn't surprised that Vaughn left—relations between him and Red Sox management had become too sour—but McAdam knew Anaheim would not fulfill Vaughn's baseball thirsts. "What did he expect?" McAdam asks. "Anaheim was the antithesis of what he's all about." Anaheim, Mo Vaughn says, is his future. He sounds like a man doing all he can to convince himself that he is happy, that being in California is the right thing for him.

"I had to turn the page, man," he says, massaging the thick rolls of athletic tape around sore ankles. "I did the job there. I came to work every day. No one can dispute that. Do I miss Boston? I miss the energy, the passion of the fans. They care. But hey, was I the first to get run out of there? I don't think so."

Will McDonough believes the Red Sox would be better if they still had Mo Vaughn, but says Vaughn's duplicitous thirst for money superceded the rhetoric of wanting to be the Last of the Great Red Sox. Sean McAdam ponders the Vaughn legacy. "I don't know if its racial—though I suspect that it is— but I've never seen a player leave here that was subject to so much *anger* as people directed toward Mo. I mean they took his leaving more personally than Fisk, Clemens, all of them." While player greed is a perennial complaint about the game, it has produced one positive side effect. Fierce competition for the best talent has finally eliminated many racial considerations.

The next two years would be a complete and total disaster for Mo Vaughn. Miserable in 2000, he hit .272, his worst since 1992, and for a third-place team. Trying to prove himself as a leader, Vaughn would injure his ankle on opening day and play with various problems in his throwing shoulder all season. Over the winter before the 2001 season, he tore his biceps muscle—it was rumored that he injured himself driving a snowmobile, an act forbidden by his contract—and missed the entire 2001 season. It would grow worse for Mo Vaughn. He would enrage his Anaheim employers by admitting during that summer that taking the money and moving to California was a mistake and that he wanted to be traded, though he still had three years and $42 million remaining on his contract. One day in September 2001, Vaughn made an appearance in the Red Sox clubhouse to a hero's welcome and made an appeal that he wanted to return to the Red Sox, where he belonged. After much luster had been worn from his image as a leader, the Angels traded Vaughn back to his beloved East Coast, to the New York Mets in December 2001. He, too, has a new beginning ahead.

Vaughn would be the last player to be groomed by the Red Sox and capture the full imagination of the city, though Nomar Garciaparra owns a similar opportunity. If Mo Vaughn wanted to leave Boston with a championship and the title of a lasting piece of the team's history, then his stay in Boston fell short of its stated goals. Yet quite possibly, Mo Vaughn accomplished something more enduring. Because of Vaughn, the Red Sox are in less of a racial quagmire than in the past. Black players, if wary, seem more open to Boston than before. Ellis Burks, ten years removed from the Red Sox, says he always asks players who come through Boston about the city's climate, "Just to see if things are different now than they were for me." Mo Vaughn proved that a black player could be a superstar in Boston, and be beloved by its dedicated, demanding fans. Vaughn had his problems with the team, obviously, but they were more the unfortunate result of a contract negotiation poisoned on both sides than irreconcilable beliefs about the city and its racial climate. He still lives in a sprawling house in Easton, some thirty-five minutes outside of Boston, and still continues his yeoman duty of charity work.

This is good news for the city, which has been as much a deterrent to the Red Sox attracting black players as the team itself. African-American professionals testify to as many cultural clashes and discomfort in Boston as a Reggie Smith or an Ellis Burks. Many stay for a moment and leave, seeking a city climate more receptive to them. This is painful for both the city and the individual, for Boston has so much to give. Tommy Harper is still as of the 2002 season coaching for the Red Sox. He believes much has changed around the Red Sox and again the outreach by Dan Duquette suggests an organization in the beginnings of a difficult but necessary transition.

After Vaughn, no player would assume the role of becoming the public face of the franchise as much as Duquette himself. Perhaps it would be a function of personality or of the complexities of the game brought on by increasing labor strife and rapidly rising salaries, television contracts and the widespread belief that baseball players were to be considered contracted entertainers, not mortar bricks important to a community. David Justice, then playing for the New York Yankees, best exemplified this trend. "Do I consider myself a Yankee? No, but I don't consider myself a Cleveland Indian or an Atlanta Brave, even though they signed me and I started my career there. I'm a baseball player, that's it. They pay me to play and I play, doesn't matter where." The time of players staying and growing up in an organization as their fans grow up with them is over. It was an era, it can be argued, which saw the beginning of its end just as Mo Vaughn entered the major leagues in 1991.*

The result is a baseball atmosphere where no one remains in one place long enough for a given club to develop much of an identity at all, racial or otherwise. Nomar Garciaparra and Pedro Martinez would take over in 1999 for Vaughn as the club's best players, but neither does a great deal more than play baseball in Boston. During his period from 1998 to 2000 as the best pitcher in the game (injuries stripped him of that title in 2001), Martinez was easily the most popular athlete in Boston. But it was Duquette who dominated the franchise. Only one player on the 2001 Red Sox even lived in the Boston area during the off-season. For decades, the Red Sox were one of the last, precious sports franchises that mirrored the city in which it was located, but now in the wake of the millions of dollars and constant player movement, the Red Sox are growing apart from its city.

In Vaughn's place, the Red Sox meandered along. Martinez would continue to be brilliant, though a shoulder injury suffered in 2001 threatens to derail a Hall of Fame career. Garciaparra fought injury but the team would lack a spiritual core, replaced by the constant specter of Duquette. The team traded for Carl Everett, the volatile black centerfielder. It would be one of Duquette's great mistakes, for after an impressive first year, Everett would never mesh well in Boston. In a case where the city's press would be too careful in treading on

---

* Research by David Vincent of the Society for American Baseball Research reveals that the free agent era has not been any less loyal to players than the reserve clause era that immediately preceded it. In the 26 years of free agency leading up to the start of the 2002 season, 48 players have played for only one team for at least nine years. Of all the players who began their careers between 1950 and 1975, the last full year of the reserve clause, 51 played for only one club for at least nine years. The argument that teams lack loyalty to established players can be made, naturally, along racial lines, where blacks and Latinos in baseball have argued longevity with one club is largely exclusive to whites. Of the 48 players who played with only one club for at least nine years during the free agent years of 1976 to 2002, 34 are white.

racial issues, little was written about a difficult personality that would have explained why Boston was Everett's fifth organization before his thirtieth birthday.

It was also an embarrassment for Duquette, for he allowed Vaughn, a true clubhouse leader to leave, while trading for Everett, a clear distraction who angered both black and white teammates. After two tempestuous seasons, Everett was traded to Texas in December 2001.

The money has changed the Red Sox, too. Today's Boston Red Sox clearly seem to lack the racial agenda that made black players skeptical of the Red Sox. Pedro Martinez, a Dominican, is the leader of the team and the best pitcher in baseball. Manny Ramirez has begun his second season with the Red Sox. When he signed his monstrous eight-year, $160 million contract in December 2000, he was the first player of color—black, Hispanic, Asian—to sign a free agent contract with the Red Sox while in the prime of his career. This would come twenty-six years after the beginning of free agency. While older generations of black Bostonians feel ostracized from Fenway, Dan Duquette felt proud that a new generation of Latino fan identifies with Fenway Park and the Red Sox. "Whatever this organization was," Duquette said in May 2001, "it is no longer. We consider that history to be a part of the past, not future of this franchise." This gentrification of baseball signals, in some way, a hope for the Red Sox even while at the same time the game's economic system inexorably detaches us from the game.

"It's all different now," Joe Giuliotti says. "I think the racial thing in the game is a thing of the past, all because of the money. Maybe for once the money has done a good thing. Today, players will play in hell if the money is right."

AFTERWORD

The end of *Shut Out* proved really to be nothing more than a beginning, and as John Henry's first year of ownership wound to a close, the dynastic edifice of Boston's old guard continued its inevitable crumble and decay.

A frosty day in the winter of 2003 would become noteworthy not because of the bite in the Boston air outside—there were too many cold days for just one to stand out that year—but because of a thawing of the arctic climate inside Fenway Park. The day was January 31, Jackie Robinson's birth date, and inside, at Fenway's .406 Club, the Red Sox renounced the shameful afternoon of April 16, 1945 by sponsoring a day of education about the life and impact of Jackie Robinson for 150 adolescent schoolchildren.

In plain sight, covered in powdery snow, was the Fenway Park playing field, the site of Robinson's first major-league humiliation, the original step toward the team's racial perdition. Here, where Robinson's hatred of the Red Sox was born, causing generations of African-American Bostonians to dismiss the club, the Red Sox and numerous politicians and civic groups pushed for Robinson to receive the Congressional Medal of Honor.

After nearly sixty years, the Red Sox had publicly repudiated the club's most defining moment and in the process made a clean and dramatic break with the Yawkeys' intractable past. During the fiftieth anniversary of Robinson's debut back in 1997, Rachel Robinson threw out the first ball at Fenway Park. That celebration, though, was a leaguewide event, mandated by the office of the commissioner. This day, however, carried much more significance, for it was a quiet afternoon without publicity.

Though over the years the organization had offered a chagrined acknowledgment that it had erred with Robinson, no one part of the old Yawkey dynasty would have dared suggest an afternoon like this one, for it would reveal too much about a too-revered, too-flawed institution. To admit a mistake would be to expose Tom Yawkey, Eddie Collins, and Joe Cronin once and for all.

Now, in a new century, change would come, in the room named for Ted Williams' miraculous achievement in the summer of 1941. Even the venue carried some meaning, for it was Williams, part Mexican himself, who had made Pumpsie Green's road easier. If Dan Duquette had once said that the Red Sox would no longer be what they once were, John Henry had now proved it with actions.

I was asked to speak at the event, and though I had readily agreed, the requisite journalistic sirens had sounded a warning against being used as part of a public-relations ploy. I had seen it before, having in the past been part of those well-meaning attempts that gave the appearance of progress while the foundation never changes. I looked upon the day with dread—community leaders droning on endlessly, patting themselves on the back, listening to themselves talk while the kids sleep.

Then everyone goes home.

Numerous other questions persisted. Had the afternoon come far too late? It was thirty-one years after Robinson's death and perhaps too distant to have any impact for those still living who had waited for it. Had too many years passed for the gesture to carry much importance, especially in a city eager to dismiss the complexities of race and move on with life? How would Robinson translate to a group of young teenagers, considering he had been dead longer than any of them had been alive? What was Jackie Robinson now, in the age of PlayStation and *Survivor*? Could he have relevance to a generation that owned cell phones before driver's licenses, or would he be like George Washington, another famous name committed to memory with no real sense of the person?

These initial questions peppered a cynical mind. So, too, came the question of the Red Sox' motivation. Penance without purpose never did anyone much good, and there existed a sense that these new owners might be trying too hard too soon. And what, really, was the club trying to accomplish? Would this afternoon be part of the larger story, where relationships improve, policies change, and the old, uncomfortable culture vanishes?

Later, in his office, John Henry was challenging, and my own fear receded under the weight of his conviction. The afternoon was a success, but neither Henry nor any of the Red Sox staff asked for a single word of publicity, putting to rest another fear. Henry is gaunt, almost frail in build and complexion. He speaks with a gentle toughness I imagine might be easy to underestimate. No one becomes a billionaire in any field without plenty of intellectual muscle and fortitude in reserve, but Henry's approach is more velvet than sandpaper. At times, he sounded an impatient chord, and at once I wondered if he would be the personality who frustrated me most in life—a person compassionate, disarming, likable, but paralyzed, lamenting the state of things without using his immense power to create change. "I think about all that we should be doing, but very few of the real numbers, the important numbers, have changed," he said, adding that the Red Sox, like the majority of professional baseball clubs, have never hired an African-American manager or general manager, and the 2003 Red Sox opened the season with more black coaches (two), than players (one).

"It is important that you not be shy in holding us accountable," he said to me that day. "It is what I expect." Henry is pale, but growing up, his sister tanned deeply, so much so that during those summers in Arkansas and Illinois some of the local whites mistook her for a black girl. Once, when he was six or seven, Henry's sister came home from Florida with a deep tan. A store clerk told Henry's sister that she'd received so much sun she might have to sit in the balcony at the theater, the only place where blacks were permitted to sit.

"You could just see the distance between the two," he said, meaning blacks and whites and colored drinking fountains, separate public seating, and the living conditions: squalid for blacks, better for whites. "And I knew from that day forward that I could not live my life in a place like this."

During that day at Fenway, cynicism quickly gave way to hope, and the fear began to melt. Looking at the young faces in the audience, one could not help but smile warmly at the irony of it all. An audience of young people, taken with stories of the gallant Robinson in Fenway Park, Boston, of all places. I immediately realized that Robinson ran no risk of becoming a dusty relic, and I felt guilty for despairing in the first place. Ten dozen predominately black and Hispanic children, dreamed about all that is possible in their lives with an innocence both unburdened and disarming. The children did not speak with presumption or naïveté; they were just armed with a conviction that few people of their races ever knew before: that the entire world stood open to their ambitions.

In me there existed no caution, no dread, no desire to shake these adorable innocents and explain to them what I knew and what they will find out as their world becomes more complicated, when those dreams are so easily crushed. I thought of my own father, who, as a black man born in 1938, could not dream so wantonly, or my uncle, who, despite achieving complete success in an American context, lived a life poisoned by the limits and presuppositions of race. Baldwin knew of this protectionist urge. He said it best: "The fear that I heard in my father's voice, for example, when he realized that I really *believed* I could do anything a white boy could do, and had every intention of proving it," he wrote in *The Fire Next Time,* "was not at all like the fear I heard when one of us was ill or had fallen down the stairs or strayed too far from the house. It was another fear, a fear that the child, in challenging the white world's assumptions, was putting himself in the path of destruction."

In those children's faces, dark like mine, dreams seemed stronger, more resilient than the ones I'd entertained at a similar age. They appeared reinforced by a support new to the Latino and black American, and by the singular, comforting truth that the entire discussion of the day, of Robinson, of infinite aspirations, occurred in a building that once symbolized all that people of color could not aspire to, those dreams that belonged to everyone but us.

When the afternoon ended, skepticism continued in various quarters, but it became clear to me that January day at Fenway Park was an understated, significant event. Three months later came an announcement: Jackie Robinson would receive his Congressional Medal of Honor.

Eras are defined by the transcendent figures that shaped the times, and sometimes only death can provide that final period punctuating one chapter, allowing permission for another to begin. Sitting in his living room watching television on January 9, 2003, a sudden, massive heart attack killed sixty-seven-year-old Will McDonough, and the most powerful and continuous voice in the history of the Boston media was silenced forever.

During his prime, some three decades, no sports figure in Boston moved without at least being cognizant of McDonough's considerable presence. In his boyhood home of South Boston, McDonough was beloved, the champion a community characterized by its insularity, mistrust of the outside, and inferiority complex. McDonough was their voice; he was the one who had made it.

He was a journalistic icon, a one-person empire forged during the days before the proliferation of cable, satellite television, and the Internet. Back when a single columnist's voice could drive newspaper circulation, Will McDonough was the must-read of the city.

McDonough was always *present*. He entered the newspaper business the same year Pumpsie Green joined the Red Sox, and he outlasted not only all of the biggest figures of the Yawkey dynasty, including Pinky Higgins, Tom Yawkey, Joe Cronin, Jean Yawkey, Dick O'Connell, and Ted Williams, but he survived the dynasty itself before passing on.

By the end, his power had waned considerably, as the old guard across the city made its last stand. Even dominant newspapers like the *Globe* lost influence in a world of competing alternative media, but Will McDonough had become diminished for two equally important reasons. The forces McDonough championed for decades stood in decline, and so too were the attitudes he catered to in his writing. John Harrington, the Red Sox longtime principal owner, had not only sold the Sox, but he'd sold them to Henry's group on the silent order of Major League Baseball. The sale sounded a bitter note for McDonough, who for years had used his position to protect Harrington and by extension the checkered legacy of the Red Sox. In his column, McDonough advocated the Red Sox be sold to local magnate Joe O'Donnell, a boyhood friend of McDonough's who had earned a fortune in the sports and entertainment concessions business. The columnist believed Harrington would ultimately agree to sell the club to O'Donnell. That was the way it had always worked in Boston—deals were done long before the press conference. McDonough was convinced O'Donnell had been double-crossed by Harrington and the Red Sox, and thus he would forever view the Henry group with deep distrust.

For decades, McDonough's *Globe* column served as something of a car wash for the Yawkey dynasty, and selling the team to O'Donnell was at least part of the payoff of a decade of cleansing Harrington. When Henry was awarded the team, McDonough used a familiar weapon—his column—to antagonize the new ownership. O'Donnell losing the team represented the latest and best example of the withering of Boston's old guard; it had been defeated by the same insider political maneuvering in which it was once so expert, and on its home field, no less.

In the first few days after his death, Will McDonough was awash in tributes. A rose occupied his chair in the Boston *Globe* offices. One radio columnist suggested a stadium be named after him. Another called for a statue in his likeness. The day after his death, McDonough's phone rang every hour on the hour. The Boston *Globe* ran days of special coverage, paying homage the toughness and impact of a Boston original. Clark Booth broadcast a trademark elegant appreciation of his close friend.

In a move reserved only for the truly universal, McDonough's body was displayed in a public viewing at the FleetCenter, the cavernous arena where the Boston Celtics and Bruins play.

Yet the overwhelming grief and celebration of McDonough's life carried within it an undertow of uncomfortable silence. For, with controversial and powerful figures, what isn't said often contains as much or more truth as what is. Peter Gammons, McDonough's longtime rival and nemesis, did not write a tribute to his old adversary. McDonough had attacked Gammons for years, personally and professionally. He would tell anyone who would listen that Gammons routinely fabricated information. In the offices of the *Globe*, McDonough's railing against Gammons was legendary to the point of being a punch line. Peter Gammons, who had fashioned a considerable legacy of his own in Boston in large part by outworking the competition, never found this funny.

In death, McDonough was as divisive as in life, revealing in a city's grief also its long-standing segregation. Mourning McDonough took on a very physical character. The black athletes who played in Boston remained curiously quiet. McDonough had defended the Yawkey way vigilantly, routinely discounting the experience of the black athlete in Boston.

During the weeklong celebration of McDonough's life, only one prominent African American was quoted in the coverage. It was Andre Tippett, the great former linebacker for the New England Patriots, who spoke in the capacity of a Patriots employee. There would be no commentary on McDonough's admirable pugnacity from the other black players who had come through town over that thirty-year period.

To the African-American community, Will McDonough was no cham-

pion, a fact illustrated by his death. He spoke for Southie and Charlestown and
the white working class, but Will McDonough never claimed Roxbury,
Mattapan, or the black half of Dorchester. Nor did they claim him. He was
powerful, someone to be feared because of his reach and connections, but those
long-aggrieved communities sought redress from Boston, from its media—
change McDonough never deemed necessary. He also owned the position to
have the last word on many issues, and anyone who disagreed was forced to sit
there and take it.

Few blacks attended his public viewing or memorial service. It was the
clearest illustration of how McDonough still divided Boston. Michael Holley,
the emerging sports columnist for the *Globe*, was asked by his superiors to write
a tribute column to McDonough. He declined, uncomfortable commenting on
a towering figure with whom he'd had little contact. In a city consumed by race
and perceptions of race, however, Holley's decision seemed, at the very least,
curious. The city's greatest sports columnist had died, and the only African-
American sports columnist in the city—who worked for the same newspaper,
no less—had refused to honor him in print.

"It would have been disingenuous for me to write about him. Jackie
MacMullan knew him well. Bob Ryan knew him well. Did I agree with his politics? No, but I write about a lot of people whose politics I disagree with. I sat
down and it just didn't feel right. I didn't have that personal connection you
need to have to write at a time like that. When my grandmother died, I wrote.
When [former NBA star] Bobby Phills died, I wrote. I don't know how it
looked, but I didn't write because I simply didn't know him well enough."

In an almost symmetrical succession, the pillars of the old guard succumbed to
time. A month after McDonough, Haywood Sullivan, the former Red Sox
catcher who became part owner of the team with Jean Yawkey during the late
1970s and '80s, died in Florida. He did not receive the attention McDonough
did, naturally, but unlike Will McDonough, Peter Gammons celebrated the life
of Haywood Sullivan. Sullivan represented a breezy baseball life of informality
that no longer exists. Like the coverage of McDonough's death, Gammons'
appreciation of Sullivan offered a glimpse into how some of the most important
elements of the franchise's history were never examined. Gammons refused to
hold Sullivan accountable for the two greatest mistakes that took place during
his watch. The first was his inability to understand the true scope of the free-
agent era, which sank the Red Sox during the first half of the 1980s. The second was Sullivan's refusal to repudiate the team's relations with the all-white
Elks Club, which embittered the few black players on the team, isolated Jim
Rice, and kept race an unfortunate and real characteristic of the Red Sox franchise decades after Robinson's tryout, Pinky Higgins, and the sins of past years.

Instead of holding Sullivan accountable while admiring him, Gammons wrote wistfully of Sullivan's Southern stubbornness, a noble, down-home virtue even though it led to Tommy Harper's lawsuit and the continuation of an embarrassing racial legacy.

Days after it was announced that Jackie Robinson would receive the Congressional Medal of Honor, the last living link to the bitter tryout of 1945 passed. Clif Keane, the venerable *Globe* sportswriter, died at age ninety on April 25, 2003, after a fall in his suburban Boston home. In death, Keane was remembered by his newspaper as brash, as the man who covered the Red Sox for thirty-six years, and as a writer who became one of the pioneers of the burgeoning talk radio industry in Boston.

Clif Keane should be best remembered for being the only journalist in Boston to recall the famous Robinson tryout that long-ago April. Without Keane's account, the story dies, lost to generations, and perhaps history changes forever. None of Keane's tributes or obituaries mentions the tryout, not even Bud Collins' farewell to his old colleague. Booth always enjoyed Keane but was completely aware of his eccentricities, for as much as Keane should be remembered for his holding the Red Sox accountable for the Robinson affair, he also personified the harsh racial climate that existed in Boston and in the press box. Larry Whiteside never forgot Keane baiting him for his lack of regard for blacks as people, and it was Keane who once referred to black Red Sox first baseman George Scott as an "old bush nigger."* Boston is nothing if not complex.

The Boston McDonough, Sullivan, and Keane have left behind, and the one Henry, Larry Lucchino, and Tom Werner have inherited finds itself in the midst of its next great transition. For decades, disturbing problems had existed within the Catholic Church. Finally, years of denial gave way to a monumental scandal, spinning the Church—one of the most powerful forces in the city— into moral and financial chaos. If the scandal proved revelatory, then so too did the zeal in which the city's newspapers reported the details of the fall of a sacred pillar. As with busing a generation earlier, the *Globe* won a Pulitzer Prize for its coverage.

Change also came when the city's newspapers ran photographs of William Bulger, a formerly prominent state politician and president of the University of Massachusetts, and his brother, fugitive mobster James "Whitey" Bulger. For years, the papers had kept the two separate, protecting William's legacy and

---

* A wonderful account of the flavor of baseball and the Red Sox in particular can be found in Marie Brenner's 1980 *Esquire* article "Confessions of a Rookie in Pearls." Brenner's story has resurfaced—along with Keane's tartness—in Glenn Stout's *Impossible Dreams: A Red Sox Collection* (Houghton Mifflin, 2003).

standing. Seeing the brothers together on the front page of both papers suggested a true shift in the Boston way.

In October 2002, I received phones call from Andy Gully and Mark Torpey, the managing editor and sports editor of the Boston *Herald,* respectively, offering me a wonderful writing opportunity that would bring me back to Boston. I accepted.

For years I'd made sure I never had to make the decision to return to Boston. When I left, following high school graduation in 1986, it was in search of a less harsh racial dynamic. Returning to Boston was never a consideration. For years, while living in Philadelphia, San Francisco, and New York, I had never applied for a job in earnest for fear of having to make that decision about coming back to Boston. I had followed everything that had happened in Boston, but from afar, and my periodic trips to the city, either to visit family or to cover a Red Sox–Oakland or Red Sox–Yankees series, carried quick nostalgia. Still, I did not fail to notice the move's historic value. Michael Holley was the Boston *Globe's* first black sports columnist since the paper was founded in 1872, and now I would be the Boston *Herald's* first, 157 years after its first edition in 1846.

Outmatched in experience, and by far in Rolodex contacts, I had still looked forward to competing directly against Will McDonough instead of in the shadowy, covert ways his eternal influence will now be felt, and to view up close what the Henry regime would do with its place in history. McDonough and I had spoken at length when I interviewed him for *Shut Out,* and he was everything I had known him to be: funny, irascible, dangerous, powerful, and completely convinced that he was right. I disagreed with him on his politics and some of his methods, but he stood for what he believed in, and he did not back down. Nor did he wilt when faced with an opposing viewpoint of equal power and conviction. During the final months of his life, he sat with the esteemed local television journalist Bob Lobel, discussing this book.

"Did you read that book?" he asked Lobel, who replied that he had.

"Well," McDonough said with the accepting evenness of a life spent throwing punches and taking them as well, "I took some shots in it."

The middle-school children from that day at Fenway Park had aspired aloud and with such range about the possibilities in their lives; I wondered if today's Boston would allow them to enter the workforce and climb. The earlier wisdom for African Americans had been just the opposite: to be successful in Boston, a black person had to leave and build a career before he or she could be taken seriously by the city's establishment. Corporate ladder-climbing in Boston belonged to whites only. It was one of the key reasons I had left.

As much as Boston had been a part of me, save for a summer spent interning at the Quincy *Patriot Ledger* I had never lived in the city as an adult, and I had a fair amount of curiosity about the current Boston atmosphere. Returns are never easy, but the complete immersion of this one seemed almost predetermined. I lived on the border between the South End and Roxbury, historic neighborhoods in Boston in both a personal and a larger context. The South End had traditionally been Boston's best hope for integration in terms of cultural makeup, and both sides of my family had grown up in Roxbury during the '40s, '50s, and '60s. It was not lost on me that as a child, my mother had played just blocks away from the neighborhood where I eventually lived.

Returning offered difficult prospects to consider, much introspection, and a fair amount of nervousness, for as much as I had monitored life in Boston, listened to the stories of change or lack of progress, these issues were just that: topics to discuss while living somewhere else. The implications had never affected me directly. Now, living in Boston once more, they would.

BIBLIOGRAPHY

Angell, Roger. *Once More Around the Park: A Baseball Reader.* New York: Ballantine Books, 1991.

Araton, Harvey, and Philip Bondy. *The Selling of the Green: The Financial Rise and Moral Decline of the Boston Celtics.* New York: HarperCollins, 1992.

Baldwin, James. *The Fire Next Time.* New York: Vintage International, 1962.

Beatty, Jack. *The Rascal King: The Life and Times of James Michael Carley (1874–1958).* New York: Addison-Wesley Longman, 1992.

Bluestone, Barry, and Mary Huff Stevenson. *The Boston Renaissance: Race, Space and Economic Change.* New York: Russell Sage Foundation, 2000.

Chadwin, Dean. *Those Damn Yankees: The Secret Life of America's Greatest Franchise.* New York: Verso, 1999.

Cramer, Richard Ben. *Joe DiMaggio: The Hero's Life.* New York: Touchstone, 2000.

Douglass, Frederick. *Narrative of the Life of Frederick Douglass.* Boston: Anti-Slavery Office, 1845.

Einstein, Charles. *Willie's Time: A Memoir.* New York: Penguin Books, 1989.

Faulkner, David. *Great Time Coming: The Life of Jackie Robinson, from Baseball to Birmingham.* New York: Simon and Schuster, 1995.

Flood, Curt. *The Way It Is.* New York: Trident Press, 1971.

Formisano, Ronald. *Boston against Busing.* Chapel Hill: University of North Carolina Press, 1991.

Gammons, Peter. *Beyond the Sixth Game: What's Happened to Baseball since the Greatest Game in World Series History.* Lexington, MA: Stephen Greene Press, 1985.

Golenbock, Peter. *Fenway: an Unexpurgated History of the Boston Red Sox.* (New York: Putnam Press, 1992.

Halberstam, David. *The Fifties.* New York: Fawcett Columbine, 1993.

———. *October 1964.* New York: Villard Books, 1994.

Haley, Alex. *The Autobiography of Malcolm X.* New York: Grove Press, 1964.

Hirshberg, Al. *What's the Matter with the Red Sox?* New York: Dodd, Mead and Company, 1973.

Kahn, Roger. *The Boys of Summer.* New York: HarperTrade, 1987.

————. *The Era: When the Yankees, Dodgers and the Giants Ruled the World.* Boston: Houghton Mifflin, 1993.

Lader, Lawrence. *The Bold Brahmins: New England's War against Slavery.* Westport, CT: Greenwood Press, 1961.

Lee, Bill, and Dick Lally. *The Wrong Stuff.* New York: Penguin Books, 1984.

Lemann, Nicholas. *The Promised Land: The Great Black Migration and How It Changed America.* New York: Vintage Books, 1992.

Lukas, J. Anthony. *Common Ground: A Turbulent Decade in the Lives of Three American Families.* New York: Vintage Books, 1986.

O'Connor, Thomas. *Imagining Boston.* Boston: Beacon Press, 1990.

Rampersad, Arnold. *Jackie Robinson: A Biography.* New York: Alfred A. Knopf, 1997.

Robinson, Jackie, and Alfred Duckett. *I Never Had It Made: The Autobiography of Jackie Robinson.* New York: Putnam, 1972.

Robinson, Jackie and Carl T. Rowan. *Wait 'til Next Year.* New York: Random House, 1960.

Schneider, Mark R. *Boston Confronts Jim Crow: 1890–1920.* Boston: Northeastern University Press, 1997.

Stout, Glenn, and Richard A. Johnson. *The Red Sox Century: 100 Years of Red Sox Baseball.* Boston: Houghton Mifflin, 2000.

Tygiel, Jules. *Baseball's Great Experiment: Jackie Robinson and His Legacy.* New York: Oxford University Press, 1983.

White, G. Edward. *Creating the National Pastime: Baseball Transforms Itself, 1903-1953.* Princeton, NJ: Princeton University Press, 1996.

Zang, David W. *Fleet Walker's Divided Heart: The Life of Baseball's First Black Major Leaguer.* Lincoln: University of Nebraska Press, 1995.

INTERVIEWS

Aaron, Hank
Babbitt, Shooty
Baker, Dusty
Bavasi, Bill
Baylor, Don
Beane, Billy
Bergman, Ron
Bernard, Harold
Black, Joe
Blackman, Frank
Bonds, Bobby
Booth, Clark
Bosley, Thad
Boyd, Dennis
Bryant, Donald
Bryant, Nona
Bryant, Tisa
Burks, Ellis
Cepeda, Orlando
Chambliss, Chris
Clemens, Roger
Cooper, Cecil
Davis, Ross
DePodesta, Paul
Downes, Edna
Downes, Luella
Downes, Robert
Downes, Stephen
Duquette, Dan
Eckersley, Dennis
Edes, Gordon
Fainaru, Steve
Fielder, Cecil
Flood, Curt
Gammons, Peter
Garces, Rich
Giambi, Jason
Giuliotti, Joe
Goddard, Joe
Goldstein, Fran

Gordon, Tom
Green, Marie
Green, Pumpsie
Halberstam, David
Harper, Tommy
Harrelson, Ken
Henderson, Dave
Henderson, Rickey
Henry, John
Hickey, John
Hill, Ken
Horrigan, Jeff
Houk, Ralph
Howe, Art
Jackson, Darrin
Jackson, Reggie
Jefferson, Reggie
Johnson, Richard A.
Justice, David
Kennedy, Kevin
Kim, Wendell
King, George
Koppett, Leonard
Lopes, Davey
Lyons, Steve
Macha, Ken
Mack, Shane
Madden, Michael
Martinez, Pedro
Massarotti, Tony
Mays, Willie
McAdam, Sean
McCarver, Tim
McDonald, Michael
  Patrick
McDonough, Will
Muchnick, David
Mulvoy, Tom
Neal, Lavelle
Nolan, Martin

O'Connell, Jack
O'Neil, Buck
Paige, Charles
Paige, Judy
Perry, Gerald
Phillips, Tony
Piniella, Lou
Poole, Monte
Raines, Tim
Rampersad, Arnold
Randolph, Willie
Ratto, Ray
Rice, Jim
Russell, Annie
Ryan, Bob
Shaughnessy, Dan
Shea, Kevin
Slocumb, Heathcliff
Smith, Dave
Smith, Reggie
Stairs, Matt
Stanley, Mike
Steinbrenner, George
  M.
Stout, Glenn
Tiant, Luis
Torre, Joe
Tygiel, Jules
Vaughn, Mo,
Walker, Adrian
Washington, Ron
Whiteside, Larry
Wilburn, Glenn
Wilder, David
Wiley, Ralph
Williams, Bernie
Williams, Monica
Wilson, Earl
Young, Leandy
Zimmer, Don

SOURCE MATERIAL

ONE

"Sure, he can hit . . ." Richard Ben Cramer, *Joe DiMaggio: The Hero's Life* (New York, Simon and Schuster, 2000), p. 188. "**Who was Stroganov? . . .**" Bud Collins, *The Best American Sportswriting, 2001* (Boston: Houghton-Mifflin, 2001), p. vi. "**They'll never be . . .**" Al Hirshberg, *What's the Matter with the Red Sox?* (New York: Dodd, Mead and Company, 1973). p. 143. "**Wrote David Halberstam . . .**" David Halberstam, *The Fifties* (New York: Fawcett Columbine, 1993), p. 556. "**Branch, you can't bring . . .**" Roger Kahn, *The Era: When the Yankees, Dodgers and the Giants Ruled the World* (NewYork: Ticknor and Fields, 1993), p. 51. "**The Negroes in America . . .**" *The Fifties*, p. 141. "**Maybe he would have won . . .**" Jules Tygiel, *Baseball's Great Experiment: Jackie Robinson and His Legacy* (New York, Oxford University Press, 1983). p. 329. "**The Red Sox are suspect . . .**" *Experiment*, p. 332. "**The primary concern . . .**" Oakland *Tribune*, April 14, 1959. "**Oh, so very preju-diced . . .**" *Experiment*, p. 286. "**Until it happens, Flood wrote . . .**" Curt Flood with Richard Carter, *The Way It Is* (New York: Trident Press, 1971), p. 35. "**Red Sox official Jack Malaney . . .**" Oakland *Tribune*, March 10, 1959. "**From night to morning . . .**" Boston *Globe*, March 13, 1959. "**Agitators may try . . .**" Boston *Herald*, April 4, 1959. "**But segregation . . .**" Boston *Globe*, March 28, 1959. "**So far as I'm concerned . . .**" Boston *Herald*, April 5, 1959. "**We want a Pennant, not . . .**" Oakland *Tribune*, April 15, 1959.

TWO

"**Reader! Are you with . . .**" Frederick Douglass, *Narrative of the Life of Frederick Douglass* (Boston: Anti-Slavery Office), 1845. p. 8. "**Nor did Arthur . . .**" J. Anthony Lukas, *Common Ground: A Turbulent Decade in the Lives of Three American Families,* (New York: Vintage Books, 1986), p. 91. "**Their common martyrdom . . .**" *Common Ground*, p. 56. "**I was afraid to speak . . .**" *Douglass.* p. 76. "**I have been in . . .**" Mark R. Schneider, *Boston Confronts Jim Crow: 1890–1920* (Boston: Northeastern University Press, 1997) p. 6.

"Welcome to the . . ." *Boston Confronts Jim Crow*, p. 7. "For two centuries . . ."
Thomas O'Connor, *Imagining Boston* (Boston: Beacon Press, 1990). "The
failure of the bill . . ." *Boston Confronts Jim Crow*, pp. 30-31. "The Southern
issue . . ." Boston *Traveller*, November 18, 1885. "The Gazette's Knoxville . . ."
Boston Evening *Transcript*, August 6, 1875. p. 1. "Gentlemen, God knows . . ."
Boston Evening *Transcript*. August 7, 1875. "I went into . . ." Boston *Herald*,
December 8, 1885, p. 8. "The Negro is a new man . . ." Boston *Herald*,
December 8, 1885. p. 8. "The final blow . . ." Jack Beatty. *The Rascal King:
The Life and Times of James Michael Curley (1874–1958)*. (New York,
Addison-Wesley Longman, 1992), p. 185.

THREE

"We are fighting . . ." Boston *Record*, March 1945, p. 1. "At the meeting . . ."
Doc Kountze, *Fifty Sports Years along Memory Lane* (Medford, MA: Mystic
Valley Press, 1979). p. 24. "Bob Quinn Sr. left no doubt in my mind . . ."
Memory Lane, p. 24. "I cannot understand . . ." Stephen H. Norwood and
Harold Brackman, "Going to Bat for Jackie Robinson: The Jewish Role in
Breaking Baseball's Color Line," *Journal of Sport History*, vol. 26, Spring 1999,
p. 124–125. "As I wrote to one . . ." The Boston *Record*, April 16, 1945. "I
know that there will be . . ." and "I think your suggestion . . ." Negroes in
Baseball file, Baseball Hall of Fame, Cooperstown, NY. "Eddie Collins is for-
getful . . ." Boston *Record*. April 16, 1945. "When the Negro Leagues . . ." G.
Edward White, *Creating the National Pastime: Baseball Transforms Itself,
1903–1953* (Princeton, NJ: Princeton University Press, 1996), p.158. "Listen,
Smith, it . . ." David Faulkner, *Great Time Coming: The Life of Jackie Robinson
from Baseball to Birmingham* (New York, Simon and Schuster, 1995), p. 102.
"Before departing . . ." The Boston *Record*, April 17, 1945. "I remember the
tryout well . . ." Boston *Globe*, July 22, 1979, p. 41. "I still remember . . ."
Glenn Stout and Richard A. Johnson, *The Red Sox Century: 100 Years of Red
Sox Baseball* (Boston: Houghton Mifflin, 2000), p. 242. "Sam told us what . . .
" *Great Time Coming*, p. 102. "In January 1951 . . ." Personal papers of Ann
Muchnick. "We all expected . . ." *Memory Lane*, pp. 46–47. "Because no
one . . ." Interview with Fran Muchnick Goldstein. "Treat the girl . . ." Interview
with David Muchnick. "Who the hell does Muchnick . . ." Jack Beatty, *The
Rascal King*, p. 485. "Wendell Smith . . ." Al Hirshberg, *What's the matter
with the Red Sox?* p. 144. "The Red Sox and Braves found themselves . . ."
Jules Tygiel, *Baseball's Great Experiment*, p. 43. "Behind the tryout was . . ."
Arnold Rampersad, *Jackie Robinson: A Biography* (New York: Alfred A. Knopf,
1997), p. 119. "Muchnick was accused . . ." Stephen H. Norwood and Harold
Brackman, "Going to Bat for Jackie Robinson: The Jewish Role in Breaking
Baseball's Color Line," *Journal of Sport History*, vol. 26, Spring 1999, p. 125.

"I never understood . . ." Interview with Fran Goldstein. "In February 1945 .
. ." Wendell Smith file, Baseball Hall of Fame, Cooperstown, NY. "This role
of progressive . . ." Interview with David Muchnick. "Bill also said . . ." Ibid.
"It's much more . . ." Interview with Glenn Stout. "Dad didn't realize it . . ."
Interview with David Muchnick. "To my friend . . ." Personal papers of Ann
Muchnick. "I'm convinced . . ." Interview with David Muchnick. "Without
the pushers . . ." Jackie Robinson and Carl T. Rowan, *Wait 'til Next Year* (New
York: Ramdom House, 1960). "was a wonderful man . . ." and "It was the
Red Sox's loss . . ." Personal papers of Ann Muchnick.

FOUR

"With Jackie . . ." and "The Red Sox are . . ." Interview with Leonard
Koppett, October 1, 2000. "The Red Sox have always . . ." Interview with
Ray Ratto, December 8, 2000. "That year the Red Sox . . ." Al Hirshberg,
What's the Matter with the Red Sox? p. 146. "There's no telling . . ." Interview
with Willie Mays, January 1997. "They told me . . ." David Nevard with
David Marasco, "Who Was Piper Davis?" Buffalo Head *Society*, February 14,
2001. "The Red Sox will never have . . ." Jules Tygiel, *Baseball's Great
Experiment*, p. 329. "Those players wanted to show . . ." Interview with Buck
O'Neil. "There wasn't much white people . . ." Interview with Hank Aaron.
"That racism was an unfortunate . . ." David Halberstam, *October 1964* (New
York, Villard Books, 1994). "There isn't an outstanding . . ." Artie Wilson
file, The Baseball Hall of Fame.

FIVE

"The police represent society . . ." Bill Russell, *Go Up for Glory* (New York:
Coward-McCann, 1966). "I had never . . ." Bill Russell, *Second Wind:
Memoirs of an Opinionated Man.* "They would try . . ." Interview with Martin
F. Nolan, July 8, 2001. "This was a great man . . ." *Sports Century: Bill Russell*,
ESPN, aired February 2002. "I mean, people . . ." Interview with Pumpsie
Green, April 25, 2000. "The unwitting center . . ." Oakland *Tribune*, July 22,
1959 (Associated Press). "I haven't made any . . ." Boston *Globe*, July 22,
1959, p. 35. "They just wanted me to say . . ." Interview with Pumpsie Green,
April 25, 2000. "Did you see that?" Interview with Pumpsie Green, April 25,
2000. "Good things . . ." Interview with Earl Wilson, June 1997.

SIX

"Hey Porter, get my bags . . ." and "Look, if someone called me . . ." Roger
Kahn, *The Boys of Summer* (New York: Harper and Row, 1972) p. 134. "I

couldn't stand the clowning . . . " Interview with Roger Angell. "By no means
. . ." Interview with Tim McCarver, June 2000. "Just throw it over the plate . . ."
The Way it Is. p. 69. "During a game against Pittsburgh . . ." Curt Flood, *The
Way It Is,* p. 70. "Too many times people think . . ." Ibid. Tim McCarver.
"Learning about each other . . ." Interview with McCarver. "Bill White credits Harry Walker . . ." Interview with Joe Torre. "Halberstam told a story . . ."
and "I'll save you some . . ." David Halberstam, *October 1964,* and interview
with Tim McCarver. "Dear Curt: . . ." *The Way It Is,* p. 73. "We don't serve
niggers here . . ." Interview with Earl Wilson.

SEVEN

"How about an autograph . . ." Bill Russell, *Second Wind.* "We have no infe-
rior education in our schools . . ." Ronald Formisano. *Boston against Busing*
(Chapel Hill: University of North Carolina Press, 1991), p. 41. "Martin
Luther King had . . ." *Second Wind.* "A lot of blue went out of the sky . . ."
Jackie Robinson, *I Never Had It Made* (New York: Ecco Press, 1995). p. 179.
Robeson "sacrificed himself, his career . . ." *I Never Had It Made,* p. 86. "In
those days on the Hill . . ." Malcolm X and Alex Haley. *The Autobiography of
Malcolm X* (New York, Grove Press, 1965), p. 42. "Any black family that had
been . . ." *Autobiography of Malcolm X,* p. 41. "Because of Boston owner Tom
Yawkey . . ." Associated Press, July 1967. "They parade on foot . . ." Alan
Lupo, *Liberty's Chosen Home: The Politics of Violence in Boston* (Boston: Little,
Brown, 1977). pp. 45–46. "I am sure that he was . . ." Bill Lee and Dick Lally.
The Wrong Stuff (New York: Penguin Books, 1984), p. 106. "A foxhole dude . . ."
Interview with Dusty Baker, September 2000. "Smith had a lot of . . ." *The
Wrong Stuff,* pp. 106–107. "Those two guys . . ." Interview with Joe Torre,
March 11, 2002. "I never felt welcome . . ." Interview with Reggie Smith,
June 12, 1997.

EIGHT

"Do you get the feeling . . ." Boston *Globe,* February 1, 1976. "I like Peter . . ."
Interview with Clark Booth, December 2001. "Joe Cronin was a friend of
mine . . ." Interview with Will McDonough, April 2000. "None had risen
above the rank of reporter . . ." J. Anthony Lukas, *Common Ground.* p. 475.

NINE

"In the Battle Royal here in Boston . . ." Boston *Globe,* September 11, 1975.
"I only hope . . ." J. Anthony Lukas, *Common Ground,* p. 495. "An impish-

looking sophomore . . ." *Common Ground,* p. 256. "He never, ever . . ."
Interview with Cecil Cooper, December 12, 2000. "The kids always . . ."
Boston *Globe,* September 7, 1975, p. 1. "He would have succeeded . . ."
Interview with Peter Gammons, January, 2001. "You were a ballplayer, yes . . ."
Interview with Tommy Harper, May 26, 1998. "To some people . . ."
Interview with Jack O'Connell, March 2002. "The writers never . . ."
Interview with Glenn Stout, November 3, 2001.

TEN

"I didn't think . . ." Interview with Luis Tiant, December 4, 2000. "I loved
Luis Tiant . . ." Interview with George Steinbrenner, March 19, 2002.

ELEVEN

"He was a man . . ." Interview with Bob Ryan, March 19, 2002. "Dick
O'Connell . . ." Interview with Dick Johnson, March 2002. "Chico Walker
was . . ." Interview with Peter Gammons, January 17, 2002. "He was one of
the fortunate ones . . ." Interview with Curt Flood, March 1994. "Red was
always smart enough . . . ," "If you conformed your personality . . . ," and
"The Celtics' pattern is painfully obvious . . ." Filip Bondy and Harvey
Araton. *The Selling of the Green: The Financial Rise and Moral Decline of the
Boston Celtics* (New York: HarperCollins, 1992). "I didn't necessarily want . . ."
Interview with Bob Ryan, March 19, 2002.

TWELVE

"Winter Haven, Fla. . . ." Boston *Globe,* March 15, 1985. "The wine has
soured . . ." Roger Kahn, *The Boys of Summer,* p. 327. "Boston Red Sox management
abhors . . ." Boston *Globe,* January 8, 1986. "There were so many . . ."
Interview with Ron Washington, August 29, 1999. "They smear the man . . ."
Boston *Globe,* April 17, 1986.

THIRTEEN

"I had a job to do . . ." Interview with Jim Rice, March 16, 2002. "Clark
Booth believed . . ." Interview with Clark Booth, March 22, 2002. "'Jimmy,'
Henderson says . . ." Interview with Dave Henderson, September 2000.
"What does being in the lineup . . ." Interview with Jim Rice. "Here I am
coming into a situation . . ." Ibid. "Maybe it was convenient . . ." Interview
with Sean McAdam, December 8, 2000. "Reggie did his best . . ." Bill Lee,

The Wrong Stuff, p. 107. "**The only thing . . .**" Interview with Clark Booth. "**He didn't want to be . . .**" Interview with Luis Tiant, December 2000. "**He put his head . . .**" Interview with Don Zimmer, August 2000. "**Jimmy was my boy . . .**" Interview with Cecil Cooper, December 12, 2000. "**He hit the ball so hard . . .**" Interview with Luis Tiant. "**The interview disintegrated . . .**" Interview with Clark Booth. "**In Whiteside's retelling . . .**" Interview with Larry Whiteside, August 24, 2001. "**Larry's position was . . .**" Interview with Joe Giuliotti, December 9, 2000. "**I must have had a . . .**" Interview with Steve Fainaru, November 30, 2000. "**People say he apologized . . .**" Ibid. "**What was I supposed to say?**" Interview with Jim Rice. "**The truth is . . .**" Interview with Larry Whiteside, March 3, 2000. "**Jeff Horrigan remembers Rice's contempt . . .**" Interview with Jeff Horrigan. "**I'd have to wait till I hear both sides . . .**" Michael Madden, "Finding upholds Harper Charges," Boston *Globe*, July 2, 1986, "**I know he and Rice were close . . .**" Interview with Joe Giuliotti. "**Jim, who was Tommy's friend . . .**" Curtis Willkie, "Rice Never Found Peace in Boston," Boston *Globe*, October 8, 1989. "**The people here . . .**" Interview with Peter Gammons, December 28, 2001. "**Peter Gammons and . . .**" Interview with Jim Rice. "**Such giants,**" wrote Harold Kaese . . . Boston *Globe*, March 1959. "**Willie Mays is the only one . . .**" "Rice's Slump is Sad, Mystifying." Boston *Globe*, May 31, 1988. "**Is there any other superstar,**" Ibid. "**In an example of how . . .**" "A Cloudy Return for Rice," Boston *Globe*, July 25, 1988. "**Ellis Burks, in his second year . . .**" Interview with Ellis Burks. "**There should be just one . . .**" "Failing on All Counts," Boston *Globe*, July 23, 1988. "**Even when healthy . . .**" Dan Shaughnessy, Boston *Globe*, 1989. "**He was the most feared . . .**" Interview with Reggie Jackson, March 28, 2002.

FOURTEEN

"**Gary McLaughlin had been . . .**" Boston *Globe*, October 24, 1989. "**Francis X. Bellotti, a former state attorney . . .**" Boston *Globe*, January 5, 1990. "**Two days after young . . .**" Boston *Globe*, November 13, 1989. "**On November 21, he exhibits . . .**" Boston *Globe*, November 22, 1989. "**There were no cameras clicking . . .**" Boston *Globe*. "**When he was arrested in Brookline . . .**" Boston *Globe*, January 9, 1990. "**Over the course of the next few days . . .**" Boston *Globe*, January 5, 1990. "**Money was the reason for the murders . . .**" Ibid. "**I love my family . . .**" Ibid. "**Dr. Alvin Poussaint said . . .**" Boston *Globe*, Ibid. "**Naturally, a pack of publicity . . .**" Boston *Globe*, January 9, 1990. "**It always made me wonder . . .**" Interview with Ellis Burks, April 11, 1998. "**I don't know how . . .**" Boston *Globe*, August 6, 1991. "**No would just let him play . . .**" Interview with Dusty Baker, June 13, 1999. "**They just never left me**

alone . . . " Interview with Ellis Burks, April 11, 1998. "Oil Can told me . . . "
Interview with Ellis Burks, December 2000. "Just be careful . . . " Interview
with Ellis Burks, March 2000. "Oil Can loved . . . " Interview with Peter
Gammons, January 2001. "Boyd was great . . . " Interview with Steve Lyons,
November 3, 2001. "I was certainly hard on him . . . " Interview with Dan
Shaughnessy, August 22, 2001. "The race thing in Boston . . . " Interview with
Steve Fainaru, November 13, 2000. "is that because of the color of their skin,
South Boston residents . . . " Boston *Globe*, January 7, 1990. "In 1990, South
Boston was 97 percent white . . . " Barry Bluestone and Mary Huff Stevenson,
The Boston Renaissance: Race, Space and Economic Change (New York: Russell
Sage Foundation, 2000).

FIFTEEN

"Bal Taylor, once told . . . " Alan Lupo, *Liberty's Chosen Home.* "Ma brought
her guitar . . . " Interview with Michael Patrick McDonald, February 1, 2001.
"In front of the audience . . . " and "The Everlasting Hurrah," Boston *Globe*,
March 5, 1995. "It will never go away completely . . . " Interview with Adrian
Walker, December 2000. "I really thought . . . " Interview with Ellis Burks,
July 2001.

SIXTEEN

"I told him he would own . . . " Interview with Peter Gammons, January 2001.
" . . . was becoming a better . . . " Interview with Kirby Puckett, February 15,
2001. "Of course you're bothered by the perception . . . " Boston *Globe*, August
6, 1991. "Say 2,356 blacks . . . " Boston *Globe*, August 11, 1991. "After reading
most of this paper's . . . " Boston *Globe*, August 10, 1991. "The new book . . . "
Boston *Globe*, December 5, 2000. "The decision was made in March . . . "
Boston *Globe*, January 17, 1992. "His mother worked with Robinson's widow,
Rachel . . . " Stout and Johnson, *The Red Sox Century.* "There was, Glenn
Stout thought . . . " Interview with Glenn Stout. "My answer to that is, Mo
Vaughn . . . " Boston *Globe*, Aug. 10, 1991. "He knew what you wanted . . . "
Interview with Joe Giuliotti. "All I can be is me. And that should be
enough . . . " Interview with Mo Vaughn. "Even then," Cooper recalled . . .
Interview with Cecil Cooper.

SEVENTEEN

"A football game was played last night . . . " Charles Einstein, *Willie's Time: A
Memoir* (New York: Penguin, 1989), p. 283. "I had to turn the page, man . . . "

Interview with Mo Vaughn. "What was I supposed to do?" Interview with
Ken Macha. "Mo did what Rice didn't do . . . " Interview with Joe Giuliotti.
"Before, the inmates ran the asylum . . . " Interview with Tony Massarotti. "I
don't know if we should . . . " Ibid. "He had an inner circle . . . " Interview
with Ken Macha. "He was the kind of person . . . " Interview with Matt
Stairs. "The plan," Giuliotti believed . . . Interview with Joe Giuliotti. "'Come
on, brother,' he said . . . " Interview with Rickey Henderson. "The Red Sox
think . . . " Interview with Mo Vaughn. "People would say that Mo changed . . . "
Interview with Tony Massarotti. "It personally rubbed . . . " Interview with
Sean McAdam, December 2000. "This stinks. Vaughn put together . . . "
Boston *Globe*, November 17, 1998. "Whatever this organization . . . " and
"All he did was talk . . . " Interview with Will McDonough, April 2000.
"These two guys . . . " Interview with Joe Giuliotti, December 2000. "When
he walked into the clubhouse . . . " Interview with Tony Massarotti, January
2001.

ACKNOWLEDGMENTS

There were numerous publications and organizations whose resources were invaluable in researching this book. They include the Boston Public Library, New York Public Library, San Francisco Public Library, The Baseball Hall of Fame, The Negro League Museum, and the New England Society for the Preservation of Antiquities. The newspaper archives of the *New York Times*, *Jewish Advocate*, *Boston Traveler*, *Boston Evening Transcript*, *Boston Record*, *Boston Globe*, *Boston Herald*, *Journal of Sport History*, the *Sporting News*, *Pittsburgh Courier*, *The Daily Worker*, and the *Oakland Tribune* were helpful in reconstructing various time periods.

There are many people without whom this book would never have evolved beyond the idea stage, but I would like to single out a few and thank them for their guidance. I thank my wife, Véronique. I am not a skilled enough writer to describe the power of her smile and presence, but I know exactly what they mean to me.

Christopher Sauceda, whose friendship and patience was invaluable: It is my hope that answering countless late-night phone calls was worth the hours of sleep he'll never regain. Glenn Stout, whom I'm sure had no idea what he was getting into that fateful day he answered my telephone call five years ago, has been more than just an ocean of information and direction, but a friend and mentor. The latter two titles are what I take away of most value from this project.

Siblings David Muchnick and Fran Goldstein are two people I had never met until the original manuscript was complete. Across numerous phone calls and hundreds of e-mail messages, both generously opened their hearts and lives to me so that I might understand both them and their pioneering father, the late Isadore H. Y. Muchnick. Their faith in me to handle, with care, the details of their family history is a treasure I will never forget. The result is what I hope to be a representative picture of a great and courageous Bostonian, and the beginning of a lasting friendship.

The work and patience—patience is a recurring theme with me—of David Kutzmann was essential to the completion of this project. A skilled and gifted editor, David carefully pored through the first and many subsequent versions of this book. His guidance provided the soothing voice that in no small part helped me find my own.

Nearing the end of the project is where you realize that you will never finish as much as surrender. Historian Annie Russell arrived late in the game—the closer, perhaps—and offered a critical eye and a perspective of both Boston and the Red Sox in the 1970s and 1980s that helped me avoid many a careless mistake. Her knowledge and insights into that particular time were invaluable.

I will always be grateful to David Halberstam for his guidance and willingness to take an interest in this project and a first-time writer. His work has always been a source of inspiration and education, his comments and critiques of immense value and guidance.

Richard A. Johnson, curator of the Sports Museum of New England, and William Chapman have my special thanks. Both used their expertise and skill to provide the photographs that appear in this book, and they made that part of this process the easiest. My thanks go out to John Cronin at the Boston *Herald* Library.

Linda Hollick and Karen Wolny at Routledge were patient and professional throughout the process, and it is my hope their time and effort has been rewarded. Thanks to Katie Monaghan, Ron Longe, and Ben McCanna for their professionalism.

I send my deepest gratitude to Brendan O'Malley and Deirdre Mullane, my original editors at Routledge, who were the first champions of this book when there were none. Brendan's faith in the project and meticulous editing of the manuscript were of singular importance. Thanks also to agent Steve Malk.

Journalists Michelle Guido and Monica L. Williams offered assistance in research, reading, and editing sections of the book as well as keeping me as close to sanity as possible. Their friendship and support were felt throughout the length of this project.

The journalists, who take the blame for virtually everything yet rarely receive any credit for both keeping the establishment honest and creating a necessary paper trail, own my eternal thanks. Martha F. Nolan and Clark Booth were most gracious with their perspectives and sharp viewpoints. Larry Whiteside is owed a debt by every African-American writer who walks into a major league clubhouse and makes the press box their office.

I thank in no particular order for their assistance: Ricardo Sandoval and Susan Ferriss; Jack O'Connell of the Hartford *Courant* and the Baseball Writers Association of America; Jeff Horrigan and Tony Massarotti of the Boston *Herald*, retired *Herald* columnist Joe Giuliotti; Dan Shaughnessy, Michael Madden, Adrian Walker, Gordon Edes, Tom Mulvoy, and Will McDonough of the Boston *Globe*. Peter Gammons, Dave Smith, Steve Fainaru, Sean McAdam, Mike Lupica, George King, Ray Ratto, the late Mabray "Doc" Kountze, Monte Poole, Mark Saxon, Stephen Buel, Brian Murphy, Martin Lurie, Kevin Hogan,

Frank Blackman, Leonard Koppett, Gary Washburn, Bud Geracie, Ron Bergman, Jonathan Krim, Mike Antonucci, Lisa Davis, Anthony McCarron, Bob Klapisch, David Pollak, and Timothy Haas. Authors Jules Tygiel, Michael Patrick McDonald, and Arnold Rampersad offered valuable viewpoints that helped clarify a complex subject. I would like to say a belated thank you to the late J. Anthony Lukas, a great writer and a constant source of inspiration.

Mitchell Krugel, my editor at *The Record*, was especially patient and allowed me the time during the off-season to complete the latter stages of the project, even during a hectic Yankees off-season.

I would especially like to express my gratitude to the baseball people who could have stayed silent on a difficult topic, but were generous with their time and recollections: Jim Rice, Mo Vaughn, Cecil Cooper, Luis Tiant, Tim McCarver, Joe Torre, Pumpsie Green, the late Curt Flood, Kirby Puckett, Ron Washington, Ken Macha, Hank Aaron, Joe Black, Leandy Young, Ross Davis, and the inspirational Buck O'Neil were especially helpful.

Dan Duquette and Kevin Shea of the Boston Red Sox were unflinching and professional in offering their knowledge and thoughts despite the often prickly subject matter.

Ellis Burks deserves special mention for his candor and recollections into a difficult time.

I thank Jim McGowan for providing friendship and unmatched writing quarters.

You cannot choose your family and I am happy for that. As lifelong Bostonians, many provided not only support but a constant source of insight into an African-American community long ignored. My parents, Nona and Donald Bryant; sisters, Tisa and Taryn; uncles and aunts, Stephen and Luella Downes, Robert and Marie Downes, and Charles and Judy Paige; grandmother Edna Downes; and the late Harold Bernard, my grandfather, were always gracious with recollections of an always changing Boston. My second family of Ted and Barbara Harris always own my thanks and gratitude. Then there is my old friend Michael Comeau, to whom I apologize for humbling in so many of our high-drama Red Sox debates.

Finally, I send out one last salute to the two greatest influences on my life: my uncle Robert Downes and mentor Charles Jackson. You are still with me.

INDEX

Aaron, Henry, 50, 63, 66–67, 73
abuse of black players, 44, 70, 92, 207
Adams, Margo, 164, 191, 233–34
Afro-American, Baltimore, 27, 29–30, 47–48, 113
All Souls (McDonald), 195
American, Chicago, 113
American League, 50–51
Angels, California, 88, 238, 249–50
Anheuser-Busch brewery, 71–73
Anson, Cap, 31, 68
anti-Semitism, 34
anti-slavery societies, 15
Araton, Harvey, 144–45
Armas, Tony, 168
Athletics
    Oakland, 139, 176, 223, 229, 243
    Philadelphia, 68
Atkins, Tom, 18
Auerbach, Red, 109, 144

Bagwell, Jeff, 153
Baker, Del, 63
Baker, Dusty, 187, 203, 243
Barnicle, Mike, 185, 198, 215–16
Barons, Birmingham, 45
baseball, major league
    anti-trust exemption of, 35–36
    books on, 212–13
    black fans and, 208
    loss of black talent, 105–6

players vs. teams in, 225–27, 251
room for blacks in, 63
segregation of, 24
silent retaliation in, 150–51, 235
smallness of, 142
traditional vs. present values in, 225–29
Baseball Writers Association of America (BBWAA), 113–14, 166
Baseball's Great Experiment (Tygiel), 36–37
basketball "three-fifths" rule, 143
Bay State Banner, 106
Baylor, Don, 151–52, 171, 179, 203, 246
Beacon Hill district, 56
Belle, Albert, 224, 267
Bellotti, Francis X., 180
bench jockeying, 62–63, 70
Bennett, Dennis, 77–78
Bennett, William, 182–84
Beyond the Sixth Game (Gammons), 107
Bird, Larry, 143–45
Birth of a Nation (Griffiths), 21–22
Black Barons, Birmingham, 45
Blackman, Frank, 227–29
black community in Boston
    assimilation in, 21
    and bussing, 116–18
    divisions within, 84–86, 198

entertainment in, 58–59, 112
and Flynn, 193–94
and Irish, 17–22, 109, 189
lack of activism in, 197–200, 203
and myth of tolerance, 13, 16
outreach to, 188, 206–7, 221–22
population of, 38, 57
professionals in, 111, 196, 25
rejection of Red Sox, 188, 207–8,
    215, 252, 266–67
Rice in, 222–23
and Stuart murder, 181–82,
    184–86, 196–97
Boggs, Wade, 164, 186, 191, 233–34
Bondy, Filip, 144–45
books on baseball, 212–13
Booth, Clark, 102, 107, 112–13, 164
Boston
    abolitionist tradition in, 7, 13–21,
        27
    city council of, 35–38
    hockey in, 9
    hope for, 248–49
    insularity of, 55
    Irish in, 17–22, 34, 55, 85–86,
        107–9, 144, 189, 197–200
    Malcolm on, 84–85
    mayoralty of, 17–18, 180, 197–98
    as media center, 208–9, 211
    myth of tolerance in, 6, 13, 16
    Puckett on, 209–10
    Russell on, 56–59, 82–84
    segregation in, 57, 192–97
    Smith on, 89, 92–94
    as tribal, 34, 162
    writers in, 95–114, 210–21
Boston College, 248
Boston Housing Authority, 193
Boston Ministerial Alliance, 7
Boston School Committee, 57, 83,
    115–18
Boswell, Tom, 168–69

Boyd, Dennis "Oil Can," 149,
    151–52, 171, 174, 188–92
Brahmin ruling class, 15, 17, 20–21,
    34
Braves
    Atlanta, 94
    Boston, 3, 25–27, 29–30
    Milwaukee, 73
Bresciani, Dick, 148–49
Breslin, Jimmy, 115–16
Brewers, Milwaukee, 125, 245
Briggs, Walter, 8
Britt, Jim, 67
Brock, Lou, 71, 93–94, 121
Brown, Dee, 209
Bryant, Erwin, 219
Buddin, Don, 3
Bulger, Whitey, 196
Bulger William, 109
Bullock, Mary, 194–95
Burks, Ellis, 105, 154, 172–75,
    179–80, 185–90, 200–206, 215,
    222, 243–44, 250, 267
Burns, Jack, 47
Burns, Ken, 212
Busch, Gussie, 11, 40
bussing conflicts, 89, 115–18, 121–23,
    162, 188, 193–94, 248–49

Callahan, Gerry, 100
Campanella, Roy, 76, 138
Campanis, Al, 153
Canseco, Jose, 224
Carbo, Bernie, 93, 120
Cardinals, St. Louis, 42, 70–75,
    93–95, 120, 212
Carter, Joe, 207
Carty, Rico, 74
Cashman, Joe, 31
Castro, Fidel, 128
catchers, black, white pitchers and,
    76

Cater, Danny, 120
Catholic Church, 17, 21, 55
Celtics, Boston, 54–59, 81–84, 97, 101, 109, 111, 143–45, 194
Cepeda, Orlando, 121, 187
Chandler, Happy, 70
Chapman, Ben, 44
Chronicle, Boston, 26
city council, 35–38
civil rights movement, 4–5
Civil War, 15
Claflin, Larry, 52, 79, 97, 124, 165–67
Clayborn, Raymond, 103–4
Clemens, Roger, 149, 152, 153, 203, 225–26, 233–35, 240
Clif-n-Claf radio show, 165–67
Cloud Nine Bar incident, 77–80, 120, 148
Cobb, Ty, 43, 68
Coffey, James, 35
Collins, Bud, 2, 6, 48–49, 97–99, 100, 109
Collins, Eddie, 6, 23–24, 28–30, 32–33, 40, 43–44, 48, 68, 105
Conigliaro, Tony, 138
Conley, Gene, 61
Cooper, Cecil, 92–93, 121–23, 128, 137, 140, 166, 223, 245
Cooper, Chuck, 143
"Coup Le Roux" takeover attempt, 138, 149–50
Cordero, Wil, 234
Courier, Pittsburgh, 8, 27, 47–48
Cromwell, Adelaide, 14
Cronin, Joe
    and American League, 51, 231
    and black press, 47–49
    and Higgins, 49
    and Mays, 45–46
    and McDonough, 108–9, 216–18
    power of, 8, 61

and Robinson, 31–33, 40, 231
    and Yawkey, 43–48, 51–52
Crowley, Bill, 148–49
Cuban baseball, 128–30
Cubans, New York, 130
Cunningham, Ed, 26
Curley, James Michael, 22, 35
Curse of the Bambino, 202, 212–13, 238
Curse of the Bambino (Shaughnessy), 212–13
Curse of Willie Mays, 187–88

Davis, Eric, 187
Davis, Lorenzo "Piper," 45–47
Dawson, Andre, 222–23, 231
Defender, Chicago, 47–48
Demeter, Don, 80
Devine, Bing, 72
Digby, George, 46
DiMaggio, Joe, 1, 9, 65–66, 175
disenfranchisement, 18
Dodgers
    Brooklyn, 4, 31–32, 39, 41–42, 138
    Los Angeles, 133, 152, 153, 212
Doerr, Bobby, 2, 9
Dorchester district, 54, 56–57, 77, 181, 199
Douglass, Frederick, 14–16, 21
Doyle, Danny, 186
Duffy, Hugh, 31
Dukakis, Michael, 181
Dupont, Kevin Paul, 98
Duquette, Dan, 208, 223–27, 229–38, 240, 242, 244, 247, 249–52, 267

Eckersley, Dennis, 176
Egan, Dave, 6, 25–26, 30, 41, 97
Eliot Lounge, the, 107
Elks Club incident, Winter Haven, 147–53, 171

Equal Employment Opportunity
    Commission (EEOC), 151–52
ESPN, 107, 211
Evans, Bill, 43
Evans, Dwight, 128, 169
Everett, Carl, 251–52
Expos, Montreal, 223

54th Regiment, 15
49ers, San Francisco, 227
Fainaru, Steve, 106, 169, 172, 192,
    214–18, 220–21
farm team system, 44–47, 68,
    121–22, 137, 139, 162, 232
Feller, Sherm, 207
Fenway Park, 92, 95–96, 119, 152,
    153, 203, 209, 211, 215, 221,
    244, 252, 266
First African Church, 15
Fisk, Carlton, 118–20, 141, 231
Fitzpatrick, Donald, 242
Flood, Curt, 10, 44, 71–75, 141
Florida, segregation in, 77–80, 125,
    147–53
Flynn, Raymond, 180–81, 184,
    193–94, 197, 200
Foggie's Barber Shop, 188
Foley, William Jr., 38
Foy, Joe, 88, 124
free agency, 137, 141–42, 158, 251–52
free agents, black, 170, 179, 207, 223
Frick, Ford, 44
front office integration, 132, 139,
    219, 245–46
Furillo, Carl, 150

Gammons, Peter, 94, 97–107, 110,
    119, 124, 148–49, 154–55,
    170–72, 188–89, 208, 210–14,
    218–19, 235
Garciaparra, Nomar, 229, 235, 237,
    251–52

Garner, Phil, 246
Garrison, William Lloyd, 13–15, 21
"gentlemen's agreement" on segrega-
    tion, end of, 1, 24, 27, 30–31,
    36, 42, 51
gentrification, 197–98, 200
Geronimo, Cesar, 129
Giants
    New York, 4, 42, 49
    San Francisco, 11
Gibson, Bob, 10, 72–74, 91, 93–94,
    121, 240
Gibson, Josh, 47
Giuliotti, Joe, 167–68, 171, 225–26,
    235–38, 241
Globe, Boston, 6, 31, 96–114, 119,
    124–25, 147, 196–200, 210–11,
    217, 235–36, 247–48
Glory (film), 15
Goldstein, Fran, 34, 37–39
Gorman, Lou, 143, 148, 150, 153,
    173, 176, 185–86, 200, 205–7,
    215
Grace, Willie, 32
Green, Cornell, 9
Green, Elijah "Pumpsie"
    and Duquette, 231
    memories of, 242–43
    and Red Sox history, 1–3, 94, 267
    return of, 52–62
    in spring training, 8–12, 167
    and Williams, 66
    and Wilson, 76
Green, Gladys and Elijah Sr., 8–9
Green, Marie, 12
Green Monster, the, 209, 211, 213
Greenberg, Hank, 63
Greenwell, Mike, 169, 186, 233
Griffey, Ken Jr., 208
Griffith, Clark, 27
Griffiths, Calvin, 240
Griffiths, D. W., 21–22

Grissom, Marquis, 207–8
Groat, Dick, 71, 75
Gross, Milton, 11–12
Guardian, Boston, 16, 26
Gutierrez, Jackie, 110

Hall of Fame, Baseball, 113–14,
    158, 159, 160, 166, 210, 244
Harcher, Billy, 223
Harper, Tommy, 123, 125, 128,
    147–53, 170, 186, 192, 231,
    250
Harridge, Will, 30
Harrington, John, 109, 206–10,
    223–25, 233–36, 238, 239, 249
Harris, Bucky, 7–8, 12, 52
Hemus, Solly, 72–73, 75
Henderson, Dave, 153, 176, 179,
    186, 231
Henderson, Rickey, 236, 244
Henry, John, 239, 241–42, 266–67
Herald, the, 2, 6, 48, 79, 97–98, 106,
    111, 247–48
Herman, Billy, 78–80
Hernandez, Orlando, 129–30
Hicks, Louise Day, 83
Higgins, Mike "Pinky," 2, 3, 10–12,
    44, 48, 49, 52, 54, 61, 62–64,
    68, 88, 108, 139, 167
Hirschberg, Al, 36–38, 45–46
Hobson, Butch, 201–2, 221
Holbrook, Bob, 60
Holley, Michael, 247–48
Horrigan, Jeff, 168
Houck, Ralph, 110, 140–41
housing for players, segregation in,
    9–12, 71–72, 74, 112
Howard, Elston, 50, 76, 88
Howe, Art, 229

"Impossible Dream" of 1967, 87–89,
    94, 95, 118–19

Indians, Cleveland, 42, 246
integration
    in baseball, 1, 11, 25–31, 50–51
    of front office, 132, 139, 219,
        245–46
    of housing, 192–97
    legal steps to, 4–5
    post–WWII, 23–24
    in schools, 20, 57, 83–84, 89,
        110–11, 115–18, 121–23,
        193–94
Irish community, 17–22, 34, 55,
    85–86, 107–9, 144, 189,
    197–200

Jackie Robinson: A Biography
    (Rampersad), 36–37
Jackson, Reggie, 142, 177
Jean-Louis, Yves, 117
Jenkins, Ferguson, 139
Jethroe, Sam, 28, 31–33, 41, 244–45
Jewish organizations, 33–34
Jim Crow segregation, 18, 20–21
Johnson, Darrell, 140
Johnson, Richard A., 38, 136
Jones, K.C., 54, 86
Jones, Sam, 86
Jurges, Billy, 54, 61, 62
Justice, David, 207–8, 251, 267

Kaese, Harold, 112
Kahn, Roger, 70–71
Kasko, Eddie, 127, 140
Keane, Clif, 32, 41, 97, 102, 112–14,
    124, 165–67
Kelly, James M., 193, 198–99
Kennedy, Jack, 34, 39
Kimball, George, 102, 124
King, Martin Luther Jr., 4, 83–84
King, Mel, 194, 197
Kountze, Mabray 'Doc," 26–28, 33,
    66, 106

Ku Klux Klan, 22, 28, 78
Kuhn, Bowie, 137

Labine, Clem, 70–71
labor unions, 17
Lacy, Sam, 27, 29–30, 47, 113
Lakers, L.A., 144
Landsmark, Ted, 117
Latino fans, 252
Lee, Bill, 90–93, 118–19, 123, 139,
    164
Le Roux, Buddy, 131–32, 137, 138,
    150, 206
Levitt, Bill, 5
Lodge, Henry Cabot, 18
Louima, Abner, 241
Lucchino, Larry, 239
Lupica, Mike, 102
Lyle, Sparky, 120, 137
Lynn, Fred, 93, 118–19, 121, 141,
    162–63, 186
Lyons, Steve, 191–92

Macha, Ken, 232
Mack, Connie, 68
Mack, Shane, 210
MacMullen, Jackie, 100
MacPhail, Larry, 8, 29–30
Madden, Michael, 106, 147–48
Malaney, Jack, 10
Malcolm X, 56, 83–86, 197
Malzone, Frank, 60–61
managerial positions, blacks and,
    132, 140, 152, 153–54, 245–46
Mantilla, Felix, 63
Mantle, Mickey, 87, 163
Maris, Roger, 87
Marshall, Mike, 201
Martinez, Pedro, 202, 235, 237,
    251–52
Massachusetts Commission Against
    Discrimination, 7–8, 151–52

Massarotti, Tony, 214
Mattapan district, 37, 56
Mauch, Gene, 11
Maxwell, Cedric, 144
mayoralty, 17–18, 180, 197–98
Mays, Willie, 1–2, 45–46, 187–88,
    228
McAdam, Sean, 212, 249
McCarver, Tim, 71–75, 120–21
McCormack, Mary Ellen, 192–93
McDonald, Michael Patrick,
    195–96, 198–99, 248–49
McDonough, Will, 68, 88, 97–98,
    100–101, 103–5, 107–9, 113,
    136, 147–50, 154–55, 175–76,
    210–11, 213–18, 220–21,
    235–36
McHale, Kevin, 143, 145
McLaughlin, Gary, 180, 183, 185
McNamara, John, 173–74
McRae, Hal, 246
Menino, Tom, 248
METCO bussing plan, 116–17
Mets, New York, 63, 153
Milk, Harvey, 227–28
Millers, Minneapolis, 9
Minoso, Minnie, 63
Mission Hill district, 180–84
Monarchs, Kansas City, 30, 136
Montville, Leigh, 98–100, 102,
    165
Morehead, Dave, 64, 76
Morgan, Joe, 110, 174–76, 187–90,
    201, 205, 221
Morganti, Al, 98
Moscone, George, 227–28
Muchnick, Ann, 33, 35, 40
Muchnick, David, 33–34, 37–40
Muchnick, Isadore, 6, 24–25, 27–31,
    33–40, 197
Mulvoy, Mark, 99
Mulvoy, Tom, 97–98, 110

NAACP, 7, 25–26
NBA, 145
Navarro, Julio, 80
Negro Leagues, 24, 30–31, 47,
    49–50, 130, 136, 192, 218
Newcombe, Don, 138
Nolan, Marty, 85
Notorious B.I.G., 236

Oak Bluffs community, 21
O'Connell, Daniel, 17, 19–21
O'Connell, Dick, 64, 67–70, 75–76,
    80, 88–89, 96, 120–21, 127,
    136–38, 140, 142, 162
Offerman, Jose, 231
Old Colony Housing Projects,
    192–95
O'Neil, Buck, 47, 49–50, 136
O'Reilly, John Boyle, 17, 19–21
Orioles, Baltimore, 42
Orlando, Vince, 172–73
Orr, Bobby, 98
Owen, Spike, 174–75
ownership
    black, 246
    maverick vs. institutional, 141

Pacific Coast League, 9
Palmer, Arnold, 160
Parker, Theodore, 15
Patriots, New England, 98, 103–4
pennant race
    of 1967, 87–89, 94, 95–96
    of 1978, 129, 131, 166
Pennock, Herb, 5, 43–44, 68
Pereni, Lou, 29
Perry, Gerald, 232
Petrocelli, Rico, 118–19
Phillies, Philadelphia, 5, 44, 50, 68
Phillips, Wendell, 13, 19–21
Phoenix, Boston, 102, 106
Pierce, Charles, 100

Pilot, Boston, 20, 21
Piniella, Lou, 232
Pirates, Pittsburgh, 138
playoffs of 1990, 224
Plessy v. Ferguson, 16
press, black, 5, 8, 16–18, 22–28,
    47–49, 66, 106, 113–14, 135,
    247–48
press, Boston
    and Duquette, 231–38
    Green and, 59–60
    Irish, 20, 22
    on Harper incident, 151–52
    mainstream, 2, 6–7, 11–12,
        18–19, 48–49, 210–21
    modern rise of, 96–114
    on racism, 153–55, 196–200,
        214–18
    on Rice, 159–60, 164–69, 203, 244
    silence of, 78–80, 97, 105–6, 113
    on Vaughn, 235–38, 249–50
    and Yawkey, 135–36
Puckett, Kirby, 208–10, 240

Quinn, Bob, 27–31
Quinones, Rey, 171

Raines, Tim, ix, 142, 207
Ramirez, Manny, 252
Rampersad, Arnold, 36–37
Randolph, Willie, 267
Real Paper, Boston, 106
Record, Boston, 6, 25–26, 96–97
Record American, Boston, 97
"red ass" player, 90
Red Sox
    as cursed, x, 100, 128, 202,
        212–13, 238
    diversity in '90s, 230–31, 238,
        251–52
    farm team system, 44–47, 68,
        121–22, 137, 139, 162, 232

lack of black players in 80s,
   200–201
left fielders of, 161
malaise of 90s, 205–7
myth and, 95
as New England's team, 68,
   95–96
and 1967 season, 87–89, 94, 95,
   118–20, 128–31
press silence and, 78–80, 97, 113
quota system on, 77
racism and, 1–2, 42–49, 61–64,
   101, 109, 135, 142, 153–55
recognition for, 99–101
regression of 1980s, 138–46, 149
sale of 2002, 239, 266–67
Southern influence on, 68, 146
stinginess of, 141
star system of, 121, 233
and winning, 1–2
writers on, 95–114
Red Sox Hall of Fame, 231
redistricting plan, 1949, 83
Reds, Cincinnati, 10, 100, 118, 131
reserve clause, 71, 141
Rice, Jim, 93, 105–6, 118–19,
   121–22, 139, 143, 148, 151,
   154–55, 157–78, 187–88, 203,
   229, 231, 244, 267
Rickey, Branch, 5, 11, 36, 40, 138
Roberts, Ernie, 98, 110, 112
Robeson, Paul, 84
Robinson, Brooks, 60–6
Robinson, Frank, 10, 246
Robinson, Jackie
   abuse of, 44, 70
   anniversaries of debut of, 153,
      246
   boycott of, 70
   Cronin at final speech of, 231
   and Dodgers, 31–32, 39, 41–42
   Green and, 1–2, 53–54

and King, 83–84
and Muchnick, 35–40
tryout in Boston, 1947, 28,
   31–33, 40–41, 112–13, 220
and Vaughn, 220
and Yawkey, 5–6, 88, 112–13
Rockies, Colorado, 203
Rosa, Francis, 98, 104
Roseboro, Johnny, 76
Roxbury district, 54, 56–57, 84,
   197–98, 217
Russell, Bill, 54–59, 81–84, 91, 111,
   143
Ruth, Babe, 202
Ryan, Bob, 97–99, 104, 135, 145,
   160, 213

Safari Hotel, 9–12
Schiraldi, Calvin, 153
school desegregation struggles of
   1970s, 20, 57, 83–84, 89,
   110–11, 115–18, 121–23,
   193–94
Scott, George, 75, 88, 167
Scottsdale, Arizona, segregation in,
   9–12, 59
scouting
   biased, 77
   foreign, 223
Seals, San Francisco, 9
Selig, Bud, 211, 245
Selling of the Green, The
   (Bondy/Araton), 144–45
Shaughnessy, Dan, 98–99, 101, 102,
   106, 119, 176, 192, 237–38
Shaw, Lemuel, 16
Shaw, Robert Gould, 15
Sheffield, Gary, 267
Skwar, Don, 214
Slade's jazz club, 58–59, 112
Slider, Rac, 122–23
Smith, Dave, 110, 112, 114

Smith, Lee, 185–86
Smith, Reggie, 75, 86, 88–94, 120–22, 124–25, 137–38, 164, 186, 231, 245–46, 267
Smith, Wendell, 8, 27, 30, 36–39, 47, 113, 231
South Boston district, 85, 97, 103, 116, 188, 192–99
Speaker, Tris, 28
Sports Illustrated, 99–100, 210
sportswriters
    black, 106, 111–14, 125, 145–46, 247–48
    racism of, 124, 167
Stanley, Bob, 176–77
Staneley, Mike, 233
Steinbrenner, George, 132, 141, 240–41
Stengel, Casey, 175
Stephens, Junior, 2
Sterling, Leslie, 206–7
Steward, Elaine Weddington, 207, 209
Stout, Glenn, 38–39, 112–13, 124, 136
Stuart, Carol, murder of, 180–86, 196–97
Stuart, Charles, 180–86
Stuart, Christopher, 180, 182
Stuart, Matthew, 183–84
Sullivan, Haywood, 131, 137, 139–42, 145–53, 206
Sullivan, Marc, 169
Sunday baseball, 29–31, 36–38

Tartabull, Jose, 75, 80, 88
Tasby, Willie, 62
Taylor, Bal, 197–98
Taylor, Silas F. (Shag), 197–98
Teague, Bob, 113
television coverage, 100, 107, 210–11

Thomas, Isaiah, 145
Thomsen, Ian, 100
Tiant, Luis, 90, 94, 118–19, 127–33, 141, 166, 246–47, 267
Tiant, Luis Sr., 128, 130
Tigers, Detroit, 5, 8, 68, 80, 140
Times, New York, 113, 213
Torporcer, George, 67
Torre, Joe, 73, 90, 93–94, 240
trades to Boston, black players' veto of, 142–43, 207–8, 267
Transcript, Boston, 18–20
Trotter, William Monroe, 16, 22
Troy, Phil, 26
Tucker, Herbert, 7
Turner, Ted, 141
Twins, Minnesota, 152, 208, 240
Tygiel, Jules, 36

Updike, John, 95

Vaughn, Mo, 108, 202, 215, 219–38, 248–52, 267
Vecsey, George, 213
Veeck, Bill, 11
Visser, Lesley, 98, 100

Wakefield, Tim, 178
Walker, Adrian, 196–200, 202–3
Walker, Chico, 140–41
Walker, Harry, 73
Wallace, George, 116, 199
Washington, Ron, 152–53
Watson, Bob, 139
Weiss, George, 4, 50–51
Werner, Tom, 239
Wertz, Vic, 52
What's the Matter with the Red Sox (Hirschberg), 36–38
WHDH radio station, 6, 97
White, Bill, 72–75
White, Jo Jo, 144

White, Kevin, 194, 197
White Sox, Chicago, 24, 41, 202
white vs. black players
    expectations of, 62–63, 76–77,
        124–25
    perceptions of, 90–93, 122–23, 163
    taking orders from, 76
    treatment of, 236
Whiteside, Larry, 106, 108, 111–14,
        125, 145–46, 167–68, 171,
        247–48
WILD radio station, 188
Williams, Dick, 86–88, 140
Williams, Marvin, 28, 31–33, 41
Williams, Donald, 199
Williams, Sandra, 181
Williams, Ted, 1–2, 9, 25–26, 46,
        49, 53, 65–67, 95, 97, 161
Wilson, Earl, 9, 48, 61–62, 64,
        76–80, 120, 148
Winfield, Dave, 207, 236, 267
Winship, Tom, 97, 104
Wise, Rick, 93, 120
Woodall, Larry, 1, 45–46
World Series
    of 1918, 27
    of 1946, 42
    of 1975, 99–100, 115, 118–20,
        128–31, 161
    of 1986, 174, 176, 191
World War II, 23–24
Wyatt, John, 75, 80

Yankees, New York, 2, 4, 8, 50–51,
        87–88, 120, 129, 131–32, 212,
        231, 240–41
Yawkey, Bill, 68
Yawkey, Jean, 137–41, 206
Yawkey, Thomas A.
    absence of black employees of,
        7–8
    alcoholism of, 3
    and Cobb, 43, 68
    and Collins, 24–25
    and Cronin, 43–48, 216–18
    cronyism of, 3–4, 10, 42, 48–49,
        138, 242
    and Higgins, 10–12, 62–64, 136
    illness of, 120
    legacy of, 135–38, 239, 241–42
    McDonough and, 108–9,
        154–55
    and racism, 43–49
    and Robinson, 5–6, 32, 40–41,
        88, 112–13
    threats to sell, 87
    wealth of, 7, 47
    and Williams, 65–66
    and Yazstremski, 121
Yazstremski, Carl, 65, 89, 93,
        118–19, 121, 128, 132, 141,
        143, 161, 164

Zimmer, Don, 131, 139–40, 161,
        244